D0943915

AMERICAN IMPERIALISM
Viewpoints of United States
Foreign Policy, 1898-1941

THE CRIME OF CUBA

Carleton Beals

ARNO PRESS & THE NEW YORK TIMES
New York ★ 1970

Collection Created and Selected
by
CHARLES GREGG OF GREGG PRESS

Reprinted by permission of Doubleday & Co., Inc.
Reprinted from a copy in The Hoover Institution Library

Library of Congress Catalog Card Number: 76-111709
ISBN 0-405-02003-1

ISBN for complete set: 0-405-02000-7

Reprint Edition 1970 by Arno Press Inc.
Manufactured in the United States of America

THE CRIME
OF
CUBA

BY CARLETON BEALS

PORFIRIO DIAZ
DICTATOR OF MEXICO

BANANA GOLD

MEXICAN MAZE

DESTROYING VICTOR

BRIMSTONE AND CHILI

ROME OR DEATH
THE STORY OF FASCISM

MEXICO
AN INTERPRETATION

The
CRIME
of
CUBA

CARLETON BEALS

WITH 31 AQUATONE ILLUSTRATIONS
FROM PHOTOGRAPHS BY
WALKER EVANS

J. B. LIPPINCOTT COMPANY
PHILADELPHIA & LONDON

Manufactured in
the United States
of America

Second Printing

W<small>E</small> <small>LIBERATED CUBA FROM</small>
Spain, but established a quasi-protectorate by forcing
the Cubans to accept the Platt Amendment as part of their
constitution.

Article II of that Amendment forbids the Cuban government to contract any debt which cannot be paid by "the
ordinary revenues" after "defraying the current expenses
of the government."

Article III gives us the right to intervene to preserve
Cuban independence, to maintain "a government adequate
for the protection of life, property and individual liberty,"
and to discharge "the obligations with respect to Cuba imposed by the Treaty of Paris on the United States."

The State Department under Stimson ratified loans to
Cuba during the Machado administration which were secured by special taxation *not included in the ordinary revenues.* One such loan involved the payment of $500,000 to
the son-in-law of Machado as manager of the Havana
branch of the New York house making the loan. The State
Department countenanced the $42,000,000 sugar bonds,
not secured by the ordinary revenues, in connection with
the Chadbourne sugar plan which has helped reduce Cuba
to economic misery but which has aided Machado.

These loans, countenanced by the State Department,
have helped to uphold a government in no way adequate
"to protect life, property and individual liberty," and in
violation of our Treaty of Paris obligations. They violated
the letter and spirit of the Platt Amendment.

These and other evils are now bearing their fruit. To-day
about fifty percent of Cuba's revenues are required to meet

payments on Cuba's onerous debt, much of which was contracted in defiance of treaty and law.

Article V of the Platt Amendment requires the Cuban government to maintain sanitary conditions "assuring protection to the people and commerce of Cuba, as well as to the commerce of the southern ports of the United States and the people residing therein."

The heavy payments on debts improperly contracted and the high costs of the army to maintain a military despotism have so curtailed the funds for sanitation that the island has been swept by epidemics, its public hospitals are closed, and even the lepers have been dumped back into the community.

In October and December, 1930, Secretary of State Stimson announced a hands-off policy for Cuba, at the very moment he was authorizing the Chadbourne sugar bonds.

We announced a hands-off policy but our Embassy was instructed to give "unofficial advice and assistance to the Cuban government" when asked, a government which for seven long years has wantonly murdered its citizens, has sent them to jail and torture without trial, has driven them into exile. The Machado despotism has overthrown the constitution, has overthrown the civil courts, has destroyed free press and the right of public assemblage, and has ruled by force and murder.

During this period that despotism was publicly praised by our highest officials; during much of that period our Embassy supervised Cuban finances; we strengthened the Machado tyranny while doing nothing to restrain its violent excesses.

Our Ambassador set his seal of approval on elections proven illegal; he maneuvered (unofficially, of course) to reconcile the opposition to Machado; and he distributed secret propaganda to malign the more honorable sectors of that opposition, propaganda openly used by the Machado-controlled press of Havana.

[6]

We have helped uphold in office a man popularly entitled "The President of a Thousand Murders."

What right have we to insist that Japan observe her treaty obligations in Manchuria when we have mutilated the Platt Amendment treaty in this fashion?

What right have we to get exercised about Hitler when we helped to maintain in Cuba, a protectorate at our very doorstep, a government which has committed far greater crimes than those which have occurred in Germany?

Armed intervention in Cuba will prove a danger to Cuba, to ourselves, and to our relations with Latin America and the world. But upon us rests the obligation of rectifying our past policy, of retiring our support from Machado, of discontinuing a false hands-off policy.

The same interests now discredited in America helped keep Machado in office against the wishes of the Cuban people, helped maintain his murderous régime, and utilized the State Department to help them in their unsavory activities. However discredited here in the United States, these same interests still maintain untrammeled sway in Cuba.

Congress is morally obligated to investigate the relations of those interests to the Machado government and the past activities of our Embassy during the Machado régime; and to formulate a program which will permit the Cuban people to recover their sovereignty and to establish a government of law and order.

INTRODUCTION

IT IS IMPOSSIBLE FOR ME TO name those many Cuban friends and acquaintances who assisted me in securing material for this volume, for to do so would expose them to persecution, imprisonment, possible death, but they will know that I deeply appreciate their good efforts in my behalf and the risks they voluntarily took in helping me to secure honest information. Already some of those good friends have been murdered, jailed or exiled.

CONTENTS

[11]

CONTENTS

PART IV
THE CRIMES OF MACHADO

PART V
AMERICAN PENETRATION

ILLUSTRATIONS

[13]

ILLUSTRATIONS

PART I
PATTERN

"With our feet on the rosary, blond head and body painted Indian and Creole, we came valiantly into the world of nations."

"There is no country which can have prouder men than our sorrowing American Republics."

JOSÉ MARTÍ
(Father of Cuban Independence)

I BLACK IVORY

1 CONTRAST

THE MAJOR TONES OF CUBA ARE black and white. The sharp blade of the sun divides the world. High-noon brilliance, as I gaze over the indigo Caribbean Sea, lifts the waters like a black wall. The horizon recedes; the sky-space is sliced by expanding steel-white disks. Chalky palm-trunks, dazzling sands, low calcium buildings transform Cuba into a shell-white island floating on a black ocean.

Even brown tree-trunks bleach, become white in tone-value; and their sun-drenched luminosity accentuates the blackness of the clotted shadows on the blanched sand, the blackness of somber foliage—so glossy and heavy it has a pulpy lushness.

This antipodean quality of earth, sky and sea, of light and shade, this vibrant cleavage in nature, is paralleled in the human order. Dominating all upper social levels is the aristocratic lily grace of the pure-blooded Spanish Creole, delicacy and pallid faces set against the dancing, singing tide of black folk. But even the negroes are not wholly black: teeth and eyes flash white; their clothing is white.

Vivid colors do belong to Cuba, but they are fused into incandescent tonality, into two realms of light and non-light. But between these antitheses flows an eternal shuttle, a constant throbbing interplay, which once understood, gives the clew to this neighboring country's secrets, its brooding saturated with mystery, its life-ways so alien in source and actuality, an interplay less intense than its extremes, but more decorative, bizarre, and occasionally balanced into peace. But mostly I had the sensation of being ever in the remorseless grip of strange black and white checkerboard coils unceasingly gliding in and out and poisonously dangerous.

The black-ivory quality of Cuba conceals the patterns. These present themselves best when the island world is hushed to lower key. On a cloudy day, the rolling landscape becomes soft-bosomed, luxuriantly green; the sharp, almost acrid, quality of the sun-days has eased off into quiet brooding, almost New England in quality but immeasurably richer.

This unexpected tranquillity of mood makes one recall submerged impressions—the lassitude, the occasional tropic stupor, that queer intermingling of blandness and cruelty— a better comprehension of many subtle interludes. All of Cuba became a blending kaleidoscope, only border outlines bitten clearly, all else in constant flux.

Cuban dawns bring a fresh minor motif—the cool mistiness, the sun rising into the rose-pearl sky beyond the Guanabacoa hills, and a soft delicacy, an alert kindliness in air and people.

And Cuban nights. Night is a reaction. In the hard white brilliance of day, every architectural scroll and gargoyle is brutally carved; the eyeballs ache from the marble sheen. Havana at high noon is a dangerous woman, thinking gainfully of sin, already dressed in glistening white satin, sharp glints in her hair, and her carmine mouth hard and bold.

With late afternoon hard surfaces and the glare break up into softer patterns: airy rhomboids of shade, like palaces thought of in luxurious dreams. Similarly cast through the prism of change, men's emotions re-form into bland intricacies.

Night brings final release from the sun's resplendent tyranny; night in Cuba is graceful, not the heavy solid night of the north. The stars seem closer, more glinting—the sensation of a splash of rainbow colors. The buildings seem melting and moving on deep, slow waters. Men float onward in the same way. Havana then is like a woman in love who has let down her long black hair in pensive and joyous expectation.

Gradually I realized what a complicated blend of peoples, ideas, and frustrations is Cuba—not the melting pot of Mexico, for Mexico is always stark; Cuba only seems stark on first acquaintance. Mexico, also in flux, displays shrill colors laid on as in modern painting—strong brush strokes against each other, but overlaid on an earth-brown background almost red. In Cuba colors flow into each other. Whatever starkness exists arises from the black and white dominant, a peculiar life-technique, utilizing many tints, yet resulting in one outstanding impression. Soon I escaped the fierce sensation of being torn between two uncomfortable contradictions, and thereafter days were golden beads; nights were solid silver, strung side by side in timelessness.

Soon I became part of the softer blending—long acres of silver-green sugar-cane, the glistening sheen of verdant rolling hills, the age-old caramel brown of flat-roofed houses, the coral pink of hill towns, tawny roads gliding carelessly among huts and vines and flambeaux trees—a world as lush as the golden pineapples, fresh as the downy green of the local star-apple.

The golden-green, ivory-black pattern of Cuba unfolds. Its inner secrets seem more important, more eternal than the surge of tyrannical politics, dollar diplomacy, sugar monopoly, and the greed and cruelty that holds the island in an iron vice of futile non-realization, denying its true evolution, its inner personality. But these unpleasant truths dominate the completed picture.

They cast dark shadows—ever growing darker through the years—on a world of strange vitality and beauty.

2 MORRO CASTLE

"No foreigner," says the pleasing writer, Jorge Mañach, "can understand the reason for our explosive joy in the lyric moment of sighting El Morro Castle when coming from abroad. . . . El Morro and its lighthouse tower are for us a symbol of the essential, immanent, immutable Havanity of Havana."

As one drifts into the beautiful bustling harbor of Cuba's capital city, Morro Castle instantly leaps into the eye. It stands aloft, garbed in ancient weather-beaten brown, sheer and stern against the eastern sky. Its rugged simplicity contrasts to the new white Baroque palaces of the Malecón speedway, curving westward to meet the sea again. And Morro Castle, long after the visitor's ship dips an involuntary salute in the harbor-mouth tide-rip, is his last glimpse of a land strangely freighted with the shadows of a long mysterious past and glistening white under eternal sun; a land of negroes toiling to cut the sugar *zafra*, singing songs sorrowful with old and modern slaveries, shaking bodies to the rumba tones of gourd and guitar and clapped hands and anklet bells; whites, proud of their pure Creole extraction, lounging on the wide Yacht Club verandas, gazing now and then with the weariness of centuries in their more pallid veins, across the smooth and vacant sea—this land of black and white, of the whiteness of sugar, crystallized out of black sweat; the blackness of tyrannies ancient and of to-day, crystallized out of shattered white hopes; and now and then the garish flash of uncomplemented colors, like the clash of worlds—old Spain, clad in medieval velvet and buckled pomp, and Africa, leaping red-blooded to voodoo sacrifice before stick and pebble gods.

Over the color pattern comes the clash not only of gourd music, but of the discord of strange tongues not Spanish and the eternal noisiness of the Cuban, almost like a tin spoon on a frying pan; until one listens more deeply and hears the deeper tide of sound, the raucous voice of primitive vitality, the low rolling clamor of a people insistent still upon a freedom never attained, forever denied them, and as remote now—nay, more remote, in these days of bullets and bankloans—as in the days of brutal Tacón and bloody Weyler.

Morro Castle stands there, a brown neutral tint, as though it had achieved a negative compromise of the sharp-cut tones of Cuba, its lofty walls a symbol of both hope and despair, of conquest and freedom, its lines unchanging, forever the same, almost seeming to chide the unruly impatience of the people within its shadow. It, of all things Cuban, seems integrated with the land, an inseparable part of the rocky promontory on which it stands— scarcely a break between the sheer sea-cliff and its own walls.

Over its embattled ramparts have waved the flags of four nations—Spain, England, America, and Cuba. Since its construction in 1597, with funds from the Mexican mines and forced labor, it has stood against the English pirates, it has housed the treasure of galleons, and in its day, with the low pink Cabaña fortress to its rear, was well-nigh impregnable. The slave labor that went into its erection has laid upon it an eternal curse; from its bloody execution room, many a Cuban patriot resisting Spain's rule was plunged through a trap-door down to the sea; under the present despotic Machado, new Cuban patriots have suffered the same fate. As if to add more irony, its harbor batteries bear the pacific title of "The Twelve Apostles."

Despite these sinister memories and actualities, those broken parapets and moldy magazine rooms are for the Cuban an abiding symbol of his very nationality, a reminder that liberty still has to be won. Whatever his national destiny, Morro Castle will still be standing guard there with its everlasting challenge. Despite its neutral tint, its eternal quiet—save for the tread and *alertas* of the sen-

[21]

tinels and its nine-o'clock gun booming over all Havana—
it seems swinging to two distinct motions, the lyrical upward sweep to its culminating battlements, and the forward
sweep, like the prow of a vast boat cutting forward through
heavy seas rolling in from the north.

To the opposite harbor-front, at twilight, along the
Malecón to the band-stand circle of La Punta, come the
Cubans, a tide of dark-faced folk in white linen, to watch
the fading outlines as the eastern clouds above the eminence and the heaving seas beneath it catch the last rose
tints of the sun setting over the Gulf. Writes the poet:

> *Three things has Havana*
> *That Madrid can never have:*
> *They are El Morro, the Cabaña,*
> *And watching the ships go out.*

3 WHITE SUGAR CUBES

Many times I have drifted
through the Havana harbor-gate, past El Morro's brown
battlements and the long pink limestone wall of the Cabaña,
past the far-glistening curve of the Malecón, to be whirled
in a *fotuto*—as Mr. Ford's creation is called—through the
narrow bustling streets, keyed to a mongrel tempo—Spanish, African, American—into a city offering breathless
glimpses through blue-tiled corridors of sun-saturated flowering patios, of ancient balconies, hallowed by centuries of
romance.

The note of romance soon fades: Havana is rather a
smoldering volcano of life, of Kaffir politics, of race and
class struggles; it is brutal, realistic, palpitating with vitality
as few cities in Latin America—the new, violent stridency
of a culture and way of life still unfulfilled, its contours
still undetermined. And as one crosses the island, he discovers the great sugar plantations in the hands of American
absentee owners, and in these hours of depression, an ele-

mentary, savage struggle for survival. Contrasts become more vivid.

Not far from the faded harbor-front tints are the new shiny marbles of the Malecón, the Vedado and the Reparto. Cuba—old and new. Parvenu Cuba—and the country always seems more parvenu than Mexico—is met with in the banking vaults of the cave-like Aguiar Street and the heavy cube of the National City Bank on San Juan de Dios Street, in the vulgar capitol building slavishly imitating Washington, in the new millionaire palaces of Marianao, on the terraces of the Yacht Club or the Country Club golf-links. There on the terraces of the richer clubs may be found, not only the new sugar baron and upstart politician of lighter hue, but also the passing Cuban plantation owner, clinging a bit grimly to the stem of his Daiquirí cocktail glass.

Not far from the newest things is ever the texture of age —tapestries on time-stained walls, the click of a flirtatious perfumed fan, a bright Persian shawl, and a lilt of black eyes that spell not merely legends of old Castile, but the seraglios of Fez and Córdoba—the side of Havana Hergesheimer caught so deftly.

The other rhythms come only with comradeship, living life in Cuban ways, rubbing shoulders even with those whom the Yacht Club habitués consider riff-raff; they come with breaking the bread of poverty and setting lips to the rim of fiery Ron Bacardi. In time, the flimsiest echo takes on significance; the gesture, the twist of shoulder, the droop of lip, have meaning in terms of survived heritage. The faint amusement and not too deep interest aroused by the first marimba and shaken gourd, heard as one idles in some side-walk café, is remembered later as a pathetic eleemosynary dulcification of that which is throbbingly Cuban however removed from the stately grace of the older aristocracy and the mores of *nouveaux riches* sugar-kings; in that ragamuffin rhythm is the whole story of Cuba surging up from water-front dives, from blistering cane-fields, from the jungles, from the far eastern shores of Camagüey and Oriente where the cocoanut trees lean back from Caribbean gales and black folk come trooping from an ancient continent. The musical *son,* not only from Andalusia, but its words in mongrel Spanish, hails through tortured centuries from the Gold Coast itself:

Ya la bi una bej
Y no la bito náaaa . . .

The larger rhythms, absorbing these minor motifs, grow in one's consciousness. Now it is caught from a group of toil-worn Canary Island *guajiros,* dressed in long, many-pleated shirts, who lift their voices in the hot restless night in that unmelodious wail which came out of Moorish Spain to haunt a race with its monotonous sorrow, a never-ending plaint that seems to wish to hold grimly on to each note even beyond the limits of breath, as though fearing the eternal silence that falls beyond.

Then, little by little, the black rhythms, the sinister Congo drums between the sharp angle of bony black Congo knees, the belly-shake of the rumba, the lilt and shout of *ñañigo,* and the rum-dum-dum of the beat of stiff fingers and wrists, palms flashing moist whiteness, the quiver of the nether belly and the twist of cinnamon loins in green-shuttered rooms in an atmosphere flavored with ginger and black sweat and the flash of white teeth and eyeballs in black faces—all these multiple inflections sweep into the long tempo to which an island rides the waves of long swells from out the Caribbean, the rhythm of a new nation, yearning to sing, and singing, yearning to be free, and free, yearning to dance its freedom.

For most Americans, Cuba is but the hieroglyphic of a ticker:

Amer. Sugar 26 5/8
Cub. Amer. Sugar 17 1/7
Cub. Am. Pfd. 18 1/5

But for me, all this inner mystery is forever imprisoned in each cube of white sugar I drop into my morning
coffee. Black Cuba and black sweat and black song and
dance, crystallized into a snow cube, held in silver prongs.

4 FEATHERED GHOSTS

Now and then I sense strange
hush in this strident Cuban world, ever so boiling up
and subsiding, and rarely meaning what I had expected.
Traveled in Hispanic American countries, I became conscious of a missing component. Most New World countries
are still rocked in the cradle of their Indian culture.

But in Cuba, however much passing faces run the chromatic gamut, there is no sign of that basic earth-brown pig-
ment; none of that soil-rooted, patient, all but stabilizing
stoic quality that holds all values in abeyance for some
final determination beyond the ken of the most inquisitive
and thoughtful—futures dim but pregnant. Cuba lives
much in the present, little in the past, even less in the
future. The Indian-Mexican lives significantly in the present, but with detachment: their past wells up and over
them, identifies them so indistinguishably with their cruel
physical environment. To our Americas they give an incom-
mensurate and infinite remoteness—something over and beyond our rush and practicality.

The Cuban by comparison is quite uprooted, has never
really struck roots. He is almost an exile in the tight little
island he calls his fatherland, shut off from ultimate harmony with it; no inevitable interflow between earth, sky,
and man, as in Mexico; no interflow with the tools of life,
as in the United States. The Cuban is whirled in an ever
swifter eddy of imperial conflict and disillusionment, and
whether he will be sucked down or tossed somewhere is
difficult to foresee.

This is why the queer hush came over me in the very

midst of Cuban pandemonium. Why does this Hispanic country have no soft-sandaled Indians? They were here once.

Scarcely an echo of them remains—like a ghost haunting a dwelling—nothing more tangible. They scarcely figure in Cuba's history. And even their solitary prominent martyr—comparable to ill-fated Cuatemotzín of Mexico—was a Santo Domingan, not native of Cuba—Chief Hatüey.

At Yara, once an Indian stronghold in eastern Cuba, where in 1868, Cuba's first rebel President, Carlos Manuel de Céspedes, raised the cry of "Independence or Death!," Hatüey was burned at the stake refusing to submit to Spanish rule.

Diego de Velázquez had sailed in four caravels from Hispaniola in 1511, with a motley crew of released criminals, also the humane and erudite Bartolomé de las Casas, the brave, grandiloquent Hernán Cortés, and others, to colonize three hundred leagues of territory and organize two hundred thousand natives, then under nine caciques. Organization meant extermination. Within a few years, most had vanished. In 1513, Hatüey was beaten down.

After torture, he was offered baptism and absolution—so he might go to heaven!

"Are there many white men in heaven?" he asked. . . . "Then I do not want to become a Christian, for I would not go to a place where I must find men so cruel."

Soon the Spaniards overran the island. By 1515 there were seven Spanish towns, including Santiago and Havana (then on the south shore). In the Templete the painter Escobar depicts the first mass in Havana, in the shade of a great ceiba tree. Indians in the background peer at the mysterious ceremony.

But by 1524 black slaves had to be imported.

To-day, a few miserable Indian survivors roam outlying eastern hills. In the Yateras mountain region around La Maya—a settlement founded by the French fleeing from liberated Haiti—the people have noticeable infusions of aboriginal blood, even the bastard French patois reveals the influence of the native dialect.

Over the beautiful rolling hills just east of Havana at the springs of Guanabacoa—itself a Siboney Indian word—in adjacent settlers may be noticed traces of Indian features. For in 1554 Governor Diego de Mazariego designated these wind-swept hills as a refuge for the fast-vanishing natives. The wretched wandering survivals were gathered here under his paternal care. For centuries Guanabacoa was known as "the Indian town."

In language, culture and physique, they were similar to the Yucayos, or as the Spaniards later called them, Lucayos; their blood was apparently mingled with those of the Yucatán Mayas; for in the museums of Havana and Santiago, in their relics, I observed decided resemblance of workmanship and theme to Yucatecan artifacts. The natives called themselves Siboneys—"rock-men"—and "Tainos"—"good men"—the latter an offshoot of the Haitian Arawaks, who centuries earlier had plied their canoes (a Carib word) across the narrow Windward Passage to Cuba.

Both groups were famed for sobriety, gentleness, peacefulness, and generous hospitality; but their sloe-black eyes betokened indolence—for why should they overwork in a balmy island of abundant food, waters about teeming with fish, gold soft for beating into bracelets, clothing easily woven from fragrant grasses and gay tropical feathers. Having no private-property institutions, they dealt justly with one another without laws, books or judge—so the records go—a beautiful anarchistic Arcadia swung in the hammock of idyllic ease. Indeed they provide us with the very word *hamaca.* Somehow they survived the fierce Guáribos, expanding from the Guianas over all the West Indies—a race Columbus called Caribs or Cannibals (hence "Caribbean"), for he saw human flesh in their pots, human limbs hanging in their huts—and who at least left some skulls and spear-heads in Cuba.

Vanished though these early people are, their influence must have been greater than later-day historians admit. The huts scattered through the island, now inhabited by negroes and mulattoes, carry the Siboney name—*bohios*—they are merely worse than those before the Conquest. Columbus' emissaries to the interior in 1492 saw the natives smoking tobacco; the weed still carries the ancient Siboney name. The *batëyes,* or sugar granges, with their machinery, buildings and outhouses, curiously have acquired a pre-historic designation. Typical rural foods, such as *gacha,* a porridge, and the *puche* (maize, yuca and wild cassava), de-rived both names and content from the Siboneys. Poorer folk still eat the plentiful *hutias,* or dumb rodent dogs, and the flesh of the *maja* snakes. And the ancient *huracana* still levels house and palm tree and disseminates death and terror. The omnibuses that careen so recklessly through the narrow Havana streets, are called by the Siboney word, *guaguas;* and the binding twine of our modern harvesting machines comes from a plant still called *magüey.* A vast number of geographical terms from end to end of the island evoke the ghosts of the forgotten peoples of Cuba, swept away by the first conquistadores.

"O Lord," prayed Columbus on his first voyage, "direct me to where I can find a gold mine."

"I came to get gold, not to till the soil like a peasant," exclaimed nineteen-year-old Cortés wrathfully on his ar-rival in Cuba.

"Let us follow the cross, and under this sign, if we have faith, we shall conquer," was emblazoned on the banners of the Conquistadores.

And bent under this Cross of Gold, the Cuban natives were swept away in the drawing of a breath—on the points of swords, over piled faggots—victims of greed, corruption and civilized diseases. The Siboney women rather than become concubines and breed slave children drank a deadly brew from the yuca root. The men withered under the lash in mine and on plantation.

A large part of Cuba was left desolate, abandoned for many centuries, thanks to this extermination and the imperialistic piratical sorties of English corsairs. As late as 1804 Humboldt noticed the "striking contrast." The original coast of Cuba, "so populous and animated, rejoicing in the visit of the discoverers," had become "a solitude." "Not a light now announces the cabin of the fisherman. From Batabanó to Trinidad, a distance of fifty leagues, there did not exist a village, yet in the time of Columbus the land was inhabited down to the very margin of the sea . . ."

II PANORAMA

1 CALENDAR

1492. Cross of Gold. October 28, the blue mountains of Nuevitas rose out of sun-haze to give Columbus, sailor of dark seas, new hope of reaching Marco Polo's golden Cipangu. On shore, he found abandoned huts, palm-fiber fishnets, bone harpoons, barkless dogs. Envoys went inland to seek the reported gold of Cubanacán. After various goldless expeditions, Columbus planted a cross on the Nuevitas hills and sailed away.

1511. Diego de Velázquez settles Cuba.

1513. Hatüey.

1524. Black Ivory. 500 negroes from the Congo and Mozambique were brought under chained hatches to replace lost native laborers.

1532. Ghosts. 4,000 original Siboneys are left. Their descendants rove remote forest hills.

1662. Pirates. Harry Morgan and 800 freebooters, cutlasses in teeth, captured and sacked Santiago. They rang the bells, reveled in the villas, looted the cathedral, danced and fornicated with black girls, and sailed away with gold, slaves and concubines, not all of them black.

1812. Smoke and Fire. Black José Aponte, emulating Dessalines of Haiti, led a revolt to free 212,000 black slaves and add them to the 114,000 free blacks. He burned haciendas, killed hacendados, made 274,000 whites tremble in their boots, finally was hanged with eight companions.

1851. Executions. Narciso López, Venezuelan, after revolts and unlucky expeditions to free Cuba, is publicly executed by the *garote* at La Punta, Havana, in sight of Morro Castle. "My death will not change the destinies of Cuba." Interpret: freedom was inevitable.

1868. "*Independence or Death!*" Death for ten long years. Carlos Manuel de Céspedes, at Yara, Hatüey's town, led a band of 147 ragamuffins into the field to throw off the Spanish yoke.

1895. "*Cry of Baire.*" February 24, veteran general Bartolomé Masó and gigantic black general Guillermo Moncada, led new raggamuffins into the field to battle Spain.

1897. Laurel Ditch. The execution ditch beside Cabaña fort above Havana harbor, already bloody from the Ten Years' War, ran anew with gore. Correspondent Stephen Bonsal wrote:

"There was a fetid, sickening smell . . . of decomposing flesh . . . clots of dark, human blood, which as we slipped on it, clung to our feet like glue. . . . (In) the wall before us . . . a thousand ghastly bullet holes . . . A negro . . . carrying . . . right jauntily on his shoulder a pitiful pine coffin. . . .

"The shooting party . . . the steady martial tread echoing through the granite gallery, and now and again the burst of dance music . . . (a) waltz in the gray dawning of that still morning, grim music of the 'Dance of Death' . . .

"Then out of the sally port came the victim . . . a young man barely twenty; very blond with gray eyes, his arms . . . tied behind his back, his bronze shoulders . . . bare, and over his heart . . . hung a little crucifix . . . The . . . corporal of the platoon . . . with a rough shove twirled the victim around, made him turn his unflinching eyes from the sight of the bare steel and the black muzzles . . . and stood him face to face with the granite . . . rampart . . . He knelt down . . . as . . . ordered upon the ground . . . damp with blood. . . ."

The Spanish officer Pedro Farón: "Not a single Cuban will remain on this island, because we shoot all those we find in the fields, on the farms, and in every hovel."

2 MERRYMACK AND MERRYSMACK

1898. Before the present persecutions by Dictator Gerardo Machado, old Professor Miguel de Araunuz had been a brilliant mathematics teacher; now in 1933, he is a baker, intermittently employed. In hoary Santiago de Cuba, we sat late one afternoon on a bench in the Alameda Michaelson, near the speckled granite base of the bronze bust of the English Admiral Sir Lambton Lorraine—a name right out of Emily Brontë. Over half a century ago the Admiral had boldly trained his guns on Santiago to stop the "dirty butchery" by Spanish authorities, executing patriots (mostly Americans) captured on filibuster *Virginius*.

Before us lay, dotted with faded fishermen's sails, the bottle-shaped harbor, historic for the battles and naval victory which determined the liberation of Cuba from Spain. Here in this ancient city, beneath the tall hills that encircle it, had flowed three centuries of Spanish rule, from the days of Velázquez to the year of Roosevelt's Rough Riders—and before that it stretched into the haze of an unknown past of the vanished Siboneys. The city is redolent with memories of the old slave trade, reminiscent of the French exiles fleeing from black terror in freed Haiti.

"Here," said the Professor, stretching out his thin arm, "was born the so-called Cuban republic. I was a young man then. Out there is where your brave Hobson sank the *Merrimac,* trying to bottle up the Spanish fleet of Cervera."

That was the dark night of June 3.

The professor continued: "The *Merrimac* steamed boldly for the harbor, guarded by entrance fortifications."

Behind him came a launch with five men in command

[32]

of Cadet Joseph Powell. Near Estrella Point the steering gear was disabled; the anchor lacing was cut by a Spanish shell. She could not make the right spot. . . . A submarine mine exploded under her keel. Torpedoes from the *Reina Mercedes* struck her. Two of the seven charges on board exploded. Slowly she sank, the Spanish ships and batteries raking her with fire. . . .

Powell steamed east and west and west and east across the harbor mouth, looking for Hobson and his men. The Spanish fire whipped around the launch. Till broad daylight, Powell cruised, then headed back for the American fleet. . . .

Hobson and the crew clung to a raft all night. At daybreak, a Spanish launch approached—Admiral Cervera himself. . . . "Guidance of a kindly fate . . ." said Hobson.

"He was a brave man," said the Professor. "In those days we thought America came to make us free; now we know you came to win Cuba for yourselves. All the island belongs to you Americans—ninety percent of its cultivable area is owned or leased by you. Our people are bowed beneath a tyranny as bad as that of Butcher Weyler. And Havana, lovely old Havana, is gone forever; your wealthy tourists have made it into a saloon and brothel and gambling house . . ."

We strolled in from the Alameda, along the Lamberton Lorraine Boulevard, turned up José Saco Street, the soft dark rustling about us. In a cheap nondescript café, we sat sipping coffee so black it stained the white shell of the cup. Near us, by the door, sat a thin negro; his bones showed through his shiny skin. He drooped there, mumbling to himself, then crooned a low mournful song.

"My friend, can't you sing more brightly than that . . ."

"Sing—on an empty stomach? The curs eat better than I."

I gave him a dime.

[33]

With a little grimace, not so much as a thank-you, he gave it a lick and with a reverential gesture stuck it in the middle of his forehead. Then, in a slow monotonous voice, and staring straight ahead of him, he said, "Sir, you have given me a day's wages cutting *zafra* from sun up till sun down under the blazing sun. That would be my wage—if there were any work. Cuba . . . Cuba . . . it's *jodido,* done for. . . ."

The Professor leaned forward. "In the United States crime is committed by gangsters. In Cuba, it is committed by the tyranny of Machado. He runs a sawed-off shotgun government. But do you know the real crime of Cuba? For nearly four centuries we were bowed under the iron rule of Spain. For nearly a century we fought to throw off that yoke. Not a spot of soil in Cuba is not drenched with the blood of patriots and martyrs.

"Then came America . . . You said, to free us . . . All you did was snatch victory from our grasp . . . Free Cuba? . . . Ha! . . . We are bound and gagged, hand and soul we are bound . . . We are bound by your dollars, by your bankers, by your politicians, by your Platt Amendment, by your greedy little politicians who pose as statesmen . . . Freedom? . . . Our government, our President, is but a puppet of your dirty dollars . . .

"And that is the crime of Cuba, my friend. For all the blood and sacrifice of our people, of your people, we merely changed masters . . . We are exiles in our own land . . . That is the crime of Cuba."

3 TOURISTS AND SHOTGUNS

1932. He was a tall bony-faced man of forty-five, very properly dressed, sitting at 2 A.M. on a high stool in the Manhattan bar on Mayor Gorgas Street. His face was flushed from gulping Bacardi. He was shaking dice with the thin-haired, bag-joweled bar-tender from Brooklyn. On high stools beside him, sat two American women of that nebulous thirty to thirty-five age, rather plain, wearing low-heeled shoes and expensive jewelry.

To me, an utter stranger, the man said out of the side of his chiseled mouth, with a backward wink: "Pick-ups." He gazed at his nearest companion. She responded with an over-sweet smile. He turned back to me, *sotto voce:* "Damn' fools, they think they're having a good time. Poor saps, they think they're enjoying themselves. They think they're seeing the tropics. The tropics—hell. . . ."

He turned to his companions again. "Say, birdie, do you know what the tropics are? You think they are romance, letting down the bars." He shook his finger at her. "The tropics are pestilence, disease, bugs, swamps, heat, fever, mongrels, brutes . . . brutes . . . brutes . . . everywhere. . . ."

Again he turned to me. "They think they are seeing romance in the tropics, coming here and swilling rot-gut rum at fancy prices. . . . Damn it, why am I paying for them? . . . The fool, she thinks she's having a good time. . . . The tropics . . . I know what the lousy tropics are. . . ."

A dapper Cuban evidently of not too decorous relation to the swarms of sultry-looking hookers at the tables to our rear, had edged up. "Pardon, Señor," he said in English. "You seem to know the tropics. Do you know Cuba?"

"Hell, no. I'm a highly trained man who sells coal to big establishments. Believing in *cultyure,* I sell coal, haven't time to know anything. I sell coal, then I drink. Bah! The filthy tropics. . . ."

"Do you know Cuba?" persisted the newcomer.

"No, I told you—"

"Yesterday I was motoring toward Managua. We hit a cow and killed it. As if by magic, folk swarmed out of the brush. They seized upon the cow, tore it apart with their hands, ripped it to pieces, and ran off with shreds of the bloody carcass. Some of them ate the flesh raw. . . . You see, they were starving. . . ."

The girl on the stool gave a little scream and crumpled.

4 MOULIN ROUGE

Aside from the exaggerated number of policemen, soldiers and mounted patrols, none of the effects of the ferocious gang-war now going on in Cuba is visible to the tourist. Thousands of them visit Havana each year. Nature made Cuba a tropical paradise —and it remains so for the American tourist. Apparently the climate is as balmy, the city as romantic, as in Herges-heimer's days. The liquor and prostitutes are as acceptable as ever.

The visitors would be shocked if told our Eighteenth Amendment had converted Havana into a gigantic saloon and brothel, or that American vested interests are ruling Cuba by fraud and murder. Rather they believe the Cubans irresponsible and depraved. They note little of the somberness hovering over the island. They dance on the Plaza roof and pick up American girls, suddenly become "push overs" because of the romance and freedom from home trammels. They whoop in and out of Sloppy Joe's and cut capers with the painted hostesses of Jigg's waterfront cabaret, sit on the palm-tree dining terrace of the National Hotel, drink free beer at the Tropical gardens. They visit the Moulin Rouge and the Alhambra theaters, respectively owned by Machado in the name of his barber, and by the Chief of Police, where the high level of Cuban culture—since the closing of high schools and University—is maintained in movies enacting scenes of sexual degeneracy, not restricted to hands and feet, and, on the stage, by naked rumbas.

The footsteps of the tourists are not likely to carry them late at night past the darker portals removed from the Prado, under which homeless families sleep in heaps for blocks on end; they are not likely to ask the meaning of the soldiers in front of the National University, their feet cocked up on the imposing bronze statue of Alma Mater; they are not likely to know that a wrecked building is the product of a "pineapple" tossed the night before. Soothed by their freedom from domestic obligations, they come back with glowing accounts of Cuba's remarkable hospitality and vigorous denials of the unsettled conditions prevailing in Cuba for the past six years.

For if they thus fail to observe the most outward signs of political and social distress, they will hardly discern the deeper indications of disintegration. They would be astonished if told that the average Cuban is so terrorized that unless he is known to the police as a tout or Cicerone, he will fear to associate with an American or any other foreigner.

5 BLOOD

On the wide Prado boulevard rises Cuba's capitol building, erected by Machado at a cost of eight million dollars plus twelve million graft, with money provided by the Chase Bank. The tourist rubs his eyes in amazement, believing our own Washington capitol has been suddenly bodily transported, so exact the imitation. Its interior decorations are an unspeakable ostentation of unimaginative vulgarity, perfect illustration of one of Veblen's chapters on *The Theory of the Leisure Class*.

From an enormous diamond—said by some to be false though charged to the treasury, and in any case a typical Cuban product—set in the polished pave of the main salon, is measured out Cuba's great central highway, which Machado built from the heliopolis of the *U.S.S. Maine* to Guantánamo, where the first American marines landed on Cuban soil to liberate the island. That highway—also built in large part by money from the Chase Bank—cost a fabulous hundred million dollars, eight times the four-fold cost of road-building in Texas under the matriarchy of Ma Ferguson.

The capitol and the road (which serves no really intelligible economic purpose) along with other ill-considered and even less creditable undertakings, represent Machado's Roman dreams of grandeur which can conceive of perpetuating fame only in material showiness.

To repay the millions borrowed abroad for such non-liquidating enterprises, as necessary as frigidaire to an Eskimo, the life-blood of the Cubans is now being squeezed out drop by drop; school-teachers and government employees have gone unpaid from four to six months; high taxes are strangling one industry after another.

I was in Machado's showy capitol on September 26, 1932, to make an appointment for later in the week with Dr. Clemente Vásquez Bello, President of the Senate. It was agreed to meet at the Yacht Club.

I would have had to consult a spiritualist medium to have kept my appointment. The following day, twenty-four hours prior to our proposed meeting, Vásquez Bello was mowed down by sawed-off shotguns.

Within a few hours some of the most honorable and respected men in Cuban public life, who had had the temerity to oppose Machado, men who had utterly no relation to the Vásquez Bello crime, were wiped out by Machado's secret Porra, or murder gang.

That afternoon I had an appointment with Leopoldo Freyre de Andrade, an authority upon the sugar question and an opponent of the catastrophic Chadbourne sugar plan, sponsored by Machado, Ambassador Guggenheim and the banks, which had helped reduce Cuba to economic misery.

I kept my appointment with a dead man. Before the sun had set, not only Leopoldo, but his two brothers, Gonzalo and Guillermo, were lying in blood on the second floor of their house, No. 13 B Street. That same afternoon, Machado's henchmen murdered another opponent, the Congressman Miguel Angel Aguiar, on his doorstep in the Vedado suburb.

And so our calendar reaches tragic 1933.

III BLACK JOY

FELA, THE OCTAROON, SAT IN the hot, green-shuttered room, clicking her wine-gold fan and superciliously smiling at Toñico. His black pulpy mandible and fig lips stuck forward fiercely across the apple-colored felt table. Alternately with heel of palm and bony fingers, he idly drummed some remote jungle time-beat.

Not that Fela—almost white—was pretentious; life had left her no time for such decorative sentiments. Out of the slim proceeds of fox-trotting with tourists at one of Havana's gilded cabarets, she supported her mother and five brothers and sisters. None of the hale back-slappers at her table, who bought drinks, exhausted her dozen words of English, then went their way, came to know her arduous personal history or to know the rhythms—so far from commercialized tunes—locked in her lovely tan and gold body. Doubtful if they even noticed—because of her finely chiseled features—that her grape-snug olive skin covered over a complex heritage much more incontiguous than merely that of Navarro in old Spain. But any one more sensitized to Antillean racial vagaries would have noticed now in the way she sat the poise of loin and limb not Spanish but African; would have caught the significance of the haze gathering in her ebony eyes as she watched the black man in front of her, a smoldering stare that revealed her terrific duality— boiling in the cross-current of her unfused blood-streams— of utter distaste and profound attraction.

PATTERN

As if trying to evade some peremptory call, hence some unpleasant decision, she relaxed; a slow uncoiling—languorous, voluptuous, falsely simulating psychic ease. Quite deliberately, she lifted her daintily manicured nails, stared intently, with a slight frown, at the large emerald ring on her third finger.

"I want a drink," she demanded tensely but petulantly of no one in particular.

I offered her cognac; her frown deepened; then Bacardi, which spilled, adding molasses odor to the heavy pistachio and narcissus perfume she used. She waved both drinks aside in absent-minded but imperious gesture—demanded beer.

Her jeweled hand stroked the velvet of her lovely throat, a downward movement, half pensive, half fearful, and her eyes—wide pools of night—looked at and beyond Toñico in vacant intensity.

Toñico had not spurned cognac. Before any one could stop him, a split bottle of Domecq had vanished in a few gulps. Now he leaned forward, a silly lascivious grin on his open fleshy mouth, three teeth missing, a veritable furnace gap. He was a big hunk of night, a mountain of darkness, beefy shoulders, sledge-hammer arms. In battering-ram posture, he shoved forward his bony close-cropped skull, composed of two half-spheres, frontal and paretic-occipital, looping up gourd-like to a form not white. Still he thrummed and thrummed.

Now hammer of calloused palm, now whang of stiff fingers, the movement quickening with a flash of inner whitish skin—like potato sprouts in a dark cellar—as his hands jumped forward and back. Faster, more powerfully went the beat; his apricot mouth writhed; his tongue lolled and smacked; he burst into song, a cracked wailing croon that rose and fell like wind over the jungle on a hot night when the moon is a drumhead of pain in the desolate sky.

Fela breathed heavily; her large breasts, distended like ripe fruit, heaved; and her sweet warm voice—like a low dark cloud in the azure sky of a tropic afternoon—came back with an answering chant, at first soft and warbling, mellifluous, as though she were struggling to remember something long forgotten. A feline glide—she was on her feet dancing. Strips of olive flesh showed through her negligee.

Toñico hurled the green-felt table aside and seized a low lacquered stand that gave forth a deep hollow sound. His stiff hands stamped into a rattle and roar; he and Fela were welded into one community of motion and sound.

She danced on and on, singing and swaying. Could it be called dancing? Her face had grown deathly expressionless, vacant eyes rolling up in mesmerized inwardness, lush red lips drawn down in a half-curve of symbolized suffering; her arms were stiff, elbows crocked out, hands rigid, fingers tight together pointing, thumbs sticking up. (Have you ever seen a black mammy munching an apple held in the full palm?) Fela's feet scarcely moved, but her body became an instrument of racial purpose quite beyond herself.

Mind and will had been melted away in that quiver, slide and wheel of the flesh-covering; a constant flexing and unflexing that stripped off, even in us clumsy beholders, all civilized layers, and left some primitive force deeper, more important even, than symbolic orgy. It thrust us, more than naked, into kinship with elemental attraction and repulsion of ions, that queer duality of matter that seeks unattainable unity in cohesion but can approximate it only by the upward spiral into form.

Toñico's beat became deafening; at intervals in the chanting, from his great gaping mouth and chest burst forth animal-like roars—guttural agony of the soul in lashing slavery in sweating cane-fields, soul defying God, fate, cursing the vast throttling hand of nature at the throat of desire, an enormous plaint coupled with the will to be free—free forever from the last trammel.

Momentarily Fela's dancing became even more significant in its lack of significance. She seemed boneless, spineless, her whole body shaking-jelly without form, as though the sheathe of her skin lost, she had freed herself from the configuration nature had imposed upon her, almost as though she rebelled at her own beauty, at her curves of womanhood.

Then—suddenly—a quiver, turn of hips, swift dive of hands, and the firm line was there again—form, rebuilt out of chaos, the spiral up from dark primal causes. The loins arched, breasts taut, legs firm, thighs like calm mirrors. A supremely creative act! She had been god unto herself; she had broken the mold of her body to re-create herself nearer to the heart's desire.

Now, back in the sheathe of new self, she wielded the precious instrument she had created—proudly.

Now, each part of her body repeated the motif of her first dissolution and reaffirmation. Little ripples started from somewhere near her chin, from out her shoulders, along her throat, then were lost like blind rivers. Her breasts—half moons suspended by unseen force in space— quivered as though denying their nexus with the body, then pressed up hard and firm. The flesh-ripple passed on into a spasm of the belly, on into vibrating loins, then moved to grip life as no human thought or will may ever capture it. An agonizing tautness, then swiftly Fela's hips turned, her body flowed into line; once more we were eased into the grace of intelligible meaning.

The black man's beat changed; the gesture of Fela's hands changed—less stiff, more spritely; the corners of her lips lift in a vagrant smile. She turns her back to the negro. Her breasts heave forward and back, grow still; then her loins . . . forward . . . retreat . . . faster. Her eyes dart fire and affection to the nearest beholder. Not only her eyes, but her whole body, now seem tender yearning, encompassing all we know as feminine—womanly mystery, mother-hood, wifely fidelity, coquettish abandon.

[43]

But presently the motion breaks into something far more mysteriously alien—quicksand underneath our smug cultural barriers. Fela's whole body began to rotate, faster, faster, in all directions, like a four-dimensional pin-wheel that is more than fire—flesh also, and more than that—the wheel of trees in the wind, the rocking of rivers, and the long concatenation of jungle sounds.

The negro behind her, not merely because of alcohol and inner abandon, is wrought to fury as he watches her ample buttocks, her simulated entreaty to others beside himself; and his song becomes a wounded elephant trumpet, but human, the roar of a man condemned to mortal pain and joys, yet wishing to leap free.

Fela sank back sullenly in her chair, grasped her tangible glass of beer firmly with the sigh of one restored to safety. Toñico fell forward over the table, sweat pouring from woolly hair over temple and cheek. His shirt was a wet rag.

Unexpectedly Fela began singing white melodies, only a faint trace of negro—octaroon songs. There was a hint of defiance in her monodies, as if she wished to be reclaimed back to her whiteness. I was amazed at this obvious, though to her unconscious, inner antagonism of bloods and cultures.

2 VIRIATO

Viriato, a heavy-set Cuban of pure Spanish extraction, prodded Toñico into new action. Viriato started a Lucumí song, drumming like Toñico, demanding the latter accompany him.

Toñico, very befuddled now from the Domecq, fumbled an answering beat not to Viriato's satisfaction. The Cuban upbraided him. The negro sullenly declared he was too exhausted. The European, bottled into the explosive and noisy Cuban jug, poured forth vitriolic abuse. When Viriato again started his song, Toñico obediently, without recrim-

[44]

ination, picked up the diapason and soon outmatched the other.

Viriato was a likeable scoundrel from the Cuban underworld, reputed to be the best rumba dancer on the island —a few steps to the accompaniment of Toñico's beating revealed masterly ease in the flow of hips and feet. He swept Toñico into chanting repartee—a sort of *Emperor Jones* travelogue. Toñico, on the eve of taking Viriato through the jungle, was warning him of the dangers,—swamps, deadly plants, enormous trees, wild beasts.

Viriato, undaunted, insisted on proceeding. As they penetrated deeper into the black wilderness amid surrounding terrors and eerie shapes leaping out of the murkiness, the beat of palm and stiff fingers in double unison became as loud as the advance of an army.

Unexpectedly Fela leapt up, seized a glass of water, and sprinkled drops on the red-tiled floor between the performers. Toñico reached down with an ape-like swing of arm, and moistened fingers and thumb; then thrust the back of his damp thumb tight against his lascivious parted lips, tapped his forehead and his head with his fingers. The song swept into a full gallop of intense drama.

Toñico, now fully aroused, left Viriato out and sang a slave song. I have heard the songs of the Mexican upland Indians, in their way also slave songs—a soft resignation which pulls at the heartstrings; but Toñico's song snapped them with its violence—guttural outbursts wrenched deep from his chest. And yet, it *was* a slave song, slave of the jungle, slave of hot plantation, slave of emotions never channelized. Despite arrogant rebellion, it held also its full cup of sorrow, the tight-clutched note of dejection and of obeisance to superior will—song after all, not action. One knew that when the last note ebbed, Toñico would bow his bloody head to fate and go forth to cut the proper number of *arrobas* of cane with an explosion of laughter and a twist of wry humor from which even the wryness would be sweated out by the toil of those massive black tattooed arms.

Viriato called to Josefina, who had taken no part in these exciting events beyond occasionally displaying a shapely bare knee. Josefina was a tall, slim Congo negress, black as Toñico, her kinky hair brushed back from her forehead and caught behind by a white ribbon. A row of white teeth and white eyeballs flashed from the pitchy black of her face —like heat-lightning on a sultry moonless night. The music, song and dance had left her little affected. She understood both Lucumí and the dance, but she was far removed from the expression of African traditions.

When Viriato called on her to accompany him in a Congo dance, she shrugged, didn't know it. In his underworld patois, then in Lucumí, he poured out on her a stream of racy abuse. What right had she to call herself a Cuban? What right had she to be proud? "Here am I," yelled Viriato, "without a drop of black blood, but I know these things, know your tongue, know your songs, your dances— because they are Cuban they are the soul and blood of Cuba, but you—you are not worth your keep. . . ." So intensely passionate was his denunciation, Josefina rolled her eyes nearly white and worked her mouth in resentful astonishment.

3 PALO-MAYOMBÉ

The negro hill-cabin overlooks a far sweep of peaceful tar-colored sea; the shore is dotted with palm-trees—like the ruff of severed ostrich necks buried in the sand.

Here, far from police wrath, gathers the *ñañigo* lodge, a secret black society, descended from ancient African religious rites, preserved hidden during the days of the slavery lash, still persisting despite governmental attempts to extirpate it.

Shabby clothes, patched wondrously, rough brogans,

workmen's drill prevail; gay shirts are leavened with home-made artistry—crossed and vertical pleats, flowered embroidery. The dancers are rigged in *diablito* costume: scarlet suit, fringed with rope-fiber—like fur—about the neck, other shaggy rings at elbows, wrists, knees and ankles. A pale pink sash with tiny sleigh-bells girds the loins, and a flat red-black hat—on the crown of it a red cross with three dots—two black, one white—is glued to the back of the head over a pointed flap that sticks up behind and ends in a tuft of rope-fiber above the conical black skull.

We sit on boxes, benches, and the flat cement circle around the base of a gigantic banana-tree with obscene magenta buds. The demijohn of fiery *ocoro mimba* rum passes from hand to hand, mouth to mouth—gaping pink caverns in black faces. For me and several apparently important persons, they bring out special *ocoro suami*, made from palm-tree pith. Vague laughing restlessness ripples through the queer group. Some of those not in special costume, but who are going to dance anyway, have stripped off their shirts, showing arms tattooed—a woman's face on a looping snake, the native *maja*.

The pave, between the banana-tree and the vine-covered stone wall, riotous with red trumpet flowers, is cleared. A fire warms the rawhide heads of the small *bongó* drum and the long narrow *tumbador*.

Presently two tall blacks advance solemnly, touch fingernails, then seize each other's hands in double clasp. With intense glances, they enunciate rapidly in *ñañigo* dialect.

"You are a divine person; the spirit of God is within you, as in all *ñañigos*. You should love your fellow-man. For him you will lay down your life. Every man is born for some other man; if he is not big enough for that mission, he must kill himself." He must assist the chosen brother of the *ñañigo* lodge with money, medicine, help in any adversity. His roof must be open to him. He will respect his friend's

[47]

wife and daughters as his own. If his chosen brother die, he must care for them accordingly.

And so, out of memory of Palo-Mayombé, "most war-like of the world"—an ancient crucifix, the stick-god of old Africa—came this dilution of rooster-sacrifice, strange hand-clasps and brotherly succor unto death in Cuban slavery. Throughout the centuries the noble side of *ñañigo* rites have been misrepresented even by most Cubans. Even a writer so sympathetic as Manuel de la Cruz calls *ñañiguismo* "a repugnant social cancer."

The drum-heads are warm. Presently the performers are beating on them. The *bongó,* later discarded for a small packing case re-covered with a special wood, is held tightly between the knees. Two players hammer the bench with two sticks; for some of the dances, two spoons, or a spoon on a frying pan. Another shakes a carved gourd.

The little orchestra is a pantomime. The tall dark negro, one black hair growing out of his chin-wart, sits before his long drum, the corners of his mouth drawn down in billy-goat gloom—a mask-like expression which never changes. The plump negro at the *bongó* constantly moves his head. The gourd-shaker's mouth is stretched in a perpetual grin. The stick-beaters go through veritable contortions—beating before and behind, under one leg, under the other, between both, head almost touching the pave. These are traditional rôles.

But the main burden falls on the man who beats the small drum. His task is so arduous he is frequently replaced. He, the *Repicador,* directs the dance, or is himself directed by the dancer. According to his beating on the drum, the dancer must alter his step, his rhythm, every twist and turn of his body.

Again, it is the dancer, who with red kerchief guides the Repicador, each gesture indicating the beat and tempo desired. This the Repicador transmits to the other players by the swift changing movement of hand and stiff fingers pounding fiercely on the box. He leans forward tensely, constantly alert, in passionate interfusion of himself with the dancer and the orchestra members. If the other performers have determined formalized expressions, his face is wholly mobile, a whirl of intense feeling, now joyous frenzy, now a ferocious frozen glare; and as the dance heightens, and he beats more vehemently, as sweat pours from kinky locks over black skin, and undershirt grows wet, his very eyeballs protrude and roll; his jaw and mouth writhe like those of a man in a fit; soul and body are kneaded by religious ecstasy.

A lean, slim-hipped fellow, rapping his mouth as a bellows, leaps out dancing, muscles rippling under his silk undershirt. He kicks off his shoes, rolls up his brown striped trousers to the knee, and dances a prayer for happiness to all and homage to God.

For my benefit, they dance not merely the *ñañigo* steps, but rumbas as well, the Colombia, Matanzas, and Poblana. One tall chap, like song set to flesh, only a black knotted kerchief falling over his handsome torso, dances with a glass of water on his head, violent big-step, kick and whirl. A swift writhe of hips, and he picks up a kerchief in his teeth; then on taut hands and feet, with even faster roll and twist of his body, now face downward, now face skyward, the movements chime in with a steady *lalalalalalaleeee* longing . . . "María de la O . . . I'm going to bathe." Kerchief still in his teeth, arms hugging his body, he gives a complete whirl and fling, touches his forehead to the floor, slapping his foot as he leaps erect . . . "I shall always love and respect you, Saint Lázaro"—for is he not "the saint of the poor, the outcaste, even of prostitute and pimp? . . ."

"The *abacuá*, the He-Man, the dancer descended from heaven . . ." comes swinging leaves of the *bejuco ubi*, a marvelous curative herb. As he dances, he rubs his whole body with the leaves—symbol of cleansing away all troubles.

The next, a heavier man, muscles like ridges, starts with the tiniest ripple of his body, with soft melodious singing and clapping of sticks. Quicker his muscles flow, with a slight heave of hips, a roll of shoulders . . . It is the Guanguancóa . . . "My child, I am dying . . ." The face falls into weeping sadness, for this in its proper time and place, is a funeral dance. As the sorrow intensifies, the steps and motions become broken, the body apparently more disorganized, falling apart, the muscles lost in the subsiding of flesh and will. The hands come to the chest in a long plaint, the held sticks droop down in an after rhythm, dying away on a moan. Then comes the ox-like drive of the head forward, the shudder and stagger, simulating, falling, dying . . .

The rain drives us inside the cabin under a slanting roof that leaks dismally. The whitewashed, peeling board walls are graced with election posters, saints, movie-stars. Boxes, rickety chairs and a green settee painted with bright flowers serve the audience. In one corner beneath crossed Cuban flags and a family picture disguising a Carabalí saint, is a little triangular cupboard bearing holy water and candles. Inside are other saints—round pebbles, "the natural form of the godhead."

But the glory of the humble room is the high red altar of Santa Bárbara, decorated Christmas-tree fashion, with electric lights, tiny plants in beribboned crêpe-paper clay pots, and little terra cotta animals and wax figurines.

Following on the heels of a long holy exhortation with frequent touching of the forehead and lips with the back of the thumb, comes the blindfolded dance to Santa Bárbara. The dancer leaps high and recklessly, with a gesture simulating snatching from above. He throws his whole body high into the air in a horizontal position and when it seems inevitable that he will be dashed to death on the stone floor, miraculously flings his feet under him. Each movement is determined by the Repicador, whose beats, hammering through to the sightless performer and guiding the shrill spoon-skillet beating, causes the black dervish of a David almost to twist his body into new rhythms in mid-air. . . . "Who . . . Who . . . Who—" wails everybody, "—who has seen the white kid stuck in with the negroes of the Merced . . . the negroes of the Merced? . . ."

The throng of watchers rocks to and fro. The words, the motion, the sounds, the music rise and fall like waves beating against a forlorn shore. The rain hammers on the broken roof. The banana tree whips dimly in the gale; the far sea is blotted out. A breath of chill dampness from the open door pervades the room, striking to the marrow.

But dumb black praise mounts through song and sweat and hoarse intoxication through Santa Bárbara to the most warlike of the world.

4 GANGÁS

It was Gustavo E. Urrutia, brilliant young colored journalist of the *Diario de la Marina* who brought me picturesque acquaintance with the Gangás. Up to that time I had seen the *ñañigo* rites, had witnessed Lucumí songs and dances, had seen the negro celebrations on the day of the Virgin of Mercedes. As elsewhere, the Church long ago learned the secret of absorbing folklore unto itself and giving pagan festivals the blessing of orthodoxy. On my first visit to Havana in 1920, I bought a vividly colored print depicting a black Christ appearing in a vision to a ragged pickaninny rocking in a tiny boat on a vast and stormy sea.

Little by little I had penetrated into various negro reunions. Various images besides white Mercedes and red Santa Bárbara are particularly venerated with appropriate colors and African names: yellow for Our Lady of Cobre, green for Saint Joseph. Through Urrutia I now met up with the Gangá legends.

[51]

Picture a gathering for the purpose of singing narrative, either traditional or improvised, and dancing. The prelude is generic song, started by the musical narrator and chorused by all present. A dance follows, which in due course is interrupted by humorous demands for the termination of the tale. Gradually, between interludes of dancing and singing, the story comes out—after all not so different from a fashionable tea-dansant with its alternation of fox-trotting, sipping, and conversation—except that rum supplants tea. The rhythm, melody and onomatopœia of the Gangá story are always perfectly molded to the action. One famous song-story is the *Siquillángama,* opening with the chorus: *"Curunguango guango curunguango guango curunguá tere me aguanó curu"*—ad infinitum, which means, "Pay attention, pay attention, attend to the extraordinary thing I'm going to relate. Pay attention. . . ."

After an interval of dancing the story begins: On the death of Gren Dami, chief of his people, his son Ecue-Ibonó became the head of the house and took unto himself twenty wives. The first wife, named Maurú, had charge of all the others. From that time since, all the distinguished men of Africa have had many wives. When a wife becomes pregnant, some young man agrees to educate the child if it is a male; if female, he makes her his wife.

Maurú and the other wives of Ecue-Ibonó dedicated themselves, like all those there, to fishing, agriculture and the care of the house. The husband was warrior and hunter, just like all the other worthy men of his country, and spent much time far off in the mountain woods hunting. Whenever he returned, his wives received him with feasting, drums and dancing.

Near the house was a very unruly river where the women fished. Once Ecue-Ibonó, on returning from hunting, found a great deal of fish to eat. He called Maurú and advised her not to catch the big fish called Siquillángama, which had castanets on its gills, because he was King of the River.

Maurú promised, but when he went back to the mountain, she got all the women together to go to the river and catch the big fish with castanets on its gills. The women went into the water with the net but freed all the small fish, trying only to catch the large one. Siquillángama fell into the net and began to sing: *"Siquillángamanga manga manga Siquillánga kurr-yón,"* "kurr" being the rubbing of the fish against the net, and "yón" his splash into the water on escaping. The chorus carries on with the music, there is an interlude of dancing, and the narrator begins anew: "Thus Siquillángama sang and escaped." But finally he was securely trapped and served to the husband at the first banquet on his return from the mountain. The head and gills were thrown into the loft of the hut to hide them.

All were at the table, but no one touched a bite till Ecue-Ibonó began to eat, for he was the man and master. He asked for soup, and putting his spoon into the clay kettle, ladeled out with the broth a large piece of fish. But on tasting it, all heard a song from the loft—the head of Siquillángama singing: *"Pacá pacá* [beat of the gills against the bars of the loft] *cocorico bandá ñama umbé umbé ñama umbé umbé ñama umbé ñama mamba sualé um"*—ad infinitum— "I am the man from the river whom you said should not be caught."

Ecue-Ibonó and all of them began to dance to the rhythm of the song; and they danced without eating a bite, until weary, late at night, they fell down asleep. The following day, on trying to eat, the scene of the song and dance was repeated, but this time it lasted three days and nights without stopping.

In view of this difficulty, the women decided to offer Ecue-Ibonó another dish—rice—to distract him from the fish which would not let them eat and which had worn them all out with his singing.

Said and done. They set themselves to shell the rice in those large African wooden mortars, big pounders more than a yard long. They sang and danced while shelling the rice: *"Yenyenó mandari fanga yenyenyó mandari mabweri bwima yenyenyó mandari fanga. . . ."* "Put the water on to boil, for now the rice is being shelled." After this chorus and an interlude of dancing, the audience hears how the women threw out the chaff to the rhythm of another joyous song. The rice was put through a sifter: *Faché faché fachefa* went the rice on the bottom and sides of the sifter; *faché faché fachefa faché faché betula faché faché fachefa faché faché umgwanga faché. . . .*

The rice is served, but Ecue-Ibonó wished to begin with soup as usual, and on tasting the fish, again he heard the head in the loft singing. He asked what fish they had served him, and the second wife related how Maurú had caught Siquillángama, the ruler of the river, contrary to her husband's orders.

Ecue-Ibonó asked for the head and saw that it really did have castanets on its gills. He assembled all his wives and obliged them to throw the head into the river. Afterwards he abandoned them.

Siquillángama resuscitated, sang his old *"Kurr-yón"* song of escape along with a few other triumphal remarks.

Ever since then men have had no faith in women.

IV BLACK CUBA

1 AFRICA WEST

As early as 1517 charles i granted the right to introduce slaves. And ever since the first five hundred under hatches from Congo and Mozambique, out of the vast African continent many different groups crowded in the pestilent "black-birder" slave ships, had been brought to Cuba. As early as 1532, the blacks formed 62.5 percent of the population. Not until 1859 was the ratio reduced to 47.8 percent.[1]

Since the expansion of the sugar industry, the immigration, legal and clandestine, of black labor may well have surpassed white. Governor Wood excluded black immigration, a policy continued until the end of Governor Magoon's administration, though many colored people were introduced surreptitiously.

Toward the end of 1912, Gómez authorized the United Fruit Company to bring in 1,400 Haitians. Under Menocal

[1] Fernando Ortiz, *Los negros esclavos*, gives the following percentages (a few points off here and there) from official sources:

(*Year and Percentage*)

1532—62.5	1855—52.2
1775—43.8	1859—47.8
1792—43.6 (50.9 correct)	1860—48.4
1811—54.5	1861—43.2
1817—55	1872—44.6
1827—55.8	1877—32.2
1830—56	1887—32.4
1841—58.5	1899—32.1
1846—52.6	1907—29.7
1849—51.5	

from 1913-21, 81,000 Haitians and 75,000 Jamaicans were admitted. Thereafter, the legal entries were:

Year	Haitians	Jamaicans
1921	12,483	12,469
1922	639	4,453
1923	11,088	5,844
1924	21,013	5,086
1925	18,750	4,747

In addition it is estimated that from 1913 to 1927 40,000 negroes a year were smuggled in. Since then and owing to the prolonged economic crisis, few have been brought in even illegally.

The companies which have brought in negroes during the period of the Republic, were supposed to send them back at the end of their yearly contract, but this was evaded. As El Pais wrote: [2] "The Haitian immigration comes for the *zafra*, but soon is diverted toward the towns and never goes back to the plantations of his own country, the result being that the following year it is necessary to introduce another contingent."

According to official statistics, 30 percent of Cuba's population is now black, the rest white. The time has been too short to reverse so decidedly the proportion between the two races. But the Cuban esteems white blood to be far more potent than do we Americans: he is classified white if he has a drop of white blood; in the United States a man is colored if he has a drop of black blood. Both systems are equally logical. The white drop is just as apt to produce white progeny as the black drop pickaninnies. And so in Cuba, at least 70 percent black according to American classification, is put down by its Creole rulers who affect no race prejudices as predominantly white. It is predominately mestizo, viz.: pure white, 25-30 percent; black, 25-40 percent; mixed, 30-50 percent.

[2] Ariquistain, *La agonia de las antillas*, 13.

The 75 percent negro and mestizo, ranging from coal black to chocolate, to tan and olive and a dirty cream color, has been variously recruited. Up to less than a century ago, old plantation lists carried after the name of each person, his or her original African nationality.

To-day, on the eastern part of the island, are found the Lucumís, from the slave coast along the Calabar River, a people with well-formed features, noses thin, not sunk as in other groups, a serious, proud clan, less joyous than the others; ingrained melancholia leads to an exaggerated number of suicides; but they are quick and sensitive. They believe faithfully in *brujo*, black magic, and can do wondrous things either for good or ill, with toe-nails, pieces of clothing, vindictive pins and other implements. Occasionally a hill-billy still tattoos vertical slits down cheek and arm.

The Carabalí, also from the Calabar River, is below medium height and *cuivrée*, i.e., less black, in complexion. He is industrious, faithful, economical and independent. Originally worshipers of the shark, they were the originators in Cuba of the religious system of *ñañigo*, an offshoot of voodooism, involving in Africa, perhaps, human sacrifice, but changed in the New World to goat or cock sacrifice. Their ancient song, dance and sacrifice have been preserved in secret benefit associations, *logias*, the inner rites of which could be successfully screened from prying whites and the authorities. These *logias* spread to all the black groups in Cuba. Rival organizations developed; gradually they became maffias, produced feuds, slave revolts and other difficulties. On the lower social fringes whites, coming in contact with *ñañigo*, formed their own *logias*, taking over the black rites. These Carabalí lodges played their part in the independence movement and have had frequent political importance. Up until the present Machado government, the *ñañigo* devotees performed part of their ceremonies in public; they dressed up in odd costumes, with flowers, fiber collars, royal headdresses and, carrying enormous lanterns, danced and sang through the streets. These harmless and joyous demonstrations are now forbidden as indecent by white officials, dwarfed by the negroes' greater vitality and honest joy; even the lodges, though still existing, are illegal.

The most intelligent, but not the most interesting, of the negroes are the Mandingás, in northern Cuba, originally from between the tenth and twentieth latitudes in Africa. One wing, especially the Fulas, had considerable cultural interchange with the neighboring Arabs; the music of both shows mutual borrowings. The Mandingás are a tall, muscular folk, amiable and faithful; but if ill-treated, they prove fierce and rebellious. The Yalofes, a war-like division, caused so much trouble, their further importation as slaves was forbidden. Like the Lucumís, the faces of the Mandingás are not so typically negroid, nose less flat, lips less prominent; the facial angle, even by western European standards, can be considered quite handsome.

The Congos and Haitians are the blackest. The Haitian immigrant is atrociously backward. The Congo is the best built of all the negroes, despite his clumsy facial features— sturdy, lusciously shaped bodies quite too elegant for clothes. Both sexes display phenomenal grace in walking and in all their movements. The Congo has great perseverance, courage and dignity, but is refractory to education. Sleepy and lazy, he shrugs off insults easily, and though often quickly treacherous, is never rancorous.

The Minas and Gangás are lighter in color. The Mina is small, with a low brow, deep-set flat nose, prominent jaw and pronounced lips. He is delicate, impressionable, rather cowardly. The Gangás, from the Calabar slave coast, though usually considered very inferior, are most interesting. They are a long-headed, large-breasted people with vigorous physiques. Among them are still found traces of the old Majá, or snake-worship cult.

2 PIGMENT

All these black cultural heritages are going into the melting pot. Cuba is not only a grist mill for blacks and whites, but for the various African groups, which despite the isolation of recent slavery and of aloofness in remote sectors, have already developed something of a common culture and a common dialect—*ñañigo.* In most places, divisions are now definitely chromatic, not tribal. In Santiago is a quite well-to-do negro club, all of whose members must be black as sin. A chocolate or high "yaller" or a white is thrown out on his ear faster than he came in. In the same city exists a "yaller" club with a very definite chromatic range.

The bond of fellowship between black and white has been historically unusually close. During much of the colonial period there was a light-hearted tolerance, which, however, largely disappeared during the nineteenth century tenseness. In earlier colonial days, on the Day of Kings, the negroes paraded the streets in gay festival, while the whites kept behind closed doors; and the Governor-General received their leaders in high state in the Palace. And except for several·bitter occasions, although there were often slight skirmishes with negroes who preferred death to the horrors of slavery under some cruel masters, Cuba has had practically no purely negro revolts.

At times, definite negro movements have sprung up. There was considerable agitation in Cuba under Viceroy Luis de las Casas (1790-96) when the blacks, influenced by the French revolution and the sweeping aside of slavery in Haiti, showed restiveness. African importations were temporarily forbidden, and Canary Island laborers flooded in to work on the plantations.

In 1812, the Aponte uprising, bent on freeing the slaves, caused the burning of a number of haciendas and the killing of their owners, until José Aponte was finally captured and hung.

In 1817 England brought pressure on Spain to abolish the slave-trade, and paid Spain a recompense of two million dollars toward this end, whereupon slave-running became as common as modern bootlegging. Later restrictions were abandoned. But that there was fear of the blacks, or at least distaste of plain speaking, was revealed when in 1827 the Havana authorities ordered the suppression of Humboldt's *Ensayo Político* on Cuba because of its observations regarding slavery.

At the same time there was a definite abolitionist sentiment among many of the whites; it crops out everywhere in the literature of the day. Anselmo Suárez y Romero, in his novel *Francisco* (1838) wrote, after bitterly describing the horrors of a sugar *ingenio*, "I tremble to find myself in a land menaced by the wrath of God for the constant irrigation of blood and sweat of an unhappy race."

By the time of Viceroy Leopoldo O'Donnel y Joris (Count Lucena, 1843-9), revolt was seething in Cuba; and it had a negro flavor. It was provoked because the whites had suddenly taken to arbitrarily dispossessing the free negroes and mulattoes, some of whom had become quite wealthy. O'Donnel struck swiftly; death and imprisonment was racked upon a group of suspected slaves near Matanzas. Many free negroes were flogged and tortured. In 1844, he put to death the famous negro poet, Gabriel de la Concepción Valdés—one of Cuba's noblest characters—and punished some 3,000 others, in all killing about 2,000—acts which inflamed the populace.

White and black, without regard to pigmentation, suffered and struggled side by side during the independence wars. Black General Maceo and black General Moncada, noble men both, had more than loyal white officers; and no man was more honored than the ex-slave Juan Gualberto Gómez, one of Cuba's finest patriots and most brilliant journalists. "The war began in Oriente," wrote Manuel de la Cruz, "because there the negro is loved, not feared." And the independence assemblage at Guáimaro voted immediate emancipation. The blacks struggled far more persistently for national independence than did the whites.

With national freedom, the whites, though grateful to the negro, were in a superior economic and intellectual condition and controlled most of the wealth. The negro, but recently lifted from slavery, less educated, was kept in a subordinate position, although the average white Creole hotly disclaims any such thing as color prejudices. A little conversation with the white Cuban soon reveals the real barrier that exists.

The American occupation at once exercised repressive measures. The negroes' lodges and other cultural activities were prohibited. In appointments the white Creoles were favored and social barriers were set up.

This division, despite the patriotic events which at times have welded the races, is long-standing and fundamental. Cuba's greatest novel, *Cecilia Valdés,* written by Cirilio Villaverde in 1833, deals with the passionate but tragic love of a beautiful octaroon for a Spanish youth of high family—a story of bitter frustration due to the strict drawing of the color line, against which the novel propagandizes. And in more recent times, straws in the wind have indicated that Cuba is not always the brotherly place its leaders vehemently insist. The negro who rises in the social scale must at least be worthy the phrase, "He passes for white."

To some extent Estrada Palma, Cuba's first recognized President, continued the Wood attitude toward the negroes; and during Magoon's administration subtle discrimination was exercised against them. By 1907 a definite movement along color lines had been provoked. In that year Evaristo Estenoz—a negro general in the 1906 revolt against President Estrada Palma's reëlection—organized the Independent Party of Color to fight for negro rights. They argued that while the negroes had provided 85 percent of the 1895-98 soldiers and constituted 75 percent of the voters, they had not been rewarded politically to a corresponding degree. They had been generously offered many things by the Liberal politicians in 1908; but after elections, ignored. Estenoz and his companions continued agitating, till in 1910 they were arrested and put on trial in April. The following month the Morúa law was passed forbidding any political party along racial or color lines.

The black leaders were released, but for two years bitterness increased—the whole movement being involved in many political machinations. By 1912 it got out of hand. It is said, but not authenticated, that President Gómez prompted its disorder that he might declare martial law to dominate approaching elections and tyrannically reinstate himself. In any event, May 20, the tenth anniversary of the founding of the Republic, Estenoz led his followers to open revolt.

Over Gómez' protest, May 31, American marines were landed at Daiquirí and other points and rushed inland to protect American property. Serious burning of haciendas and of a large sugar mill occurred. Though 4,000 armed negroes took the field, by July 18 the last body of them had been cut to pieces or captured—after 3,000 had perished. But though Gómez was victorious, he immediately granted many negroes important political jobs.

Thus, the race question runs submerged in all Cuban politics. The Conservative Party, represented by exiled ex-President Menocal, is dominantly a white Creole plantation group; the Machado Liberal Party, whatever atrocious things may be said about the present despotism, undoubtedly more generously includes the mestizo and negro elements. Only the Liberal Party has ever given full-blooded negroes prominent positions.

Though the negro Martín Morúa Delgado held a high post under Conservative Estrada Palma, socially he was discriminated against; but under Liberal Gómez, Morúa became President of the Senate and Secretary of Agriculture; and his very black wife was admitted to the highest official and diplomatic ceremonies. At his death, much to the shocked disgust of the white Creoles, President Gómez rode beside his two black brothers at the funeral.

At the present time, General Manuel de Jesús Delgado, Secretary of Agriculture, is a full-blooded negro, a most capable and unostentatious official. For the first time, a negro has been given a diplomatic post, a career hitherto closed to him—Ramón Vasconcelos, commercial attaché in the Cuban legation in Paris. Negroes have come to occupy other important appointive posts.

But in the winning of high elective office, they have been less successful than immediately after independence. This is in part due to cumulative corruption beginning with Governor Magoon during our second occupation. To-day, votes—especially negro votes—are a matter of barter; it requires 40 to 50 thousand pesos for a candidate to buy his way into the Chamber of Deputies. Few negro candidates can afford this amount, despite the fact that through the allotment of lottery graft, the returns of the office would far exceed the sum mentioned. On the other hand, the ordinary negro has learned to demand a definite monetary price for his vote—he knows he will get nothing more in return—and from a certain angle, this can be considered an advance in civic consciousness.

The *guajiro*, the Cuban peasant, with the exception of Canary Islanders and other ethnic elements and many mestizos, is usually black in skin and culture. He is the serf on the big sugar and tobacco plantations, but occasionally achieves some sort of semi-independence. This class dwells in poorly made leaky *bohios*, the floor muddy from the indriving rain and cluttered with half-naked smeary babies, dogs, chickens, even pigs. His clothing is cheap cotton trousers and unadorned shirt; his wife, without underclothes, wears merely waist and very long skirt, bare feet in ragged slippers or fiber *alpargatas*. He stacks up wood with a little cross over the pile to burn for charcoal, transports goods on donkeys and mules to remote corners, or cuts tobacco stalks, bamboo, or cane; and fortunate in the eyes of his neighbor is the one possessing a yuca or *malonga* patch. Often they have no food in the house; and the unwary traveler may go far before he finds sustenance.

In 1849 the Cuban Economic Society used the phrase, "150 negroes produce 400 tons of sugar." And as Márquez Sterling adds nearly a century later, "The slave served as the machine. Machines later freed the slaves, but did not free the blacks; and this most miserable slavery which weighs down the spirit of the country, from which both blacks and whites suffer, spreads through the land, carpeted with sugar-cane, ignorance, superstition and poverty."

3 SÓNGORO COSONGO

Much of Cuban culture is definitely negro in origin—music, folklore, dancing, some of the food. Music is a golden net which entangles the feet of every Cuban; the negro has given Cuban music a cachet recognized the world over. Father of our modern jazz, Cuban music has reached refined interpretation for both Cuban and Paris concert hall and operetta in the work of Moisés Simón, who also has written some of the best danzón tunes, based on negro melodies, and is best known in this country for his *Peanut Vender*.

In the plastic arts, negro influence, though as yet twice removed, also enters. The Cuban intelligentsia took up fervently the *vanguardista* movement in sculptoring; this has influenced the work of such artists as Sicre but especially Navarro. Many of the *vanguardistas* who might not have been so receptive of the new tendencies had they been derived directly from Cuban negro sources, unwittingly hailed with enthusiasm African forms delivered via Paris; but the basic negro inspiration in them has perhaps caused such work to be more intelligible, hence more at home in Cuba, than in other New World Latin countries.

The Cuban negro possesses little literary tradition. In Africa literature was monopolized by a special class which carried on the group traditions. This protected class naturally never fell into the hands of the slave-traders, hence the negro was brought to the New World shorn of his literary heritage, though popular song and dance and many old memories have been preserved. These have been recorded by, among others, that indefatigable folklorist, Dr. Fernando Ortiz, forced into exile because of the intolerance of the Machado régime.

The first notable negro in Cuban belles-lettres was the ill-fated Gabriel de la Concepción Valdés, who besides flaming love-poems and proletarian cantos, which made him the idol of all Cuba and carried his fame to far Hispanic lands, was a salty political critic. His biting polemics landed him in a prison cell, from which he continued to pour forth plaintive lyrics. Finally he was executed at the early age of thirty-five in the year 1844.

A group of modern younger negroes has recently become literary conscious and are turning out interesting work. The journalist, Gustavo E. Urrutia, for the first time, has turned public attention to basic facts in the negro problems of Cuba. The poems of Regino Pedroso, though inspired by the modern proletarian movement, have definite negro roots, form and phraseology. Of them all, the most outstanding is Nicolás Guillén, whose slim but brilliant book of verse, *Sóngoro Cosongo,* is a violent, singing, lilting outburst of the negro heart. The lines swing to the rhythm of the rumba, of *ñañigo* dancing, to the beat of drums and rattles and dusky hands pounding out jungle music. Guillén represents a complete rupture with traditional Castilian verse-forms and a definite attempt to express negro sentiments, thoughts and life in typical negro-Cuban Spanish. Though not prolific, he has written the most vital poetry of modern Cuba.

The patriotic mulatto Maceo said on being asked if he resented being classed as a negro: "When the black man is not ashamed to be black, there'll be no shame in being black."

V WHITE CUBA

1 SILVER BUCKLES

THE TRAGEDY AND CHARM OF upper-class white Cuban Creoles reside in their belonging to a past of velvets and silver buckles not intrinsically their own. They are, as one of their intellectuals remarks, "offspring of a racial trunk whose dense foliage of ideals and medieval mysticisms did not rot in time. We were born and grew up in a house of ruined grandees."

However much the Creoles may have engaged in modern professions, or associated themselves with American business initiative, or promoted sugar production, their activities, mentality and emotions float in a vague middle world, neither Cuban nor Spanish. That world has definite contours, a geography; yet, infolded, it despairingly attempts—despite trappings borrowed from Paris and the United States—to be culturally self-sufficient. Many members of this group affect great disdain for all things Cuban; that most vital and human about them, albeit untutored, they decry as barbaric and disgusting. They hold their fatherland up to the mirror of modern Europe and America and find it frayed and crude, even though they themselves, however much they may ape foreign ways, are powerless to break the mold of their own inadequate cultural compulsives.

They do add grace to Havana and a few other centers by cherishing older traditions, while Cuban life patently disintegrates before the smashing impact of northern initiative. That very grace, clung to with forlorn tenacity, crumbles before swarming, pushing American tourists demanding both coarse and snobbish joys, before the swirl of black folk in the shoddy low-roofed *barrios,* the pushing peseta-grabbing raucousness of the poorer Spanish immigrants, and the mongrel tide of mixed offspring—Chinese, African, Spanish, challenging the chromatic range of the rainbow.

Paradoxically, they are both more of the modern world and further remote from it than their Mexican cousins, who have been fused and blended, shaped and reshaped by the hammering incoherence of a hundred years of independence. Mexico enjoys slightly more autonomous political reality than Cuba, caught in a series of static tyrannies attempting the undignified rôle of avoiding any offense to the United States or to the powerful banking and sugar companies that are the final courts of appeal.

Thus, from the standpoint of pure patriotism, the white Creoles are a bit stodgy and unpleasant, politically more pathetic even than the actual custodians of their national sovereignty—those brutal governors for absentee American capital. Yet for all the Creole Toryism, the clinging to dubious and unreal privileges, this maladjusted group has preserved much that makes Havana delightful to eyes enjoying the rococo and mid-Victorianism stripped of sensual rigidity.

But there is something non-vital and pitiable about their distaste of actual political brutalities, their wistful consciousness of the ebb of an era and the ebb of their own cultural significance—that vacant reminiscent stare, that helpless weary flow of the hands—inarticulate resentment at threatening economic disaster and fear of the inscrutable dark future of their country. They are a class still-born into the brief epoch between the downfall of Spanish rule and the Republic and enjoying a gilded, non-creative renascence during the sugar booms, but never at all comprehending the dilemma of race and politics involved in their country's pseudo-independence.

Such a one is my dear friend Dr. José Camargo. When he was an industrious sugar-planter, a large-scale *colono*—before the absorption of the industry by the banks and the present sugar debacle—he must still have preserved the ruggedness I have observed in this hardy class of rural white Cubans who have fought so long for their patrimonies no more successfully than he. But now his defenses have cracked on all fronts. Big law-firms, with far-reaching political and financial tentacles, monopolize most of the island's important legal business; if Camargo cannot be a *colono,* neither do twenty-five years of solid connections now help him much in his legal practice. Even more in youth, he must have had a fine courtesy, sensitivity about human relations, well-meaning faith—all the best-foot-forward of an inherent soul-weariness. Those likeable traits have not deserted him, but the fumbling bewilderment behind them has now oozed through the mask; and this tinge of melancholia, of frustration, has become almost Oriental passiveness—its maximum achievement the slow delicious savoring of his inordinately long Larañaga cigar. Suddenly his ideas seem pudgy; evasion casts nebulosity about him.

The younger generation—though youth prevents ultimate despair—is even more caught on the prongs; it finds even fewer doors open to it, the harsh economic circle ever narrowing. This is sad, for they have better intelligence by far than their elders; but no real economic or political leverage commensurate with their capacities. Among their peers, competence reigns and functions, but does not carry over, either in comprehension or functioning, into the administrative or creative life of Cuba. The Yacht Club balls, the various social functions, maintain properly polished grave joy. Those dapperly dressed handsome youths, with long fine hands, white skins, sleek plastered black hair, were born with the aura of self-assurance and dignity; capable for any task—facing a firing-squad, directing a Santa Clara sugar plantation, or matching wits and elegance against the best of any country—somehow they are excluded from any vital relation to the dull forces mastering Cuba for the ends of power and exploitation. Yesterday exploitation was their divinely appointed rôle—save that they imparted to it feudal éclat and noblesse oblige and leisurely appraisals not crudely greedy. But the machine age is not their toy. Their usefulness as major-domos for American capital diminishes as the pivot of political gravity shifts from them to more ruffianly militarists and *mestizo* riffraff, who, less intelligent, but more vigorous and aspiring, can whole-heartedly and without compunction perpetrate the atrocities of rule demanded in a country sodden with financial absenteeism.

Nor can they properly participate in the new, deeper struggles for liberty, inevitably proletarian and dark-skinned. Their participation but misdirects and vitiates that struggle, tries to swing it around the circle into a belated Fascist survival of feudal prerogatives.

Their day has been brief enough. What little expansion they enjoyed was won gradually, painfully, from Spain, subsequently by coöperation with American overlordship. They were a flash between two eras. A goodly share of them were Tories during the independence struggle, refusing to assist the fearsome ragged patriots of Maceo and Gómez; but others, despite personal sacrifice, to which they are not willingly prone, were a valiant part of the long fight for free Cuba. Both reactionaries and libertarians won doubtful rewards from the new era, though better by far than those of the masses. Now their day is irretrievably passing.

2 BLOOD OF THE COLONY

The independence struggle had grown out of the iniquities and economic stupidities of the colonial régime—little changed despite previous loss of all the rest of Spain's New World empire. Though Spain, during the nineteenth century, had been shaken by gusts of liberal and Republican sentiment, essentially the Spanish government and hierarchy still formed a social complex based upon monarchy and super-domination of the State, submergence of the individual to the *cives romanus* status—privileges but neither rights nor responsibilities. It involved feudal aristocracy; a pre-Renaissance Church denying the individual religious self-expression; a colonial system drinking the blood of subjugated peoples—Cuba, the last, was most suffering. Spain was still steeped in traditions of official cruelty, disguised by romantic sentimentalism and false chivalry and filled with racial and religious hates.

In Spain, as Elias Entralgo has pointed out in the *Revista Bimestre Cubana* (XVIII, 1, 132 ff.), social order is not the result of harmony between authority and liberty, but variously derivative of individualistic attraction for military chieftainship (*caudillaje*), tyranny, or anarchy. This was the typical cycle of Spain in the nineteenth century: Ferdinand VII (tyranny); militarism of the revolts; interludes of anarchy. Outside of the political sphere, the Spaniard shuttles between the authority of the State and the authority of Religion.

The Indians killed off, negro slaves imported, Cuba from 1511 to 1899 was held under Spain's iron rule and was governed—more often misgoverned—by civil and military grandees. Their portraits reveal a notable series of powdered perukes, velvets, ruffs, gaudy uniforms, medallions, glittering spangles, and silver-hilt swords. From them were derived many of the traditions and customs of the better-class Cubans. The Viceroys ruled arrogantly, enriched themselves and the Church, sent back a stream of gold, sugar, tobacco and tropical fruits to the mother country. The first gold of the Americas glistens on the ceiling of Santa María Maggiore in Rome; the Escorial is lined with mahogany, ebony and other precious woods from Cuba's forests.

The Viceroys established the Inquisition, built fortresses and convents, discovered copper mines, grew tobacco, punished smugglers trying to evade the monopolistic trade-acts, established the Santa Cruzada order against vice, died of the black vomit, took the census, fought English and French buccaneers sailing over the horizon under Drake and Jacques Sores, and imported ever more and more slaves. Pleasant days of plaza promenade at the hour of retreat; high-comb señoritas in white lace mantillas, skirts spread wide in their spanking two-wheeled *volantes;* festivals and music and feudal intimacy, featured the life of those days.

Even after splendid living, palatial elegance and corrupt orgies where comely black wenches danced naked in hilarious balls, the Spanish governors by 1838 poured ten million pesos annually into the Spanish Exchequer, garnered in part by beating free colored men to death and driving black slaves ever more harshly under the lash.

For more efficient exploitation, caste lines were closely drawn. All offices, religious, civil and military, were plums for Crown favorites. The division between things Spanish and colonial was almost uncrossable. A Spaniard born in Spain—be he an ignorant Extremadura peasant—was superior to the native whites, whatever their category. The merest Spanish clerk was socially above the wealthiest Creole.

As the latter could achieve no distinction in government, Church or Army, gradually he came to consider himself— as early as the end of the sixteenth century—Cuban rather than Spanish. Though no idea of political separation filtered in, on occasion the Creoles vigorously defended their ideas and rights. In 1717 some five hundred of them rose in revolt to oppose a proposed tobacco monopoly. They captured Jesús del Monte, not far from Havana, before being persuaded to lay down their arms. In 1721 and 1723 two more Creole tobacco uprisings occurred. These clearly indicated growth of Creole self-consciousness—inevitable outcome of economic and political discriminations, the strict rule of favoritism, and the trade regulations benefiting only the mother country.

Too, the Creoles were held, so far as possible, in intellectual as well as economic inferiority. All books on the Index Expurgatorium were prohibited from leaving Sevilla, the one port which could have commercial or other relations with the island. The Edict of Delaciones specifically prohibited Bibles, the Alcorán, the Talmud, Luther, Molina, Ario, Voltaire, Rousseau, Voleny, Diderot, Crébillen. All reading material was carefully given the once-over before being allowed to pass to the New World. Charles IV declared that "learning should not be made general in America," and in 1799 (reiterated in 1802) forbade Cubans to send their children to study in the United States.

Elementary education in Cuba, mostly in private schools, had as the chief text the catechism; for the girls, mostly embroidery. The University curriculum remained very theological to the very end of Spanish rule.

Despite such restrictions, the Creole, blood-brother of his Spanish overseers, was far above the mulattoes; for notwithstanding strict caste lines—interbreeding had increasingly taken place as the centuries rolled by. The lowest in the social scale, with little legal or economic protection, were the negro and mulatto slaves. All these social and racial barriers greatly complicated the cause of Cuban freedom; and not until Spanish tyranny began leveling all colonials, did these walls temporarily break down enough for the common cause of national freedom to embrace all Cubans irrespective of color or creed.

3 FEMALE FACES

Independence witnessed temporary American political domination—far more race-prejudiced than Spanish. Creole snobbery reasserted itself. But even more than under Spanish rule, the economic roots of "the aristocracy" in the productive life of the country were cut by the double-edged knife of Spanish immigrant commercialism and American economic imperialism. The Spaniards, it is said in Cuba, can take out the heart of a competitor, scrape off the fat, and replace the organ without the owner's knowledge.

Expediency and contemporizing on our part (as elsewhere in Latin America) have alone caused casual alliance with this class by American capital as a stabilizer while the basic resources could be monopolized. To-day the need for this utilization is fast disappearing. For industrialism inevitably, sooner or later, wars on medieval feudalism. It turns, when the time comes, to the less couth mestizo; as in Mexico, to Calles. Machado represents the preliminary unenlightened inauguration of this new era.

Not that the white aristocrats did not have their brief belly-full fling at wealth under the Republic. The white marble palaces of the Malecón, the double-decked mansions of the Vedado and the luxurious villas of the Reparto attest to their expanded scale of living. They swung on the upgrade of the prosperous sugar wave during the World War and the subsequent "Dance of the Millions"—the 1920 postwar orgy.

But up to that time there was as yet little to stamp Cuba as a typical tropical country exploited economically by foreign capital. Foreigners, Spaniards, Cubans, even negroes, had made and lost fortunes since the day the Spanish flag was hauled down from Morro Castle. But 1920 was the peak of dizzy credit expansion, when the card-house collapsed. American capital has gathered in the fragments until to-day, the iron ring of American banks, public utility interests and sugar Centrales, has been forged to an enduring yoke. Step by step the Creoles have been shoved aside.

Suddenly the Creole discovers himself a stranger in his own house. He never has had too defined a rôle in Cuban independence life, certainly none comparable to that in other Latin-American countries. He came too late on the world scene. In Mexico even to-day, despite this class's elimination from power and former wealth, it is fiercely traditional. The Cuban Creole has always had more grace and less efficacy than that. He should be Catholic, and is—but in a casual way more befitting a cosmopolitan gentleman unaddicted to extreme dogmatism. His churches have none of the historic interest or grandiose sumptuousness of those in Mexico; his convents have become warehouses, smelling of tobacco, molasses and onions in bulk. Impossible to imagine Cuba shaken by a religious struggle which even up until the last decade devastated a large part of Mexico, and is still a political issue.

The Creole women, too, are between worlds; though in Cuba, as elsewhere in the Hispano-Moorish world, women's faces stare longingly from ancient balconies. But a few, for better or worse, have sought a modicum of emancipation. Swimming and sports claim such in the swank seashore clubs; a few swing golf-clubs. Others will be found —chaperoned it is true—dancing on the Plaza roof to jazz bands, where the musicians, bedecked in fake Hawaiian wreathes, bang tunes thrice removed from their African source but still bearing a trickle of twice-removed Cuban music. And a few, emulating northern sisters, have founded the Lyceum, where occasionally the military authorities permit innocuous addresses and art exhibits. Unwelcome divorce has even stuck its foot in a door never to be closed.

But those female faces of Cuba, of Latin America! Behind their lattices, in their barred windows, they hint at the Oriental seraglio, at mystery and romance. The glimpse of a shawl, the suggestion of artistic coquetry and alien ways fortifies this impression of the delightfully exotic. But the initiate knows that the system that imprisons female faces behind bars, however strange, is prosaic. As elsewhere, romance must be captured individually rather than collectively.

In time, those faces, as Mañach points out, fall into common categories: faces a bit wan from seclusion, most of them, despite olive-hued skin, slightly pallid, wistful as though striving to be properly distinguished from a distance; faces with large black eyes wearing virginity's expectancy; matronly faces still hopeful of some break in daily monotony. Those in higher balconies seem resigned to a dream-like existence; their glance, more platonic, bespeaks merely idle curiosity. Those on the street level, since masculine eyes come closer, are more alert, more captivating; practice has made them flirtatious—souls less settled, more disturbed.

Except for certain morning shopping hours, Havana is still largely a male city. The tide of pedestrians along narrow Obispo Street with its cavernous cool dark stores, or under the Prado portals, wall-papered with magazines and multicolored lottery tickets, the idlers in the open-air cafés —nearly all are men in white linen, now and then a bright tie under a dark chin shaded by a straw hat tilted effectively. Women seated alone in the cafés are either Americans or prostitutes, the latter quiet and reserved, the former legs crossed, smoking, listening to the ambulating orchestras, but despite apparent receptivity, less courageous than their Cuban sisters in affairs of the heart.

On Thursday and Sunday nights, the complexion of the throngs changes. Then the Cuban brings out his family— bejeweled portly wife, beautiful slim daughters dressed in diaphanous organdie, eyes sparkling with pleasure and amorous expectancy, children of all ages—to listen to the café orchestras and sip *naranjadas*.

4 CULTURAL WEDGE

The grace and restrained animation of Cuba's respectable levels comes precisely from this rhythm of habits of the cultured Creoles. The center (in a sense never understood by Americans caught in the haste of industrialism) is the home, for even those Vedado mansions with their elaborate high stucco ceilings, their deplorable taste for scrolled furniture in sets, marble-top tables, gold vases, portraits in gaudy gold frames, heavy hangings and general air of palatial nobility, remain intimate refuges. There in Cuba, the Ausländer is more likely to be promptly admitted and banqueted than in any other Hispanic country; and he finds hospitality and courtesy, however lavish, far more sincere than elsewhere. For the upper-class Cuban is the most approachable of all the New World aristocracy south of the Rio Grande.

Despite parvenu ostentation and bad home taste, family ties of wife, children and relatives are imperatively binding. There in flowering patios, scented, and melodious with song-birds, in the cool rooms, laddered by light from almost closed shutters, the home becomes an oasis of peace during the hot siesta hours. Little disturbed by the gusts of a feminism, not yet evolved into graceful solutions, or by the factory system of haste, the Cuban can still properly savor connubial and domestic delights; both sexes escape into proper spheres with equal ease.

In these more intimate family reunions, too, a real stimulation springs from feminine sweetness, gentleness and vivacity—outstanding traits of the Cuban woman—which our American sisters would fain deny any one raised in such apparent captivity.

The Cuban woman loses pseudo-equality, gains something by the very narrowing of her interests. Far more than the Mexican woman, she surmounts her obstacles: her conversation is spritely and keen, for to interest men she must depend upon, besides her beauty, warmth and sweetness, finesse rather than variety—the human foibles, nuances of sex; art and literature, perhaps.

But she also has her courage in public questions, and in hours of darkness has not hesitated to step boldly outside of her traditional rôle. During the independence wars many fought shoulder to shoulder with the men, went to jail, died in battle and before the firing squad. In 1807 they signified their adhesion to the insurgent cause by cutting off their hair; in 1868 they showed their loyalty to the Yara revolution by going through the streets with their hair down over their shoulders. Such names as Marina Manresa, the filibuster Emilia Teurbe Tolón, Lola Garí Ayala de Betencourt, Teresa Mendoza de Domenech, "Manana" who accompanied Máximo Gómez, and gave birth to a daughter Celemencia, "in the smoke of battle," Magdalena Peñarredonda, Luz Noriega, and others are legendary in Cuba for their courage and sacrifice. The companion of the martyred Cirilio Villaverde, Emilia Casanova, in 1868, founded the first feminist organization in Cuba: "The Workers Society, League of Daughters of Cuba." And during the present Machado despotism, the women of this class, above all others, have not hesitated to speak their minds, to demonstrate publicly, and to suffer atrocious imprisonment and maltreatment.

Where not submerged by American influence, central Havana bears the full impress of the Creole class. According to Hergesheimer, it has become a mid-Victorian Pompeii: "marble façades, inadmissible architecturally, yet together holding surprising and pleasant unity . . . Spain touched by the tropics, the tropics—without tradition—built into a semblance of the Baroque."

Tucked in the interstices, around the fringes, facing the water-front, is the world of negro and mulatto and Chinese slums, of brothels and pornography, of dives and cabarets, ñañigo and rumba and snake-magic. But Havana's facade is Creole. The marble Malecón, the sea-wall, the La Punta bandstand ring, the Prado and the shaded Paseo de Martí with deep stone benches—here, during twilight and early evening hours, after the post-siesta visits to the clubs, circulate the social élite as in colonial days. At the horse-races, the women come modishly dressed, trying to be chic and foreign and succeeding with a flourish all their own, as if for lawn-parties or soirées; not with the English sport air, ready for tramping across sloshing turf.

The Creole keeps up the Conservative tradition of the theater as opposed to the more vulgar neighborhood rumba stage. Though his class has given no new creative impulse, they sit genially in the boxes listening to stale Spanish comedies. They subscribe to poetry-readings of the visiting Spanish literati, who—just as the second-rate English novelists raid the American lecture platform—inflict their mediocre talents, with a comparable air of superciliousness on a properly impressed Latin America. Now and then our best people are found watching a hotly contested *quiniela* between Azules and Blancos at the exciting Jai Alai Frontón.

Thus the Creole aristocrats are a sort of cultural wedge between the Cuba of the past and the Cuba of the present, cherishing the real Spain as opposed to the new Spanish immigrant such as the Canary Island cane-field workers. Though in the elbow duties of life, Spaniard and Cuban are quite hail-fellow-well-met, scarcely distinguishable, past feuds completely buried, socially the Cuban Creoles still keep somewhat aloof—however much their smart balls may overlap—from the wealthy Spaniards gracing those ornate marble interiors of the Gallego and Asturian clubs on the Parque Central; for however self-made, the Spaniard is clanny, has not quite forgotten that he is intrinsically superior to the highest Cuban; though often he is but a poverty-stricken immigrant grown wealthy, who has made no effort to improve his culture. In social and intellectual

[79]

lines, the Spanish casino and the Cuban Lyceum are practically non-communicating rivals; the first is chiefly for recreation, the latter for education.

The Creole represents the last remnant of cultured Cuba colonial and European in tradition, that had a slight glimmer after independence—a glimmer that has steadily faded. Whatever European éclat Cuban life still holds, apart from that which is American and native, is still in his hands, a charm constantly being trampled under foot by new alien forces and shaken by the more earth-rooted hosts.

To survive he must inevitably submerge his destiny with that of all Cubans; must go into the market place and politics, not to conserve his ancient privileges, but to battle for the righting of the wrongs of his country.

The younger intellectuals, even many more mature, have already, despite persecutions, lifted up a new banner of faith. The oldest of all, the philosopher Enrique José Varona, is as young as any of them, always ready to lend his pen to any righteous matter; Dr. Fernando Ortíz (now in exile), folklorist, jurist, economist and penologist, is a mind that would honor any country. Nor should one forget that turbulent enthusiastic spirit, the brilliant journalist, José Antonio Fernández de Castro, the clear, forceful insight of Roig de Leuchsenring, the indefatigable labor of that more than noble character, Félix Lizaso, reviving the work and patriotism of Martí, the poet Juan Marinello (long imprisoned, now in exile), that fine proser—the best in Cuba to-day—and equally fine character, Jorge Mañach. The list is far from complete. Some of these and others have found their new rôle in Cuban life courageously.

VI THE CUBAN AS HE IS

1 MELTING POT

THE SPANIARDS CARRIED TO the New World the blood of Celt and Iberian, Roman and Visigoth, Moor and Jew, Basque and Mauretanian. Conquest brought into the main stream the blood of the Siboneys: the people of eastern Cuba are still called *Indios*. During many decades of the last century, Mayan captives from Yucatan were sold by droves to the Cuban plantations at twenty-five pesos a head. The 30,000 French from Haiti at the end of the eighteenth century and others from Florida, at its transfer to American sovereignty, provided new ethnic ingredients. During the nineteenth century Chinese added to racial complexities. The Count of Pozos Dulces, writing of cheap labor in Cuba, remarked to the Junta de Información in 1886: "To the African violently torn from the forests has succeeded the Asiatic, docilely contracted and added to the peasant proletariat of America."

Intermixture of all these on a large scale over centuries has created a color range from the blackest *bozal* through the "tobacco-leaf" complexion and the *cetrino* (vying with the citron in hue) to the blonds from Valencia and Asturias.

Out of this melting pot is emerging the true Cuban type, into whose hands the destinies of the island must ultimately come. Between these racial, economic, and cultural extremes is encountered the Cuban in the making—in this mestizo middle ground.

Here, more than anywhere else, is tradition less binding. The mestizos make Cuba seem a very parvenu country— agitated, shoving, casual, informal. If the Cuban has much in common with all tropical dwellers, to other Latin Americans and to those of the New World in general, his attributes nevertheless have an individualized *cachet*.

To disembark in Cuba is to drop into noisy pandemonium, docks full of shouting, gesticulating people. The hotel-runner, baggage man, taxi-driver jostle and shout in your ear even before you open your baggage in the customs and call you life-long friend with the ease of a boyhood chum. Jovial, full of camaraderie, they introduce you to a country of little false dignity, of gay comradeship, of reckless enjoyment, of hit-and-miss living, of real vitality.

The pandemonium of the docks continues within the city. A place of 600,000 inhabitants, Havana in normal times has five times the traffic and animation of Mexico City with its million. Its itinerant orchestras, the raucous shoe-shiners, peanut and lottery venders, have Neapolitan vehemence. The cafés are loud and garrulous. Havana ever presents the spectacle of bustle, of darting taxis, of hasty shouts. But it reminds one of flitting fish, its industriousness a bit meaningless, circle-chasing, not the ponderous onroll of Fifth Avenue nor the anarchic but purposeful whirlpool of Paris.

On my first visit to Cuba, I felt I had arrived in a tropical setting devoid of etiquette, gravity or perspectives, among a people of no circumspection. Like we Americans, hail-fellow-well-met—though in a much different way—the Cuban has a heart-on-the-sleeve friendliness. Essentially democratic, he ever tries to annul all social barriers. This, coupled with a *dolce fa niente* attitude, a sense of personal independence, a love of hedonism, brings resistance to all social subjection. Of delightful frankness, he likes his ordinary acts open to his neighbor's gaze. Among poorer classes, homes are wide to the streets, permit the stare of every curious passer-by. The heat itself defeats personal seclusion. Air is more valuable than privacy.

The dignified reserve, the polished courtesy of the Mexican toward all strangers, the careful watchfulness over the sensibilities of others, have no place with the average Cuban. Part of his natural breeziness, his apparent rudeness, so different from the hidalgo tradition, is merely confidence in his own ego. Just as he accepts himself as an independent functioning entity, so he expects the next man to feel the same, hence no need for exaggerated politeness. The Mexican (not the Indian elements), though equally an egotist, also has self-assurance; but it is jealous, suspicious, doubtful of itself, giving rise to ingrained brooding, a baffling interplay of arrogance and inferiority, so absent from the Cuban. The Mexican is the great introvert of the Americas; the Cubans and we Americans are the extroverts.

The Cuban's lightning cerebration is free of the intricacies of most allied peoples. If superficial, he is more alert. In both his lassitude or his violences, he is less sustained than the plateau Mexican. Eternal heat gives him a nervous jerky quality. Not persevering, he darts from activity to activity with gypsy gusto; ever is he avid for new sensations of a hardy, often brutal sort, the unique, the adventurous. But he is the surf, not the sea; and the patterns of his life are multiple and often beautiful, though inconsistent. Reckless of means, never conservative of energy, thought or money, all he has generously belongs to all. He is a delightful, stimulating companion.

Were it not for the Cuban's heartiness, honesty and sheer love of living, plus a decidedly invigorating skepticism, he would be stamped as shallow. For he simply refuses to take life seriously. The profound person is considered a bore; the consistent person, annoying.

The Cuban's irresponsibility may be ascribed in large part to the lack of balance and consistency in both his political and economic realms. His country has gone through cataclysmic shifts of prosperity and depression. Fickle Crown trade regulations no sooner promoted commerce than they as quickly destroyed it. During the War and post-War booms, Cuba rode on the crest of extravagance; in off years it has hit the nadir of misery. The popular saying is, "Cuba is a cork"—meaning it will always bob up again.

As a result, the Cuban too exclusively worships the god of chance. An inveterate gambler, he will spend his last copper for lottery tickets, though he knows dishonesty rules the drawing and that it sustains political tyranny. Usually hopelessly in debt, he is ever borrowing from Peter to pay Paul. But why worry? To-morrow the wheel of fortune will turn. Convinced that life is but a series of violent ups and downs, he takes it as it comes with an easy shrug. Thus he is good-humored even in dire disaster. Penniless, he can still sing and dance.

The Spaniard—from Moor and Roman Catholic Church —has always been a fatalist. The Cuban's religion undoubtedly contributes to his idle hopefulness; he expects manna from heaven, not by the sweat of his brow or by sustained civic effort.

The political situation greatly contributes to this same psychological approach. The Cuban, aware that his country is a protectorate of the United States, that his government functions in a realm of unreality, that the final resort is American banking interests and our State Department, refuses to get profoundly excited about politics. Rightly or wrongly he believes any solution answering basic Cuban needs can meet only failure. This has led to ever greater divorce of power from popular will, to constantly diminishing honesty and efficiency in government.

This has engendered a thoroughgoing cynicism about all important public questions. No decent man can play a self-respecting part because the final determination is outside of him, his group, and his country. The proud man can only throw monkey-wrenches, never assume responsibility. Solemn politics is reserved for the sycophants, petty tyrants and grafters.

Only recently has the bitter anti-Machado struggle altered and deepened the attitude of the younger generation. But desperation is often as poor a counselor as indifference or iconoclasm. A few elements to-day in Cuba have staked their lives, their futures, upon the patriotic solution of Cuba's plight, their old devil-may-care attitude metamorphosed by the bloody facts of the present tyranny. For the first time, as a native writer remarks, some Cubans are really coming to have souls. Slowly the realization is being born in that only through years of sacrifice, years of persistent struggle, can Cuba emerge from its present disastrous condition to attain any measure of freedom. Something of the fierce, deeply patriotic and fearless attitude of the Ten Years' War Cubans and the 1895-98 patriots has been fanned into flame again. Those past years of struggle proved that a Cuban cannot be surpassed for valor, abnegation and determination.

2 CHOTEO

Yet the keynote of the majority is still gay irresponsible insouciance—the Murad gesture, perhaps though but a mask for deeper values which frustration in personal and national life prevents him from realizing.

This contradictory attitude is best exemplified by *choteo,* an airy persiflage and conduct uniquely Cuban. To analyze this—and I turn in part to Jorge Mañach's brilliant little study—is to illuminate very fundamental truths.

Choteo has considerable resemblance to the shrugging *vacilada* or flirtatious inconsistency of the Mexican of mixed blood, which I analyzed in *Mexican Maze.* But the

[85]

Mexican inconsistency has deeper life-roots, a richer philosophical heritage, and represents more action than the Cuban conversational trait. Mexican *vacilada*—caricature tinged with paradox—is rooted in the intrinsic duality of existence, its impossible contrasts and juxtapositions—the goat's horns on a saint, egocentric hedonism and sorrow buffeted between extreme extravagances, a cactus growth of hybrid racial expression. More a non-organic fusion than a negation, it interweaves the ridiculous with the sublime, vulgarity with purity, quite in defiance of all European logic; always it is shot through with passionate mirth, a self-protective distortion. It reveals real desperation, a psychic dominant of bitter humor and passion, shaken like a fist in the face of God.

Cuban *choteo* is not so penetrating, more on the surface, less sophisticated, more childish. Not so instinct with life's complexities, its lower forms are merely impish; at best, express cynicism and resentment.

But it also is a decidedly hybrid product. *"Choto"* is Andalusian for "little goat." *"Chota"* means "to suckle." Hence *choteo* would mean etymologically "to act like a little goat," implying thereby a certain vulgar sexuality, intimacy with all procreative acts and subsequent nursing. The negro dialect, Lucumí, has the word *"chot,"* "to talk," and the Pongué dialect, *"chota,"* "to spy upon." All these suggest sex, intrigue and derision wrought into a burlesque of conversation. When *choteo* is merely airy persiflage, akin to Irish blarney, it is healthy, external, easy-going, though often connoting intellectual laziness. Its essential characteristic, however, is to take nothing seriously, to toss everything nonchalantly to the winds.

Choteo is far more a Creole than a negro approach. Yet the negro does contribute primitive lackadaisicalness, *laissez faire* joy, perhaps the very ingredient that has caused Cuban Creole litmus to change color. For otherwise, the negro brings solemnity, seriousness, respect, and his joy is sensual, free of pessimism, a generous giving devoid of Creole frustration and selfishness. *Choteo* is a hybrid product.

Behind the Cuban's mask often is a soul as sensitive and credulous as a child's; but if on certain occasions the Mexican enjoys displaying his deepest emotions, the Cuban prefers ordinarily to appear flippant, to show disrespect, to ignore surrounding persons, ideas and objects—an exacerbation of the normal critical spirit of the Creole. *Choteo* demands that the user be "agin" all things without considering their intrinsic values, a sinister ingenuity to prove that nothing is worthy of respect. Patriotism, the home, culture, bring a sarcastic, often pointless remark, "sheer romanticism." Even though the speaker think differently it behooves him to deride—a socially obligatory approach.

Often the Cuban admires that which he most ridicules. He merely hides aborted volition, a disinclination to bend body or mentality to any defined goal. Hence he is really expressing resentment, impotence to achieve a desired end. Such invidiousness is quite European, but in the Cuban it quite disrupts the connection between interior appreciation and outer conduct.

The joke, however, is not an attribute of children, monkeys or dogs; it implies competence, mental agility and experience. But it is often a subterfuge to escape the strong, evasion permitting temporary escape from a difficult situation, an affirmation of one's own personality against that which is superior or reputedly equally powerful. This, too, finds much of its source in Cuba's general political dilemma.

Cubans have an unusually quick sense of the comic, a trait common to all peoples of extra-rapid mentality, but rather than attempting to plant barbed satire, they often merely irritate rather than amuse. Style, restraint, rhetoric, serious planned living increase the subtlety of humor; this is why humor flourishes in England, not in Sevilla. It is likewise a manifestation of consciousness of superiority, discipline, assurance, the generosity of people strong enough to cede many things. "But in a small country," remarks Mañach, "the feeling that because of its weakness it is not respected, causes all within it to respect each other less, destroying the contrasts which invite humor."

For *choteo,* as the vulgar comic and a mere required social convention, is a very low form of joking. The perpetrator discovers things funny where no one else does, discovers the absurd in all authority when often none exists. *Choteo* does not attempt, as does humor—which has such far-reaching apperceptions of cause and effect and life's difficulties—to meet clever controversy by greater *esprit,* and failing, abandon the contest; but comes back, if necessary, with a desperate jocose insult. Not a species of dialectic but of attack, it belongs to the corner-grocery type of so-called humor, and although in no sense practical joking, it is decidedly mental slap-stick, amusing at the first blow, subsequently boring, its *savoir faire* quick to evaporate.

Choteo often becomes mere bad manners. For no reason at all in a public gathering at an impressive moment, some one gives a loud guffaw, an audible yawn, or shouts an offensive phrase. He is determined, for no intelligible reason, to run counter to the audience. Of a sudden he demands some artificial excitant, perhaps to defeat the leveling lethargy of the tropics—his resentment at the overwhelming fatigue of thin blood.

Reflex laughter usually results from some unexpected but not serious accident, but *choteo* does not restrict itself to accidents upsetting dignity; it is uproarious at any upset of disorder, however dangerous. The Cuban is ever delighted at the overthrow of concord and hierarchy, for order is synonymous with command, discipline, obedience, external composure. In disorder the individual may express himself more freely, with less restraint. How much more comfortable one feels on entering a stranger's room slightly topsy-turvy! The Cuban's more vulgar humor expresses enmity toward any limitation whatsoever on the individual's expansion and whims. A spirit of extreme personal independence is always simmering in the dregs of Cuban banter—the word "caprice," like *choteo,* comes from *cabra*—"goat," i.e., to jump around like a goat.

Three escapes for individualism exist: rebellion or rational conformity or the achievement of personal power. *Choteo* is disguised rebellion inadequate to rebel. Our parlor radicals should take lessons.

Any studied application, any profound attitude toward any problem, any love of disciplined living, is a limitation upon irresponsibility. The Cuban, not wishing to be bound by even his own emotions, is therefore quick to render asunder his own sentiments as well as those of others. But did not Stirner point this out as the true road to the true ego? The Cuban solves it by subjecting the pathetic to an immediate guffaw, an ever alert denial of true feelings.

A Cuban historian has stated that Cubans are only apparently obstinately frivolous; but because of their innate individualism, they have real difficulty to deliver themselves whole-heartedly to accepted attitudes or opinions or to devote all their powers to any given end.   Unfortunately deeper implications, the more remote nexus, escapes them.

3 BEEFSTEAK DEATH

Mañach tells of a Cuban in a Paris crematory who shouted, as a body was thrust in, "Let me turn him over and over!" Instinctively he wanted to reduce the cadaver to a beefsteak category, to strip it of all sentimental attachments and dignity. Latins, in the company of death, must ease their terrific emotions by repartee and laughter. Mexicans assume an open camaraderie with their dead, which often they cannot assume toward living friends. This is sane—far superior to our horrible nerve-racking Protestant ceremonies, but the Cuban carries this attitude to the point of burlesque. Though the black hearse will gleam with gold; the coachman wear scarlet coats trimmed with gold and black cock-hats on flaxen wigs; the horses be draped in black nets with golden tassels (he must have his theater, too) his jokes at a wake are notoriously disrespectful, perhaps a defiance of death, a desire to prove that the lost life-companion is still with the watchers.

The Spanish General Concha declared that Cuban happiness consisted of a "shrill little guitar, a little game cock, and a little deck of cards." The Cuban propensity for amusement and gambling reveals little regard for the day after to-morrow. They so want independence—but not the bold and brave sort demanding long sacrifice, only the placid, evasive sort—that they are content with not being bothered; for this immunity they will fight obstinately.

Yet all this psychological discussion is perhaps too much a picture of the uprooted city Cuban. The picture is not complete without the hardy, soil-wise poorer *colonos*, those lowlier white and mestizo cultivators of rural Cuba, still pathetically resisting disinheritance by foreign corporations and battling day by day with the elements and an economic situation that spells eternal defeat—almost. The "leading families" of a passing rural scheme, they struggle on the mountain slopes of Oriente and Pinar del Rio, harvest their citrous fruits in the Isle of Pines. They live simply, often in *bohios*, but well-built, three or four of them hitched together, tightly thatched. The furniture is mostly home-made and solid, chair-bottoms and backs of rawhide. An ornate saddle and other harness are stacked in the corners. If more prosperous, they have more solid quarters, a porch lined with colonial pillars and plants in tubs and tins covered with tissue paper and bows. Wherever the traveler goes, from laughing Sagua to haughty sad Santa Clara, from severe harsh Guantánamo to young bold Manzanillo, along the country roads, women leave their sewing machines by to stand in the door, curious and smiling, their long white calico dresses covering even their shabby country-made shoes.

The men are clad in light washable trousers, many-colored shirts, linen on holidays, with an ornate shirt-like coat split at the sides over the hips, pleated and with pearl buttons and an intricate embroidered monogram. Their Panama hats complete "Cuba's national costume."

All of this indicates a reciprocal influence between the character and experience of a people. Custom, modes of thought, differ with locale. And they have varied with the ups and downs of Cuba's prosperity. Out from the depths of national idiosyncrasy are called forth the situations and conduct most adequate for different situations. During the liberation wars, the Cuban revealed taciturnity and irony— now garrulousness, frankness, bantering cynicism. These various attitudes are transitory, not anthropological characteristics. Now he is entering upon a new phase.

For another source of Cuban superficiality is not merely the unreality of foreign-controlled institutions, but lack of roots, due to his alienation from the soil and the tools of life, and equally the over-night establishment of the Republic—which we would up and set going. The American colonies had long prior training in self-government; Cuba, none. The noblest and most capable Cubans had been killed off. Yet a new government had to be knocked together without prior experience. Schools had to be founded with teachers snatched from the very rim of the uneducated. Professionals had to be polished off in a day. Art and literature revealed hurried attempts to express something worthy of the new freedom. The new void had to be hastily filled with little or no training, with no comparative standards, everything led to superficial improvisation. Lawyers and doctors with meaningless diplomas were able to achieve prestige easily. Politicians without antecedents sprang into the breach with empty pockets to fill them quickly. Newspapers sought to be witty and succeeded only in being pornographic or burlesque. Cubans were pressed into cultural activities in chain-gang style. Now, these opportunities hedged about, a deeper realization of the inadequacy of past efforts is entering Cuban consciousness.

For Cubans, "the hour has come," declares Mañach, "to be critically joyous, audaciously disciplined and *consciously* disrespectful." A new cross to bear, they, a reënslaved people, must now face their mature needs.

PART II

¡CUBA LIBRE!

"The Antilles freed will save the independence of our America and the honor, already tainted and wounded, of Anglo-Saxon America."

José Martí

Five months before the Spanish-American War:

"I speak not of forcible annexation, for that cannot be thought of. That by our code of morality, would be criminal aggression."

William McKinley

During the war:

"While we are conducting the war and until its conclusion, we must keep all we get; when the war is over, we must keep what we want."

William McKinley

VII THE CRY FOR FREEDOM

1 THREE NATIONS

THE FINAL WAR FOR CUBA'S freedom had begun. February 24, 1895, a band of patriots rose in arms in the little sprawling town of Baire in the palm-flecked Contramaestre vale of eastern Oriente province. April 1, the noble mulatto emancipator, exiled General Antonio Maceo, disembarked near Baracóa, in the very teeth of Spanish guns. Ten days later, General Máximo Gómez and the great poet-liberator, José Julián Martí y Pérez, leapt ashore at Playitas.

Soon their guerrilla bands galloped from end to end of Cuba. For three long years the island was harried by steel and fire. Flames swept miles of cane-fields. Sugar mills went up in smoke. The black death of typhoid, malaria, small-pox, every sort of pestilence, stalked over the starving island. The terror of the Spanish firing-squads echoed around the world. The bull-pen camps of "Bloody" Weyler shocked decent men everywhere.

The destinies of three countries were altered: a new nation was born; the balance of power in the world was realigned; America entered upon her career of over-seas imperialism.

For the patriots, 1895 was a hopeful and courageous year. For the frightened Spaniards and wealthy Creoles, "a war of negroes against whites."

"Mere bandits already in flight," said the Spanish Minister at Washington to our State Department. The revolters in Baire were led by aged veteran General Bartolomé Masó, a rich hacendado of Manganuillo, and by gigantic black General Guillermo Moncada of unbelievable bravery; both were veterans of the earlier Ten Years' War to free Cuba, which had terminated in 1878 with the Treaty of Zanjón. These two were holding the cause together until the arrival of the two outstanding leaders, Maceo and Gómez.

Maceo—a handsome black fellow with a King George beard—came with twenty-two companions on the little schooner *Honor* from Fortune Island to the eastern tip near Baracóa. Still forty miles out at sea, the eager passengers sighted the flat anvil crown of steep Yunque de Baracóa. Anxiously they scanned the tropic shore, the silver-plated cliffs, of their native land. Their prospects of encountering immediate aid were slight; the possibilities of being captured, great. They brought little but faith and courage.

Soon they had need of all their courage. A Spanish war-vessel crowded them upon the rocky coast. A smashing wave lifted and drove the *Honor* well upon the shore.

For fourteen days, bitter, relentless pursuit of Maceo and his companions kept up across rugged hills, through valleys choked with forests of tall coconut palms and humid banana groves. Maceo lived on sour oranges and green bananas. One day he had to fight his way through the cordon of his pursuers seven times.

His brother General José Maceo became separated, endured incredible hardships. Antonio's companions were killed, others captured. But Antonio himself—twenty-five wounds recorded his reckless staunch fighting during the earlier Ten Years' War—once more came through safely.

He finally took charge of a little band in an unremitting struggle against unbelievable odds—until shot, December 7, 1897, too soon to witness the final triumph of his cause, but long enough to stamp him the greatest military leader in Cuba's history.

On the stormy night of April 11, the Dominican General

Máximo Gómez—also a Ten Years' veteran—accompanied by Martí and four other companions, was dropped off a German freighter in a small boat at the eastern end of the island to battle through a stormy black sea to an invisible shore. But for sighting lights in a cabin, they would have been engulfed. Toiling frantically at the oars with blistered inexperienced hands, they were finally flung ashore in a crash of surf.

They fell on their knees. Gómez kissed the sacred soil of Cuba. They looked up to see a few stars glimmering through inky clouds.

They, too, now had a long Odyssey; but Gómez—a small athletic man, keen eyes, eagle nose, flaring white mustache, and high-strung ways—pressed forward till they met faithful followers.

The return of Maceo and Gómez reanimated the insurgents. Men sprang to arms everywhere.

The Army of Redemption had no uniforms; the soldiers marched in rags. Half had no weapons, only the curved machetes of cane-field slavery. Their arms ranged from shotguns to sport rifles. But they marched behind Maceo, "The Lion," and Gómez, "The Fox,"—names known and loved in every Cuban home; and they were fighting for the ideals of liberty set forth in the joint proclamation of Gómez and Martí, written March 25 in Monte Christi, Santo Domingo. Its brotherly love message embraced all Cubans whatever their race and creed in a crusade against Spaniards, without bitterness for Spaniards, for in "the Antillean breast there is no hatred"; only sympathy for the soldiers of Spain, torn from their homes as conscripts to assassinate the sons of a liberty for which they also aspire.

Gómez was the wise, hardy leader of Cuban independence; Maceo, its Garibaldi; Martí, its Mazzini.

2 DAWN

The new fight for freedom was the continuation of a hundred years' struggle. Against the aspirations of Creole, mulatto, and negro, free man and slave, Spain had utilized all her stern machinery of government. Absolutism and centralization were the cornerstone of her colonial policy. All functions of government, even in local affairs, even including Church administration, were concentrated in the Captain General, a royal appointee.

Economic life was hedged. Spain permitted only noncompeting products to be raised, and until the end of the eighteenth century, monopolized all commerce through one given port—Sevilla—permitting but one ship a year, a condition ever more irksome as the developing United States became Cuba's logical market and supply-house. Much of Cuba's trade had to be clandestine; smuggling activities, facilitated by frequent wars between Spain and England, were often as romantic as those of American rum-running.

Under Charles III (1759-1788) Spain made concessions, but later these were partially withdrawn. Not until 1801—then for only eight years—was Cuba really opened to world commerce. In 1818 the bars were again somewhat lifted, though heavy export and import taxes were imposed; numerous discriminations favored Spain. Not until 1891 was a reciprocity treaty drawn up between Cuba and the United States, the island's best customer; but in 1894 this was abrogated; new special advantages for Spain helped precipitate the 1895 revolt which led to freedom.

Thus trade restrictions, arbitrary heavy and antiquated taxation, the exclusion except for minor posts of all Cubans from the government, and slavery, were the chief causes of nineteenth century discontent.

Ideas of independence inevitably dawned. During the 1810-20 colonial independence wars, Cuba might have joined in the general movement, save that the country, an island, was separated from all friendly succor, and being a strategic key for all Spain's overseas possessions, was more firmly held. Also the Aponte negro revolt and Bolívar's proclamation freeing slaves, frightened Cuban Creole sugar and tobacco growers dependent upon a large cheap labor supply. Before their very eyes were the recent bloody scenes of Haiti's independence—the murder or exile of all whites; and the 1817 census in Cuba gave over half the population as black.[1] In 1823 Royal Minister Calatrava told American diplomatic representative Kilpatrick: "The fear the Cubans have of negroes is the best weapon Spain has to guarantee its domination in that island." [2]

Fear of the blacks and complete trade dependence on us fostered in the breast of the separatists the hope of annexation to this country. During the Hispano-American independence wars and subsequently, secret societies worked toward this end. "The Electric Chain" was the name of one discovered in 1822; and when Governor Francisco Dionisio Vives arrived in 1823, he found the island honeycombed with them. The most famous, "Suns and Rays of Bolívar"— due to Ferdinand VII's restoration of colonial tyranny— planned revolt August 16, 1823, to establish the Cubanacán Republic. Leaders were arrested; others fled the island. Though resuscitated in 1829 as "The Black Eagle Legion," the society accomplished little, for Vives—though Cuban society became progressively more corrupt, disorderly and degenerate—ruled with an iron hand.

Cuban bitterness was further heightened by the odious rule of his successor General Miguel Tacón (1834-8)—most appropriate name: *tacón* means "heel." His chief claims to fame were his beautifying of Havana—part of the Prado Boulevard; his deportation of the brilliant Cuban scholar,

[1] 688,000 inhabitants; 250,000 black slaves; 115,000 free colored.
[2] Manuel de la Cruz, *Estudios históricos*, VII, 25.

José Antonio Saco, "the first to teach the Cubans to think"; and his cruel administration.[3]

During Tacón's period, liberal revolution in Spain restored the 1812 constitution which provided for Cuban representation at the Cortes. Tacón smothered the idea with arrest and exile, insolently announced, "I am here, not to promote the interests of the Cuban people, but to serve my master, the king."

Revolutionary movements gathered force. Numerous juntas plotted from American soil. In 1848 the Partido Anexionista advocated exchange of Spanish for American sovereignty; so did the leading 1849 revolutionary junta; and from 1848-53 the columns of La Verdad (New York) warmly advocated annexation. After the turn of the half-century, the Order of the Single Star, the Cuban Junta of New York and of Havana, as well as the papers El Cubano and El Filibustero, clamored to come under the Stars and Stripes.

From these beginnings arose the first noteworthy armed attempt to free Cuba—the López conspiracies of 1848-51. Narciso López, native of Venezuela, had risen to a Spanish generalship during the independence and Carlist wars. He married in Cuba, became identified with wealthy Creole interests, plotted revolt in the hopes of annexation and to buttress up the Cuban plantation slave system by its incorporation in the American South. American southerners, eager for a new slave state, abetted his plans, offered him supplies—never delivered because of both American and Spanish vigilance. Discovery of his plan to revolt June 24, 1848, caused him to beat hasty exit to New York.

He worked for armed support and found many Ameri-

---

[3] Oriental whimsicality featured many of his decisions. A wealthy profligate count seduced and abducted a charming young woman betrothed to a very poor man. Tacón gave a decision in favor of the count, but ordered immediate marriage and his return to his plantation with his bride. A Tacón emissary murdered him on his way. Thus the girl got the man of her choice plus the estates of her abductor.

cans, still thrilled by the capture of Chapultepec in Mexico, eager. The *New York Sun* obligingly ran up the five bar single star banner of free Cuba on its flag pole, but the north feared a new slave state. López went south, offered command of his expedition to Jefferson Davis, to Robert E. Lee, to Governor Quitman of Mississippi, each of whom ultimately declined. Late spring, 1850, López set sail with nearly 600 men, mostly Americans, some of them Mexican war veterans.

Spiritedly they attacked Cárdenas east of Matanzas. López lost sixty men; no Cubans sprang to his aid; strong Spanish reënforcements obliged him to reëmbark his troops for Key West. A new expedition set to leave April, 1851, was held up by the American authorities.

Early in July, Joaquín de Agüero, having expected López to arrive, raised the cry of liberty in the public square of sumptuous Camagüey (then Puerto Príncipe). The fifteen men who responded were easily put to flight. But in a nearby town, the several hundred who gathered to hear Agüero read a declaration of independence, drove back an attacking Spanish column and two days later fought a successful engagement at Guanamaquilla. But ere long Agüero went to his death on the scaffold; other companions were shot.

López finally landed in Pinar del Rio with 400 men, but was soon captured and executed.

After 1868, under the liberal Spanish governments of Amadeo, of the 1873-4 Republic, and the limited monarchy restoration of the Bourbons (Alfonso XII, 1874-1885), the Cubans petitioned for constitutional home-rule, freedom of the press, the right to hold office in Cuba, and to be represented in the Spanish Cortes. No heed was ever given to these demands.

3 TEN YEARS

Cuba remained relatively quiet until 1868. October 10 Carlos Manuel de Céspedes of Bayamo (birthplace also of the great Cuban soldier, Saco, and of Estrada Palma) burned his Demijagua sugar hacienda, and gathered his guajiros about him—147 men and fewer guns—and pronounced for independence. The famous revolutionary assemblage of Guáimaro (April 10, 1869) drew up a constitution, Céspedes became President. It was voted unanimously to emancipate the slaves at once. Black recruits flocked in.

But the provisional government, soon driven from Bayamo, its capital, was harried from pillar to post. The Presidency was passed from hand to hand, to Salvador Cisneros, Francisco Aguilera, Tomás Estrada Palma (subsequently first President of the freed Republic in 1902) and others.

By the close of 1869 Céspedes' 147 men had grown to 26,000, fairly well-armed. President Benito Juárez of Mexico sent him two veteran officers of the war against France and the Empire. Santa Clara, Camagüey and Oriente were in continual turmoil for ten years; no place in the country was really safe.

Spanish Count Valmaseda, under whom Weyler was then serving, decreed, "Every man over fifteen found beyond his farm will be shot, unless his absence can be justified. Every uninhabited hut will be burned . . . Every hamlet not hoisting a white cloth . . . will be reduced to ashes."

Secretary of State Fish to the Spanish Minister: "I hope the document is a forgery. . . ."

November 27, 1871, eight medical students, arrested on a trumped-up charge by the Spanish authorities, were put to death amid the cries of a bloodthirsty mob; others sentenced to hard labor were marched through jeering throngs to their tasks. But it was a Cuban acting substitute governor

[102]

who signed the death warrant! To-day a monument at the foot of the Prado commemorates their martyrdom with the simple word: *"Inocentes."*

General Máximo Gómez, gaining many brilliant victories, came to the fore as the principal patriot leader. Antonio Maceo aroused admiration for his reckless audacity.

But in 1875 Gómez was roundly whipped in Camagüey. The war dragged on another three years. Most of the Creoles killed or having made peace, only the negroes and poorer whites kept up the struggle.

In 1877 Governor General Martínez Campos won the sobriquet of "The Great Pacifier" by persuading the Cuban leaders, assembled in a ruined farmhouse, to accept the Zanjón pact, pledging full amnesty, negro emancipation and political reforms.

A few, Maceo, Calixto García, refused to recognize the treaty. Maceo finally went into exile. García, on the verge of capture, put his revolver to his chin and fired. The bullet came out between his eyes, leaving a hole in which later he always wore a bit of floss.

Desultory fighting continued until 1881; there was a slight outbreak in 1885; conditions remained permanently insecure; a woman visitor in 1887 to the leading American sugar estate of Edwin Atkins observed that every one traveled with rifle and pistols and that the place was surrounded by armed guards.

The Zanjón treaty was only a truce. The Ten Years' War had offered up 50,000 Cuban lives on the altar of liberty; 208,000 dead Spaniards also lay at the foot of the altar. Spain expended $300,000,000; $700,000,000 went up in smoke. By blood and sacrifice, the Cubans had laid the cornerstone of freedom, had proven to themselves they could cope heroically with Spanish military power.

But not until May, 1902, the American occupation terminated, was Gómez finally able to say over the tomb of Céspedes in Santiago: "At last you have a country."

Fortunately he died before having to witness the shame into which the government gradually sank deeper during the twenty years of so-called independence; before learning how little the Cuban people had gained from all his heroic efforts, his country's tragic sufferings.

4 TIGERS

The guerrilleros of insurgent General Agramonte dashed into the bivouac of a superior Spanish force to rescue the patriot leader Sanguilly, wounded and captured. Afterwards the general remarked: "My soldiers did not fight like men; they fought like tigers!"

That was during the Ten Years' War. The 1895 struggle, precipitated by Masó and Moncada, and carried on by Maceo, Gómez and Martí, was to prove even more bloody and devastating. The Cubans, fighters and civilians, suffered losses and brutalities. The island was laid waste.

At the very outset the patriots suffered many misfortunes and tragedies. López Coloma was seized and later shot in the "Laurel Ditch" beside the grim walls of Cabaña fortress in Havana. The brilliant negro journalist, Juan Gualberto Gómez, was sent for fourteen years to an African penal colony. Numerous veteran leaders of the Ten Years' War were placed under precautionary arrest. The earlier revolters were harried from place to place.

But by May 3 the insurgents were able to give real and successful battle at Jarajueca on the open plains of Boca de Dos Ríos. Costly the success. Martí—after a lifetime of patient indefatigable publicity and organization to make possible this final blow against Spanish power—was shot down in his first battle.

His body, despite desperate efforts by Cubans to retain it, was captured. Spanish Commander Ximénez Sandoval was a Mason; so was Martí, and to Gómez in the Cuban camp was said to have come the simple two-word message: "Martí . . . Sandoval . . ." beside each of which were sketched a rose and a cross—to indicate decent Christian burial. Years before Martí had written: "It is necessary to live and die embracing the truth. Thus, if one falls, he falls in beautiful company."

Martí had been the breath, the soul, the brain of the cause. The Cuban sculptor Juan José Sicre has caught a characteristic pose and expression. Martí's large head has the full high curve of intellectuality; he is looking down studiously and compassionately, eyes deep under bushy dark brows. The large mustache and small beard lend distinction.

On Martí's birth, January 28, 1853, his father—who later repudiated all his son's ideals—had immediately resigned from the Spanish army: he didn't want his boy to grow up to accuse him of serving the "tyrants." Before he was sixteen, Martí was arrested in Havana for publishing seditious articles and poems:

> Oh, how sweet it is to die when one dies
> Fighting audaciously to defend one's country!

He was sentenced to six years' hard labor with ball and chain in the quarries—No. 113 in the first White Brigade, the black "death hat" on his head—an experience of which he afterwards wrote: "The pen describes with blood what I saw; but bloody truth is also truth." From there, he wrote in verse to his mother, telling her not to weep over his fate —he was merely "a slave to his years and his doctrines. . . . The life of noble souls, my mother, is to struggle and die honoring the fatherland; to save it, if necessary, one must tear out his own entrails."

Friends succeeded in having him incarcerated on the more benign Isle of Pines and later secured his deportation to Spain. He arrived there in 1871 on the *Guipúzcoa,* sick and penniless, but immediately hastened to study in the Universities of Madrid and Zaragoza. Frequently he issued —especially after the first Spanish Republic was founded— a futile appeal to the Spanish people for justice and freedom for Cuba.

He made his way to Paris, to Mexico, to Guatemala, writing for papers and magazines, did not take part in the Ten Years' War, but after the Zanjón pact, returned to Cuba. Spanish General Blanco soon called him "a crazy man . . . but a dangerous one . . ." and September, 1879, shipped him off to Santander a prisoner on the *Alfonso XII*.

Ere long he was in New York, "where the unprotected always find a friend and a helping hand." . . . A trip to Venezuela. Dictator Castro drove him back to New York. "A foreign land is somewhat like a ship. Hard that sensation of indefinable disgust. One feels the ground rock and shake under his feet. . . . One walks staggering, one's spirit out of balance."

Again he wandered—through South America—everywhere agitating for Cuban freedom, everywhere royally received, already famous on three continents. Uruguay, Paraguay, and Argentina made him joint consul in New York, and his modest stipend and writings now enabled him to concentrate most of his efforts upon creating an effective independence movement. He made the warm friendship of Charles A. Dana, editor of the *New York Sun,* who opened his columns to his writings and to the Cuban cause.

Martí's first great hour came when he was flung that stormy night upon his knees on the beach of Playitas, once more embracing his native soil. His second great hour came when he perished for the cause to which he had dedicated his whole life.

In one of his verses Martí hoped to die with his face to the sun, the flag of his free country on his tomb with a spray of flowers. When the war was over, the Cubans put up a marble monument in Santiago with the new Cuban flag in a glass-covered niche, and there school-children some-times, when they remember, lay fresh flowers beside the flag.

Spain rejoiced tumultuously at his death. The Queen Regent and the Minister of War cabled congratulations to Sandoval. He replied that the revolution had received its death blow.

Instead, a thousand new patriots sprang to arms. Over in Tampa, Florida, the poor but loyal cigar-workers—for whom Martí had been the one great idol and who for years had uncomplainingly contributed their pittances in behalf of Cuban freedom—now responded with their last pennies. A new and fiercer determination carried on the struggle. Brave death begets bravery.

Estrada Palma took Martí's place as head of the Cuban Revolutionary Party. By July '95, four months after racing through the jungles as a fugitive, Maceo found himself at the head of 16,000 men not badly armed. The same month, in the battle of Peralejo near Bayamo, he routed the Span-ish forces decisively, killing General Santoclides; Captain General Martínez Campos barely escaped capture.

Cuban constitutional delegates at Jimaguayu approved a new Magna Charta of freedom (September 16). Salvador Cisneros Betancourt was elected President; Máximo Gómez was confirmed as Commander-in-Chief; Antonio Maceo was named Lieutenant General.

To these revolutionary efforts, Spanish Prime Minister Canovas del Castillo retorted: "Cuba shall remain Spanish though it takes the last man and the last peseta." Troop shipments increased; at one time over 200,000 regulars were on the island, not to mention local militia and Tory *vol-untarios*.

Thus the Cuban struggle represented a much more bril-liant, arduous and self-sacrificing effort than our own Rev-olution. The Spanish royal forces were far more over-whelming. Whole regiments of so-called American patriots threatened to return home unless their back wages were fully paid up and they received a cash bonus for reënlistment; the Cuban patriots fought the war through without pay. Far more resources and abnegation were needed than to achieve our own freedom.

5 FIVE MILLION PILLS

With a mobile force of 200 men, Gómez dashed west and slipped through the famous Trocha. This cyclopean barrier dividing the island, stretched from the south coast at Júcaro to the northern fort of Moron, then was completed by the Robles River flowing into the sea at the Romano Keys. The Spaniards boasted that its frequent blockhouses, barricades, trenches, fox-pits, barbed wire, heavy garrisons, constant patrols would never let the Cubans through to the western provinces.

On Gómez' heels, Maceo's army battled its way west. Out of far eastern Oriente province, Maceo crossed the Jobabo River into Camagüey. With a relatively minor skirmish, he broke through the Trocha full force into western Camagüey, clear into the rich plains of Santa Clara. The rebels, a ragged enough crew, singing the triumphant *La Invasión,* had ventured into the guarded domain of 180,000 trained Spanish soldiers.

The Spanish press immediately found consolation in the failure of the Trocha to isolate the campaign: "At last they are where we want them!" The two chiefs would soon be bottled up, their forces quickly exterminated, their very bones picked.

But to have insurgents in the heart of the wealthy sugar area was alarming for both Spanish and foreign owners. All clamored for protection. To curtail Spanish revenue, Gómez forbade mill-owners not paying taxes to the independence government to cease grinding cane. Few obeyed. Their haciendas were burned; if caught they were shot.

The rebel march became a cloud of smoke by day and a flame by night as they marched "West, ever West!" Before the end of the year, the smoke of burning fields could be seen from Havana itself.

December 15 in Mal-Tiempo, the revolutionists smashed the Spanish forces with cold-edge machete charges, capturing 20,000 rounds of ammunition. They pressed on, tearing up railroad tracks, requisitioning fat cattle and grain.

Before the year was out, Gómez and Maceo again met full Spanish forces in the heart of Matanzas province, only a hundred miles from Havana, in Coliseo, a town of the "Milk and Honey" valley, surrounded by rolling hills blanketed with gray-green sugar-cane fields. Again Martínez Campos was sent flying—clear to Havana itself.

By the new year, Gómez, hot on Martínez' heels, crossed into the Güines district, destroying as he went; by January 5 camped in Marianao, on the western outskirts of the capital. Maceo pressed still further west into Pinar del Río province. Every part of Cuba was now up in arms, had a provisional independence government.

"Supplies, more supplies!" cried Gómez to the civil government and the New York revolutionary junta. Despite virtual blockade by coöperating American and Spanish authorities, supplies were run under the very noses of revenue cutters and frigates—but never fast enough.

"I need five million quinine pills!" cried General Calixto García—President at the time. Impossible to send enough, thousands of troops died from malaria.

Ten thousand cartridges came through. "Never has there arrived, more timely for a sick man, the medicine he needed for a cure!" exclaimed General Boza.

The Cubans were now triumphant almost everywhere. Spanish General Salcedo was astounded at "the simultaneous and audacious advance" of Gómez and Maceo, "the aureole of cane fires in their vanguard." The Spaniards now found themselves "pursuing an enemy perfectly mounted, with expert riders." The "drafted" Spanish infantry hardly knew how to use its weapons. Salcedo lamented the careless defense of the Trocha, a "superb military bulwark . . . an impassable barrier. . . ." Now "victoriously" they had invaded Matanzas province itself, had destroyed the railway system, "not barbarously as alleged but as is demanded by the modern art of war." They remounted "fresh horses from the towns, estates, and pastures of that rich territory" and astonishingly "threw themselves at last courageously on the provinces of Havana and Pinar del Río."

The Spanish troops, far more handicapped by the climate, were more afflicted with disease. Yellow fever took a toll of at least 10,000. Too, the Spanish officers treated their subordinates inhumanly. They grafted on all possible supplies. The soldiers' rations were cut down to the starvation point; they had no sanitary protection. Lacking canteens, they drank out of green and muddy pools.

Deputy Sol y Ortega shouted in the Spanish Cortes: ". . . the troops are starving . . . but the generals . . . they bring back so much gold with them that they have actually caused a drop in the gold quotations."

Eusebio Blanco cried: "The poor leave here illusioned and return dying. They are thrown into the sea by dozens and hundreds like rotten fish. . . . When . : . [the] mothers of Aragón were the first to protest, crying, 'Let the rich also go!' they were branded as unpatriotic and put in jail, as was Blasco Ibañez in Valencia."

The Spanish conscript was dirt beneath the heel of the military aristocracy; not a few sympathized with the Cubans they were fighting.

6 PENNSYLVANIA AND POCAHONTAS

Spain, alarmed at domestic criticism and disastrous events on the island, recalled Martínez Campos, "the Peace-Maker," and sent over "The

Butcher," General Valeriano Weyler y Nicolau, apprentice of ruthless Valmaseda during the Ten Years' War.

The Bishop of Barcelona blessed him, placed his army under the protection of the Virgin, prayed for victory over the Cuban patriots.

Under Weyler's command were now five lieutenant generals, nine division generals, twenty-six brigadier generals, and two marine generals. To back up this gold-braid collaboration had already been sent over 191 cannon, 76 million rounds of ammunition and 176,000 soldiers in addition to those enlisted in Cuba.

Hardly had Weyler arrived than he executed the prisoner López Coloma, who died shouting, "¡Cuba Libre!" The firing-squad worked overtime.

Determined to stop at nothing to achieve pacification, Weyler, who knew the powerful secret aid of a hostile population to an enemy, extended Valmaseda's old order to women and children; and civilians were herded into military bull-pens. He was merely following the approved usages of war.

General Weyler marched with 6,000 men into Pinar del Río to end Maceo. The insurgent struck lightning-quick at every Spanish unit, then rushed to the coast to receive a shipment of 450,000 rounds of ammunition and a dynamite gun, brought by the indefatigable gun-runner, *The Three Friends*.

Wearying of pursuit, Weyler turned to Gómez to drive him east, catch him in a nutcracker, his back to the fortified Trocha.

But October 11, '96, Gómez stormed Cascorro. Ensign Luis Rodolfo Miranda, first in the final charge that captured the main block-house, shinnied up the 18-foot flagpole. Sizzling fire sent a bullet through his hat, smashed the hilt of his machete. He yanked down the Spanish flag and flung out the Cuban colors.

Weyler's aims were not achieved, but his maneuvers

scattered the insurgents badly. He reported all Cuba—save for guerrilla bands—pacified as far as the Trocha.

Gómez retorted, the war had already cost the Spaniards 36,502 men, made fun of Spanish tactics, promised to keep enemy troops, suffering frightfully from fever and dysentry, constantly on the move. "I count upon my three important allies—June, July and August"—the rainy reason when malaria and yellow fever were ever rampant. A smallpox epidemic hit the Spaniards, missed the Cubans.

Despite such favorable allies, despite arms shipments from the United States, despite secret sale of Spanish materials to the insurgents smuggled through the lines from Havana itself, despite the fact that prostitutes—whom the Spanish soldiers paid in cartridges instead of cash—turned over the proceeds of their carnal sales to the patriots, the revolution was increasingly in desperate straits, impotent against the overwhelming numbers and resources of the colonial government.

The darkest hour came when December 7, Maceo, reviewing his troops, only eighteen miles from Havana, was shot from behind a wall. His men got his 210-pound body on to a horse; the animal was shot down; they were dispersed. His aide, young Francisco Gómez, son of the Commander-in-Chief—though himself wounded, his arm in a sling—braved enemy fire to drag the corpse off. He and another officer finally tied it to the tail of a mare; an enemy volley killed this animal also. In the face of whistling bullets, though given superior orders to retire, Gómez still persisted in trying to save the body. Shot through the chest, he fell over Maceo's corpse groaning in death.

General Máximo Gómez proclaimed of Maceo that Cuba had lost "the most glorious of her sons; the army, the first of her generals." Later, free Cuba put up a lofty monument of marble and bronze to their negro liberator; there he rides still on the Malecón, his back to the sea, his face toward the land he loved—"Famous captain, blameless patriot, chief of the brave whose valor equaled their loyalty."

Weyler told the *New York Herald* correspondent this was the greatest loss the Revolution could have suffered; Maceo was "a valiant man, a fighter, indefatigable, tenacious. . . ." Gómez was "old and sick."

The old, sick man set forth on a new whirlwind campaign.

Over in Tampa the cigar-workers again took bread from their mouths to buy more arms. At a meeting of Cubans, humble Martín Herrera emptied out his purse—all his money; then proceeded, since his country needed "every possible sacrifice" to remove his watch and guard chain, his cuff-links, even his wedding ring. Calling his wife America, and his daughters, Pennsylvania and Pocohontas, he had them contribute their jewelry.

Gómez after Maceo's death became such a raging fury of purpose that he kept a trusted aide by his side to mutter *"Ave María!"* to calm him at the first sign of loss of temper. His difficulties with the Civil Government, dodging in safe places, and with his representatives in the United States did not increase his good humor. But by June the following year, the Cuban cause was again on the upgrade. After a three-day battle, the Spaniards were routed in Saratoga.

VIII "REMEMBER THE *MAINE!*"

1 SUGAR, BONDS AND JESUS

Big business and official Washington did not want war. A borrowing not a lending country, we had as yet little surplus capital to export. Washington wanted peace and order in Cuba, not war with Spain, not intervention, least of all Cuba's independence. Our government still preferred Spanish rule if that could maintain satisfactory conditions. The motives of our boss-ridden government—under the Mark Hanna gang and McKinley (yes-man for Ohio public-utilities)—may not have been very laudable; but the war did not originate in the White House; there it was opposed, not quite to the last ditch. It did not originate in Wall Street; there it was fought until, inevitable, it was then utilized for new garnering of wealth.

The Executive branch of our government was pulled by powerful interests opposed to the termination of Spanish dominion. Should Spanish rule crumble in spite of all, then many officials hoped annexation would result. Not in harmony with his own American people, McKinley knew nothing about the Cuban people, was blinded to the fundamental issue.

To placate American sentiment, and not a little annoyed, Washington brought pressure on Spain to set her "pesthouse" in order, but coöperated with Spanish spies here to harass Cuban patriots and block arms shipments. Manuel de la Cruz, active in the New York Junta, declared: "The revolutionists have to struggle on the Cuban coast with the Spanish fleet; in the United States ports with the official zeal of the American authorities," notwithstanding that test cases had proven the Cubans within "the laws which govern(ed) the commerce between Spain and its colonies and the United States."

Thus our government's policy—compounded of desire to please privileged groups favoring Spanish rule or, as an alternative, annexation—led to an evasion of every claim of humanity and freedom and contributed greatly to our finally being flung hastily and unprepared into an unjustifiable war, half hypocritical, half idealistic; led us to found a pseudo-Republic, half free, half enslaved, doomed to political and economic failure up until the present time.

What powerful interests had twisted American policy out of line?

The American sugar people—traders mostly, not producers—manipulated eloquent advocates in Congress to denounce the "Cuban bandits," the pet term then as now for independence patriots.

Already under Cleveland, American policy owed most of its outlook to Edwin F. Atkins, the leading American sugar-producer in Cuba, who boasted that Secretary of State Olney (fellow Bostonian) was "always willing to listen to what I had to say. . . ." An Atkins letter was embodied verbatim in one of Olney's reports to Congress. Atkins had very close relations with John E. Long, Mark Hanna and Charles Francis Adams; through them he worked to prevent recognition of the Cuban insurgents—not supported "by the Conservative elements in the Cuban population." All of Olney's Boston sugar friends wanted, not Cuban freedom, but the immediate suppression of the revolution. Atkins, near the outbreak of the Cuban trouble, had seen 10,000 tons of his cane go up in smoke, and a year later 200,000 arrobas went the same route. He feared the insurgents more than the Spanish authorities.

The budding tobacco trust, not yet in the Cuban field, was decidedly opposed both to Cuban freedom and to bringing Cuba into the Union.

Cleveland obeyed these special interests.

McKinley leaned to the bankers and big corporate interests, then as now, so remote from control of the Republican Party. American brokers held Spanish-Cuban bonds and equities in Cuba properties, which they feared would be lost if independence came. Despite the graft paid to Spanish authorities, American business men, inspired by the bankers and having trade with the island—in 1893 over $100,-000,000—held similar fears. They merely wanted Spain to end the revolt.

Our diplomatic representative Stewart Woodford complained to a Madrid minister in March 1898 that before the disorders, the United States, getting nine-tenths of its sugar abroad, had purchased this from Cuba, which bought back flour, meat and manufactures. But all this commerce was "practically destroyed." Americans had large capital investments there ($30,000,000 to $50,000,000) and loans to Cubans, holdings "valueless" with the existing civil war. He emphasized "the tremendous pecuniary loss" our people "must suffer until peace is restored."

Too, the powerful Catholic Church strongly supported Spanish domination.[1] The Queen Regent was a devout Hapsburg. The godfather of Alfonso XIII was Pope Leo. Church officials had blessed the Weyler expedition and other troop-shipments, had asked God to give them victory. At the beginning of the century, Spain had agreed to indemnify the Church for valuable properties seized by the government—in bonds. The Cuban union of Church and State brought the Church liberal annuities from the colonial budget. Bonds and subsidies were powerful persuasives in determining the Church's position. Naturally it brought

[1] Later when diplomatic relations between Spain and the United States became strained, the Pope appealed for clemency to the Cubans.

full pressure to bear on its members in the United States. Manuel de la Cruz states that an eloquent priest was forbidden by express Archbishopric orders to address a Cuban meeting in Wilmington.[2]

The Spanish-American War, therefore, was a popular sentimental crusade, not due to Wall Street machination; a hysteria of the American people, not of its elected officials or its financial and business powers. If ever the Socialist fallacy that wars could not occur if the people could first vote on them, was revealed, it was in the case of the Spanish-American conflict. As E. L. Godkin of the *Post* wrote: "An immense democracy, mostly ignorant and completely secluded from foreign influence and without any knowledge of the other states of society, with great contempt for history and experience, finds itself in possession of enormous power and is eager to use it against any one who comes along, without knowing how to do it."

The United States had turned violently jingoistic in the late 'nineties. Why?

Ignorant of foreign relations, the American public had suddenly developed an excess dignity in an imperialistic world. In 1889 a remote clash of petty naval dignitaries, epaulettes bigger than their brains, led to the Samoan affair in which the antique American squadron in Apia was facing the German imperial fleet, prideful, new and efficient. No engagement casualties, but our backwoods gloated when our diplomats snubbed the Iron Chancellor himself at the Congress of Vienna. We ordered our first modern battleship.

On the heels of this, an outrage to Admiral Schley's sailors in Valparaiso, Chile, threatened war, with the chances highly in Chile's favor. And two years later (1893) we discovered our empire builders in far parts displaying characteristic enterprise. American planters in Hawaii, led by Dole of pineapple fame, seized the government and de-

2 Obras, VII, 3.

manded annexation, for the "Hawaiian pear is now fully ripe . . . golden hour . . . to pluck it." President Harrison tried hard to pluck it in the name of "the peace of the world." Thanks to Congress, it remained unplucked and the world tranquil in that quarter, until we ourselves upset the peace with Spain.

Before that happened, Olney was telling England, in a way that tickled the tobacco-juicers of the plains and made England lift her eyebrows at America's provincial cheek: "The United States is practically sovereign on this continent, and its fiat is law upon the subjects to which it confines its interpretation. Why? . . . Its infinite resources combined with its isolated position render it master of the situation and practically invulnerable against any and all powers."

Bewildered by growing signs of American truculency in the best Kaiseresque manner, the *Journal of Commerce,* a big business organ, not yet aware that war spells big profits, asked, "What is the occasion for all this militant insanity . . ." and navy jingoism? It decided that the "naval officers were impatient to use their new fighting plans."

The sources of our jingoism were varied. The frontier had disappeared; the last Indian war had been fought; the lonely spaces were gone. We were attuned to a disappearing spirit of adventure.

And the quickening tempo of industrialization, even before our national psychology had changed, was demanding new tropical products and new foreign markets and bringing new foreign names into our provincial cosmos.

Some beneficent effects were already visible: the Interstate Commerce Commission, created in 1887; the 1890 Sherman Antitrust Act; hullabaloo about high tariff (McKinley was stump-speeching: "Cheap merchandise means cheap men and cheap men means a cheap country"); and the stiff 1890 schedule. By 1894 Coxey's army had camped in Washington. In 1895, not Coxey but J. P. Morgan was called in by Cleveland as a consultant, and the Morgan-Belmont bond-sale to save our precious gold was floated amid the Nebraska cry of an "infamous contract with Satan." In 1895 the Federal army was browbeating the Pullman strikers and a harmless soul named 'Gene Debs was to go to jail under a barrage of newspaper vituperation; the Populist and free silver agitation was shaking the West.

Another factor was the series of gold rushes which checked the downward trend of prices.

All in all we were growing up—rather painfully—and had a sudden touchy dread of being considered inferior. An orator at the World's Fair glowingly announced that the beauties there now entitled American genius to claim rank with the artistic culture of the Old World. The American word "bluff" began to be seized upon by foreign peoples as an accurate description of American character. And so we prated about our "peculiar mission," to save the world from injustices, as we unfurled the flags for a hurrah war with Spain. In the eyes of Europe, not our own, our aim was purely aggrandizement. Of course we were really only serving God and humanity.

Thus the Spanish-American conflict was a product of hinterland passion, nobly put through the hoop by yellow journalism and Teddy Roosevelt imperialists. War thereafter was easily pricked into life by an accident to an American battleship, the cause of which was known perfectly to all the corner-grocery spittooners fulminating about the accursed Spaniard.

The yellow press, founded by Pulitzer and Hearst, had to provide thrills for a society no longer able to seek them on the wild and woolly frontier and not having yet developed golf as a substitute. War with Spain admirably filled this void. The circulation of such papers "grew upon bloodshed." The *New York World* climbed to nearly a million circulation. At the very outbreak of the 1895 Cuban trouble, the tall, chilly-eyed William Randolph Hearst, with

$7,500,000 jingling in his pockets, arrived in New York and bought the almost defunct *New York Journal*. He jazzed up the Cuban cause, and boasted he spent a cool million on the *Journal* to bring on war.

It gave good meat, well illustrated by that great artistic genius Fred Remington: virtuous women stripped by vile Spanish officials, and infants held up by the heels and hacked to pieces by *machetes*.

New jingo public men were emerging. Teddy Roosevelt was the pivot of a small group of Republicans, backed by Cushman, Davis, Lodge, Walter Hines Page (editor of *Atlantic Monthly*), Whitelaw Reid (editor of the *New York Tribune*), Leonard Wood—Anglophiles all of them. Shining lights among them had served at the Court of St. James where—their own letters reveal—they had imbibed genteel snobbery and a distrustfulness of all other European powers. Whatever England did, thought this group, was worthy of emulation; though England itself, if necessary, should be chastised. They emphasized high-born privilege and aristocracy, paraded civic ideals and *belles-lettres* rather than mere business and grab. Roosevelt, saber-rattler of the first racket, had on previous occasions evinced an almost pathological desire for war; and his Mussolini-esque poses had captured the imagination of the yokels. He himself wanted to shape our foreign policy to drive off this continent every European power, beginning with Spain. When prospects of war over Venezuela brightened, his spectacles grew moist as he shouted: "I don't care whether our seacoast cities are bombarded or not; we would take Canada. . . . This country needs war." This group saw that if we fought Spain and seized the Philippines, we too would be a worthy companion of the Great Catch-and-Grab nations of the Pacific. Alarmed that Germany had tagged the Philippines for a future colony—a menace to dear England's Australia—Roosevelt, already discerning in the Teutons our potential enemy, declared with the others that we needed the islands for strategic reasons (against Japan); they were the key to the Chinese trade. Now we know they weaken us strategically, that they have nothing to do with the Chinese trade.

2 SCISSORS AND BLOOD

What did we really want? Why did we go to war in April 1898 and not on far more provocative occasions? Were we interested in the property of plundered Americans? Most of the claims had arisen in 1896; some were already settled. Were we provoked at the illegal arrest of Americans? Most such Americans were Cubans with fraudulent naturalization papers. They had been released in 1898. Were we interested in suffering humanity? Then we should have gone to battle during the Ten Years' War, or in the present instance, during the Weyler Reconcentrado brutalities before Spain permitted American relief agencies to operate freely. Were we interested in annexation? Conditions had long made possible serious purchase negotiations. Purchase for annexation, almost as sodden as conquest, violated self-determination, but it would have avoided unnecessary bloodshed. Were we truly interested in real Cuban independence by Cubans? We could have recognized Cuban belligerency—what the Cubans really wanted, to enable them to float bonds and freely ship war material. Even after breaking with Spain, we could have recognized the patriot government.

Such recognition was proposed many times. In the summer of 1896 Congress called upon Cleveland to take this step. But Olney—Atkins' shadow behind him—argued that the insurgents once independent would quarrel, precipitating a race war and the resultant establishment of two republics, one black, the other white, "enemies from the start," never to rest "until one had completely vanquished the other." Cleveland rebuked Congress sharply with a good bounce on that rubber cushion known as international law, but negotiated with Spain for reforms, to appease the American people.

McKinley feared that if we recognized Cuban belligerency and subsequently had to intervene, "our conduct would be subject to approval or disapproval of such a government. We would be required to submit to its direction and assume to it the mere relation of a friendly ally." Terrible prospect! An attitude that accounts for many of our subsequent failures in Cuba.

When in May 1896 Estrada Palma and Horatio Seymour Rubens, attorney for the Cuban Junta, presented an argument to the State Department for recognition of belligerency, Secretary of State Olney fixed a severe cold eye upon Estrada Palma and attacked him for rebel destruction of American property, threatened to prosecute him, warned him to put an end to such a situation.

Rubens, while Olney opened and shut a pair of scissors with little snipping sounds, tried to impress upon him that the new Cuban constitution guaranteed property protection to the citizens of such countries as recognized belligerency. Olney brusquely terminated the interview.

In that barbed triangle of American Big Business and affiliated interests, of the active Cuban revolutionary Junta in New York, and of growing popular sentiment, official Washington—in the good Cleveland-Olney days of brutally executing strikers and the fat corporation days of Boss Hanna—did its best to side with the biggest campaign contributors, a practice which has since disappeared. Both the Democratic and Republican administrations, revealing the great gulf in their policies, gave out arbitrary advice to Spain as to how to restore order, hopeful messages to the American people, and harassed the Cuban patriots in this country. If both administrations, wiser than the American people, tried to avoid war, this was not from any exalted motives—merely the policy demanded by powerful back stage interests.

3 SELFISH CENTURY

Just as Cuban independence was the normal outcome of over a century's growth of national consciousness, so our own failure properly to meet the Cuban crisis—aside from the pressure of powerful interests just mentioned—was a continuation of a long century of official twisting. Our uncertainty was largely due to fear of European powers and desire for annexation. Selfishness on our part, as much as anything else, probably kept Cuba under Spanish rule for nearly a whole century of bitter repression. This, plus big business, in the end robbed our victory of whatever idealism was involved in the armed struggle. We retarded, then aborted, Cuban freedom.

As early as 1810 Governor Claiborne of Louisiana had expressed a fervent desire to see the flag of his country "reared on Morro Castle," for Cuba was the real mouth of the Mississippi. "Give me Cuba and the American Union is placed beyond the reach of change."

Jefferson, ever enthusiastic advocate of annexation, in 1809 announced, "We must have the Floridas and Cuba."

July-August, 1820, the *London Morning Chronicle* ran articles by J. Freeman Rattenbury advocating Spain be forced to turn over Cuba to England—indemnity for the harm done by the Florida transfer to us—to serve as a "depot of thunder" to awe the United States. But Cuba, as a *London Courier* writer expressed it, was still the Turkey of trans-Atlantic politics, "tottering to its fall and kept from falling only by the struggles of those who contend for the right of catching her in her descent." Such ideas made John Quincy Adams, formulator of the Monroe Doctrine, believe the best policy was to let Spain keep Cuba until the United States could get it without risk of losing it. The annexation of Cuba ". . . almost in sight of our shores" was "indispensable to the continuance and integrity of the Union itself."

During the early nineteenth century Latin-American wars for independence, revolutionaries in Colombia and Mexico projected expeditions to free the island. The United States invariably opposed these moves. The belated American delegates to Bolívar's 1826 Panama Congress carried instructions to oppose Cuba's separation from Spain. Then and subsequently we feared European annexation, and we feared Cuban slave liberation might stir trouble in the United States.

President Polk, not satisfied with great accretions of Mexican territory, wished to crown his glory with Cuban annexation. Vice-President Dallas openly toasted annexation. A Senate resolution was introduced authorizing purchase. Secretary Buchanan wrote Minister Saunders in Spain regarding America's anxiety to prevent Cuba from becoming English and our desire to obtain it. The Spanish Prime Minister replied: "Sooner than see the island transferred to any power," Spain "would prefer to see it sunk in the ocean."

All through the century American irritation was fostered by trade-restrictions, seizures of American ships, killing of American citizens, medieval law enforcement, and difficulties and delays of diplomatic negotiations—messages shuttling from Washington via Spain to Cuba, back to Spain, back to Washington. October, 1854, Pierce and Secretary Marcy countenanced the sensational Ostend manifesto by three American diplomats, Buchanan, Mason and Soulé, urging "immediate acquisition" of Cuba for not more than $120,000,000, as of "paramount importance" to the United States. If Spain should decline this far too generous price and her rule endangered the "internal peace and existence of our cherished Union," then "by every law, human and divine," we would be justified in "wresting it from Spain." The newly formed Republican Party promptly stigmatized the Ostend manifesto, the "highwayman's plea." Buchanan declared that "only cowards" feared and opposed expansion.

During the Ten Years' War most South American countries recognized insurgent belligerency. Peru bought $200,-000 of revolutionary bonds. Mexico, Chile, Venezuela, Bolivia, Peru and Salvador received the banner of the Republic in their ports. Colombia contributed $25,000 to General Quesada and $50,000 to the cause. The President of Santo Domingo gave aid. Grant wished to follow suit but was blocked by our annexationists. Some of our better aristocrats did not like the smell of the rebels: their barbarous methods made Caleb Cushing's blood "run cold."

The Ten Years' War strained American patience.

In 1873 we almost went to war over the shooting of Americans on the captured filibuster *Virginus*. In 1875 Secretary Fish, blundering, recited American grievances to to six European governments to incite them to persuade Spain to end the war to avoid American intervention. All, including Britain, gave us the cold shoulder.

We were also upset by commercial difficulties. From 1876 to 1891 inclusive, our trade with Cuba had totaled well over a billion dollars. But we imported nearly five times what we sold. It was cheaper to ship Mississippi flour clear to Spain, pay outrageous duty there, then reship to Cuba, than to send it direct to Havana. Grafting inroads were added to exorbitant tariffs and taxes. During Cleveland's administration though Spain slightly liberalized her policy, annexation sentiment was again prevalent. In 1890 Spain sharply increased duties on American goods. After much agitation, a reciprocity treaty was signed in 1891. American commerce jumped over night. But in 1894 the treaty was withdrawn. The shock to Cuban business, plus the 1893 depression, plus our unexpected 1894 sugar tariff, threw Cubans out of employment, were fundamental causes for the revolt of Gómez and Maceo.

4 MCKINLEY'S ELOQUENCE

Official Washington had been propelled in the direction of annexation for nearly a century. The American public, ignorant of the economic forces involved, had long had a vague pro-Cuban sentiment. Now various resolutions were introduced in Congress; for inquiry into conditions, for recognition of belligerency, for intervention, for recognition of independence.

By election time in 1896 popular sentiment overwhelmingly favored Cuba's freedom. The Republican platform stated that Spain had "lost control of Cuba," was "unable to protect the property or lives of resident American citizens." The American government "should actively use its influence and good offices to restore peace and give independence." The Democratic platform extended "sympathy" to the Cubans in their struggle.

Cleveland's 1896 message mentioned why the United States should be interested in Cuba's proximity, $30,000,000 to $50,000,000 investment, trade $103,000,000 (1893), $96,-000,000 (1894). When Spain should demonstrate "that her sovereignty is extinct in Cuba for all purposes of its rightful existence," then our obligations to the sovereignty of Spain would be superseded "by higher obligations." These we could "hardly hesitate to recognize and discharge." But that same year, April 8, 1896, Olney informed Spain we would look upon the final triumph of the insurgents "with the gravest apprehension." He wished to coöperate with Spain to establish "local self-government."

Spain suggested we detach the insurrection from popular support in the United States, suppress the New York Cuban Junta, and more effectively prevent gun-running.

McKinley's 1897 message said the Weyler Reconcentrado system "was not civilized warfare; it was extermination. The only peace it could beget was that of the wilderness and the grave." He demanded Spain take steps to improve the

[126]

situation and to placate the revolutionists, but refused to take any responsibility if the proposed steps did not work. Translate: Take our advice or we will fight. If our advice is bad, we will fight.

American sentiment, much to the annoyance of the Spanish authorities and insurgents, caused money to be raised for the Red Cross to relieve the Reconcentrado victims. This annoyed Spain because it cast reflection upon her tactics; it annoyed the insurgents because the starvation was really their weapon more than that of Spain. This charitable activity naturally focused greater publicity on Cuba in this country. Spectacular incidents contributed to our interest.

One woman, Evangelina Cossio Cisneros, fired the American public with her miraculous escape from death. Cubans had beaten up a Spanish officer who tried to rape her; he then slaughtered groups on the streets and announced rebellion. Evangelina was brought to Havana charged with murder.

The American press thundered. Prominent women, Mrs. Jefferson Davis, Julia Ward Howe, even Mrs. McKinley pled for the girl. The English prohibitionist, Mrs. Ormiston Chat, led her 200,000 blue-ribboners to a protest.

Hearst correspondent Karl Decker rose to the occasion, cut the jail bars, lifted Evangelina from prison to a nearby roof, had her disguised as a boy, and smuggled her out on the Ward Line *Seneca* for New York. There she was greeted by tens of thousands in Madison Square Garden, and wined and dined by the great. The public gloried in Evangelina, adored her—virtue triumphantly snatched from the claws of the grisly Dagoes. Mr. Hearst gloated: "An American Newspaper Accomplishes at a Single Stroke What the Best Efforts of Diplomacy Failed to Bring About in Many Months." Quarter page drawings showed pensively sorrowful Evangelina in prison garb and ordinary dress—"Before and after fifteen months." [3]

[3] The Machado tyranny has again exiled her and confiscated her property.

Despite the reports of the bad situation, the American relief agencies began to get a better view of the situation. American sentiment against Spain seemed abating. One soon wishes to wash his hands of the object of charity. For Spain, October, 1897, heeding the furor over Weyler, replaced him with Ramón Blanco y Erenas. Abolition of the Reconcentrado system was promised and officially fulfilled November 25. Spain was earnestly trying to placate the United States, however much doubt it may have had regarding the efficacy of our proposals. Conforming to our demands, it agreed to a species of home-rule with large powers to an elected legislature. The autonomist law went into effect January 1, 1898. It had the support of liberal Spaniards and wealthier, more conservative Cubans—the Tories opposed to independence. The reactionary Spanish colony was bitter over the concession. Autonomy helped divide the anti-Spanish movement McKinley did not wish to recognize; he was relieved by the moves which thus staved off need for American action. Atkins, the sugar man, was sure this pseudo-independence would solve the whole question.

This even seemed probable. Cuba, despite the proddings of the Democrats, was slipping from the front pages of the newspapers.

We told Spain these steps would satisfy us. But our good State Department and Navy officials were busy.

5   TSAR REED INVOKES THE LORD

Commander Converse (*Montgomery*), peddling belated reports of the Weyler period, sent word, February 6, 1898, that in Matanzas, 50,000 of a total population of 253,616 had died from starvation; 98,000 more were starving. Captain Sigsbee (U.S.S. *Maine*) heard February 8 that "half the people of Cuba" had died. He himself estimated from the outlook tower of his ship that 500,000 people, or one-third of Cuba's population, had perished, 200,000 of them being pacific Reconcentrados. Woodford, using his spy-glass from Madrid, wrote that when the revolution broke out there were 1,600,000 people in Cuba. Though 200,000 troops had been sent over, not a million souls remained alive on the island. October 20, 1897, eleven days before the arrival of Blanco, Vice-Consul Joseph A. Springer visited the Los Fosos Reconcentration camp: 500 women and children, some at the breast, were crowded into a space suitable for 200. He "saw one orphan family of ten little children, boys too weak and emaciated to stand; much nudity and indifference to common decency; everywhere hunger, misery and starvation. . . . The condition of those still in the country towns is inconceivable."

American Consul A. C. Bryce at Matanzas reported (also before the arrival of Blanco): "In some towns a third to half the population has disappeared." In Colón a third of the 6,000 Reconcentrado prisoners had perished from hunger; and he enclosed a clipping from the local paper giving a pen-picture of two weak children carrying their dead father to the cemetery in a cod-fish box tied together with rope.

When the American authorities after occupation examined the Havana prison, the women had no place to sleep except on the floor and were "without clothes to cover their nakedness; and they came before the inspector one by one, passing the same garment from one to another." [4]

Conditions were bad, but not entirely due to willful cruelty so much as to maladministration, lack of funds, carelessness, and the general callousness of war days. Our own 1899 census of Cuba revealed a decrease of only 68,985 from the 1892 census, or only 3.6 percent. Most of this was probably more than accounted for by emigrés and the return of the enormous Spanish population to its homeland. This decline was only 200,000 less than the normal increase

[4] Elihu Root, *Military and Colonial Policy of the United States*, 201.

would have provided, never present in war-time anyway. Our good official and naval representatives may have been over-enthusiastic about the number of Cuban deaths.

The Reconcentrado system, aside from the spiritual shock of uprooting people, really had many humane features. It removed civilians from the area of conflict. Weyler in each case ordered housing, rations and zones for refugees to cultivate their own food. True, if Spanish officers grafted off their own soldiers, they would do no less with the consigned rations. But often the Reconcentrados had more opportunity to grow and harvest their crops than in the war zones. People were starving anyway. The insurgents had orders wherever possible to destroy the cultivated grounds of the Reconcentrados. Atkins recorded a case near Cienfüegos where the insurgents slipped through the wire one night and uprooted every plant. War is war. Curiously it was really the insurgents who were utilizing the starvation weapon to stir the people into action.

And we by our insistence upon the ending of the Reconcentrado order at such a time merely made things more of a mess. The revocation came when harvests would have been reaped. The Reconcentrados were cast forth, uprooted a second time, to drift about, this time with utterly no Spanish responsibility for their welfare and more starving than ever.

God had a hard time those days.

Senator George Vest cried: "Are we to wait until the island is devastated by fire and sword? Sir, if we do it God will curse us."

Tsar Reed: "If the Lord has not intervened to protect these Reconcentrados, why should we?"

Congressman Harry Skinner, voicing the noble sentiments of his South Carolina constituents: "I tell you, Mr. Speaker, the Cubans look upon the [United States] flag to-day as the emblem of Christianity; wherever you would advance the cross to establish Christian religion, I take that flag as the counterpart of the cross, as the emblem of liberty. I would place it over Cuba . . . in every land, on every sea, not only in America, but over every people on this continent who ask for the blessings of liberty."

March 27, 1898, when most of the brutalities had been mitigated and our relief agencies had decidedly improved the situation, McKinley rediscovered the Spanish crimes in Cuba. Secretary of State cabled Minister Woodford in Madrid: "The President's desire is for peace. He cannot look upon the suffering and starvation in Cuba save with horror. The concentration of men, women and children in fortified towns, where they are permitted to starve, is unbearable to a Christian nation geographically as close as ours is to Cuba." (Distance does diminish horrors.)

Blanco officially reported that deaths were due to disease, not hunger, and hinted that some clients of the Red Cross had been killed by overeating. Spain reminded us the Reconcentrado system had been altered four months previously.

6 SPAIN'S SADDEST DAY

Our Havana Consul, Fitzhugh Lee, a fervent annexationist, became alarmed at the bitterness of the Spaniards towards resident Americans due to our backing of the autonomist program. He actually discovered an anti-American conspiracy in Matanzas and asked for battleships at Florida Keys to be ready at a moment's notice.

No conspiracy developed.

But January 12, perhaps disconcerted, he magnified an attack on a newspaper office (according to Lee, four offices) by army officers incensed at criticism and advocacy of autonomy, into an ugly demonstration against resident Americans. His telegrams were vague but alarming. It was a minor riot soon in hand. But he wired Captain Sigsbee of the *Maine*, "Two Dollars" (the code word prearranged for such a momentous enterprise for him to come at once to Havana). This was countermanded for all Lee could report the following days was "excitement and uncertainty," though it was doubtful whether Blanco could "control the situation." Pressed for details he laconically continued wiring, "All quiet."

Nevertheless the *Maine* proceeded to Havana January 25 for a courtesy call, and like most courtesy battleships sent in critical places where they are better absent, was to cause no end of trouble. Had it stayed at home it is doubtful if we would have had a war with Spain.

Anyway no one lacked in courtesy. The proper calls were made. The Acting-Captain General (Blanco was in the interior) sent Captain Sigsbee a case of fine sherry. Captain Sigsbee gallantly returned a copy of his book, *Deep Sea-Sounding and Dredging.*

Two events now exacerbated American feeling.

February 9, 1898, Rubens, legal adviser to the revolutionary junta, made public in Hearst's *Journal,* a stolen private letter by Spanish Minister Dupuy de Lome, who criticized the "ingrained and inevitable coarseness" with which McKinley's message repeated the vulgar press, concerning Weyler. McKinley was "weak, a bidder for the admiration of the crowd, besides being a common politician who tries to leave a door open behind him while keeping on good terms with the jingoes of his party." Spain promptly recalled de Lome; but our national pride was overtly aroused by the very accuracy of the depiction.

Before our anger died down, February 15, at 9:40, just as ship Captain Sigsbee was licking the envelope of a letter to his wife in his hot quarters, an explosion knocked him off his feet. The *Maine* had mysteriously blown up. Before dawn the New York linotypes were sizzling, and "Extra!" woke the city.

Spanish Governor General Blanco, up in the old Palace on the Plaza de Armas, smote his desk: "This is the saddest day Spain ever saw!" And he came out of his office to meet Fitzhugh Lee with tears streaming from his eyes.

7 IN THE NAME OF HUMANITY

"Remember the *Maine!*" swept the United States. People went out of their heads. Frenzied patriotic feeling raised the cry of vengeance. Barnstormers rallied public hate. *"Remember the 'Maine'!"* buttons were sold everywhere. The soda-jerkers complained bitterly because McKinley "couldn't be kicked into a fight." The American Methodist congregation in Mexico City offered itself to the flag and evidently to Christ as a "sacred and significant sacrifice on the altar of humanity."

"Remember the *Maine!*" was the final mob cry of American sympathy for the Cuban cause. For years we had looked across the narrow waters separating us from Cuba at a war gone on from bitterness to brutality, wholesale slaughter. The Spanish government had tried doggedly to smash insurrection by all the devices of civilized war, as practiced up to that time. Trade, business, investments, humanity—everything suffered. But it was "Remember the *Maine!*" that set our marching boys in motion.

Without permitting any joint investigation of that catastrophe, without heeding Spanish overtures for peace carried to the point of utter humility, without recalling that most of our grievances had already been met, we plunged headlong into conflict—and thereby changed our entire destiny and that of Cuba.

Was the Spanish War an unnecessary conflict? April 15, 1898, Secretary of Navy Long wrote to the editor of the *Boston Journal* that the President had obtained from Spain a concession on every ground asked except independence. She had "released every American prisoner; recalled Weyler; recalled de Lome; changed her Reconcentration order; agreed to furnish food; and ordered an armistice." The previous six months had shown "constant steps toward her retirement" (from Cuba). If McKinley had had a free hand, independence would have come "without a drop of bloodshed, as naturally as an apple falls from a tree."

A week later, Long was issuing orders to blockade Havana. The Spanish-American War had begun.

While the public howled, and the navy painted its ships gray, McKinley, though he got Joe Cannon to put through a $50,000,000 army and navy appropiation bill, held out, bewildered and timidly, against the clamor. Not until March 27, when the *Maine* naval investigation commission returned a report of blown up from external explosion (the Spanish commission had reported the contrary) did he rediscover all the Cuban horrors and demand that while the United States did not seek the acquisition of Cuba, Spain should consent to an armistice until October 1 to permit peace negotiations with the rebels; that the Reconcentrado system be ended and immediate relief for those in the camps be instituted. In case Spain and the Cubans should not have reached an agreement on the date named, the United States offered to be final arbiter.

March 31, Spain reminded us that the Reconcentrado system had been abolished (at our demand) for all western Cuba, but suggested impartial investigation and arbitration to fix responsibility for the *Maine* disaster—a terrible affront to the cause of truth, peace and national dignity. Plans would be taken up by the new autonomist legislature (set up at our demand), to meet May 4, for permanent pacification. The communication raised no objection to the work of American relief agencies, but Spain would not grant an armistice until the insurgents asked for it. Give us a little more time, pleaded Spanish premier Praxedes Mateo Sagasta.

The Pope offered to mediate—and this was fatal. McKinley knew that to heed that quarter would arouse Protestants to disappointed rage, and then good-by Republican

Party. In the act, the newspapers whooped up military preparedness and "no Popery."

The European powers at the eleventh hour presented "pressing appeal to the feelings of humanity and moderation of the President and the American people." McKinley told them he was very interested in humanity and wished to end a prolonged situation; the *Review of Reviews* righteously warned of the "dangers" of even having allowed these devious Europeans "to communicate with us at all in the collective sense." The American people could "never consent to have the concert of Europe, as such, act diplomatically in any affair which concerns us."

McKinley, bedeviled on every side, did not know which way to turn. Teddy Roosevelt was boiling—"that white-livered cur up there . . . has prepared *two* messages, one for war and one for peace, and doesn't know which one to send in!" On another occasion he remarked McKinley had no more backbone than a chocolate éclair. Congress was champing at the bit for war. The states were voting enormous defense funds. The papers clamored. The President, Vice-President, Speaker Reed from Maine, Senators Hale (Republican Senate leader), Allison, Aldrich, Fairbanks, Platt, Mark Hanna, and practically all of the Cabinet, except the incompetent Secretary of War, Russel A. Alger, dreaming of personal and pecuniary glorification, were opposed to war; they swung to the other view only when the party hacks had shown that it could be capitalized for Republican power; when they were convinced that the nation was too eager to save humanity with bullets to be influenced. Besides, Germany had seized Kiaochau, China, March 6; and Russia, Port Arthur, March 31. The Rooseveltians howled for action. Atkins, the sugar man, fresh from Cuba, tore around sweating, trying to swing the "better elements" in Congress to peace.

Woodford, on the heels of the Spanish reply, informed Washington that Spain was prepared to "go as far and as fast as she could." He was sure that if she had "time and reasonable liberty of action," he could, "before next October . . . get peace in Cuba with justice to Cuba and protection to our great American interests." And by the November elections sober reconsideration would have veered public opinion to a course "which must be approved at the bar of final history." He hoped nothing would be done to humiliate Spain; she would cede all along the line practically anything demanded. But once more Spain had asked for an impartial *Maine* investigation!

The fear displayed by McKinley and subsequent administrations towards this perhaps explains in part why he did not try to pour oil on troubled waters by publishing the last Spanish note. If after so much hullabaloo and diplomatic high-hatting it were discovered that negligence or defective equipment resulted in disaster or—as it has been charged—certain elements blew up the *Maine* precisely to provoke war, we should have cut a sorry figure before the world.

McKinley still could have played a strong card by giving full publicity to the new attitude of Spain, but he had capitulated to the war party, and he went to Congress the very day following Woodford's strong communique. His message meant war—nothing else.

Several years later Elihu Root told the people of Canton, Ohio, "McKinley with a soul of tenderest sympathy, straining to the utmost the efforts of diplomacy to secure justice for bleeding Cuba [but not independence], was forced to become the leader in a dreadful war in the islands of the East and the islands of the West." Thereby he established the sad truth that a reactionary imperialist power could show more respect for decent international dealings and restraint in the face of provocation than could the new western democracy.

April 11, the destinies of the United States were altered. The shabby victorias of Washington, with their drowsy negro drivers, stood in the shade under the Japanese cherry trees in full blossom. The windows of the red brick fronts had been thrown open to spring. The marble corridors of the capitol were cool and quiet. But unknown to Washington's placid dwellers, even to some of the politicians, the giant of commercial empire was knocking at the gates. McKinley carried the ultimatum of the newcomer in a folded document in his Prince Albert, down hushed corridors to Congress.

Suppressing all but slight reference to the new Spanish communication and falsely stating that our last overture for peace had had "a disappointing reception," the President now told Congress intervention was fully justified; "the fire of insurrection," though it might "flame or might smolder with varying seasons" could "not be extinguished by present methods." The only hope was "the enforced pacification of Cuba." He continued eloquently, "In the name of humanity, in the name of civilization, in behalf of endangered American interests . . ." [climax or anticlimax?], the war in Cuba had to stop. But recognition of the independence of the insurrectionary government was neither "wise nor prudent." [We had just demanded Spain recognize them through an armistice.] The insurgents were merely to be steam-rollered by us, not Spain.

He and others evidently hoped for annexation, wished to sidestep any disclosure of any ultimate purpose of American intervention. Eager as Congress was, it took two days to bring in the House Resolution dutifully ignoring the thorny question of independence. But in the Senate, friends of Cuba had been busy and secured insurgent recognition. This created a "riot" in the house, and the throwing of at least one "big bound volume" at a colleague, and the adoption April 16 of an even more bellicose resolution. The resolution was delayed again in the Senate and passed interminably back and forth between the two bodies, with great crowds of spectators shuttling to and fro with the fateful paper. In the interums, some fifty Representatives awoke echoes with patriotic songs, *The Battle Hymn of the Republic, Dixie, Hang General Weyler to a Sour Apple Tree.* They forgot that Weyler had been recalled long ago. "Soldiers bivouacking about the camp-fires in the enemy's front could not have been more enthusiastic," said a press report.

Real friends of Cuba and the revolutionaries, mostly un-enthusiastic, were hourly more alarmed as recognition of the insurgent government was laid aside.

Largely through Rubens' efforts, the Teller Amendment (article IV) was finally adopted against the administration's wishes: The United States disclaimed all "disposition of intent to exercise sovereignty jurisdiction or control over said island except for the pacification thereof." This accomplished, the island should be left "to its people." Also was retained the curiously emasculated Senate phrase, "The people of the island of Cuba are and of a right ought to be free." Though the Joint Resolution, signed April 20, did not quite respect the President's wishes, the long-sacrificing patriots were left out of the picture.

April 21, relations were broken off. April 22, the American fleet left Key West, sighted the low western Cuban hills and Morro Castle at 3 o'clock.

8 GOD'S FORCE

The people wanted war. Wall Street wanted peace, looked with apprehension upon our aggressiveness.

As late as April 2, the *Commercial and Financial Chronicle* voiced big-wig bank opinion, "the proposition to settle this series of events by the indiscriminate slaughter of the armies and navies of two nations" was a "stain on our country's good name." Stock prices fell. "Peace-at-any-price telegrams of the most abject description"—as Roosevelt characterized them—were pouring in from New York and Boston business men.

It was the roar of the hinterland and the Roosevelt-Lodge-Hay-Reid Anglophile jingoists that turned the trick. It was the sulphur fumes of the yellow press. It was the work of the party-hacks, who feared that the bungling record and unpopularity of the administration would cause the G.O.P. to be swept from office in the 1898 and 1900 elections. General Grosvenor of Ohio asked if any one thought that the "great party in power" was going "to be unfaithful to a trust" which if properly discharged would "bring glory to the Administration"—glory and the plums of office.

The speeches of our statesmen from the corn and Bible belts reeked with alternate sentimentalism and jingoism. The Populist Senator Allen from Nebraska even called himself "the jingo of the jingoes!" Spain did not possess enough gold "to compensate for the insult . . . or for one precious life lost. . . ." Ergo, shed more precious lives. He was but a magnavox for the real jingoes, the commoners of the mid-west mudflats and the great "nigger" humanitarians of the South, all the hard-fisted go-getters-and-spenders of Zenith. Congressman Mason S. Peters of the Kansas sun-flower prairies saw in the war "a blessing to the world," in it the opposing forces at work "shaping human destiny through the ages"—"the divine rights of man versus the divine rights of kings."

Senator Thurston of Nebraska, not a jingo, believed in Christ's doctrine, hence wished merely to intervene. Intervention meant force. Force meant war. But as it was in behalf of humanity and liberty, it would be God's force. Nor did Thurston forget how Christ embraced the temple money-changers: "War with Spain would increase the business and earnings of every American railroad, it would increase the output of every American factory, it would stimulate every branch of industry and domestic commerce, it

[139]

would greatly increase the demand for American labor, and in the end every certificate that represented a share in an American business enterprise would be worth more money than it is to-day." [5]

By all means—"remember the *Maine!*"

[5] Jenks, *Our Cuban Colony*, 53-5.

IX OUR HIGGLEDY-PIGGLEDY WAR

1 BLOCKADE

Five days after the joint Resolution, Congress declared that war with Spain had existed since April 21 of the year of Our Lord 1898. The country whooped to battle, bands tumultuously playing *There'll be a Hot Time in the Old Town To-night*.

The result of the war will be, Cleveland wrote Olney, "a depreciation of national standing before the world . . . at home, demoralization of our people's character, much demagogy and humbug, great additions to our public burdens and the exposure of scandalous operations."

In Kansas City a shoemaker was duly mobbed for hanging crêpe on his door, "closed in memory of a Christian nation that descends to the barbarity of war."

Europe bitterly criticized us, but in the United States, editors, Christian preachers, politicians, contractors, business-men—all were courageously standing behind the President, and doubtless would also have risked their lives. By April 26, Pulitzer's *World* was selling 1,300,000 copies a day. That old-vintage *Atlantic Monthly* blazoned with an American flag on the cover. The chorus at the Knickerbocker Theatre, "Unchain the Dogs of War!" nightly brought the audience banging to its feet. Everybody was joyously drunk with patriotism.

But also every one was demanding something, better

billets, special equipment, favors. Roosevelt was very busy. And "every section of the country," wrote Long in his diary, "although patriotic, has an eye on the main chance." The coal-transport companies demanded so much more than the agreed prices, we finally had to buy our colliers from the British. Mules doubled in price overnight. Later, a Congressman demanded that a battleship—there weren't so many—be stationed off Jeckyl Island, wealthy resort and game preserve, to protect those patriotically shooting ducks so the nation would not starve to death.

In his diary, George Cortelyou, McKinley's secretary, wrote: "The President is looking careworn . . . the struggle for place among the ambitious gentlemen who desire to serve their country in high-salaried and high-titled positions . . . the usual bickerings among the officers of the army and navy . . ."

In all the fanfare, the Cuban insurgents were the least jubilant, far from anxious to have the United States step in and reap the fruits of their years of sacrifice. General Gómez desired that no American troops be landed in Cuba, only perhaps some much-needed artillery and ammunition. Thereafter Gómez was religiously ignored.

No one knew exactly what steps should be taken, though then and subsequently the War Department blithely announced all its plans to the world, including the Spaniards. The first great proposal was, not to help the insurgents, but to blockade Cuba, though but a few weeks previously we had been arrogantly insisting on sending food to the starving Cubans. But how could one have a proper naval war without blockading something or other? This had the advantage, though, of letting starvation and the doubly-starved Cubans do the fighting, while we came in at the glorious finale to occupy the island and set up a different government from the one they already had. As an afterthought, a member of the Cabinet said that when the Span-

ish supplies had run out we would take steps to furnish
Gómez' soldiers with "sufficient hardtack" to fight.[1]

Gradually our ambitions increased. It was decided that
early in November (this would not expose our dear boys to
yellow fever), we would send General Miles, knee wounded
in 1890 Indian fighting, with the bulk of the American
forces to surround Havana, to be simultaneously blockaded
by our naval forces. The War Department had to depend
upon Spanish maps of ancient vintage. Then it discovered
that Spain had nearly 200,000 trained fighting men on the
island. Our standing army of 26,000 men had rusted since
the Civil War, had no brigade formations. The States and
National Guards were not much asset; they spent most of
their time bickering over making officer-jobs political
plums, and would have nothing to do with stuck-up West
Point officers. The New York state guard flatly refused to
enlist as part of the Federal army. Secretary of War Alger
had to devote all his time to politicians, relatives of enlisted men, concession hunters and had only nights and
Sundays left for conducting the war.

The Department had to be dissuaded from sending
50,000 men in heavy blue cloth uniforms; cooler khaki
and drill were then ordered and were ready when the war
was over. The dye of the blue uniforms ran in the rain, and
we had a real peacock army. No sabers; Wood had to buy
machetes. And thus the Burnside whisker officers and War
Department officials blundered along the dark cobweb
chambers of inefficiency. Civil War veterans, still in the
service, unlimbered their rheumatic joints; at least one long
white beard "waved free in the wind" in the El Caney
charge. We went into the fray as if carrying on an "absent-
minded comic opera."

But what Federal officialdom lacked, private initiative
supplied ruggedly. The Wall Street white collar boys organized a regiment. One financier "gave" a regiment to the

1 Millis, *The Martial Spirit*, 146-7.

war. Mrs. Helen Gould plunked down $100,000 for the Navy lads. Mr. John Jacob Astor gave a battery of artillery. The *World* and *Journal* chartered whole squadrons to keep the public informed, pilot the bewildered navy about, and give advice to Washington. Hearst, with a specially-granted ensign's commission, sailed as an admiral of his own navy, one flag-ship and the verbal cruisers of the *Journal,* and ordered his London correspondent to sink a vessel in the Suez Canal so the Spanish fleet couldn't get through to the Philippines.

Volunteers were flung into unprepared camps—"Rough-tough, we're the stuff." Teddy's Terrors, successively re-christened "Rocky Mountain Rustlers" and "Rough-Riders," descended on San Antonio in charge of Colonel Leonard Wood, while Roosevelt held the Washington front. The camp contained "twelve hundred as separate, varied, mixed, distinct, grotesque and peculiar types of men . . . ever assembled in one bunch . . . millionaires, paupers, shyster lawyers, cowboys, quack doctors, farmers, college professors, miners, adventurous preachers, gentiles, Mexicans, Indians, West Point graduates, Arkansan wild men, baseball players, sheriffs and horse-thieves." And it was noted "one, possibly two—Democrats."

To concentrate the army, the Department first chose Key West till it discovered there would not be standing room for 12,000 men and that no water was on the tiny islet. Tampa was chosen with its dismal huddle of huts and giant Planter Hotel of ornamental brick and silver minarets, statuary, potted palms, circular stuffed sofas around columns, and gingerbread piazzas. This hotel served us admirably to see us through "the rocking chair" period of the war. The lone embarkation pier was miles off connected by a one-track railroad.

For trains to get to Tampa, officers fought and seized them, ousting passengers. Supplies tangled. At one time transportation was blocked as far north as South Carolina. Fifteen cars with uniforms were sidetracked twenty-five miles from Tampa. Miles informed the Secretary of War that "several volunteer regiments had come without uniforms, others without arms, some without blankets, tents or camp-equipage." The First Missouri had many men without shoes or socks, some without underwear. [None of our statesmen remembered previous aspersions about the ragged Cuban insurgents.] Five of General Guy Henry's regiments, continued Miles, were unfit to go into the field. "Officers were obliged to break seals and hunt from car to car to see if they contained clothing, grain, balloon material, horse equipment, ammunition, siege guns, commissary stores, etc." Five thousand much-needed rifles were miraculously discovered.

For months the soldiers milled around the foot-deep sand-streets. "Confusion, confusion, confusion," Wood wrote his wife, June 9. Neither men nor horses could get proper food.

2 "GUSSIE"

The navy was doing better. By May Dewey had sunk the Far Eastern Spanish fleet in Manila Bay. St. Patrick's Cathedral in New York, between its lofty Christian spires, flaunted the largest flag ever displayed in the city (40 x 35), doubly impressive for during the first week of the war all the bunting supply in the country had been exhausted and the price had since jumped at least 300 percent. The restaurants served battleship ices à la Dewey; and the dear ladies appeared in striped red-white-and-blue waists and blue skirts with buff cavalrymen stripes down the side.

Admiral William T. Sampson had hurried to Puerto Rico to look for Admiral Cervera's fleet at the rate of six knots an hour, the boilers of our prize ship *Indiana* leaking badly, the *Terror's* steering-gear almost out of commission, and towing two useless, ponderous, revamped Civil War monitors.

Sampson fired at almost defenseless San Juan till he couldn't see through the thick black-powder smoke, killed a few civilians, and hastened home.

The navy was copping all the publicity. The Navy Department, to show its mettle, hurried with great fanfare to send the old side-wheel walking-beam river-boat *Gussie* to land arms in Cuba. But it could effect no contact with insurgents and after wandering along the Cuban coast for three or four days to the amazement of all who saw her, it returned to Tampa, her supplies all safe and sound.

Anyway the army was not really expected to get to Cuba until fall when the climate was safe. In the meantime we had shipped thousands of men to annex the Philippines; the climate in Puerto Rico was good; take that "first," Andrew Carnegie advised General Miles. The poor Cubans, whose miseries we had set out to end, could wait till the braver needs of empire were attended to.

3 EMBALMED BEEF

Cervera had proceeded from Spain via Martinique to Santiago harbor in southeast Cuba. If America was enthusiastically inefficient, the Spaniards were impressively so. Cervera wrote the Minister of Marine, April 22, 1898: "You say you have given me all I asked. The *Colón* is without its big guns, and I asked for a poor gun if there were no others; the 14 cm. munitions are bad except for some 300 shells. The defective guns of the *Vizcaya* and *Oquendo* have not been changed. We have not one Busta-mente torpedo. . . . This is already a disastrous affair, and we may fear the worst soon. . . . The *Vizcaya* now hardly navigates and is like a boil grown on the fleet. . . . We have no charts of the American seas."

May 23 Admiral Schley's Flying Squadron was ordered

to fly from Cienfüegos to Santiago. He began flying the night of the 24th at about seven knots, his vessels in great disrepair, and not until the 26th did he arrive within twenty miles of there. Then, suddenly worried about his coal supply, the next day he raised the flagship signal to go to Key West and telegraphed the War Department he could not obey its orders. By the 28th he changed his mind and sailed back, this time really looked into Santiago harbor—there was the *Cristóbal Colón* anchored [since the 25th] right across the entrance.

June 7 Admiral Sampson came with the rest of the fleet —"his Bargain Counter Squadron"—and soon sent the despatch: "Have silenced works quickly without injury of any kind, though stationed 2,000 yards. If 10,000 men were here city and fleet would be ours within forty-eight hours."

Schley's shilly-shallying was played up in the home press as a brilliant maneuver to make Cervera think he had left disgusted, and thus take "the bait" and run into the harbor to be bottled up [which he had done before Schley ever appeared].

General Shafter was ordered to embark "regulars and volunteers"; and General Miles rolled back from the Washington front in a special train, accompanied by Mrs. Miles and Miss Miles.

Soldiers at Tampa hurriedly thrust themselves on to the transports, without control or system. First come first served. Pitched battles for trains and boats. In those days of coy word compounding, "biff-bang-do-it-right-now-can-not-put-it-off-another-minute" Roosevelt confiscated train gondolas to get to the pier, fought through the milling mob— "Hell won't be no more crowded on the last days"—and holding the gangplank against all comers grabbed the *Yucatán,* assigned to the Second Infantry and the Seventy-first New York volunteers. The Seventy-first, for its part, had also seized a train, holding it at the point of the bayonet against its rightful consignees, the Thirteenth. Somehow

815 officers, 16,000 men and 89 newspaper correspondents crammed on board the boats.

Suddenly a cable from Admiral Remy at Key West warned of Spanish vessels north of Cuba. For a week the troops, profusely swearing, were held up on the transports in hot crowded unsanitary quarters. The undiscoverable "Ghost Fleet" later proved to have been three American naval vessels.

June 14 the Fifth Army corps took off in its transports at a snail-like pace—seven miles an hour, "with long pauses for thought and consultation." "Painted ships on a painted ocean," wrote Wood poetically. "Imagine three great lines of transports with a warship at the head of each line, streaming in long lines, 800 yards from each other over a sea of indigo blue. . . .

"A good daring Spanish commander could get into this fleet and put out a good portion of it. . . ."

And easier later, as the transports began straggling out on the "burning and brilliant sea." Still easier at night, when all the lights were lit blazing "like a harbor" and the bands pounded out ragtime.

Damnably hot. Foul water. No place to sleep. The canned beef stank. On the *Segurança,* three-hundred-pound General Shafter sweltered in his woolen uniform and never removed his sun-helmet.

Secretary of Navy asked Secretary of War what provision had been made for landing troops and supplies and was informed the army could tend to its own landing.

Despite rebuff, the Secretary of Navy ordered assistance rendered. Admiral Sampson and General Shafter (the latter's great bulk on a little white mule "with a brave little heart") visited General García's camp, and Cuban troops advanced to Siboney and Daiquirí, sixteen miles west of Santiago, the places selected for landing.

The fleet laid down a barrage, smashing up trenches already evacuated. And while fourteen armored navy vessels stood by, thirty-five transports, far out in the open road-stead, landed 16,000 men through the surf "higgledy-pig-gledy," to camp amid palm trees and nastily scuffling land-crabs, between a tropic sea and mountains "singularly rem-iniscent of Arizona." Preparations were so inadequate it took from June 22 to 26, day and night, to disembark the whole force. In the glare of searchlights, half-naked figures shouting, singing, half obeying stentorian orders, scram-bling ashore, amid Coney Island screeching and tooting of whistles. Many of the chartered merchantmen kept running away and had to be constantly chased for miles and rounded up.

Shafter rushed General Lawton forward through June heat and tropic night deluge to occupy the Siboney railway crossing, then to a strong defensive position on the Santiago road till transportation could be organized. But Wood's Rough Riders, obeying Wheeler's conflicting orders, dashed on ahead (though Lawton managed to hold up the regi-ment's dynamite gun), and fell into the brush to be at-tacked at Las Guásimas almost as from ambush in a cross-fire of Mausers. Though the Rough Riders had had no practice with their new Krag-Jorgensen smokeless rifles (the only ones in the whole army), the Spaniards, after causing large and unnecessary loss of life, finally retreated (as they had planned to do anyway) toward Santiago behind their grim outpost forts. Mr. Edward Marshal, *Journal* corre-spondent, shot through the spine, came back on a stretcher, bravely singing *On the Banks of the Wabash Far Away*.

Teddy hastened to write a senator, "The mismanagement has been maddening. . . ." "Shafter was not even ashore." In thus pricking plans and extending the lines, Wheeler, Teddy and Wood had caused the demoralization of the entire supply service and prevented all possibility of prop-erly organizing the landed troops and regulating their ad-vance.

The Americans, who had thrown away their blankets and food supplies, upbraided the Cubans for not having food ready. García had led his 2,000 men across a completely devastated area; his followers had learned to live on boiled grass, snake flesh, and grasshoppers. Even so, the Cubans in turn were sullen because the Americans had no supplies at hand.

Told to fetch their own supplies from those disembarked in Siboney, at once the Cubans started a long line of ration-runners through the American forces. Our own transport of new provisions by packtrains—the wagons were still on the transports—was inadequate and tardy. Hungry American soldiers, refused food by the Cuban runners, were angered by the apparent selfishness of those they had come to save. One quartermaster did raid clear back to Siboney and rejoined his outfit at 4:30 in the morning; but lost his cache; Roosevelt "appropriated the dump."

The whole force milled around the muddy stew that was the road to Santiago, a narrow trail where not four men could march abreast. The terrific rains engulfed the men; they shivered blanketless in the cold damp nights. Frightful heat, rain, and rapid spread of fever prostrated thousands. Others died from so-called "embalmed beef"—that was before free and easy packing-house days had been ended by Upton Sinclair's *Jungle*. A court of inquiry whitewashed this whole rat-meat scandal.

4 BLUFF AND VICTORY

The Second Massachusetts was pushed forward to El Pozo Hill, the approach to fortified San Juan eminence. Equipped with only old-fashioned Springfields, they could poorly return the heavy Mauser fire raking their ranks. Captain Grimes' battery—still using old-style black powder with its thick revealing smoke—was easily located by the Spaniards, who pounded the American guns, killing many too-closely stationed Rough Riders and Cubans.

Later, light artillery was actually put in front of trenches, and the frightened artillerymen repeatedly beaten forward to their guns after each firing.

At nearby El Caney (appropriately meaning "Sepulcher"), hampered by lack of sufficient artillery preparation, Lawton's men, hungry and having had only four hours' sleep, dashed again and again in a frontal attack on the stone fort held by only 500 Spaniards skillfully protected by fox-pits and barbed wire. All day the combat raged. When the attackers finally uprooted the wire-entanglements and overwhelmed the fort in a last rush only one Spanish officer and four men were left alive. The American dead were far more numerous than the entire corps of Spanish defenders.

The Americans at El Pozo advanced on to Las Guasimas River, in all 10,000 men milling in a narrow sluice of mud, ever under fire. The whole Seventy-first New York lay down in the mud, rifles thrown aside. General Kent called it "highly irregular," and ordered the Wikof brigade not to pay any attention to it. Said another officer mildly, "I infer they were in this position for the purpose of avoiding exposure to bullets." Major Derby, riding in splendid isolation in his basket above the mêlée, led a captive balloon down to the river and anchored it at the ford, drawing Spanish fire where the troops had to cross—"the Bloody Ford." The balloon was ultimately punctured. Derby stepped out smiling. "The aerial phase of our war with Spain was over," remarked Millis.

It was death in the roaring road or at the ford. It was death to cross unknown terrain—the exposed tall grass meadows before San Juan. There, trapped in barbed-wire defenses (and having no wire-nippers), cavalry and infantry swirled in ever more confusion, exposed to murderous fusillades from all sides. About a thousand men were uselessly sacrificed.

Panic ruled. The troops could not plunge back into the heaving road; they could not go forward. Advance and retreat orders arrived at confusing intervals. Petty officers finally acted on their own; the men leapt forward in disorderly advance. Generals Kent and Hawkins came to the rescue. General Wheeler rose from a sick bed and wandered around at large. A fantastically courageous and unscientific rush stormed Kettle Hill, the San Juan outpost, and took it.

Despite grammar-school text-book engravings, Roosevelt, bravely busy elsewhere, did not reach even Kettle Hill until after it had been seized by the Tenth cavalry, and did not take San Juan.

At the crest of San Juan hill a Cuban dashed bravely forward to cut the last barbed-wire defenses, sacrificing his life, and the troops boiled over the summit. Secretary of War Alger later falsely said this was the only Cuban in the attack.

Santiago still lay on ahead, secure behind its barbed wire, gun positions and forts.

One thousand four hundred and seventy-five men had been thrown away.

That night Wheeler wrote Shafter: "The lines are very thin, as so many men have gone to the rear with the wounded and so many are exhausted."

Wood wrote in his diary: "No effort to get up artillery . . . a most awful state of affairs . . . only partial rations . . . criminally negligent . . . absolutely sickening . . . no head. . . ." Rain and more rain . . . "roads and trails . . . absolute canals of mud. . . ."

But Senator Lodge wrote Teddy . . . "I hear talk all the time about your being run for governor and congressman . . . anything you wanted. . . . I think you would find it without much difficulty the road to the Senate."

Shafter cabled the War Department he was going to with-draw five miles.

Wood snapped, "What we need at this point is less brains and more guts"—a bit contradictory in view of what had happened.

Disturbed under-officers secretly asked García to take command to save such bloodily won positions. He would not withdraw his own force, he said, but had no right to com-mand American troops.

But before retreating, Shafter got the idea of sending a bold demand for surrender. "Characteristic American spirit," Secretary of War Alger announced, but "vulgarly called bluff," appended Rubens. Yet, appalled by his own blunders, fearing the Santiago breastworks, patiently Shaf-ter bluffed his way to final bloodless capitulation.

But nerves were bad. A rift had developed between Shafter and Sampson. Sampson demanded Shafter hasten his advance, capture the shore batteries and cut torpedo-control wires so he could enter the bay and attack the Span-ish fleet. Fat, plethoric Shafter, ever bewildered, still with-out heavy artillery and supplies, suggested that the navy could risk its men as well as the army and should enter the harbor as had Farragut with "Damn the torpedoes!" In-stead, Sampson sent Hobson to try to seal up the harbor en-trance by sinking the *Merrimac*.

Eight thousand Spanish reënforcements now walked into Santiago right under Shafter's nose. He upbraided García, though June 27 he had refused to let García send 2,000 Cubans along the coast to intercept the column, saying then that if reënforcements entered Santiago he would bottle them up also; the sooner would Spanish rations be con-sumed. He would starve them out, he advised the War De-partment. As it was, García already had held off vastly superior forces and had fought thirty prior engagements, effectively barring all previous Spanish succor for Santiago.

The first part of the Santiago assault almost unnerved

the American forces, including vacillating Shafter himself. The wounded had to be carried to the rear—only three ambulances were available—in rough-floored ox-carts, which shook them together in painful bloody heaps. Medical supplies were not removed from the transports until July 30, two weeks after the capture of Santiago. No lights were at hand; the doctors had to work on packing cases by the light of the moon or candles.

July 3, Cervera, warned by General Blanco to leave the port before the enemy blocked the mouth (despite the Admiral's repeated protest at such "a useless hecatomb"), hauled up his winches, and with the Spanish blood-and-golden battleflags flying bravely, sailed out of Santiago.

Sampson had sailed off in his flagship for one of his spats with Shafter. Admiral Schley was elated at his opportunity. His vessels closed so joyously on the Spanish fleet that in the clouds of dense smoke they got into each other's range, swung in circles, and the *Brooklyn* was almost rammed by the *Texas*.

But once untangled, the *Brooklyn*, with only half her power available, and the *Oregon* kept up the chase, while the rest of the fleet, including Sampson's flagship, struggled to catch up with the fast disappearing battle.

It looked as though the swifter Spanish ships would get away. But under the first heavy rain of shells, their wooden decks had burst into flames and could not be extinguished. One by one, before blowing up, they had to be beached from six to fifty miles along the coast. The crews leapt off to save themselves. Admiral Cervera swam ashore in his underclothes.

We fell to rescuing the wounded and drowning, capturing the shore prisoners. The Cubans were falsely accused of trying to assassinate them, though Cuban delivery of prisoners to an American superior has been properly certified. Ensign Hearst leapt pantless from the press flagship, rounded up twenty-six dripping Spaniards and delivered them at the point of the pistol to Admiral Schley.

Captain Philipps led a thanksgiving service on the *Texas*.

The wreck of the Spanish fleet lay along the shore that Columbus long ago had sailed in his caravels. Their black hulks were also a symbol of the final passing of Spain's power in the New World.

5 SURRENDER

July 16 Santiago surrendered.

The Cuban troops, on the grounds they might commit reprisals, were refused entry into the city. To the surrender ceremonies, General García was invited in such terms he could not accept—gross and unfair insults. The invitation was sent so late to Sampson that the latter's chief of staff arrived panting to find everything finished.

A comic opera surrender. Shafter, entering, spied press-photographer Sylvester Scovil perched on a roof and profanely ordered, "Throw him off." Scovil, right in front of gold epaulettes and clanking swords, just as Old Glory was to be raised, punched Shafter's head. He was arrested and temporarily perched on a statueless pedestal in the burning sun, two bayonets guarding him.

Shafter reappointed Spanish officials to govern Santiago. García protested, announced withdrawal. Shafter (who had completely maligned him in his reports to cover up his own egregious blunders) expressed his regrets, declaring official reports had done complete justice to him and his "brave" army.

Shafter and Sampson squabbled over the shipping in the harbor, the navy wishing to collect the prize-money. Shafter's men held off the marines with fixed bayonets. Sampson got the Alvarado gun-boat away on a fake order.

Shafter sent a tug full of soldiers panting fruitlessly after her.

The war was about over. The troops after much urging and scandal were replaced, taken out of the yellow-fever and malaria atmosphere to wallow and die of typhoid in Chickamauga, Alger and other camps.

"We had," remarks Millis, "acquired a foreign policy almost as fatuous as the most elegant examples of monarchical Europe. We had seized a colonial empire in a manner entitling us to recognition by the very best diplomats."

Our conduct of the war had few of the glowing text-book aspects ascribed to it.

6 PEACE

July 26 Spain queried via France regarding peace-terms. President McKinley demanded with regard to Cuba: relinquishment of sovereignty and immediate evacuation, immediate armistice, and a peace commission.

October 1 five commissioners each from the United States and Spain met in Paris to draw up the final treaty. They soothed their arduous labors by *Le Figaro* "Five-o'clocks," with singing and Spanish dances. President McKinley was swinging around the circle to back them up with speeches about the flag and Dewey's victory. He discovered that we had to have the Philippines, a revelation that came to him after walking the floor night after night till midnight and going down on his knees to pray to "Almighty God for light and guidance. And one night it came to me . . . there was nothing left for us to do but take them all, and uplift and civilize them . . . by God's grace do the very best we could by them, as our fellow men for whom Christ also died . . . I went to bed . . . and slept soundly."

Soon after, Tsar Reed was amusing himself writing imaginary communications from General Weyler to Congress asking that body to give him due credit for having originated our methods.

By December 10 the Paris Congress had settled all controversial points.

Spain wished Cuba annexed to the United States to guarantee greater security for Spaniards. The commissioners refused. For the time being only the United States would act as trustee for the island, assuming responsibility for life and property.

The suppression of the Cuban debt was another great "moral" achievement, though far short of what the Cubans wanted.

The Cuban treasury had been the scapegoat of all Spanish administration. Cuba's half-billion dollar pre-1898 debt was in excess of the entire real estate value of the island, and included costs of the Ten Years' War and of trying to suppress the recent revolt, Spain's expenses for General Prim's ill-starred 1862 Mexican expedition, for successfully fighting revolution in Santo Domingo (1863-5), for the 1866 Peruvian expedition, for part of the Carlist wars. Cuba was also charged with the maintenance of the Fernando Po penal station and the annual cost of the entire Spanish diplomatic and consular corps in the Americas. The treasury inroads ran from a pension to Columbus's heirs to the annual expenditures for administering Cuba badly. Current income did not suffice. Loan and bank advances had to supply constant deficit, ever more swollen by accumulating interest charges. Much of the 1886 and 1890 loan issues, payable in gold, were still outstanding. The Bank of Spain was sunk to the tune of $160,000,000 utilized fighting the insurgents. An additional $70,000,000 was due on the floating debt.

Despite the war, expectation of American victory and recognition of at least the bonds had sent them up on the market, so the American bankers had been able to get out from under. But we refused to recognize any of Cuba's past obligations. Had we taken the high moral stand since taken toward the Soviet Union, we should have insisted upon Cuba paying her debts, some of which were more valid than many of our own recent loans in Latin America or to the Machado government. We forgot also that for thirty years we had been inciting Spain to spend money suppressing the Cuban people, saying we would not look with favor on a free Cuba, whom now we could not consent to be crushed "by a burden created by Spain . . . to oppose their independence," while at the same time we were refusing to recognize the existing government which had fought long and hard for independence.

Bluntly we refused to arbitrate this phase of the question. As a peace-loving nation we believed in arbitration, but— The Spaniards wished at least to extricate the non-military portion. Our cause was too just to consider that either.

Commissioner Castillo said to Commissioner Reid: "Cruel, most cruel; pray God that you may never be likewise vanquished," and put his silk hat on his head and vanished down the plush-carpeted hall.

To get the Philippines and another bloody war, we salved our conscience by paying Spain $20,000,000 and called ourselves noble and generous.

Certainly the treaty would have been more worthy, its moral foundations solider, had we invited the Cuban patriots to the peace conference to participate in the solution of Cuba's future.

Dr. William Graham Sumner acidly repeated the bitter truth of all wars for righteousness: "We have beaten Spain in a military conflict, but we are submitting to be conquered by her on the field of ideas and policies."

"Who made us," demanded young Representative John Sharp Williams, "God's globe-trotting vice-regents to forestall misgovernment everywhere?"

Senator Hoar added his voice: Were we "a cheap-jack

country, raking after the cart for the leavings of European tyranny?"

But by this time General S. B. M. Young and others had discovered that the Cuban patriots we had come to save were "a lot of degenerates, absolutely devoid of humor or gratitude . . . no more capable of self-government than the savage of Africa," rather quaint after all our urgings about autonomy to Spain. In Santiago American and Spanish troops fraternized in mutual admiration for each other and contempt for the Cubans, who were carelessly booted around. Newspaper correspondents were discovering that "the better class in Cuba favors . . . annexation."

X ANGLO-SAXON BLESSINGS

1 TORIES

THE TASK OF SETTING UP CUBA as a going concern now faced the United States. McKinley now had to notify the insurgents regarding armistice terms, hence had to engage in official intercourse. He sent that good hack politician, Charles E. Magoon, to confer. Estrada Palma held out for his official title; McKinley, much annoyed, had finally to treat with him as Minister and Plenipotentiary delegate to the United States, and through him to cable Bartolomé Masó as "President of the Republic of Cuba."

Aside from that, we ignored the Cuban revolution. The patriots who had bravely fought for freedom, who had risked death, who had sacrificed themselves, their families, their property, their future, to carry on the war in the face of colossal odds, were elbowed aside; and we turned chiefly to the Tories, the respectable Cubans, the people who had looked with apprehension upon a free Cuba, who had either done nothing or had opposed freedom—in other words, to those whom history has ever branded as traitorous to the fatherland.

Had France, after helping us become free, kept its troops in the thirteen colonies to set up a constitution and government to its own liking, at the same time shoving aside George Washington, Benjamin Franklin, and the other patriots while calling upon the services of those neutral or favoring British rule, the later-day history of this country

[160]

might have been far more troubled and unsuccessful.

For a time our government was apprehensive lest it have a new revolt—a Cuban Aguinaldo, to repeat, as in the Philippines, the same evils of which we had accused the Spaniards. There were unfortunate riots; the army considered the islanders dirt. Máximo Gómez toured the island, acclaimed everywhere, "The Americans have embittered the joy of the Cuban victors with their forcibly imposed tutelage." The whole Independent Cuban Assembly followed suit—especially Manuel Sanguilly and Juan Gualberto Gómez, a very remarkable ex-slave negro, and Fernando Freyre de Andrade (whose three sons were recently murdered by the Machado government), a man of great personal and family prestige, all good orators, communicated their ill-feeling to the populace.

We finally saved ourselves from the irony of ironies by reaching an understanding, after much bickering, with General Máximo Gómez to have his troops turn in their arms and pay his army $3,000,000 as a step toward pacification. It split the Cubans.

Gómez' under-officers were furious at his "betrayal." The Assembly was very bitter. Though it now took its stand on the questionable issue of a larger army-bonus, the real animosity was rooted in America's high-handed determination to rule in its own way. More trouble was feared. But after deposing Gómez as Commander-in-Chief, the Assembly disbanded April 4, 1899.

January 1, 1899, Spanish General Adolfo Jimánez Castellanos, Blanco's successor, had formally turned over the island to the American military governor, General John R. Brooke, and amid some rioting by disappointed Cubans, we ran up the Stars and Stripes on Morro Castle. By February the last Spanish soldier had left the island.

2 BUZZARD FOOD

The Spaniards left Cuba fit for buzzards. In the last months of their dying administration, they had but one thought—loot, the final shakedown before they got out. Everything was gutted. Public buildings lacked even a stick of furniture. By personal appeal to his Spanish predecessor, the American official in charge was able to get a chair and desk. As Willis Fletcher Johnson has said (IV, 133): "They destroyed the plumbing and lighting fixtures. They broke or choked up the drains. They left every place in an indescribably filthy condition. There was nothing in all their record in Cuba more unbecoming than their manner of leaving it."

Famine and disease rode death-steeds triumphant. Children wandered about like wild animals. Roots, branches, herbs were gnawed with delight. Unclean and repugnant animals were frenziedly hunted and devoured. Children pawed over the street dirt to find a few grains left after feeding cavalry and devoured these raw. Despite the efforts of the police, they carried off carcasses of animals that had died of contagious diseases. These people were the relics of the country folk brought into the concentratoin camps by Weyler, whom we had forced Spain to un-concentrate.[1]

With the ex-Bavarian, ex-newsie, ex-doughboy, Frank Maximilian Steinhart, "cherubic as an innkeeper and astute as a mandarin," ever at his elbow, Brooke immediately took steps to alleviate this misery. Temporarily twenty thousand people in Havana were fed free. Sanitation was immediately tackled. Accumulated garbage was removed from streets grown impassable. Over twelve hundred cubic yards of rubbish were removed from the customs house alone.

In rural areas the distress was just as bad. Agriculture was paralyzed, the sugar industry in ruins. Domestic animals had disappeared. The cane-fields were abandoned, machin-

[1] Martínez Ortiz, *Cuba*, I, 15.

ery out of commission, mills smashed. New tariffs by the United States and European nations, just going in for beet-sugar, aggravated the situation.

Though Brooke utilized mostly Cubans, put most au-thority in the four administrative chiefs constituting his cabinet, inevitably there were many frictions, especially as those who fought for independence often received the cold shoulder. The average American expected Cubans to sing peans of praise for what we had done and for the oppor-tunity to acquire glorious American institutions—at the time of course, the best on earth and ordained by God. But the Cubans were merely impatient at not having full inde-pendence. Our provincialism and lack of experience in colonial affairs plus Cuban unpreparedness for self-govern-ment created a complicated situation, both technical and psychological.

Even so, Brooke's administration has been characterized even by Cuban opponents as a model of honesty and good intention. Little by little he tried to slip into the back-ground and let the Cubans hold the stage.

Before he left an American officer wrote, "City for city, the towns of Cuba are more peaceful and orderly than those of the United States. There was never a more docile, quiet people . . . Our troops have practically nothing to do . . . The pacification has been accomplished."

We were not merely concerned with destroying lawless-ness, but in setting up a government to guarantee property investments. Though much of Cuba's population was white, there was much talk of "the white man's burden." Our mission became that of building up a republic "by Anglo-Saxons in a Latin country where approximately seventy percent of the people were illiterate," a republic "modeled closely on the lines of our great Republic." [2] In reality this meant putting a loaded pistol into the hands of the Cubans; it meant giving them a mechanism they could

[2] Gov. Gen. Wood, 1902 Report, I, 271.

misuse, not one forged out of their own intelligence and needs.

But it was considered a very necessary and laudable undertaking, especially as American and other capital was now pouring into the island. The pressure of business interests, of the Monroe Doctrine, and the Treaty of Paris demanded that we set Cuba's house in order and make it safe for foreign dollars.

3 THE PRACTICED WILL

After the capture of Santiago, Wood remained in charge of the military occupation of Oriente. Even before becoming a "successor of Cortés and Ponce de León" he had been quite impressed by his Oriente patrimony. "God's own country . . . Beautiful as a dream —great mountains green to their tops, valleys filled with coconut and royal palms . . . dear, quaint little towns, hundreds of years old but so dirty. . . ."

How dirty, he soon realized. He found people dying by thousands from disease and starvation. Gaunt shapes stretched pitiful arms from the windows, beseeching bread until they fell back dead. "Long lines of wan, yellow, ghastly-looking individuals dragged themselves wearily up and down the filthy streets, avoiding the dead animals and heaps of decomposing refuse . . . The very air . . . laden with death." Wood himself paid fourteen dollars gold for his first meal—of horseflesh.

And while the wine of victory flowed at the Café Venus and the San Carlos Club, Wood took care of the sick, fed the starving, buried the dead. Every man shall have work or food was his motto.

With the help of Red Cross Clara Barton and the ex-circus-man, Major George Barbour, he cleaned up Santiago.

The death-rate was over two hundred daily. Many cadavers lay for days undiscovered. "Men could not bury the dead fast enough," wrote Wood, "and they were burned in great heaps of eighty or merely piled high on gratings of railroad iron and mixed with grass and sticks. Over all were turned thousands of gallons of kerosene, and the whole frightful heap reduced to ashes." Kerosene jumped to a dollar a gallon, until Wood laid down the law to forty assembled merchants. Ninety hours, day and night, were required to clean up just one street. The drinking-water cistern at the Spanish hospital where lay 3,000 sick soldiers was found to contain human and animal bones, old shoes and rags. The dilatory Spanish health engineer was yanked out of bed and brought before Wood in his nightgown. Barbour smashed in the doors of private homes to clean up and publicly horsewhipped citizens carelessly unsanitary.

Wood stamped out epidemic after epidemic, laid sewer pipes, till "even the flies starved to death."

And though the transport crews talked mutiny till they had to be put in irons on bread and water, Wood went ahead reëstablishing municipal government and courts, started public works, especially road-building. He not only strung telegraph lines along the royal palms through the jungle, but combated the Cuban temptation to utilize the wire for baling grass by putting offenders to work on the roads. He supplied country-folk with tools and seed and food and sent them back to their farms.

He founded schools, created rural guards, shot a looting American soldier, ran Cuban newspaper critics out of town. He told García to disarm his troops; García threatened to fight. "That might be the best way out of it," retorted Wood. Gradually the soldiers laid down their arms.

By the end of the year, his jurisdiction was "orderly, capable, and self-sustaining."

"Ever since I have been in Santiago," he said, "I have prescribed liberal doses of the United States constitution, and the treatment has been remarkably efficacious." He even issued a Thanksgiving Day proclamation; and his staff met for gratitude and strip poker on his despatch boat. The losers went home at dawn in newspapers, and the police, under Lieutenant Matthew Hanna, scattered the curious.

When Brooke was appointed Governor General, the two men immediately quarreled. Wood resented interference, and made a trip to the States to attack his chief and schemed secretly, pulling wires everywhere, and promoted underhanded attacks to get his job.

The Santiago press was permitted to roast Brooke. Brooke angrily ordered Wood to suppress such papers. Wood refused to do so. "I have always permitted the press . . . to criticize freely in decent language. . . ."

On his trip to the States, Wood stirred up a much-deserved ovation. At the Metropolitan Club's dinner Archibald Hopkins burst into poetry:

> *American all the way through,*
> *Bone blood and muscle, nerve and will,*
> *The brain to plan, the pluck to do,*
> *The steady hand, the practiced will. . . .*
> *(Seven stanzas)*

Wood bucked Brooke's financial arrangements, refused to submit proper accounts. "Your estimate for August is wrong," Brooke advised him. "You must submit estimates for each distributing office in your department . . . The haphazard methods heretofore existing . . . must cease instantly . . . absolutely correct forms will be insisted upon for every disbursement. The accounts rendered for the last six months are a disgrace to the army," and he held up funds pending compliance.

Wood went over his head, demanded a court inquiry. Brooke thought this—because of its effect on the Cubans—unwise.

"He crawled abjectly," wrote Wood to the Adjutant General.

Wood was reënforced by his Rough Rider record and by solid achievements in Santiago.

Roosevelt too was giving him a constant boost, holding pro-Wood banquets and meetings, and soon was bombarding McKinley constantly to oust Brooke and promote Wood. December 13 the appointment went through.

4 JAI ALAI

December 20, 1899, Wood glided into Havana at six o'clock in the morning under the saluting guns of Morro Castle . . . to be received by swarms of American and Cuban politicians, and bands beating out the *Star-spangled Banner* and the *Hymn of Bayamo,* and rode to Hotel Inglaterra beside General Rodríguez of the revolutionary army.

When made Governor General, Wood was still a young man, thirty-eight years of age, a tall handsome Hercules with iron hand-grip. He rested by taking gymnastic exercise. Bold and self-confident, he feared no situation; despite any criticism, he never swerved from any decided course of action. He was a rule or ruin type, also an indefatigable worker, a high-powered organizer and a man of great integrity with a fine sense of justice—save where his will, ambitions or prejudices were overtly aroused.

Too often he took credit for the labor of others. Undoubtedly peremptory, he sent most subordinates home in a huff that created smoldering animosity that lost him proper recognition in the World War and caused Woodrow Wilson to write: "Wherever General Wood goes there is controversy and conflict of judgment . . . absolutely unable to submit his judgment to those . . . superior in command."

But as new Governor General in Cuba he made an excellent impression by suppressing his annexationist sentiments too obviously displayed in Santiago, and appointing a cabinet made up purely of "revolutionists." But he soon showed he meant to run absolutely everything himself. He did get things done, till the weary Cubans said in doggerel:

> Don't stop to drink or spit,
> To smoke or scratch your ear.
> Go work while the stars are lit!
> Come home when night is near.
> There is no time for food,
> Write till the ink runs dry.
> The man who works for Wood
> Is one who wants to die.

Politically tied up with the Roosevelt Republican clique, he dared step on a Boss Hanna hireling, Estes G. Rathbone, for postal frauds, fought the case courageously through against the Ohio gang, and sent him up for ten years.

He continued cleaning up Havana, established systematic sanitation under Major Gorgas; Doctors Reed, Lazear, Carrol and Agramonte, at great personal risk (death for Lazear and Carrol) verified the theories of the Cuban doctor, Carlos Findlay, regarding the *Stegomyia* mosquito, and stamped out yellow fever, long the bane of the island and our southern ports.

Already under Brooke, with an able school-law drawn up by the Cuban scholar Enrique José Varona, a decentralized school system under Alexis Everett Frye had been inaugurated, new schools started almost recklessly, old Spanish barracks being turned into schoolrooms; a corps of teachers—partly (under Wood) through Harvard generosity—was built up in record time. Under Spain enrollment in the schools had been 36,306 (only 21,435 in 1899) with an attendance of little over 15,000. June, 1900, enrollment totaled 143,120. Frye was enthusiastic, hard-working, believing firmly in enlightened Cuban independence.

Wood, imperialist to the core, soon interfered, and sent Lieutenant Matthew Hanna, an ex-Ohio schoolteacher, out to inspect the schools and their pernicious ideas and new methods. Hanna to centralize the school system drew up a severe school code, based on the Ohio State law, but including unpleasant salary and fine provisions.

And so Root could declare in his 1900 report: "The courses and methods of instruction are those most approved in this country. The text-books are translations into Spanish of American text-books"—probably an improvement over the previous catechism, but hardly more intelligible or appropriate.

Centralization proved more costly: $26.50 per pupil as compared to the $22.50 American.

The teachers and Frye protested the changes angrily and in vain. Wood calmed them by certain new proposals never adopted.

At the same time the schools were rigorously reorganized; incidentally teachers too fervent for early Cuban independence were eliminated. When some of the teachers protested the Platt Amendment, Wood accepted Frye's resignation, and reported angrily, "He was a very dangerous man on the island, and his influence on the teachers and children was in the direction of the most intense radicalism as to the future relations between Cuba and the United States. . . ."

Under Brooke and Wood taxes were honestly collected, justice more properly administered, habeas corpus introduced. Wood reformed the jails and prisons; the insane "confined in cells in the jails all over the island, filthy and ragged . . . treated . . . like wild beasts . . . collected and taken to the large insane asylum in Havana."

In accordance with an election law which applied "the best examples of our American elections statutes to the existing conditions of Cuba" [3] municipal self-government was initiated. All in all a very solid, admirable record.

But Cuba had not, by the time of evacuation, been restored to its 1895 prosperity. Uncertainty of American tenure retarded normal economic expansion. More road-building, agricultural loans and similar enterprises might

[3] Root, *Military and Colonial Policy*, 194.

have been more beneficial than so large an emphasis upon schools to educate the electorate to obey a foreign-inspired paper constitution and to exercise prerogatives they would —as subsequent events have demonstrated—have very little opportunity to exercise.

Nor did the intervention satisfy all the patriots. Wood arrested and set to breaking rocks on the streets the two editors of *El Reconcentrado,* Augustín Cervantes and Ricardo Armantó, a fact recently cited by Secretary of State Orestes Ferrara to warrant the repressive tactics of Machado.[4] And Wood suppressed at least one paper criticizing the Platt Amendment. To his wife he wrote in October, 1899, "The *Cuba Libre* is preaching blood and war . . . say frankly they want to raise a spirit of revolution . . . I represent the perfidious United States and hence they intend to oppose anything I advocate . . . I want to exhaust all civil means before resorting to military force . . ."

And to another editor he said, "The moment you attack the government, I small put you in Morro Castle and keep you there."

Our own patriots were happier. Cuba was good pickings. Business enterprise puffed its idealistic throat. Waves of American civilizers, burdened by their whiteness, descended upon Cuba. Newspapermen were followed by property owners anxious to salvage their damaged estates. Realty offices boomed. Merchants, eager to open or reopen connections, flung out a skirmish line of all sorts of persons "eager to help Cuba by helping themselves." The island was literally "floated on new and endless stock companies." There were pitched battles to control new or existing concessions.

Cuba was looked upon as fair game for big business. The War Department, as guardian for our new ward, decided to control all plums from Washington. As early as February, 1899, a board, headed by General Robert P.

---

[4] Ferrara, *Las enseñanzas de una revolución,* 44.

Kennedy of Ohio, was formed for this purpose—to advise upon the "sale or gift of franchises, either local or inter-provincial; railway grants; street-car line concessions; electric light and other municipal monopolies."

But Congress, a spark of idealism left, battled its way across the vested trenches of Mark Hanna and the administration plunderers, and in March pushed through the Foraker Amendment to the military appropriation bill prohibiting the granting of concessions of any kind during the occupation by the United States. Dreams of sudden wealth were blighted. If rapid reconstruction was retarded, the intervention was kept pure of shady deals and scandals; and business men became advocates of an early termination of intervention.

Civil Order No. 53, February 8, 1900, made clear, however, that General Wood did not consider that the amendment forbade the purchase of land and the building of a railway on it, or that revocable permits for such lines to cross public highways and streams were in the nature of concessions; and thus-wise Sir William Horne started the Cuban railroad from Santa Clara to Santiago, opening that very rich productive area up to development—all in all a commendable evasion of the Foraker restriction.

Nor, as Jenks points out, did the amendment prevent the revocation of past concessions to open the way for interested parties later on. When Governor Brooke discovered that the Spaniards shortly before evacuation had provided for a waterworks and a dock, he canceled this, indignantly calling it a fraud on the rights of the United States. Straightway he sent troops to the dock and engineers to the waterworks without so much as advising the owners or adhering to the Spanish law that confiscation demanded recompense. Washington finally, after our evacuation, recognized the original waterworks title, but retained the dock —for there American ships could moor. If the owners did not like this, they could appeal to the Cuban courts, by that time bound by the Platt Amendment to validate every act of the occupation.

Nor did the Foraker Act prevent the granting of a ten-year monopoly to the Jai Alai company which proposed introducing the famous Basque game to Cuba in connection with open gambling. Despite its illegality, General Wood, himself an enthusiastic player, so strongly interested himself in the concession, he returned the petition three times to the judge-advocate-general for his authorization and quite misrepresented the matter to Washington by suppressing the facts regarding professionalism and gambling. The concession was finally printed as a *fait-accompli* in the *Gaceta Oficial,* May 9, 1902, eleven days before General Wood sailed away with a $5,000 silver tea-set from the grateful concessionaires to face a dust-cloud of emotion in the United States raised by selfish beet interests over the fact that he had utilized Cuban funds to pay a Washington propagandist in behalf of lower tariff.

Compared to the contemporary corruption in our own large cities and the procedure of European powers in the Near East and in Africa, our first intervention in Cuba— and I say this without irony—stands as a model of fine trusteeship. Its basic evil resided, not in its worthy deeds, but in Washington's failure to recognize and aid the insurgent government.

XI FROM THE ASHES

1 CUBA'S APPENDIX

Hon. DAVID J. HILL, LL.D., Assistant Secretary of State, told the Rochester Chamber of Commerce, December 8, 1898, on the eve of the establishment of American military government in Cuba: "I cannot believe it an evil for any people that the Stars and Stripes, the symbol of liberty and law, should float over them." The Cubans should be glad to remain under that banner. Patriotic orators, from then on, shouted our flag should never come down.

Wood himself was at heart an annexationist. He wrote Roosevelt, "Clean government, quick, decisive action and absolute control in the hands of trustworthy men, establishment of needed legal and educational reforms, and I do not believe you could shake Cuba loose if you wanted to." Even after a constitution had been drawn up he was still hopeful. "There is an extremely strong sentiment for annexation," he wrote Root October 16, 1901. "Annexation talk grows apace," he wrote Roosevelt October 7. "I always tell the people, however, that they must talk annexation through their own government when it is formed."

Powerful American interests, opposed to our original entry war, desired this step. Robert Porter, special 1899 McKinley representative to arrange terms with Gómez, later to report on economic conditions, publicly advocated such action—the Spanish merchants desired it, all "the best" people of Havana. Many Americans "believing we had declared the merchants free and independent," announced that the Cubans did not want to govern themselves.

Official Washington looked with as much trepidation upon the experiment of a free Cuba as did Europe at a Republican United States in 1776. But contrary to the expectations of Europe and not a few disappointed Americans, we did get out; our restraint gave greater face to our democratic annexation of Porto Rico and the Philippines against the wishes of "bandit" Aguinaldo, who had done most of our fighting for us, but who had ungratefully declared the Philippine Republic unappreciative of McKinley's lofty Christian purposes.

True, there were a few heretics. At Faneuil Hall Moorfield Storey asked embarrassingly, "Why should Cuba with its 1,600,000 have the right to freedom and self-government and the 8,000,000 people . . . in the Philippine Islands be denied the same right? . . . Is Porto Rico more indebted to us than Cuba? Is the commandment 'thou shalt not steal' qualified by the proviso 'unless it is necessary'?"

If not annexed, then Cuba could succeed only by being "bound to us," McKinley stated in his December 5, 1899, message, "by ties of singular intimacy and strength. . . . The new Cuba, yet to arise from the ashes of the past"— said our poetic guardian of reactionary business in words of singular eloquence—could not be turned "adrift" as a "loosely framed commonwealth" to "face the vicissitudes" of "weaker states whose natural wealth and abundant resources are offset by the incongruities of their political organization" and the sapping of their strength "by internal rivalries"—in effect, he argued (in a weird assemblage of monstrously long words elbowing each other rhetorically), Cuba would have to become our ward to be kept orderly that its wealth might be properly exploited. For decades most of our communiques to Spain had revealed as our dominant motive the safety of capital and investments.

Even some Cuban revolutionists were not averse to a relationship to guarantee rapid rehabilitation and governmental success. If for no other reason than to stand in Washington's good graces, these wished to attract American capitalists. Estrada Palma, February 1, 1898, wrote Andrés Moreno de la Torre: McKinley had been advised that while annexation was not desired, the American government should "in some manner provide a guarantee for internal peace" so the Republic might "inspire confidence among foreign capitalists to encourage them to invest large sums. . . ."

Promptly we set to work to establish the proper big-brother relationship. Two great intellects evolved the necessary paternalistic paraphernalia: Senator Orville H. Platt of Connecticut and Secretary of War Elihu Root—a Roman Emperor type "imperfectly acclimated to democracy and barely tolerant of its inefficiency and rabble." To establish a legal right for intervention which even Europe would be obliged to recognize, they worked in the traditional policy of imperialist Seward, the ante-bellum Whigs, and the Monroe Doctrine. "Thus," remarks Jenks, "the mind of Elihu Root moved from first principles toward conclusions indistinguishable from those reached by unphilosophical persons who merely wished investments to ripen in Cuba." [1]

The April 20, 1898, Joint Resolution had declared Cuba was and of a right ought to be free and its government vested in the people. February 25, Root's new tablet of stone was dragged down from the War Department Sinai to the Senate Chamber and tied to the tail of the 1901-02 Military Appropriation Bill, a nice tandem of implied force and idealistic oats. After two hours' debate on the 27th, the bill was passed; after favorable House action, was signed by the President, March 2.

"We are going to impose upon them obligations which the Federal Government has never thought of imposing upon any of the States of the Union," complained Senator

[1] *Our Cuban Colony*, 74.

John T. Morgan of Alabama. Senator Edward W. Pettees of the same state said sadly: "Free and independent. . . . We are disgracing the name of the American people." And Representative De Armand of Arkansas cried: "Ignoble House! Miserable despotism! Never was there a day so full of fatality for liberty since the United States was formed . . . infamous measure . . . cowardly renunciation . . . commercialism. . . ."

A Cuban constitutional convention was then in session. It had been convoked under the benign patronage of Leonard Wood by Order 301, June 25, 1900, of the General Headquarters of the Cuban Division. He at once toured the island to see that proper men were elected to it. For the most part Wood was satisfied with the resultant personnel; but the people had, he advised Root, "also sent some of the worst agitators and political rascals in Cuba."

The delegates had been asked to fulfill Articles I and IV of the Joint Resolution and to consider what form future relations between the two countries should take, these to be adopted as part of the constitution.

Such a demand at once aroused the fear of Cuban patriots. Those more outspoken denounced Wood as a "quack doctor," his talk of Cuban independence as "hypocritical," that the constitution was just a sop, that its tail would wag the dog. Relations with a specific country were not constitutional questions.

February 21, 1901, invoking the blessing of God, the Constitution of the New Republic, containing 115 articles and seven Transitory Dispositions, established the conditions on which Cuba entered the concert of nations— except for the United States.

Discussions regarding Cuban-American relations had been started February 12. Although the convention as a whole was dominated by elements fairly critical of the United States, many proposals, practically all friendly to us, had been presented. The Convention clearly desired

that we guarantee Cuba's independence. It wished to con-
ciliate American economic interests upon which Cuba's
future development depended and to prevent the island
ever being used as a base for foreign aggressions against
us. But the convention speakers betrayed gloomy forebod-
ings that the United States' desire to make Cuba a protectorate was likely to insist upon relations incompatible
with Cuban sovereignty.

They already had an inkling even before Mr. Platt's
fatherly concern for Cuba had manifested itself. Already
Wood had warned the convention (so he advised Root
February 19) that these conditions (later a few others were
added) were "the only ones" the United States "could at
present consider." But the convention looked sourly upon
these pre-Platt terms, and Wood wrote Root that as our
demands were "liberal, equitable, and just," they "should
be insisted upon throughout." He urged sending a forcible
communication.

February 27, his tone hardened. "I have told them flatly,
of course unofficially [blessed word], that the United States
felt that it had performed its duty here with exemplary
fairness and liberality and cautioned them against appearing to slight or ignore what had been done for them. The
political element are an ungrateful lot and they appreciate
only one thing, which is the strong hand of authority, and
if necessary *we must show it.*"

The forcible communication was the Platt Amendment,
embodying the Wood-Root demands. Our fairness and
sense of justice were so god-like, it was foolish even to
imagine the Cubans would even expect the generosity of
discussion. March 2, less than three weeks after the convention started considering the matter, the Amendment
determined exactly what the future status of the island
would be with reference to the United States. It was presented for adoption to the convention by General Wood,
March 7.

The delegates then discovered what they had long suspected: that though they might talk, nothing they might propose would be given the slightest consideration; neither their coöperation nor bona fide future coöperation between the countries was in the least desired. The hand-embroidered towels of free Cuba's hope-chest were too shabby for her imperial consort.

Wood took the committee on relations away "from the murky political atmosphere of Havana" to Batambo on the *Kanawha* fishing-boat to impress upon them what they would have to do—an ultimatum. This interference with the convention was highly to be criticized; that body openly declared it had been "insulted," the orders "pitched" at them.

They were quite dismayed. Where was the freedom of action which had been pledged? Was there not time enough for the United States to object to the convention's opinion after it had been formulated? One patriot, Salvador Cisneros Betencourt (Marqués of Santa Lucía), President during the Yara revolt and again during the Baire revolt, proposed returning the document forthwith. Some wished to introduce a resolution asking for Wood's recall, others wished to adjourn *sine die*. The oratory of the negro Juan Gualberto Gómez swung the assemblage against immediate acceptance. Certainly the Amendment violated spirit and letter of the Teller clause of the Joint Resolution. Nor was the Amendment demanded, as Root insisted, by the Treaty of Paris. Article II of that treaty—in which the Cubans had no voice—obliged the United States to protect life and property; but Article XVI specifically limited this to the duration of occupation; on its termination, we should "advise the government established . . . to accept the same obligations."

Wood wrote Root he was "bending every effort to rush this thing through," and on another occasion he advised his superior he had the "unquestionable" feeling of the rural people being in his favor but "in the large cities—Havana, Cienfüegos, Santiago—where the agitating element is gathered, one hears only outspoken opposition to the military government."

A Cuban cartoon published in *La Discusión* depicted Cuba nailed to the cross between General Wood and McKinley as thieves; Roman centurion Platt proffered the Amendment sponge on a spear.

Wood in apoplexy closed the paper for a day and had the editor brought before him under arrest.

But brow-beating was bringing our pro-consul nowhere. The delegates were constantly getting more and more on their uppers. To calm them down, the majority of whom hotly demanded modifications, Root, fearing the hook might not be swallowed at all, took up the smooth handle that Wood in his brusqueness had disdained. April 3, Wood transmitted to the convention President, Dr. Domingo Méndez Capote, a new cable from Root that the Amendment was "not synonymous with intermeddling or interference with the affairs of the Cuban Government." The United States would intervene only to preserve Cuban independence and maintain a proper government.

A bit mollified, still not satisfied, the convention sent a commission headed by Méndez Capote to Washington to learn the real intentions of the United States and secure modifications, at least barter trade reciprocity for acquiescence.

In Washington, Root reassured the delegation that the Amendment gave the United States no right not already possessed and exercised; it merely enabled us better to act for Cuba with reference to foreign nations to protect Cuban sovereignty. After praying to God the need for intervention might never arise, he swore it would only be contemplated in case Cuba, lacking government, should fall into anarchy, or a foreign menace should arise—no meddling with internal administration.

If our intentions were so benevolent, inquired the commissioners, why a tantamount ultimatum, why such pressure to secure immediate consent to exercise a right the United States would exercise anyway?

Root replied, "Good diplomacy consists in so handling the way in which a conflict arises between two nations that it is its adversary which has violated the law"—of course European nations, not the United States.

The commission returned with these and other interpretational baggage and reciprocity promises from the President, Root and Platt. It was clear the American army would not be withdrawn until they capitulated; the Cubans were quite free to choose the Amendment or American military rule. May 26, the delegates, still trying to hedge, finally adopted a revised version of the Amendment by 15 to 14. Root sent a letter to be submitted reiterating his position.

Wood said nothing would be gained by further discussion. "Yes or no . . . to the Amendment." The time had come for an "ultimatum," of which there would be no further consideration or discussion. The ultimatum was delivered. By a vote of 16 to 11, June 12, 1901, the provisions, with the sad resignation of the patriots, were written word for word, not a letter changed, into the Cuban constitution as an "Appendix." Two years later, as the Amendment and Appendix provided, this was embodied in a permanent treaty. For five months the delegates had resisted. They finally had to bow to Root's infallible wisdom, Wood's "strong hand," and our superior power.

2 THE SPONGE

The Platt Amendment, thus forced down Cuba's throat, forbade the Cuban government to enter into any treaty with any foreign power or powers which would even tend to impair independence; no foreign power could be permitted to obtain by coloni-

zation or for naval or military purposes, lodgment or control over any portion of the island. (This really meant—any
foreign power except the United States.)

Though the Cuban constitution already included sovereignty safeguards, also that no loan could be issued without Congressional authorization and provision for permanent taxes for interest and redemption, we forbade any
loans not amortizable through an excess above current
revenues.

We also retained the right to intervene "for the preser-
vation of Cuban government" for "the maintenance of a
government adequate for the protection of life, property
and individual liberty," and to insure fulfillment of the
Treaty of Paris obligations.

The Cubans were obliged to ratify and validate all acts
of our military occupation.

All existing plans for sanitation were to be completed
and amplified to prevent epidemics endangering the people and commerce of Cuba and of our southern ports.

The Isle of Pines, always part of Cuba and thus administered by Spain, was "omitted from the boundaries of
Cuba," its future ownership to be determined by treaty.
We were given the right to buy or lease lands necessary
for coaling and naval stations.

It froze for all time the relations between two developing supposedly sovereign states. Imposed by the strong
upon the weak, purely legalistic, devoid of the comprehension that no law which overrides the wishes of a people
has moral validity, it was unimaginative, stodgy, bureaucratic, unnecessary. No room was left for Cuba's evolution,
for the evolution of its relations with the United States or
for adequate future relations between us and Latin America as a whole. It is one of those static patterns which delight the Sir Oracle mind and New England puritanism,
and has had only disastrous effects upon Cuba.

It was a unilateral document giving us rights and Cuba

duties. But can any right ever be justly exercised without assumption of its corresponding obligations? Can we even interpret that document without thereby incurring definite responsibilities regarding every Cuban government? For the interpretation of the intervention privilege was held strictly in our hands—we alone could determine when a government violated life, property and individual liberty, when it was proper to intervene, when a loan was inadvisable, when a foreign treaty was inimical. In short, it was the establishment of a definite protectorate which has the advantage of similar relationships (as that of Egypt or France in Morocco) in that it enables us to shirk our responsibilities and avoid blame for all evils, but accept plaudits for fine achievements.

One Cuban stated, it was "equivalent to delivering up the key to our house, so that they can enter it at all hours, when the desire takes them, day or night, with intentions good or ill . . ." If the United States alone can determine when a government is "adequate," then "only those governments will live which count on its support and benevolence."

The policy of the United States to oppose all revolutions in Latin America and not recognize governments coming into power by such means, whether the revolution is justified or the new government represents popular will, leads inevitably to local tyranny, doubly so in Cuba's case. This policy forces us to become solid allies of the worst tyrants, the ones who best profit from such a static control.

When we imposed on Central America the 1907-23 treaties, when we applied the Platt Amendment in this manner in 1917 in unjust behalf of Menocal, we merely recognized existing governments which had seized power in the fashion we supposedly opposed, thus helping to perpetuate non-elected governments, while denying the people the right to remove them. Such tyrannies are further assisted, as in Cuba, to buy unlimited war materials in the United States, often with the proceeds of loans from the United States, true of Cuban Presidents Menocal, Zayas, and Machado.

For this to approximate a just, democratic and enlightened policy, we would have to guarantee ·honest elections, obviously impossible and entailing further injustices and violations of national sovereignty. Hence this policy, embodied in the Platt Amendment, merely utilizes the United States' power to maintain directly and indirectly a condition constantly favoring tyranny, corruption and American capitalists at the expense of human liberty. This has been and is the situation in Cuba. This is the fundamental explanation of the present Machado dictatorship.

Thus when Secretary of State Stimson and Ambassador Guggenheim announced in 1930 they were merely following the Root interpretation of the Platt Amendment, they were confessing, for every one in the slightest informed, that they were upholding the Machado tyranny.

PART III

LIBERTY TO LOOT

"It is not known which are the direst ambitions in a country not yet born—those of the soldiers or those of the civilians."

"What I must say, before my voice is silenced and my heart ceases to beat in this world, is that my country has all the virtues necessary for the conquest and maintenance of her liberty."

JOSÉ MARTÍ

XII PROBLEMS

1 CHILD OF THE TROPICS

José MARTÍ, INTELLECTUAL father of Cuban independence, was essentially a child of the tropics. His fervid words, though he illuminated many subsequent pitfalls, were but a vehicle for the pain of the tropics, not for its realistic problems.

Cuba, far more bland, despite diseases and hurricanes, partakes greatly of all semi-tropical characteristics. Any one ever enthralled by rural life on that island will grasp part of Martí's intellectual dilemma. For what is more beautiful and painful than the contrasts of each dawning day—the fresh early morning filled with warmish white fog, the gradual sun-bright quickening world, steaming in spirals as though the earth's very crust were about to bubble? Soon heat lays heavier hand over everything, like a cap of hot untouchable metal; and each human toward noon, as the hours grow stale, feels sodden lethargy, almost stupefying inaction, shot through with sensuous and lovely images—the glint of sky and vivid raw colors, the majestic, white-limbed trunks, the sun sharp-etched on cane-fields, feathery palm trees moving softly in a breeze overly warm and caressing, the slow-moving folk in bright clothes, brown and black flesh more humid and darker than the earth itself. Easy enough to suffer all things, resist all things, enjoy all things, be part of all things, but not to dominate, control or improve. All too easy to sink into a pattern far too perfect to be changed.

[187]

Martí and other revolutionists did not sink into any such pattern because for them it had been disrupted, made ugly, by aliens; and because the Cuban, whatever his kinship with the rest of the American tropics, is far more of a parvenu. Both because of the very closeness of the independence movement and Cuba's proximity to the piston-like civilization of the United States, he is more frothily agitated in spirit and life.

But the rupture of tropic peace explains in part why to Martí and others it was sufficient if their country were only free. Spanish shackles once thrown off, the people would automatically be reintegrated with the soil and growth of Cuba. To that the patriots were loyal, not to the mere mechanics of government or justice.

Martí was a Mazzini, an advocate of extreme political liberalism. For him whites, mestizos and negroes were all Cubans, equally to be cherished; but he did not halt to consider the racial, cultural and economic problems that would spring out of differences of pigmentation and historical origin. He wanted no idle odium toward the Spaniard, but never considered what would ensue in a free Cuba with business still dominated by aliens.

Beyond simple brotherly formulæ, he did not delve deeply, very little into the economic and social requisites to make ideal citizenship effective. The trends of the '48 in Europe, of the Paris Commune, of capital and labor, of economic penetration of foreign capital, were never pondered by him. He belonged still, noble soul that he was, to the age of the Physiocrats, to Emersonian platitudes and hoary generalizations regarding liberty, mostly far removed from the functioning forces of active social control. And though all his thoughts and deeds were on a lofty plane, placing him beside Cuban heroes and her most courageous thinkers—Arango y Parreño, Félix Varela, Saco, José de la Luz y Caballero, Conde de Pozos Dulces—yet his very idealisms were intellectually and historically a bit anachronistic.

Ideologically the Cubans were unprepared for their new freedom. Spain's strict control over the intellectual life of the island, the low state of public education, the barriers set up against intercourse with the United States, not to mention the rest of Latin America, gave no proper philosophical, let alone practical, enlightenment for the new duties of self-government.

2 CHANGO

In justice to Martí, to this day none of the serious problems confronting Cuba have been honestly faced by her leaders—only partially by some of her thinkers, and now by some of her younger revolutionists. The generation of rulers born of the independence revolt—the most militaristic and unscrupulous elements of that effort—have merely led her ever deeper into degradation.

Nor could our American occupation be expected to consider basic economic problems. The American official mind had not learned to think of governmental responsibilities in those terms. *Laissez faire* was at its apogee; as yet we know nothing even of Roosevelt's fake trust-busting days or the Wilsonian regulatory schemes.

What were and are the problems of Cuba's political independence?

As independence came late, this, plus American ideas of definite separation of Church and State which canceled previous government subsidies to the Church, permitted Cuba to avoid the bitter religious struggles which featured the first half century and more of Mexican and Central American independence, an issue still to be fought out in many South American countries. Even so, Wood was rightly condemned for paying $2,000,000 and authorizing other payments from the Cuban treasury for Church mortgages and buildings confiscated half a century earlier by the

Spanish authorities, a lien canceled by the financial clauses of the Treaty of Paris. But Cuba was freed from the onus of a religious struggle.

Other questions were not so brightly disposed of.

Is there a negro problem in Cuba? Cubans deny it. Americans have never faced their own race question; the military occupation, unlikely to think in such terms, did not.

The majority of the negroes were not freed until the 'eighties; many were not really freed then. The influx of blacks continued almost up until the close of the slavery period—the Magoon census still showed 7.958 African-born negroes. Despite prohibitory legislation, the black-cargo traffic continued with negroes from Haiti and Jamaica down through the period of the Republic. Hence a vast portion of the negro population, foreign in thought and customs, has never been properly rooted in Cuban life. Cuba was and is two countries—black Cuba and white Cuba.

Though the two races have rarely been opposed on a militant basis, the negroes, during Spanish rule and since, are far more uneducated, on a far lower economic scale, and far less prepared for the tasks of self-government. They were the cannon-fodder of the revolution, the beasts-of-burden of the sugar and tobacco plantations. Manumission never gave this large black population a settled economic status. Before and after being freed, they were uprooted by the wars, a disorganized mass frequently addicted to political instability, a vast reservoir of demagoguery and future revolution. The negro runs the whole social gamut from ferocious atavism to intellectual brilliance; but to this day, the mass remains culturally apart, ignorant save for lustrous exceptions, inevitably economically discriminated against, politically inferior. Only mulattoes are accepted socially, and must pretend to be white.

The following news item should not be taken too seriously in these Machado days of governmental criminality, official assassinations and terrorism, but it is indicative not only of the negro problem but of some of the root causes of present political atavism in high white circles.

"Five little white girls from four to eight years old disappeared from . . . farms near Havana last week. . . . In a deserted barn near Caimito, twenty-two miles from the capital, the children's dismembered bodies were found . . . also a crude altar of stones and seashells, a hideous statue of the goddess Chango, and twenty-eight half-crazed negroes, two of them with bloody robes and blunt stone axes. . . . José Delgado described what had happened:

" 'For three weeks Chango has been demanding white blood lest a curse be cast upon us. . . . While we had the girls, we fed them raw potatoes, sugar and water, for that is what a sacrifice for Chango must have. . . . It was decided to hold the sacrifice to-day because of the search being made for the girls.

" 'After praying and dancing around Chango's image and singing hymns to Chango, the girls were brought before the altar. Some of them resisted but others just screamed and cried.

" 'Heavy ropes were tied around their hands and feet and they were placed side by side. Then Chango's bodyguards beat them with royal palm switches. There were about fifty persons present. They danced, yelling and singing and clapping. Two *curanderos* [medicine priests] cut the bodies apart with stone axes. We could see Chango smiling and satisfied as the *curanderos* sprinkled her image with blood. Then police appeared. . . .' "

But March, 1933, an almost exactly similar case among the white "long-tongue" sect in the Mason and Dixon area of these United States occurred. Religious fanaticism is not a racial but a social product correlated with ignorance.

Inevitably Cuban government was to be controlled by the better-prepared white Creole classes. Wood fostered the white Creole tendency, ignoring as far as possible basic revolutionary forces and catering to the more wealthy cultured groups, better educated, more responsible in a conventional way, but for the most part Tories, unthrilled by freedom, dreading its responsibilities and intrinsically non-Cuban in spirit.

Wood wrote to Root January 19, 1901: "Our policy toward Cuba has rendered it impossible for the business and conservative elements to state frankly what they desire. . . . Let Congress set a definite date of withdrawal . . . and I will make every effort to bring the conservative and representative elements to the front. . . ."

The race-prejudices of our occupation were continued by our dutiful successor, Estrada Palma, long-steeped in an American outlook. Though black Martín Morúa Delgado held high position under his administration, Estrada pointedly denied Señora Morúa corresponding recognition at official functions.

The Creoles, quick to realize their true rôle in the new Republic, became partners and agents in American business enterprises and soon, increasingly dominating the government, utilized political leverage to maintain their social status by a species of bartering and unholy concessions to foreign capital. They thus have become official parasites, contemptuous of Cuba.

Mexico achieved independence by the treachery of Crown officer Iturbide, who tried to initiate the Creole class into absolute power; something similar occurred in Cuba by the side-tracking of the autonomist movement and the usurpation of power by the American intervention.

3 SOLDIERS AND PEASANTS

Cuba's essential economic problem is agrarian. Her life or death depends upon the future of her rural population. Their economic security eventually would have meant more than all the new schools modeled on the Ohio system and knowledge gleaned from translations of American texts. At the outset the occupation slightly aided the peasants, provided the soldiers with a bonus, here and there gave farmers seed and tools. But Wood naturally did not think deeply of Cuban needs in relation to the soil. Until our recent depression, because of vast still unexploited areas, we have never had an inkling, except here and there locally, of such a thing as an agrarian problem. Our frontier was scarcely closed to settlers. But the land problem is inherent in a seagirt island, might have been apparent even to Wood, had it not been obscured by racial and political factors. After all, the mass of Cuban peasants were and are negroes.

The independence leaders, eager to attract American capital, did not stop to remember that such capital inevitably would flow into large land-holdings and large-scale agrarian industrial activities. To-day Cuba still has a population of miserable serfs. Even if foreseen, probably limitation of the size of holdings would have been blocked by foreign selfishness.

The twentieth-century experience with regard to one-crop production—though England had faced this problem in Jamaica and Barbados long before—were not particularly in evidence. Most of Latin America due to backwardness and peripheral situation to the world's major industrial development, has been the victim of single crops in given areas—Mexico, oil; Yucatán, henequén; Chile, nitrates; Brazil, coffee. The single crop has buttressed up its political parallel, dictatorship—the single-crop idea in government. Overdependence upon one product has resulted in alternations of extravagant prosperity and overwhelming depression, automatically precipitating corresponding political disasters. Cuba was to travel this road with sugar.

Failure to look ahead in agrarian matters is linked up with Cuba's military problem. The peasant masses of Cuba, fighting for freedom, or else pitiably dislocated by the Weyler Reconcentration camps, had in part lost their sense of affiliation to the soil, were badly dislocated. We provided temporary dollars-and-cents' solution for Gómez' soldiers but failed to foresee the future rôle of the veterans in public affairs. Improperly demobilized armies ever return like locust plagues.

Cuba's military problem could not manifest itself during the American occupation, but neither could three years extirpate the rebellion habit, ingrained for a century, especially as no substitutes were really provided. Estrada Palma's first administration went along fairly smoothly, but largely because he opened the treasury to the veterans and secured a foreign loan to dish out the fantastic sum of over $50,000,000.

Inevitably the claim of having been a soldier against Spain was to bring prestige to old leaders and seriously block political advancement for the younger generation. The virus of militarism ate its way almost imperceptibly into Cuban life; the poison already planted there had not been eradicated. The strong injection of American paternalism merely drove it temporarily into more hidden recesses of the body politic. The sore was to fester, by the time of Machado was to become a running ulcer. Cuba long prided itself on its superiority to its Latin-American neighbors in this respect; it had merely closed its eyes to realities. Having done so, it now groans beneath armed tyranny. As a recent A.B.C. manifesto summarizes it:

"Thanks to the indifference of its accidental and powerful ally, Cuba found itself after emancipation with an army of veterans deprived of every pacific means of gaining a livelihood, with a legion of émigrés who had lost their properties or the capital to exploit them, the country desolate, a rural population reduced to misery by the Reconcentration, and a native middle class completely ousted by that from Spain and reduced to a parasitic condition. . . . Emancipation had added a third to the pauper population of Cuba. Cuba had gained its political independence at the cost of its economic independence."

Spanish rule had been vitiated by most scandalous corruption. Graft was ever rampant. The Spanish governors, with no intrinsic interest in Cuba, were engaged in ruling with no obligation to the ruled. Thus every official transaction was accompanied by the most venal graft. The Brooke-Wood administration was essentially honest; that of Estrada Palma perhaps more so, but seven years did not destroy the evil.

It was tolerated, even abetted, under the second intervention of Magoon, "who taught the Cubans how to steal." He did not teach them. He merely weakly bowed to an ancient system reasserting itself, and added a few pink bows of American boss-ridden politics. Misappropriation of public funds increased steadily during the remaining period of independence up until the present, any occasional curtailment being due merely to depleted revenues, not to honesty.

In other ways, the conventional Latin-American pattern has been repeated. After the first fairly united Estrada Palma government, the struggle for power revolved not about principles, but was a sordid scramble between ins and outs.

The inane character of Cuban political struggles has been fostered by the Platt Amendment, which makes the United States the final court of appeal. With the growth of American capital holdings, the Cuban government has moved ever further from that which is intrinsically Cuban. With each concession to foreign capital its roots have become shallower. It merely placates the people or batters them into submission. As our interests and those of the Cuban people are largely antithetical, the people are more often battered than placated.

XIII BULLETS AND BOODLE

1 VETERANS VERSUS PROGRESS

"THE AMERICANS," REMARKED
Ramiro de Maeztu, "fight for the power of money; the His-
pano-Americans for the money of the Power." Which
merely means that with us politics are subordinate to business; that in Cuba the biggest business is politics, and a
closed monopoly at that.

In name, Cuba was free, but Martí's ideals still remote.
Not that the Presidential elections celebrated by Wood,
December 31, 1901, were not technically honest, or that
Estrada Palma, joint candidate of the Nationalists and Republicans (backed by Máximo Gómez), did not honestly
win the election, or that the United States did not get out
on schedule time, or that subsequent disasters were due to
our direct mismanagement or meddling; nor can too much
attention be paid to the charge of American electoral favoritism for Estrada which was made by the anti-Platt Amendment candidate, former Provisional President, Bartolomé
Masó, the first to take the field for freedom in 1895.

Undoubtedly Wood's sympathies were warmer for a man
who docilely accepted the American program—now written
irrevocably into the Cuban constitution—than for one who
still stormed against it.

The Cuban revolutionary leaders—such names as Máx-
imo Gómez, Domingo Méndez Capote, Manuel Sanguilly,
Emilio Núñez, Ricardo Dolz, Martín Morúa Delgado, and
Gonzalo de Quesado—felt probably that the weight of our

intervention leaned in many subtle ways to Estrada Palma; but being human and enthusiastic, they wished to have a part in the first independent administration of their country, and were willing with the prospect of our early withdrawal to sacrifice differences for harmony. Estrada Palma was felt to have the confidence of the United States; he had been head of the Revolutionary Junta in New York, had engaged in the Ten Years' War, was known to be scrupulously honest, in a sense had inherited the mantle of Martí.

Masó, shorn of party backing, rounded up partisans outside the Estrada combination—among others, Spaniards, the old Autonomists, and the negroes, not very happy bedfellows.

Wood pointedly refused to alter the composition of the Electoral Board of Scrutiny (containing only Nationalists and Republicans, all backers of Estrada) to include members of Masó's new group. More flexibility would have saved the elections from all charge of partiality and would not have created the precedent of iron-clad partisan control, later to be utilized in such funereal ways.

This gave Masó and his supporters an excuse not to go to the polls. Estrada Palma won uncontested—bad augury.

Congress met May 5, 1902, to ratify the candidates elected. May 20 at noon, streets jammed with rejoicing Cubans, the Stars and Stripes tumbled down; the Cuban flag was run up on the Palace and Morro Castle. The bands played *La Bayamesa*. A salute thundered from the fort and the war vessels; cheers echoed the crash of the guns; and shortly Wood and the American soldiers—"different," as Root insisted, speaking of Cuba, Puerto Rico and the Philippines, "from all other soldiers of all other countries" —sailed away on the *Brooklyn,* the shore black with cheering crowds.

Estrada Palma faced many obstacles and now had to govern with a political mechanism, devised by well-intentioned minds schooled in English and American practices, alien from Latin traditions. Our military government had left over a million in the treasury. But sugar and agriculture in general were far from a healthy state. Cuba, now cut off from Spain, was also cut off from the American market by the tariff. Sugar had to win its way back against an augmented beet-sugar production in Europe and the United States.

The veterans, despite the difficult situation, despite revenue possibilities or other governmental functions, at once began treasury raids. Congress' first concern was to create new jobs and though we had already paid $3,000,000 to disband the independence army, it enacted a bonus bill, one dollar for each day of service, extravagant sums for officers.

This bad precedent opened the way for vicious peculation, especially when Cuba's 1903 Speyer loan of $35,000,-000 was negotiated. Over half of it was to pay off this veteran debt. Delays in payment exasperated would-be recipients. High officials bought up their certificates at discounts as high as 60 percent, immediately collecting the full account from the treasury. Twenty-six thousand one hundred and three veterans, about half, sacrificed their claims. Also men who had never fought were listed as veterans, the service periods were padded, ranks arbitrarily raised, even imaginary names appeared on the rolls.

General Máximo Gómez and Chief of Staff Boza, from their Quinta de los Molinos estate, for patronage purposes, issued wholesale endorsements to every comer—even to those suddenly become Cuban patriots after the American squadron smashed Cervera, even to former open enemies of the insurgents.[1]

Despite the veterans, Estrada Palma's first years' expenditure was less than Wood needed annually, and for the remaining three years—excluding the Speyer loan—very little in excess. His administration showed real achievements; after only six months, he reported road-building, docks,

[1] Luis Octavio Divino, *Pro-patria*, 122-3.

light-houses, dredging, public buildings, etc. In all, he built 328 kilometers of road; Wood, 98. A fourth of the budget was devoted to education. Sanitation continued to reduce mortality, already lower than in the United States. Soon a reciprocity treaty with the United States caused the 1903-4 sugar crop to rise from 636,000 to 850,000 tons. Camagüey and Oriente were, for the first time, developing into enormous sugar centers. By 1916 there was a treasury surplus of $25,000,000.

Yet the President saw breakers ahead. By 1905, he stated, "In Cuba we have a Republic but no citizens." By the end of his term, he was seriously alarmed over the drop in school attendance.

The inrush of American capital had taken up unemployment slack. But that in itself ultimately meant dispossessing the Cubans, making the country dependent upon one-crop vicissitudes and foreign influence. The land problem, the veteran problem, the political problem were all in the offing to cause trouble.

2 MONSTROSITY

First elections under Estrada —1904—fulfilled the ill augury of the Wood election. Both sides resorted to fraud, utilizing the *copo,* i.e., "cutting off the enemy's retreat," by installing unanimous majorities from the districts controlled by each party. Senator Ricardo Dolz of Havana and General José Miguel Gómez (no relation to Máximo Gómez) Governor and boss of Santa Clara took a fairly moderate position under the Conservative-Republican banner, mildly supported by Estrada Palma. The National Liberal Party, supported by Máximo Gómez and Emilio Núñez, had as its leading plank "abrogation of the Platt Amendment."

But January 17, 1905, Máximo Gómez was carried to his grave on a gun-carriage, smothered in wreaths and flying purple streamers, and followed by President Estrada Palma, his cabinet, Congress, the diplomatic and consular corps—on foot. The police and rural guards pounded back the people, rising like a turbulent sea, demanding to carry the general on their shoulders.

Núñez, who had hoped to have his backing as presidential candidate in the 1906 elections, buried his ambitions and joined the official Moderate Party. This had just been founded by Dolz and Méndez Capote, to replace the Conservative Republican Party and eliminate José Miguel Gómez as a presidential aspirant. Gómez had at once swung the remnants of the Conservative Republican Party—which he controlled absolutely in Santa Clara—over to the hostile National Liberal Party. This, after Núñez' defection, became the new Liberal Party, with Gómez and Alfredo Zayas as candidates; the program, immediate abrogation of the Platt Amendment.

The Moderates put up Estrada Palma for reëlection. Like more brilliant men, he considered himself the only leader able to uphold the true state of liberty. He at once polished the sacred vase with the excrement of ruthless suppression to insure his continuance in power.

The surface issue was ambitions for jobs, the conquest of the twenty-odd millions of the treasury. But the new political division represented two tendencies buried by our occupation, hidden by the apparent unity of the first independence government. The Moderate wing of the revolutionary movement was allied with the Tory elements revived by American military patronage. The Liberals represented more the mestizo and mass tendency.

By August, 1905, armed revolt was brewing. "Serious disturbances of public order" necessitated an extraordinary session of Congress. September 13 a band of men rose up in Sevilla, near Santiago, hoping to seize the President and demand immediate full veteran payments. Estrada Palma told Congress "doubt" had been thrown "on the seriousness of our institution" and independence jeopardized.

But he himself had already trodden those institutions under foot by traditional Latin-American political brutalities, now unfortunately common in most of the world. In February, 1905, he had reorganized his cabinet with only moderate politicians—the "Fighting Cabinet," chief manipulator Fernando Freyre de Andrade, the revolutionary patriot, active, courageous, but uncompromising and violent. Determined to reëlect Estrada, Freyre resorted to police coercion and supervision of all municipalities and seized control of the electoral machinery everywhere to shut out Liberals. All non-Moderate government employees, even school-teachers, were fired wholesale.

The Liberals—already riots and other violences had occurred—raised cries to high heaven, talked revolution. Liberal Representative Enrique Villuendas openly charged the Moderates with brutal repressions, citing numerous shootings and the appointment of two pardoned murderers to the police and rural guard forces. September 22 he alleged a Moderate plot against his life. Two days later he was shot down by the police in his room in Hotel Suiza.

The Liberals withdrew from the preliminary September 23 elections. With no opposition the Moderates successfully polled, in some cases, more votes than the total number of inhabitants. Their total for the Republic was a third of the entire population—"a monstrosity," declared *La Discusión,* "the paternity of which should be denied by its various perpetrators, because it gives them the title of idiots." December 1, the Moderates walked away with the elections without opposition.

Freyre, later questioned by Taft about the 150,000 surplus voters, remarked "impossible to hold an election in Cuba without fraud."

Soon bullets replaced ballots. Between November 21 and 27 four armed uprisings in Havana and Pinar del Río provinces were suppressed. February 24-5, 1906, on the out-skirts of Havana some thirty would-be revolters broke into the Guanabacoa barracks, killing several guards and seizing horses and arms. According to Estrada Palma, apparently present giving them personal I. Q. tests, these disturbers were men of "very low stamp, mostly illiterate."

Liberal candidate Gómez had rushed off to the United States to give out bitter interviews about Estrada: interven-tion and honest elections would prove 80 percent of the Cubans were Liberals—this from the great opponent of the Platt Amendment.

Presently employed by American capitalists to establish a large sugar mill, he returned quietly to Cuba. Unexpect-edly asked to give up his new task, again he became "the soul" of the brewing revolution.

At the April, 1906, opening of Congress, the remaining Liberal deputies, led by General Faustino ("Pino") Guerra, after an unfavorable vote on the validity of the elections, walked out in a body—"There is nothing for us to do here; we must seek justice somewhere else."

Estrada took office May 20. The Liberals planned to seize the Havana police station, a swift coup to forestall Ameri-can intervention. But Pino Guerra hurried into revolt in Pinar del Río, raising aloft the Cuban flag, draped in crêpe —"the little War of August." Soon other bands were in the field. The government arrested Liberal leaders including Gómez; but revolt gathered headway. The local *American Telegraph* whooped up the disturbance, hoping for inter-vention and annexation.

The great Cuban scholar, Enrique José Varona, flayed both groups, prating about "the good of the country, the honor of the country, the liberty of the country" and yet releasing upon it "the greatest calamity—war."

The association of veterans of independence, represented by young Colonel Mario Menocal (manager of the enor-mous Chaparra property for the Cuban-American sugar interests) rushed in to attempt a compromise, suggesting that all government officials except President Estrada Palma and the Vice-President resign. The President, until the rebels laid down their arms, refused to consider proposals and sent Menocal off curtly.

3 MARINES AND TAFT

American Minister Edwin V. Morgan was away on a vacation. But the U.S.S. *Denver* plowed into Havana harbor, decks cleared for action, and swung to, her guns pointing up O'Reilly and Obispo Streets, menacing dense crowds of Americans, grinning, and Cubans, faces dark with hatred.

Soon our young Chargé d'Affaires, highly alarmed, feel-ing overly responsible, with Estrada Palma's consent, had marines swarming on shore, dragging a little field-gun be-hind them. All night long, in pairs, white splotches in the dark, they patrolled up and down the black silent avenues. Next day, President Roosevelt curtly ordered them back on shipboard, and put all decisions into the hands of Consul General Steinhart, an overt interventionist soon to rise to great financial power.

September 8, 1906, Steinhart sent an "absolutely confi-dential" message to Washington that Estrada Palma, unable to protect life or property, requested two war vessels im-mediately for Havana and Cienfüegos. He reiterated the request two days later.

The Court of St. James was not inactive; British engines of the Cuba Central collided head on full speed, and West-ern Railways bridges were dynamited.

Assistant Secretary of State Bacon hurried to notify Stein-hart two ships were being sent. "The President directs me to state that perhaps you do not yourself appreciate the reluctance with which this country would intervene." Sep-tember 11 Bacon repeated more forcibly that President

Roosevelt considered "actual immediate intervention out of the question."

Steinhart, with Estrada Palma's encouragement, daily more urgent, September 12, transmitted a Cuban memorandum asking for the sending of 2,000 to 3,000 men "with the greatest secrecy and rapidity." The following day Steinhart reported that Estrada Palma officially asked for intervention and offered to turn the government to an American designate.

Root was off on a good-will mission to allay Latin-American ill-feelings over the Platt Amendment, the rape of Panama, the seizure of Puerto Rico and the Philippines; and here we were being dragged into new intervention. For a few days Roosevelt manfully resisted. In an open letter to Gonzalo de Quesado, Cuban Minister at Washington, he urged the Cubans to sink their differences. He was sending Secretary of War Howard Taft and Bacon to Cuba to aid in a peaceful solution. "Whoever is responsible for armed revolt and outrage, whoever is responsible in any way for the condition of affairs that now obtain, is an enemy of Cuba." Intervention would come only when Cuba herself had shown "she has fallen into the insurrectionary habit, that she lacks the self-restraint necessary to insure peaceful self-government, and that her contending factions have plunged the country into anarchy."

Both sides rested on their arms awaiting Taft and Bacon. The veterans made a final unsuccessful effort to effect compromise. Political prisoners were released. Zayas, given guarantees, came out of hiding.

Taft, Bacon, and the American minister arrived September 19, 1906, interviewed everybody who might throw light on the situation. Though the elections had been utterly fraudulent, Taft favored Estrada Palma as representing "the regular and constitutional government because the election was held under the forms of law," but this would cause us to fight "the whole Cuban people."

Zayas, rebel spokesman, refused the persistent Estrada Palma demand that the rebels lay down arms before discussing terms and asked for reformatory laws, new elections, that every one except the President and Vice-President resign. A deadlock, plus—as Taft described them—"kaleidoscopic" changes. Roosevelt, stroking an oar from Washington, opposed encouraging the revolutionists; but in the next breath was taking Taft to task because he insisted upon a "constitutional" solution. "Do we need to bother our heads much about the exact way in which the Cubans observe or do not observe so much of their own constitution as does not concern us?"

Estrada Palma, feeling Taft's lukewarmness, announced his irrevocable decision to resign. Taft lost part of his smile trying to dissuade him, was chagrined that the Moderates were willing to "scuttle" the government, preferring intervention to any compromise.

Congress met September 28. Estrada Palma resigned, went his way to a pauper's grave. To avoid appointing a successor, the Moderates broke the quorum.

September 29 Taft proclaimed that Cuba, left without a government "at a time when great disorder prevails," would be governed provisionally by us long enough to restore order, peace and public confidence. So far as possible all governmental functions would be left in Cuban hands, the Cuban flag still waving.

Taft now became alarmed at the character of the Liberals still under arms. The prospect that they might have to be treated as a government *de facto* made him "shiver at the consequences." They were "an undisciplined horde of men under partisan leaders . . . the movement is large and formidable and commands the sympathy of the majority of the people of Cuba, but they are the poorer classes and uneducated." The appointment of insurgent generals to office would be "a circumstance most grave in itself."

Yet when our intervention terminated, it delivered the

country, after an honest election, into the hands of these "disreputable" Liberals.

The politicians, provided their claims could be recognized or the opponent smashed, were not adverse to intervention. Wealthy Cubans wanted it, but criticized the United States for not standing stalwartly behind constituted authority. Rather Americans than Liberals, rather intervention than civil war, have been attitudes which have corroded the dorsal cord of Cuban self-reliance. Estrada Palma himself had written that stable government was more important than independence. He spoke of political "dependence" insuring the "fecund boons of liberty" as preferable to a "sovereign and independent republic discredited and made miserable by the baneful action of periodic civil wars." Estrada Palma—one of the foremost fighters for Cuba's independence—was the first to deliver the island anew into the hands of a foreign government. He was "more Pope than the Pope, more Platt than Platt." As Luis Ariquistain has said: [2] "The Yankee danger—it is imperative to say it—is not always in the United States; at times . . . it is in . . . the moral vileness of Hispanic governments, parties and individuals who to remain in power or reach it, have no scruples in soliciting alliance and armed intervention of those who soon become the hangmen of the fatherland.":

The real factor was that Cuba had become "a factory governed by Cubans and exploited by foreign capital." Above all else capital wanted as before peace at any price, protection of its investments. More than any legal or moral aims, we desired to stay civil war to prevent further damage to American-owned property.

The American press was more strongly in favor of annexation than for Estrada Palma's "dependence." Resident Americans and business-men were unanimous. As Jenks noted: brokers, recommending securities to their clients,

[2] *Agonia Antillana*, 234.

openly declared that "the possibility of the establishment of a protectorate or annexation" lent "additional speculative value to Cuban securities." Cuban bonds and the internal debt, bought up at a song in Havana shortly before, were now being peddled abroad at fancy prices.

But the Cuban flag was still flying. Washington even went through the passes of transacting official business through an American Chargé d'Affaires in Havana.

4 STAR WITHOUT LIGHT

October 12, 1906, Charles E. Magoon, Root favorite, succeeded Taft as Provisional Governor. Magoon, a Minnesota politician, had been governor of the Canal Zone.

Lozano describes him as "a magnificent example of Yankee honor: gross in type, rude of manners, a profound ambition, greedy for constant rapine. He falls like a buzzard on the Cuban treasury and devours it. He falls like a hurricane of administrative immorality upon everything and infects it all; he is a Jew who fondles gold like a sweetheart."

Barbarossa called him "a star without light," who as a lawyer won his only suit in Cuba with "the assistance of the Washington politicians, that of the millions Estrada Palma accumulated in the treasury." Morally he was "a man of wax. Pliant and amiable with all" but an "astute diplomat" and "waster" of the revenues.[3]

Physically Magoon was tall, massive of abdomen, small eyes, pleasant smile, face round "like a California apple." He liked to set a good table for friends with an occasional bottle of champagne.

Magoon made no attempt to go to any root problems any more than had Brooke, Wood, Estrada Palma or Taft. He was there to see there was no "Cuban problem" to disturb Taft during his election to the Presidency, and to reëstab-

[3] Chapman, *History of the Republic of Cuba*, 230.

lish some government able to function without immediate insurrection.

To save trouble, Magoon, aided by Steinhart, "the man behind Magoon," ruled Congress without a cabinet, without opposition parties, without any of the responsibilities commensurate with his unlimited authority—a hundred times greater, wrote Márquez Sterling, than that of the Tudor of the Netherlands.

But he leavened absolutism with complacency. A good politician, he catered to every one, at the expense, naturally, of the Cuban treasury. He administered Cuba as a Tammany problem in patronage. If the revolutionists' objective was jobs, then they were entitled to them, and he accepted all the recommendations of the Liberal committee for positions as rapidly as opportunity arose. All other factions were inducted into the banquet at the earliest opportunity. Discipline was thoroughly corrupted as the *botellas,* or "sinecures," were handed over ever more recklessly to the feeble politicians recently weaned from power who now had to take their nourishment from the bottle of the malted-milk treasury. New and unnecessary posts were created for the buzzing seekers. The creation of an unnecessary army (nonexistent under Estrada), introducing the menace of militarism which has since engulfed the Republic, provided many new berths. As plums were handed out, political groups split into ever more infinitesimal factions, alleging improper favoritism. Magoon, himself said to have been personally honest, tried to be kind to all. He anticipated the Texas Ferguson in the matter of pardons; in 27 months 1,250 were granted, 46 a month. And the Cubans and Americans were permitted to steal to their hearts' content.

All this occurred with Cuba facing economic depression. The grand 1907 crash descended upon us and the island. In Cuba crops were bad. Cyclones all but wiped out the fruit industry. The 1907-8 sugar crop dropped from 1,400,-000 to 960,000 tons and brought a lower price.

Nor had the Republic in any way as yet improved the lot of the peasant, the *guajiro*. Old-time Spanish landholders had squeezed the country, were still doing so. Heavy mortgages owned in Spain still were sucking large sums across the sea. Now Americans were stepping into their shoes. Rather than remedy elementary abuses, Magoon resorted to costly public works, the expedient of all governments unwilling to destroy economic injustices or antagonize powerful interests, and thus increased public debt with inadequate returns. Magoon spent thus wise over $11,000,-000, and converted Estrada Palma's surplus—$13,000,000 above the loan fund—into a final floating debt of $12,000,-000. The historian Chapman unfairly turns Estrada Palma's surplus into a deficit, stating that part was already pledged and the rest affected by existing legislation.[4] But Magoon not only did not leave funds for future designated uses, but put the treasury in the hole. He anticipated the R.F.C. by meeting financial crisis with government funds. At Steinhart's suggestion, he distributed five millions among the Havana banks, taking up bonds to 90 percent of their value and giving the money without interest to July 15, 1908. Cuba was thus enabled to ship $12,000,000 to help out the crisis in the United States; sugar planters could borrow money to harvest crops; but it began a financial speculative spirit to culminate in later scandals.

The most active administrator was Colonel Enoch Crowder, controlling State and Justice. He drew up myriad new Cuban laws to regulate the 1901 constitution in the best American manner. His electoral code was such a "perfect" instrument "against frauds and election abuses" that our Minister Gonzáles later confessed to Márquez Sterling, he had found only four men able to understand it. Repeated tinkering failed to make this democratic machinery work.

As the Magoon administration drew to a close, it hastened to dish out contracts for the coming period of restored in-

4 *History of the Republic of Cuba*, 237.

dependence. Cuba became the happy hunting-ground for every disreputable concessionaire. One immediate task of the subsequent Gómez government—perhaps not for public morality but to besmirch our administration and benefit the new Cuban clique—was to revise all these "privileges" and "irregularities" based on "profound immoralities."

In a Cuban weekly Dr. Luis Marino Pérez exposed these "immoral" contracts, which Washington naturally was energetically defending. Said Pérez, the American public should know that "this sort of contract . . . is creating embarrassment of a political and financial nature to the new Cuban administration."

The subsidized English language paper of Cuba, the *Havana Post,* ever back-slapping every one in power, during Magoon's time was frankly annexationist. No praises were too high for the great Magoon. Henry Watterson, typical time-server, filled its columns with peans. "Magoon, the Magician," he enthused ". . . has caused two blades of grass to grow where but one had grown before." He had found Cuba "clouded by the smoke of burning property and military campfires," and he left it "echoing with the hum of industrial activity and overspread by the aroma of nearly one hundred mills grinding day and night." But the Liberals Watterson called "riffraff; injin, nigger, beggar-man, thief—'both mongrel, puppy, whelp and hound, and cur of low degree.' " These had been Olney's fears regarding the Cuban insurgents, Taft's fears of the revolutionists—the typical common American colony attitude toward the people they exploited. Yet history teaches that riffraff rarely becomes anything more than riffraff except through it own benighted efforts and sacrifices. Nothing in the four centuries of Spanish rule had been done to aid them. Except for sanitation and some education—both of which have gone by the boards under Machado—nothing has been done for them since.

January 26, 1909, Magoon turned the administration

over to President-elect Gómez, chief of the "riffraff," and sailed away with the waiting American battleships—one of them the new *Maine*. Behind him he left the undisguised "rage and hate" of every decent Cuban. As Irene Wright says, he "handed Cuba over, a sacrifice to the Republican Party in the north, into the power of her worst elements"— a swarm of rapacious officeholders. "If ever another American intervention such as this second one is threatened here I will go out and fight," declared Fonts Sterling, one of the two honest men Taft admitted he met on his first arrival. ". . . They have ruined us, but prostrate as we are, we'll stand no more such treatment."

The American press direly predicted Magoon would soon be back.

To make such a contingency impossible, President Taft evolved a new policy for Cuba—continued up until 1923— the so-called "preventive." Better constant steps to forestall intervention than intervene; better meddling—despite Root's solemn never-never promise—than letting nature take her course. The basic evil of course resides in the Platt Amendment, and the economic disinheriting of the Cuban people—these dual determinants make any and all policies by us palliative, hypocritical, inconsistent, doomed to failure.

XIV GRAB BAG

1 SHARK

J OSÉ MIGUEL GÓMEZ WAS TYP-
ical of the pseudo-libertarian audacious chieftain who has
inevitably captured the affections of his compatriots regardless of his abuses. Estrada Palma's precise airs of an ex-
physics teacher were replaced by the rough clothes of the
cow-puncher, silver spurs and broad Panama hat—Cuban
equivalent of Jeffersonianism.

A ruined planter, Gómez utilized politics to amass great
wealth. In the 1895 revolt, already experienced from the
Ten Years' War, he put himself at the head of the Sancti
Spiritus brigade (named from the town of his birth), and
operated effectively in Santa Clara Province. Afterwards he
dug himself in there as an all-powerful military and political
cacique. To his side he attracted a group of clever young-
sters, all to become Liberal leaders—Orestes Ferrara, Gerardo Machado, Carlos Mendieta, José Monteagudo. Gómez
was a member of the Cuban assembly, then civil governor
under our first military administration, delegate to the
Wood constitutional convention, then elected governor
under the Republic.

A typical, ruthless boss, he used strong-arm gangs to win
elections, seized cattle to repair his fortunes; opponents
mysteriously disappeared.

A likeable energetic man, probably with a strain of negro,
he loved recreations, gambling, good fellowship, kept magnificent open house. "A miracle of smiles," he was called,
and himself said, "All my life, I have been jovial in spirit,

a smile on my lips." Though lacking formal training he assimilated knowledge easily and however inexact his insight into social problems, he was quick to grasp situations, an excellent judge of men—"I study men as others study books." His rival, Zayas, called him a "model for tolerance of spirit," which Lozano translated as "very well tempered for meandering through the labyrinth of politicians without mistaking his way."

Much to the disgust of Washington, Latin America made a gala affair of his inauguration, and sent special envoys to help celebrate Cuba's recovery of her freedom.

The Liberal group Gómez represented was rooted in the mestizo element in Cuba; and its rise to power represented, however disguised, the typical *caudillo,* or military chieftain, rule, so characteristic of Latin America. Naturally, after the interruption of normal development by our two occupations, original insurgents inevitably reasserted themselves and their right to rule the Republic; but only the militarist politicians had the *putsch* to recapture the battlements, not the intelligentsia. The emergence of this type led to crass looting governments, continuously more degenerate through the years.

Fortune smiled on Gómez' administration (1909-13). Economic conditions were excellent; crops, not a single bad year; the world market, in good shape.

After the corrupt loose-spending of the Magoon period, Gómez had promised economies, no new loans, but kept neither pledge. Soon, to carry on sanitary tunneling and paving in Havana and Cienfüegos (demanded by us), he contracted a new $16,500,000 Speyer loan at a ruinous rate netting him about $14,500,000 cash. The money was squandered, the work left uncompleted. Considerable funds were spent to build up the army (from private to general made up of Gómez Liberals), to establish a military academy in Morro Castle, and a small navy.

Gómez continued Magoon's policy of creating new sinecures (among other things unnecessarily expanded the diplomatic service to take care of all his *cuneros,* or political "foundlings." General budgets constantly increased; expenditures, still more rapidly. Though he built a few highways, he let old roads go to ruin. With a $6,000 kilometer government subsidy, the Cuba railroad built the Martí-Manzanillo line. Gómez initiated other lines and fomented many enterprises, reduced taxes and duties on agricultural machinery, raised them on soap, shoes, paper, beer, and food products to promote native industry. He built bad workers' homes and tried to establish accident insurance, but abandoned the scheme entirely when scandal disclosed he was trying to control the company to handle it.

He restored cock-fighting—in fact the Liberal Party emblem during the 1908 campaign had been a rooster on a plow, a clever appeal to lovers of the great sport and to the negro *ñañigos* for whom the cock is sacred.

Gómez' supreme talents lay in lining his own pockets. Entering the government poor, on leaving he spent $250,000 on a marble palace-home on the Prado; his investments in mines and sugar were estimated at about $8,000,000.

His private secretary, Lieutenant-Colonel Avelino Sanjenís, disgruntled that Gómez did not give him "the most meager crumb of bread in that splendid banquet of four succulent years," wrote a vicious attack entitled *Shark:* "Deaf to the requests of friends, avid of wealth, obstinate and tenacious acquiring it, he employed all means, including sacrifice of his most intimate associates, to create a fortune." Sanjenís records the opulent life of Gómez after leaving office, his mansion, private cattle-farms, purchases of costly art, his wastrel trip to Europe.

Graft, which laid the basis of his fortune, was involved in navy vessel purchases, the Speyer loan, dredging projects, the Júcaro-Morón railway (over the line of the old Trocha), monopolization of lottery collectorships, personal evasion of customs, construction of a presidential palace, rental of buildings, bids for arms, cannon, horses, ammunition, the Territorial Bank project, the telephone concession, road building, the Havana bridge, various aqueducts, the Columbia camp, sewerage and paving, innumerable other subvention contracts and pardons—even junk iron sales. A scandalous steal was the exchange of public arsenal lands, fronting Havana harbor, for those of Villanueva (English United Railways) along the south end of the Prado. The company agreed to build five docks and a garbage incinerator; the government proposed to build some $6,500,000 of public buildings. This grandiose proposition, involving perhaps a governmental loss of $4,000,000, was opposed by Washington, probably not so much because of the graft but for the harbor and dock features.

2 PATRIOTIC PRECEDENT

In his September 22, 1908, platform, Gómez had argued against reëlection. As late as January 29, 1911, he stated, "I wish to have the honor of being the first opposed to his own reëlection. I wish to give that example to my people . . . as prudent, foreseeing and patriotic." April 25, 1912, he wrote General Gerardo Machado, a member of his cabinet, he would not be a candidate. But like Estrada Palma he became enamored of the gilded presidential chair. From the very first, as later analysis reveals, his every step was directed toward reëlecting himself.

His administration had not been without difficulties. The night of March 15, 1909, Manuel Lavastida, former Rural Guard captain, said to be plotting, was arrested at Placetas and given Ley Fuga, i.e., shot in the back supposedly attempting to escape. His assassins were acquitted. Lavastida's associates in the Rural Guards were rounded up and condemned to death. The Santa Clara Audiencia ordered them liberated. Furious, Gómez removed all but one dissenting judge.

April 11, Secretary Knox, from holy Pittsburgh, who had journeyed to Havana, gave the Cubans a lofty address on civic virtue.

Politics was boiling under the surface. In accord with an election pact, Gómez had given the Zayas faction four cabinet posts and other high positions; but soon, despite pledges to support Zayas in the 1912 elections, he eliminated these elements from his government. Zayas partisans soon found themselves ever in greater difficulties; Gómez became increasingly dictatorial.

January 31, 1910, Congressman Orestes Ferrara introduced a national defense law to muzzle the press. Concerted journalistic protest caused the bill to be withdrawn; but even so Gómez arbitrarily laid a heavy hand upon public expression—in February, jailed the editors of *La Prensa* and *El Gordo,* and fined the editors of three other papers.

Two revolts: July 25, 1910, Conservative General Vicente Miniet rose in arms; two days later was captured near El Caney. July 3, 1911, General Guillermo Acevedo attempted unsuccessful revolt in Havana Province.

Gómez' worst thorn in the ambitious Zayas faction was General Pino Guerra, head of the army. Gómez offered him a lucrative mission to Europe. Guerra declined. And so, the night of October 22, 1910, when leaving the palace after a game of billiards with the President, Guerra was wounded in the leg by would-be assassins. The aggressors, though known even to the general public, were never punished. Guerra resigned. General Monteagudo, enemy of Guerra and Zayas, close friend of Gómez, was appointed in his place.

When it became very patent Gómez was determined to hang on to the power, Machado resigned from the cabinet, denouncing reëlection in a flowery open letter, obviously not penned by his own prosaic brain. The Zayas wing of the Liberal Party, suffering ever more persecutions, openly formed a new group. Gómez also found himself opposed by the organized veterans, led by the political aspirant General Emilio Núñez, who fulminated that the government still harbored not true revolutionaries but various dubious guerrilleros and even ex-Spanish sympathizers during the independence wars.

The situation grew more critical. Dollar Diplomacy Knox hastened helpfully to warn Cuba of the United States' grave concern; the laws should not be "defied"; Cuba ought not to force our government "to consider what measures it must take."

General Núñez at once capitalized this, blatantly announcing he would fight to the death against any American interference. The American embassy began meddling in all departments, insisted that the Secretary of State further new laws; Cosme de la Torriente, head of that department, resigned. But the veterans desisted from their campaign against actual office-holders.

Disturbed conditions were also heightened by the 1912 race-war—perhaps promoted by Gómez himself. In answer to the terrified American property owners, May 31 marines were put ashore at Daiquirí near Santiago and hastened inland. They remained several weeks.

Gómez declared national martial law, denouncing the "ferocious savagery" of the rebels, and within two weeks wiped them out. Amnesty was granted and numerous jobs were lavished on negroes, ever since prominent in Liberal politics.

Despite Gómez' personal schemes, the Liberal Party nomination was seized by the foxy Zayas. Gómez dropped his pretentions to reëlection, but secretly, since Zayas, he said, stood for "dissolution, ruin and rout," backed the Conservative Party led by the candidate General Mario Menocal, who was further aided by the bolt of the Asbert Liberals into his camp and by the support of Núñez.

In the due course of elections, Gómez handed the government over to Menocal, and making virtue of necessity, reiterated his own self-abnegation and patriotism: "I glory in having been the first ruler in Latin America to establish such a patriotic precedent."

3 MORE AMERICAN THAN CUBAN

President Menocal, a veteran who had fought under Máximo Gómez, Maceo and García, attaining the rank of major-general, had distinguished himself in the victory of Las Tunas and had great influence with the veterans. For the Cuban-American sugar company, he had developed the Chaparra plantation, largest estate of its kind in the world, a great aristocratic feudal patrimony. He was, so to speak, promoted from sugar to the Presidency, a relation which seemed to guarantee the proper government in those lush pre-war years. One of our publicists, George Marvin, even declared he was more American than Cuban—a remark meant as high praise.

Menocal and his Conservative Party represented the Creole in government. From the better white classes of Havana, Menocal threw his offices ever more to the aristocrats. Through extravagant nepotism—he had myriad relatives—and favoritism, he converted party and government ever more into a purely personal machine. For this purpose, far more than Gómez, he utilized the National Lottery, dishing out the collectorships, involving much graft, to dutiful supporters—a form of patronage bribery since perfected by Machado.

He faced severe economic crisis; but the World War soon brought excessive demand for Cuban products. By 1915-16, the sugar crop had risen to three million tons; trade from $302,000,000 (1913-14) to $604,000,000 (1916-17) with a favorable balance ($108,000,000) in the latter year. Cuba was then importing from the United States more than the South American A.B.C. countries combined, more than one-third of all our exports to all Hispanic America. No country in the world had so great a per capita wealth—mostly in American hands.

Like Gómez, Menocal had faithfully promised not to seek reëlection; but by 1915 it was already clear he proposed to disregard this pledge. But his party, already cracked from his excessive personalism, split. The scholar, Enrique José Varona, Secretary of Agriculture General Núñez (still with Presidential aspirations), José Antonio Gonzalez Lanuza, Wilfredo Fernandez, José de la Maza y Artola, were strongly opposed to his reëlection. Nevertheless, by packing the Conservative convention with the old Estrada Palma Moderates, Menocal captured the party nomination and made Núñez his running-mate.

The Liberals were also divided. But Zayas, despite Gómez' opposition and that of the new Unionist wing, directed by Machado and Colonel Carlos Mendieta, again won the nomination. Gómez, in return for promised control of various cabinet positions, decided to support him; as did also the Asbert faction now backing the fold. The Liberals barged into the campaign shouting "Zayas or Revolution!"

Menocal rapidly ousted Liberal officials by installing military supervisors in the provinces and towns. Riots and deaths were soon occurring. A million names were put on the voting lists.

In the elections about 800,000 ballots were cast. (Three years later the census disclosed there were only 477,786 eligible voters.) Even so all evidence pointed to a Liberal landslide. Menocal's secretary even sent congratulations to Zayas for his victory. But at the very last moment Menocal was persuaded to ignore the vote and capture the election at all cost. Incoming returns were illegally diverted from the telegraph office to the Secretary of State, who issued doctored figures. Then returns ceased being given out all together. By one means or another the election was stolen.

The Liberals carried the matter to the central election board and brought charges before the Supreme Court. Despite apparent submission to Menocal, the court accepted evidence that ballots had mysteriously disappeared in Liberal strongholds, parts of Santa Clara and Oriente; it gave the Liberals a majority in Santa Clara of 1,164. That alone guaranteed Zayas' victory—our Minister William Elliot Gonzáles informed Washington—for the reëlections ordered by the Court in various precincts, could not possibly destroy the Liberal lead.

But Menocal used new violence. Criminals were pardoned, heavy troops rushed in to terrorize the Liberals. Booths were hidden away in the woods.

Feeling ran high. Menocal offered to withdraw if Zayas, "unworthy the Presidency," would follow suit. (Four years later he unjustly boosted Zayas into that high office.) Spirits could not be calmed. Both sides were preparing for the violent *chambelona,* as the expected mêlée was called.

The United States was more than usually interested in Cuban peace. It feared revolution at the time of the sugar harvest for war with Germany was looming. Lansing called on the parties to settle their differences, cited to the Cubans the Hayes-Tilden case—where a minority had been successfully seated without bloodshed—an intimation he would support Menocal whether elected or not.

Menocal now jailed Liberals on the false charge of a conspiracy against his life and suppressed the Liberal press. Soon the Liberals were up in arms.

The dormant Platt Amendment woke to the thunder of cannon and joined forces with the would-be usurper, Menocal. Our Minister Gonzáles, through the press, immediately issued peremptory orders to the rebels. The United States would give its "confidence and support" only to "constitutional" governments; it would never recognize revolutionary success—this on the eve of our war to make the world safe for democracy.

Although the government's tactics had obviously pro-voked revolt and the elections promised to be notoriously crooked, the failure of the Liberals to await the voters' verdict was given as an excuse for our attitude. But though condemned to defeat, the leaders could not, would not, re-treat. The movement spread into every province.

A new Gonzáles note supported Menocal, branded the revolt as lawless, but responsible for injury to foreign in-dividuals and property; no revolters could ever expect any future personal consideration from the United States. We also permitted Menocal to purchase 10,000 rifles and five million rounds of ammunition.

Without such assistance, Menocal would soon have col-lapsed. Now, despite armed occurrences, he proceeded with the Santa Clara election farce (February 14), securing 2,427 votes out of a padded list of 2,401! Subsequent elections in Oriente showed similar surprising conversions of all Lib-erals to the Conservative Government.

Gonzáles told Washington we should at once occupy "ten or twelve ports and keep open the Cuban Railway, an American corporation." The Manatí Sugar Company, Atkins and Company, the United Fruit Company, the Cuba Company, Bethlehem Steel, and others constantly peti-tioned for protection, demanded marines—seventeen folio pages of telegrams tumbled about Secretary of State Lan-sing's ears. Even so, he resisted. The Commander of the U.S.S. *Montana* at Guantánamo tried to call a parley of two forces. The rebels declined. Other naval officers revealed friendliness and a spirit of compromise. Immediately after Commander Reginald R. Belknap arrived in Santiago with the *Petrel,* February 15, he actually recognized the insur-gent commandant of the province and forbade all military operations which barred Menocal from suppressing the re-volt. Many local Americans there favored the insurgents. The navy officials discussed amnesty and elections, sent proposals to Washington which went far toward fulfilling rebel demands.

But by the end of the month the navy began to swing over to the State Department position. February 26, marines were landed at Guantánamo. Later others were landed in Santiago from the *Petrel*. They forced the leader, Rigoberto Fernández, out of the city to ultimate defeat at Conservative hands. Fleeing to Haiti, there Fernández was seized by American officials and deprived of $194,000 in his possession. Soon American forces occupied Guantánamo, Manzanillo, Preston and Nuevitas; bluejackets tumbled off the *Connecticut* at San Francisco; others went inland to El Cobre mines to protect American property.

March 1, Lansing instructed Gonzáles, to his disgust, to have Menocal, coincident with the laying down of rebel arms, proclaim new elections in Santa Clara and Oriente. Menocal opposed amnesty, ignored the election request. Gonzáles, likewise opposed to new elections, misrepresented the whole electoral situation to Washington. Lansing then thought new elections only in Oriente would suffice.

Gómez retorted via Commander U.S.S. *Paducah* that if new elections were not guaranteed, he would proceed to destroy American property. But now hampered by the marines, he was badly defeated March 8, at Placetas, Santa Clara, and two hundred of his followers captured.

Our Minister hastened to announce the "destructive policy" had been nipped, quite underestimating Liberal strength and determination. Liberal bands continued harassing the country.

Washington offered Menocal military aid and to send Crowder to supervise elections. To his credit, Menocal declined.

Washington seemed to waver toward the rebels. Bitterly Gonzáles criticized any compromise, asked Washington to make another "unequivocal declaration." This would cause "general and immediate collapse." March 23 a strong statement was published that the rebels need expect no American aid; we could and would hold no communication whatsoever with them until they laid down their arms.

The Liberals felt that this repudiation of various naval officer negotiations connoted bad faith. Cane-burning and property destruction increased. Now a sharp note was addressed to Menocal to send adequate forces "immediately" to give proper protection. The Liberals were jubilant and encouraged.

April 6 the United States declared war on Germany; Menocal followed suit April 7. The Gómez movement was at once played up to our wise electorate as a Liberal-Germanic plot, a most acceptable explanation. Immediately Menocal could stigmatize his foes as pro-German. We feared, rather ridiculously, the establishment of a German submarine base in Cuba.

Gonzáles recommended that 1,000 marines be brought from Haiti to the Guantánamo naval station to police American properties and free Menocal's soldiers to put down the rebels.

But the Navy Department had no additional marines to spare for Cuban duty. May 11 Washington informed Menocal that since he had aligned himself with the United States, we would be "forced to consider as our own enemies those persons in revolution against the constitutional government unless they immediately returned to their allegiance," and would send troops.

Menocal declined the troops. Gonzáles was instructed to advise him sugar-production "must not be interrupted" and published a new note to the Cuban people. About 1,600 U. S. soldiers were thereupon landed in Oriente, a thousand in Camagüey. They remained until 1922. With their aid, Menocal continued to the end of his rule, long after the so-called Peace of Versailles, to exercise extraordinary war-powers.

Zayas, it has been said, early betrayed the revolt after the promise (presumably involving the American minister) that he would be greased into the Presidency four years later. He returned unmolested to Havana to live at the castle of Madame Abreu, a lady "who also maintained there [as a pet], the only chimpanzee born in captivity." Gómez remained in prison till September 24, 1917. Other revolters (though later pardoned probably due to American pressure) were condemned to death.

Despite war-prosperity, every worthy governmental activity degenerated. Education. Teaching jobs—now mere *botellas,* nursing-bottle sinecures—had doubled since General Wood, but the schools reached a new low level of neglect. The army, grown to 10,000 men under Gómez, was now increased to 15,000 in 1916, to 18,000 in 1919. Menocal spent almost as much on highway construction as his three predecessors combined, but built less than any one of them. Existing roads deteriorated. He reintroduced gambling on a grand scale with corresponding official rake-offs. Ricardo Dolz was given a horse-racing concession. The Mayor of Havana, Ernesto Asbert, murdered a critic of his gambling activities.

But foreign trade grew to over a billion dollars with the United States alone. Revenues increased from $37,000,000 (1913) to $108,000,000 (1920). That year Menocal, thanks to his two 1917 loans, spent $182,000,000. For an enormous palace to serve as the President's residence was spent $3,750,000—more than double the cost of the White House; further sums furnished it splendidly—$100,000 for linens alone; a commission of $60,000 to one of Menocal's cousins for a weird painting of his famous Las Tunas battle. Payments were made for fictitious roads and bridges. A score of banks were looted, while the directors and government stood by, arms folded. "Half a billion in taxes were collected while he was President, but the only signs of progress

. . . that remain are the presidential mansion and a bronze and marble statue of Antonio Maceo."

A "Dance of Millions!" From this Dance of Millions, even before Menocal left office, the country headed directly into disaster and moratorium. Banks failed. The very bottom dropped out of Cuba.

4 NEW ELECTIONS

In the midst of these disasters, new elections hove on the horizon. Zayas, "the Bryan of Cuba," discredited in his own Liberal Party, organized the new Popular Party, which noisily advocated "non-interference" of other nations in Cuba's affairs—the old anti-Platt Amendment program. Menocal, evidently having made prior promises to both Zayas and Núñez, sidetracked the latter to throw the joint Popular-Conservative Party nominations to Zayas, his 1917 opponent. Núñez, double-crossed, flopped over to the Liberal Party which nominated Gómez.

Menocal by now knew how to win elections—355 criminals were pardoned, 44 of whom were murderers. In 73 of 112 municipalities Liberal mayors were shorn of their powers and replaced by military supervisors. The army was set in motion—it "shot to kill," said the American official observer, Herbert J. Spinden. Concessions were made to the negroes to wean them from their normal Liberal moorings; restrictions on meetings of the *ñañigo* lodges and the *Conga* dances were lifted; negro murderers were pardoned.

Gómez, the Liberal candidate, ordered his followers not to participate in the polling. Washington, despite obvious lack of fairness, practically ordered him to participate or forfeit all rights to the presidency. Official observers were promised to avoid intimidation or fraud.

The observers came and observed; but as they had no authority, violences, intimidation and fraud were perpetrated under their very noses. "There can be little doubt but that this [election] was stolen," reported observer Spinden. Numerous tricks were resorted to, early closing, intimidation, disqualifying of Liberals on every pretext.

Despite this, the Conservatives carried all of Cuba by only 10,585 votes out of 312,765. The Liberals requested a new election under direct American supervision.

Without prior notice to the Cuban authorities, Crowder, unasked and unwanted, appeared on the scene (January 6, 1921, in the battleship *Minnesota*) to "confer with President Menocal with respect to the political and financial conditions of Cuba." Cuba protested, but Crowder did not budge. He came on the heels of a Morgan debt default and collapse of the Cuban banks.

Four days later he sent a long communique to Menocal, in which he objected to delays in the electoral disputes (pending before the Supreme Court) and suggested rapid expedition along indicated lines. If the new legal government were not installed by May 20, intervention was threatened.

The situation was one of "great gravity." The existing financial crisis constituted "a menace to the National life, calling for extraordinary remedial measures." The Supreme Court soon cleared its dockets and annulled the elections in some 250 precincts, about 20 percent of the total.

The voting lists were ordered revised: humorous cynicism was revealed by such names as Christopher Columbus, Arsenio Martínez Campos, Valeriano Weyler, and to add a touch of nobility, Simón Bolívar—all of whom, despite the "new deal," were allowed to vote anyway. Crowder forced Menocal, Gómez and Zayas to sign a "pact of honor," to abide by the results. Military supervisors would not be used, only inspectors from the central electoral board.

Feeling ran high. The Liberals charged coercion. A week before election at Colón, Matanzas, a veritable battle between the two parties occurred. The Liberals, remembering our unfair partisanship in 1917 had cost them victory, refused to go to the polls. Zayas—certainly not the choice of the Cuban people, in no way entitled to the office—won, was given the office, they say in Cuba, the one time he wasn't elected. (Worthy of note: the two most corrupt governments in Cuba were those of Menocal's second term and Zayas' coming administration.)

Gómez hastened to the United States to appeal for new election supervision. Though Crowder himself admitted the Liberals were the victorious party, Gómez' petition was denied; April 17 we formally recognized Zayas as elected.

Bitterness continued. The Liberal candidate for Governor of Havana province was murdered; so was Zayas' private secretary.

Gómez, disillusioned, died in the United States June 13, to become a Liberal "martyr." A two-mile procession in Havana carried his body to the grave amid a riot of partisan feud and a riot of flowers.

5 SYMBOL OF GOOD

Zayas, for many years a slippery politician, was popularly called "the peseta stealer," i.e., a petty grafter, and a man of "especially morbid sensual proclivities." In April, 1913, Gómez had given him a $6,000 salary to write a history of Cuba; he collected some $20,000 for which he finally produced, May, 1916, thirty-three worthless pages in *Cuba Contemporanea*—about $30.00 a word—perhaps the highest paid writer in history.

But now Crowder was there to keep him in line—as Charles E. Chapman, his best apologist, relates—the symbol of "good" as opposed to Zayas, the symbol of "evil." Using the leverage of a proposed loan and State Department backing, Crowder enforced many proposals.

But Zayas, not the popular choice, obliged to govern with a hostile Congress, had to win his way by bestowing spoils. Crowder, "so honest he leans backwards and some day may injure his spine," could be holy precisely because he had the whole United States at his back, did not have to face political realities, did not have to assume the actual responsibilities of government; and having in view the placing of a new Morgan loan with State Department support, could insist eloquently and constantly upon administrative rectitude regardless of party problems.

No Magoon this time! Although in his prolonged dealings with Cuba, Crowder had not learned to speak any Spanish, he began a virtual dictatorship. Impatient for quick results, he always expected the people to act as Anglo-Saxons, he could deal with undisciplined, individualistic Cuban traits only by ultimatums. Believing his legal nostrums, based on the logic of honesty and perfection but not on Cuba or human beings, would promptly work miracles, he was "cast down when high-class men" would act "just as disgracefully as their more lowly fellows." His January bank-liquidating acts fell through, in part, because they disturbed too many influential people; perhaps too because the Cubans disliked to make him too much of a success.

Zayas, facing a hard road, had found the treasury bankrupt, immediate claims exceeding cash on hand, an enormous floating debt, $12,000,000 of government funds tied up in the ruined Banco Nacional, back salaries unpaid, interest and principal of $2,000,000 due on internal debt issues and $200,000 a month on external loans. Menocal had left everything, owing even $25,000 for ice for the Palace and $280,000 for meat—"dark flesh and white." Since Cuba needed money urgently, Zayas eventually had to submit to the humiliation of Crowder dictation.

He resisted for a time, avoided default on foreign obligations by issuing treasury checks instead of drafts. But by June 30, 1922, payments had fallen in arrears to the tune of $4,500,000. Zayas in his inaugural address recommended that the 1918-19 budget of $64,460,000—a decided reduction—be adopted as the basis for the coming fiscal year.

Crowder, although even the higher figure meant serious curtailment of jobs and public works, demanded it be cut to $55,000,000. Zayas wished to cover his financial difficulties by issuing an internal loan, less costly than dealing with international bankers. July 3, 1921, Crowder urged Washington to withhold consent to any loan until the Cuban government agreed to allow the American minister to inspect and be informed as to the annual budget and all additional Congressional or Executive credit—in other words, enduring financial control.

The Cuban government squirmed. It sent a mission, headed by Minister of Treasury Sebastián Gelabert, to Washington. Zayas, it alleged, had made a real effort to meet the situation. But Washington, while it abandoned overt financial control, disapproved of the internal loan and reiterated Crowder's contentions that the budget be cut to $55,000,000 and be balanced by provision for additional revenues, reorganization of the customs, and elimination of graft.

A special session of Congress in consultation with Crowder formulated a legislation program. A loan of $50,000,000 was authorized, also $60,000,000 to buy up and hold off the market unsold sugar, for sugar control was one of Crowder's hobbies—a most unfortunate one for Cuba. Closely linked with American sugar interests and the banks, Crowder was catering to interests nearly always against the true needs of Cuba.

The Zayas government appealed to the house of Morgan to buy a few bonds at 7½ percent. Dwight W. Morrow, accompanied by Norman Davis (whose prior profitable deals in Cuba will be considered later), immediately went to Cuba.

Immediately he saw the utter unwisdom of buying the old sugar crop. Crowder and Davis (whose Trust Bank held sugar contracts and equities) were hard to convince, but capitulated.

October 7, 1921, Morrow arranged a $5,000,000 credit to become part of a later $50,000,000 loan. Zayas agreed to cut the budget to $55,000,000 and to bring up receipts $10,000,000 in excess of expenditures. Cuba rescued from default, could now continue paying up on the older Morgan loan to Menocal, but nothing fundamental had been done.

In February, 1922, the United States asked Cuba formally to recognize the Platt Amendment right (quite a stretching) to make critical investigation of any departments it chose. Zayas protested, but Crowder converted his anomalous position into a roving commission to set the republic to rights. Soon experts arrived buzzing and produced rabbits out of hats. John Hord's little bunny was a gross sales tax to raise $20,000,000 at the expense of the consumer; it actually did bring in $10,000,000. W. P. G. Harding, retired chairman of the Atlanta Federal Reserve Board, spent several months devising banking bills and a system of American control.

Between March and June Crowder sent in various peremptory secret memoranda to Zayas. The first that has ever come to the attention of the public—largely in the dark regarding the sub-rosa intervention—was No. 13 (April 8, 1922). Recounting Cuba's bad financial condition, it emphasized the need to meet all debts, called for budget economies, removal of various officials, elimination of graft and frauds in the customs house and internal revenue bureau, judicial reform, canceling of bad contracts, moralization of the lottery, suspension of the civil-service law to prosecute grafting employees. It demanded the Hord gross sales tax, the establishment of a national banking system controlled by American stockholders and our Federal Reserve Board, the reorganization of municipal government, supervision of Havana home-rule. Little indeed that Crowder did not nose into. He had the penchant of a zealous reformer, plus the cold appraisal of a bank emissary—efficient but imaginationless.

Hostility to him at once took on larger proportions, doubly so because of rumored close relations with American sugar interests. Zayas complained to Harding. A cartoon depicted Zayas, hesitating, pen in hand: "Which name shall I sign: Crowder or Zayas?" Another entitled "The Obligatory Loan," showed *Liborio* (Cuba) strapped to an operating table while an American banker administered the loan through a cup held by Uncle Sam. June 20, the Senate adopted the Wilfredo Fernández resolution, stressing friendship with the United States, but objecting to Crowder meddling in violation of the original interpretation of the Platt Amendment.

Already the entire Cuban cabinet had resigned, and Crowder installed his own preferred men, the so-called "Honest Cabinet." In contrast to Magoon, some attempt was made to cancel old and check new unsavory contracts. But now these were Cuban contracts. Naturally graft was disclosed: a paving contract to a company in which Zayas' son and an intimate friend were heavy stockholders, a Camagüey province road-contract to Zayas' brother, a dredging contract to a client-company of Zayas' law-firm, which received 8 percent of all amounts, the Camagüey city paving contract, held by a dummy for the Senate president . . . No worse than contracts let by Magoon, Gómez and Menocal, some of which we had upheld through diplomatic pressure. But Crowder did enforce some cleaning up to reduce part of the floating debt, now (largely thanks to Menocal) totaling nearly $70,000,000, a necessary preliminary for the proposed loan—the real pot of gold at the foot of the rainbow. Bankers dote on getting commissions for changing floating debts into bonded debts with coupons, especially after the proper people have bought up the loose obligations on the bargain counter.

Corrupt 1922 elections went into history, but most of

Crowder's demands were eventually met, including the unjust gross sales tax, refusal of which, Zayas was told, would create "a serious situation." The new $50,000,000 loan was fully authorized—but without the excellent rapid amortization feature of the proposed Morrow loan.

Crowder sailed home, to return shortly (January, 1923) as accredited ambassador. By August, Cuba, thanks to the new loan, had paid up her war-debt in full; and Charles Mitchell, that moral fellow from the National City Bank, hailed Cuba as "a solvent nation, enjoying an excellent administration."

6 "MENOCAL WENT BUST"

Loan in hand, Zayas refused longer to be coerced. Honesty could be enforced with the loan-bait, not afterwards. With a cry of nationalism, he eliminated, over Crowder's and the State Department's protests, the so-called "Honest Cabinet." Placing fourteen members of his own family in strategic places, as Crowder's buddy, Menocal, had done, Zayas laid normal siege to the public treasury. $367,000 were spent repairing non-existent bridges. He purchased the Santa Clara convent from the Church at the exaggerated price of $2,350,000—estimated graft, one million. Zayas himself profited from his incumbency to an amount estimated by his enemies at from two to fourteen millions; the discrepancy indicates the loose gossip bandied about. But if he put long fingers into the coin of the realm, he was royally helped by American contractors, concessionaires and so-called respectable business-interests.

Yet—and this is not to whitewash Zayas—he stole far less than Menocal; his administration has been besmirched perhaps because his officeholders had to do their looting in two short years, and because, unlike his predecessors, he did not suppress the newspapers even though they reviled him bitterly. Also, Crowder apologists in Cuba and in this country have strained furiously to exaggerate Zayas' peccadillos to make our American draft-boy wear a more golden halo.

Chapman declares that all available portions of the loan and $81,000,000 of national revenue were exhausted with the public servants still unpaid, before overdue coupons on the debt could be taken up, before paying $400,000 due to the United States post-office.

Anxious to add luster to Crowder, Chapman neglects to point out that most of the loan-funds were held in the National City vaults, that that institution charged Cuba 5½ percent, while giving but 1½ percent on moneys held; that the $50,000,000 took care of the previous $5,000,000, which had also taken care of a previous Morgan debt; $7,000,000 to pay *"services rendered the Republic"* previous to July 1, 1922; $9,000,000 to replace the fund of Special Accounts; $2,000,000 for pensions; $18,000,000 for past obligations; $3,000,000 for amortization and interest of the internal debt bonds; $6,000,000 for reconstruction, repair, and, if anything left, for public works. Practically every cent of it went for obligations not created by Zayas! In addition to facing economic crisis, falling revenues, Zayas still had to cope with much of the old floating debt.

Thus, to exonerate Magoon and his deficit, Chapman argued that Estrada Palma's surplus was all tagged for future obligations; to exalt Crowder and damn Zayas, he disregards the fact that Menocal left no surplus, but a terrific deficit, accumulated bills and a mountain of debt, which the loan did little to cover.

Zayas' government, despite the loan, lived from hand to mouth; any honest examination of the budget soon reveals he did not have nearly the leeway for graft of his predecessors. And he was constantly hampered by the bitter animosity of Crowder.

Whatever Zayas' errors, he retrieved his country's credit, funded much of the floating debt, left cash in the treasury, averted intervention, gradually wormed out from under the Crowder incubus, and secured definite title to the Isle of Pines after twenty years' delay. Despite vituperation, he did not arbitrarily mistreat the press. His administration merely represented the culmination up to that time of governmental corruption, but if anything he was much better than the general trend of social and political life about him, advancing so rapidly toward decay. As Jenks says, "There is not likely soon to be a government in Cuba or elsewhere so closely accomplishing its real intention in the face of bankrupt treasury, foreign censorship, bank catastrophe and a major economic depression."

And Crowder was constantly pricking from behind. A prolonged conflict grew up between Zayas and the Veterans and Patriots Association over pensions and other questions. Crowder abetted the agitation, hinted to the government's opponents that their movement would be recognized. The office of the American military attaché and of General García Vélez, leader of the Association, were side by side and used indiscriminately.

As Crowder's antipathy to Zayas and sympathy for the agitators was known, everybody hastened to board the bandwagon—peasants, hacendados, bankers and intellectuals. Much money was raised, and large purchases of arms, vessels, even tanks and aeroplanes, were openly bought in the United States in a surfeited post-war market from speculators close to official circles.

Asked the wiseacres, Whom would the United States aid, the Veterans and Patriots who had adopted the latest Crowder reforms, or the Government of Zayas, who no sooner discovered what Crowder wanted than he did the opposite? Disorder and Crowder's personal vindication, or order and no intervention. Coolidge chose the latter course.

Was it because the veterans' organization had suddenly taken a stand against the pending iniquitous Tarafa law (to benefit the Rubens-Lakin-Woodin-Rockefeller railway interests at the expense of independent sugar producers)?

Zayas arrested some of the organization, temporized, put down a revolt started by Federico Laredo Bru, April 30, 1924. General García Vélez, off buying arms, was publicly accused of squandering the funds of the organization in New York cabarets. Pot calling the kettle black.

Among his missteps, Zayas, though he had five times asked Congress to pass a law forbidding reëlection, was bitten by the usual vanity bug, and schemed to capture the Presidency again. Once more he became the candidate of the Popular Party, and stood for the Conservative nomination. But Boss Menocal garnered that unto himself.

The Liberal Party, after Zayas' earlier defection and Gómez' death, had fallen completely into the hands of the Unionist group; but this in turn had split between the personalities of Gerardo Machado and Carlos Mendieta. The latter, known for his unimpeachable honesty, was the rank-and-file choice of the party, for Machado was known to be greedy for personal wealth and was too closely linked up with American electrical interests, recently grabbing up public utilities with Machado's aid. Machado declared Cuba's future depended upon its going hand in hand with the United States, made many promises, disbursed liberal lobby funds, derived from Power Trust friends and other foreign business interest, bought Zayas' support for $80,000 and got the nomination.

Undoubtedly the country was Liberal and that party would have controlled the government ever since Gómez had it not been for the 1912 split and subsequent violations of popular sovereignty by the United States government.

Now, with the President in power backing Machado, plus popular support, plus American business aid, the outcome was assured. Though the customary riots, official coercions and falsifications of votes occurred, there is no doubt but that in 1925 Gerardo Machado was the honest choice of the Cuban people, and remained so until his assassination of Armando André. Above all others the people hated Menocal. The Machado program jibed four-square with popular demands: administrative honesty, public works, no increase in the public debt, no reëlection. He was to violate all these pledges except public works, and dearly they have cost the Cuban people. But now he carried easily every province except traditional conservative Pinar del Río. The popular refrain expressed the general rejoicing:

> *Menocal went bust,*
> *For this time it was different,*
> *Gonzáles wasn't minister*
> *Nor Wilson, president.*

PART IV

THE CRIMES OF MACHADO

"To many generations of slaves must succeed one generation of martyrs."

"The independence of a people consists in the respect which the public powers show toward each and every one of its sons."

JOSÉ MARTÍ

XV SAWED-OFF SHOTGUNS

1 NERO

In chicago, wholesale murder is carried on by underworld gangsters. In Cuba, wholesale murder is carried on by the government of Gerardo Machado against innocent citizens who dare criticize his terror. Students, professors, lawyers, doctors, labor-leaders, members of Congress, editors, business men, leaders in every profession and walk of life, have been shot down ruthlessly in their homes, on the street, or in jail by his hirelings.

Machado runs a sawed-off shotgun government. He is called "the President of a thousand murders," a conservative estimate of the number of lives sacrificed that this twentieth-century Nero might continue to rule.

As Elías Entralgo wrote in 1931, "Double reincarnation. Vives misrules again. Tacón commands once more."

In that repository of junk, known as the National Museum of Cuba, may be seen carefully preserved under glass, the toothbrush of one of the patriot generals who fought to free the island from Spain—pathetic testimony that Cubans have taken liberty seriously. But the final balance-sheet of the promise of freedom we gave during our holy crusade against Spain, is a Cuba now ground under the heel of one of the most monstrous dictators in the history of the Americas and—evidence by trade and production statistics—leveled to relatively greater economic disaster than during the period of bloody Weyler.

Despite the fact that Machado was virtually put into office by campaign contribution of American corporations and could not stay in office except for our State Department approbation, he conceives of himself in more grandiose rôle. This present-day ruler of supposedly freed Cuba, not willing to permit his post-mortem fame to depend upon a chance toothbrush, has taken good care to perpetuate his greatness in more heroic tangible forms before the termination of his earthly career.

One major outdoor Havana sport is changing street names, not to hallow Cuba's honored dead but to sanctify patriots still buzzing at the honey-jar. Unfortunately revised street names are easily pegged up by each newcomer; even a toothbrush is a more lasting memento. Machado has given more difficulty to his successors. To be named after himself, he picked out one of the longest, broadest avenues and along its length were set up heavy concrete cream-colored posts, "Avenida Presidente Machado." At its junction with the beautiful Malecón sea-front boulevard was erected a massive square monument with the carved motto: "The Beginning of Avenida Presidente Machado." On the pavement around its base was painted a wide circle to indicate a national military zone eternally guarded. Whoever steps across that red circle commits a military offense. To eliminate the new monument would require blasting.

Thus far the only service rendered by this monument has been as a refuge for two guardian policemen who ducked behind it to save themselves when the bullets flew in the 1932 assassination of Police-Captain Miguel Calvo y Herrera. Only temporarily did this save one tan-colored body beneath its nickel plaque. Promptly arrested, one soon after hung himself in jail—his fellow cops, who would have braved bullets fearlessly, apparently wished to purge their corps of any stigma of cowardice and to erase the record that a monument to brave Machado should be stained by any such pusillanimity.

In contrast to Machado's bold monument, a modest ex-hedra in the wall opposite the first Malecón glorieta informs the curious that the broad sea-boulevard, extending from the dry-moat La Punta fortress and flanked by glistening white palaces, was constructed in 1901, when General Leonard Wood was governor. The Malecón also harbors such noteworthy monuments as that to the U.S.S. *Maine* and to the great negro emancipator, Maceo. Why not one to the living Machado, greater than all predecessors? This is not Machado's only claim in stone and gold. One should not omit mentioning the hundreds of marble slabs with which the benevolent President has furnished the local cemetery.

Who is this figure of force, murder, and strange vanities who, despite his atrocities, continues to command the respect of our government? Who is this stocky, bespectacled, prosy-looking individual, who has violated every preëlection promise, who has ridden rough-shod over the constitution, who has murdered, imprisoned and exiled opponents, and yet who continues to enjoy the praise of our statesmen and the cordial attention of our ambassadors? Why does he have to travel in a $30,000 armored car, a veritable army afore and aft? Why is the Palace sown down with machine guns, packed with police and soldiers armed to the teeth?

Already in office seven years, his term will expire in 1935. Already he has announced that any one aspiring to the presidency at that time will be considered an enemy of the fatherland. Enemies of the fatherland are unceremoniously bumped off or fed to the sharks.

Gerardo Machado and his father, turbulent elements in the province of Santa Clara, were known as cattle raiders before the independence wars. Gerardo Machado by participating in the armed movement against Spain, converted cattle raiding into a patriotic enterprise. Subsequently he was elected mayor of Santa Clara. One of his first acts was to burn down the Audiencia containing the records of a criminal accusation against his father.

During the Gómez administration, he was Minister of Interior, a key political post, which gave him much experience in controlling political machinery. This department handled all light and power concessions. Machado dished these and other public utility privileges out right and left, with pecuniary benefit to himself. In some enterprises he was awarded promotion shares; he was half-owner of the Santa Clara Light Company.

When in 1921 the Electric Bond and Share Company began buying up Cuban utilities, it found that one of the most experienced men in the field, influential in many enterprises, and a dominant figure in the so-called Liberal Party, was Machado. It made one of his close friends, Mr. Henry Catlin, president of the Cuban Electric Company; Machado himself became vice-president. By the end of 1923 they were serving more than eighty communities with electricity, gas or water. With Machado's aid, both before and after his becoming President, a series of complicated reorganizations and stock-waterings were effected involving the Cuban Electric, the Havana Electric Light and Power Company and the Havana Electric Railway Company. The telephone system of Cuba came into the hands of the Cuban Telephone Company, a subsidiary of the International Telephone and Telegraph Company, like the Electric Bond and Share, sponsored financially by J. P. Morgan and Company. The principal docks in Havana harbor are the property of the Port of Havana Docks Company, managed by the Behn brothers, big shots in the I. T. and T.

Catlin, who previously departed from another Latin-American country rather unceremoniously, was also legal adviser of the Chase National Bank for the arrangement of loans to Cuba. The 1932 Senate Finance hearings on the sale of foreign bonds and securities (IV, 1959) reveal a payment to him for services; more important but unmentioned fees are said to have been paid.

Machado's hand-in-glove relationship with Catlin and those interests was a fundamental reason for his election. President Menocal had been an official in the large Cuban-American sugar corporation and owed his political success largely to that connection. But with the shift of control, during Zayas' administration, to the banks and public utilities interests—especially as important sugar properties had been absorbed by the large banks—Machado became the representative of these interests, not of the Cuban people.

Catlin provided Machado with half a million for his campaign expenses; affiliated interests put up another half million. Also, from Machado, an important realty property, originally rifled from the nation through complicated transactions, was purchased by Catlin interests at many times its value. With such funds and the active backing of the electric and banking interests, Machado was easily elected.

Furthering his own financial interests, Machado promptly showed his gratitude. Through arbitrary governmental pressure, the remaining independent light and power plants were crippled and easily seized. Machado's own brother presented a bill in Congress to grant the light companies "perpetual" concessions, "exempting them from all taxes, present or future." This measure could not be pushed through, but the government remitted taxes to the light and power interests to the tune of several million dollars. The new law excluded workers' insurance and all protection, abolished the most onerous taxes, and granted other extraordinary facilities. In these efforts, Catlin was always at Machado's elbow, even "in orgies and bacchanals" and the power of the electrical interests over the island was thoroughly cemented. To-day, despite special privileges, Havana must pay 17 cents a kilowatt hour; the rest of the island from 20 to 30 cents.

Such outlandish rates led to a consumers' strike in Havana, sponsored by the Rotary Club and the newspaper, *El Mundo*. It ended briefly. Machado threatened he would accuse the leaders of blackmail, would "tear off their heads if necessary." Despite such threats other cities boycotted the company. The military authorities, hurrying to protect Machado's private interests, and those of Catlin and the companies, declared such movements "seditious," prohibited all public gatherings to discuss the matter, forbade all press comments, and gave orders to fire on sight upon any one who disconnected any wires. Despite such stern repressive measures, to-day in Cuba some twenty cities are dark—both home and street—because the people and the city administrations will not or cannot pay the high lighting costs.

Catlin and friends also bought up about seven million dollars of worthless Zayas paper at a few cents on the dollar, it being promised that these obligations would be recognized. Hard-pressed for funds, Machado delayed. Catlin kept pressing the matter, finally called up Machado by long distance from the Biltmore Hotel to advise him that if his promises were not kept within thirty days, he would withdraw his friendship. Within less than a week, Machado ordered payment, as recorded in the *Gaceta Oficial*.

In short, murderous Machado has been not so much President of Cuba as good representative of the Power Trust and the banks.

2 BLACKJACKS

How did Machado consolidate his power? What is the secret of his success?

After brutally trying to squelch the activities of opposition parties, after browbeating them at the polls, after assassinating such independence heroes as André Masó, after murdering people wholesale during 1926 and on, Machado utilized more terrorized opponents to form a conciliatory pact of coalition control with the Conservative and Popular parties. Non-conformist heads were ejected and proper minions substituted and by decree he forbade appointment of new party officers, making the rank and file powerless to throw out any of their renegade heads. Machado thus appropriated the party names, their headquarters, and active machinery. The Nationalist Union, which sprang up in opposition to these maneuvers, is absolutely proscribed, its members have suffered death and constant persecution. No new party can be formed. The famous Crowder election law was unconstitutionally set aside. All public assemblages were forbidden. No paper can print independent opinion. Even cultural organizations cannot function.

Machado also won over most of the existing Congressmen and Senators by large-scale corruption. This consisted in distributing the lottery collectorships among them, with the right to sell the tickets at from 30 to 50 percent above their marked price, in all an illegitimate profit, in which the President, military officers and other favorites also shared, totaling in good times nearly a million dollars graft a month, nearly $10,000,000 a year—equivalent to nearly a fifth of the national budget. This device to assure perpetuation in power of the Prince was never dreamed of even by Machiavelli himself.

Thugs, armed with guns and blackjacks, have invaded the sessions of such private organizations as the bar association, the federations of doctors, dentists, pharmacists, the society of engineers, and the academies of Science and of History, in most cases to impose pro-Machado officers. The lawyers were obliged by such methods to accept the corrupt and bitterly disliked Rafael Guas, imposed by Machado as President of the national Chamber of Deputies. (He finally resigned March, 1933, when the lawyers jumped over the traces, protesting the sending of Martínez Saenz to the Isle of Pines.)

Machado's attempts to use similar methods to control

sport and social clubs met with more stubborn resistance. So, December 28, 1930, the aristocratic Havana Yacht Club, which dates far back to Spanish colonial times, was closed, soldiers placed at its doors, its directors accused of conspiracy. Subsequently it was allowed to reopen.

During his first two years Machado destroyed all bonafide labor organizations of the country, jailing and killing recklessly. This was easy because the cry "Communism!" could be raised, though scarcely a handful of the numerous labor leaders now languishing in jail without trial for years knew the slightest thing about communism.

3 JOBHOLDERS AND JOBLESS

The Chadbourne sugar plan and the economic crisis, causing wholesale unemployment, were Machado's allies in lowering wages and destroying the labor movement. Unemployment has been further aggravated by the stopping of most public works and the discharge of thousands of government employees, without having received their pay for prior months. But the Chase bank, with the aid of high discount extensions, has been faithfully paid. Government wage-scales were reduced 50 percent in 1931, a step enforced by Ambassador Guggenheim, who had promised he would thus salvage the government's economic position; and employees have suffered three cuts in all.

Business concerns and government employees are taxed to help the jobless, but little of this money ever reaches its destination. Responsible persons have estimated unemployment at 500,000 out of a population of less than 4,000,-000. City laborers' wages have fallen from $3.00 to fifty cents a day; rural wages, from $1.50 to $2.50 to from three to twenty-five cents. The former rarely have six days' work a week. The latter are lucky to get one month's work a year. Skilled cigar workers get a few days' work a week at

$1.00 a day. Strippers make from 30 to 40 cents. Factory workers—textiles, candy, chocolate, soap, drugs, etc.—receive 20 to 25 cents a day. Common laborers work for food and shelter or for from 15 to 20 cents a day.

It should be remembered that the cost of living is in Havana as high as that of a city in the United States of comparable population. Undoubtedly wages would never have reached such low levels, despite the depression, had it not been for Machado's ruthless suppression of labor organizations, all of which are now illegal, as are strikes and public assemblages. No concerted action can be taken. Small groups anxious to maintain decent living conditions must meet secretly, and now have no means of influencing the large aggregate of workers.

The army has closed all labor headquarters, leaders have been killed, deported or jailed, some of them for years without trial. The few labor organizations that exist are run by Machado's paid henchmen, and likewise have little influence. A recent labor conference in Cienfüegos was actually organized by the secret police.

The Cuban labor movement during the time of Gómez, Menocal and Zayas had come to occupy a recognized place in the scheme of Cuban life. Organizations ranged from Communist and Anarchist down to most conservative groups. But in 1925 Machado called the army out to crush the Camagüey railroad strike; some thirty labor leaders are said to have been killed at that time. Since then any worker who lifts his head has disappeared or been otherwise summarily dealt with.

In 1927 Chester Wright, editor of *International Labor News,* organ of the American Federation of Labor, and English Secretary of the Pan-American Federation of Labor, brought to Washington the account of 147 assassinations committed by the Machado régime. This evidence was given much publicity. The New York port-workers voted to sabotage Cuban sugar arriving in the port. Then something happened.

Machado hastened to Washington and met Green in the Belgian legation. Green thereupon issued a public statement that from this date on the condition of Cuban workers "would be improved." After all a great labor leader must feel honored when a President calls upon him regardless of the fate of mere workers.

Wright presently was out of his two jobs, and despite the fact that the conditions of Cuban workers has grown steadily worse, that assassinations have continued, that men then jailed are to-day in jail without trial, Green never once has lifted his voice in their behalf.

All labor organization, except a few groups patronized by the government and without any following, mere paper organizations, have been driven underground. The Confederación Nacional Obrera Cubana (CNOC), member of the Latin American Trade Union Federation, affiliated with the Profintern, comprised about thirty-five unions of all trades. The Havana local of the CNOC, the Federación Obrera de Havana, had thirty trade unions and about 8,000 members. Some of these unions were under communist influence, others were reformist, as the street-car motor-men; affiliated restaurant workers were under anarchist syndicalist influence.

About 30,000 tobacco workers were organized, the leading group being the Federación Nacional de Torceadores.

The Railway Workers Brotherhood, ever since the breaking of the organization with troops in 1925, has been a more or less paper organization with leaders appointed by Machado. It belongs to the Pan-American Federation of Labor, manipulated by the American Federation of Labor.

The Union of Bakery Workers, under anarchist influence, and the shop-assistants union, about 800 members, were unaffiliated.

Two pseudo-labor organizations should be mentioned:

the Federación Cubana de Trabajo and the Unión Federativa Nacional Obrera. The Federación Cubana was a fake Machado organization claiming several thousand members, which joined the Pan-American Federation of Labor. It was formed by two paid Machado men, Juan Arévalo and Fabregat, who later quarreled over which should be city-councilor. Arévalo then made rubber stamps for an organization called the Unión Federativa Nacional Obrera. No trade unions are affiliated with the Unión Federativa, but Arévalo published his *Acción Socialista,* full of pictures of Machado, "the true friend of labor." Despite his quarrel with Fabregat, neither got the councilorship, instead Machado appointed Urrubia, a government henchman of the Railway Brotherhood.

Arévalo and Fabregat became disgruntled. Arévalo constantly published in *Acción Socialista* accusations that Fabregat was all the time in the pay of the police. Fabregat issued manifestoes and leaflets with photographic reproductions of Arévalo's letters to the police with lists of workers to be expelled or arrested, all of which recommendations were executed. Despite these revelations, Fabregat's union is still an accepted member of the Pan-American Federation of Labor.

Despite the government's persecutions, murders, "kidnaping of workers," organization has proceeded more or less underground, without much opportunity for expression. In 1930 a twenty-four hours' strike of 200,000 workmen in all industries was pulled off as a protest against the crushing of labor. In 1932, when the tobacco trust attempted to return to a 1914 wage-scale, the cigar-workers walked out. The companies retaliated—though also impelled by impossible taxes—by removing their establishments to New Jersey.

Strikes are now utterly taboo and the least sign of protest is met with bloody repression. When the school-teachers threatened to strike for their six months' unpaid salaries, the government announced it would use the army against them.

4 ARMY MULES

The chief instrument of tyranny has been the army. As soon as he came into office, Machado weeded out all army officers not personally loyal. Officers—mostly trained in American military academies—were granted lavish privileges: salaries higher than American officers, good uniforms, comfortable homes, servants, the opportunity of buying most things below cost. Even the common soldier is the pet of the Machado system. Teachers are unpaid, jailed, or killed, but the Cuban barracks have become commodious clubrooms. All equipment is up-to-date, and includes a modern air-force.

The army mule receives a food allowance of 38 cents a day; the public hospital patient, before all such institutions were closed, but 12 cents. The salaries of public employees, after being cut over fifty percent and further reduced by exorbitant taxes, are from four to six months in arrears; but the army receives its pay on the dot; new munitions are bought constantly.

The army is not only favored at the expense of every other portion of the starving Cuban population, but its functions are continuously expanded. As the university, colleges and preparatory schools were progressively closed, soldiers were placed over them. In the few elementary schools remaining open, military supervisors were installed. Military supervisors were set over the provinces. By March 15, 1932, this was extended to the towns; army officers were put into the city halls, with full jurisdiction over civil authorities. To-day every department of government has its military supervisor. The meat and milk monopolies, among others, are under complete military control. Local police have been absorbed into a national militia. Cuba is one vast armed camp.

The army's functions now include nearly all civil functions. From time to time attempts have been made to legalize these unconstitutional steps. Thus, the afternoon of February 16, 1932, not a regular session-day, in the absence of the President, Vice-Presidents, secretaries and stenographers of the Chamber, a group of deputies approved the law subjecting civilians to court-martial. Machado signed the bill the following day.

In 1932 Machado published a decree creating the new office of military majorship to dictate proclamations and regulate citizens' lives in each province. The army officer in charge was given absolute sway except in so far as direct orders might be issued by Machado himself. Any citizen failing to obey the military proclamations is subject to arrest or arbitrarily imposed fines against which he has no legal appeal. To leave towns or cities, even to travel to Havana suburbs, all except tourists require special military permits.

Though legally the police should be at the disposal of the various mayors, these military majors absolutely control the local corps, which are automatically part of the national militia. This status was created in part to prevent civil courts, then still with some functions, from chastising policemen committing abuses and murders. Havana Province has as its Military Major, Colonel Federico Rasco, besides the Military Supervisor, at present Colonel Rogerio Caballero, who controls the national police force, the secret and judicial police, and the gang of convict sluggers known as the Porra.

Among policemen indicted by civil court was Israel Pérez, who murdered the American citizen Arthur T. Tagle at Virtudes and Prado streets right near the Havana American Club. Held without bail by the Judge of the First Instance, he mysteriously escaped. Machado and Congress put into effect an amnesty law for all militiamen and policemen who had committed any transgressions. Pérez, in defiance of justice and affronting the American Embassy, is now back on the force. What is an American citizen or two—if he doesn't own property?

Another Machado decree forbids more than three persons to assemble without military permit. Though people go on with their dances and so on, the government can arrest almost any one it wishes to. Thus, December, 1932, Carlos Fernández and Carlos Martí, President and Secretary of the Association of Commercial Employees of Havana (over 40,000 members), were arrested and each sentenced to fifteen days and $50 fine for having assembled with other executive members of the organization for social purposes without the required permit.

Extensive espionage causes frequent arrest of people for inadvertently expressing their opinions in restaurants, clubs, theaters, sometimes in private homes. Immediately put under military jurisdiction, sometimes they are tried, sometimes merely held indefinitely. At one time the government discovered that a certain group of young oppositionists were accustomed to go without hats. A police-decree provided for the arrest of any one on the street without a hat; numbers of innocent persons chancing to be bareheaded were savagely beaten by the Porra.

Often people are arbitrarily sentenced to jail without hearings. Thus, Dr. Orfelia Domínguez Navarro, prominent criminal lawyer, head of the feminist league, early in 1932 was taken out of her home from a sick bed on a stretcher, being advised by the military authorities she had been sentenced to forty-five days in prison, but without being told her offense. She has suffered similar sentence and imprisonment on other occasions. Her case is far from unique.

The following extract from a *bando*, or proclamation—order of the military commandant of Havana, posted late in 1932 on the walls of the city, indicates the military concept of law and justice.

After citing the names of Martí and Maceo, without which no Cuban manifesto would be complete, and reciting the military and police officers who had lost their lives, it states: "And as this military commandancy has reports that in this *comarca* there exist various persons who take orders from this band of savage terrorists . . . as soon as one of these terrorist acts occur which endangers the life of any citizen, there will be arrested and shot, without previous trial, all those who form part of so terrible an organization because they are considered enemies of the Fatherland and of Humanity."

The result of this has been the police-murder of any number of law-abiding members of the community known merely to sympathize with the opposition.

5 SCALES OF JUSTICE

All who have attempted to argue cases in behalf of prisoners before civil or military courts have been arrested and held incommunicado, as Pedro Herrera y Sotolongo, or assassinated, as Professor Gonzalo Freyre de Andrade.

For a time the Supreme Court valiantly attempted to maintain its independence and support constitionality by handing down brave and honest decision on freedom of press, habeas corpus, trial of civilians in civil courts, the closing of the university, etc. Under the strain of attempting to uphold his innate convictions against the Machado terror, President of the Supreme Court, Dr. José Luis Vidaurreta committed suicide. His successor, Dr. Juan Gutiérrez Quiroz, soon resigned, March 29, 1932, after denouncing "the usurpation of the constitutional life of the country," and declaring that the military authorities had appropriated the punishment in cases properly corresponding to

THE CRIME OF CUBA

civil jurisdiction, had refused to heed habeas corpus or to permit investigation of official crimes. This last accusation referred particularly to the fact that Major Arsenio Ortiz of the army, after having been indicted in the Circuit Court of Santiago for forty-four brutal murders, was protected by the army and promoted by Machado.[1]

Machado then appointed his former Secretary of State, Dr. Vivanco. Though known as a dutiful henchman, within a month and a half the Supreme Court declared again that the military jurisdiction law was unconstitutional, null and void.

Machado thereupon put into effect a new but essentially similar law. Prisoners under the old law were released and rearrested.

Since then the Supreme Court has been completely a creature of Machado's will, though recently it has shown new signs of independence. The lower courts had long since been converted into Executive rubber-stamps.

[1] Gutiérrez, in his final memorandum, March 29, declared that the Judicial Power demanded that the Executive issue general orders that: [condensed]

1. The courts of justice always be properly respected and their habeas corpus orders complied with.

2. All departments maintain respect and confidence in the court decisions.

3. All authorities promptly answer judicial communications and expedite cases before the court.

4. Measures be adopted to respect the lives of prisoners.

5. Prisoners be not required to make any declarations except to the proper court.

6. No fortress be used as a provisional prison and no prisoner be held incommunicado.

7. Arrested persons be no longer held indefinitely but be released or tried promptly.

8. Immediate modification of the February 17 law (military court jurisdiction).

9. Immediate modification of the habeas corpus law giving greater facilities to the judges and determining the manner to make the orders effective.

10. Constitutional amendment reforming the organic law of judicial powers.

11. Immediate approval of the laws reforming judicial appointments.

12. Exclusion of all civilians from military jurisdiction.

6 INTERNATIONAL INTRIGUE

Turn back a few years. After having unified political and military control, already having acquired considerable sums from American bankers (despite his preëlection promise not to increase Cuba's debt) Machado prepared to perpetuate himself in power. A new Presidential election was to take place in 1928, but after consultation with Kellogg and other American officials, Machado decided to obviate this necessity by throwing the constitution completely overboard and extending his term two years.

Utilizing his personally controlled committees of the parties, in April, 1928, he assembled a hand-picked constitutional convention, presided over by Dr. Antonio Sánchez de Bustamente, and though according to the Cuban constitution—Article 115—amendments can be adopted by such a body only if proposed by Congress and submitted to a plebiscite, the new body hastened to carry out Machado's minutest wish—despite the objections of unconstitutionality formulated by the leading lawyers in Cuba. Most of these lawyers soon spent varying periods in jail, some without trial and without ever being told the reason for their arrest.

Instead of proroguing his term two years, the constitution was altered, permitting a six-year term without reëlection. Machado, made an exception, was allowed to reëlect himself.

Through this illegal maneuver and through a fake election in November in which he was the only candidate, Machado was given a new term to run from May 20, 1929, to May 20, 1935.

In this violation of the entire legal system of Cuba, with the good wishes of Washington, Machado has had the opposition of every literate Cuban except the army and a small clique on the government payroll and a few others directly benefiting from his tyranny.

It was well known in Cuba that this illegal creation of dictatorship followed on the heels of secret financial and political maneuvers. By the early part of 1928 the Chase National Bank had over $20,000,000 laid out in unpaid work certificates, which they feared to lose and which they wished to convert into a revolving $60,000,000 credit. Machado's term was coming to an end, trouble was brewing, and the enormous graft of his public works utilizing Chase money had aroused universal hostility. A successor might delay in cleaning up the Chase obligations; he might also have to make electoral promises which would prevent him from going ahead with the Chase financing.

The second factor in the creation of illegal tyranny in Cuba was the Sixth Pan-American Congress to be held in Havana in January. In the Fifth Congress in Santiago de Chile rather sharp opposition to American policies had arisen. Now American marines were battling bloodily in Nicaragua; hatred of the United States was seething in all Latin America. Even sharper criticism was expected in the new Congress. On the other hand many countries were planning to boycott it entirely, denouncing it as an imperialistic body. Both prospects were not pleasing to Washington, which was arguing in Europe for disarmament, the rights of small nations, and non-aggression. What was to be done?

We might be pressing Nicaragua's face in the mire, but it was necessary to make a gesture of nobility. Suddenly Cuban Ambassador Orestes Ferrara at Washington began propagating the idea that in the Congress the Platt Amendment treaty would be denounced with Washington's consent as a preliminary to its abrogation, that the sugar tariff would be lowered, that the Cuban debt would be negotiated on a reduced basis. The Sixth Pan-American Congress would back up all of these demands, provide the leverage for the State Department to go successfully before the United States Congress.

Machado hastened to Washington personally to invite Coolidge, his "great and good friend," to attend. Conferences were held also with Ferrara, Kellogg and others, and high Cuban officials in the know declared privately that the agreement was then reached to permit Machado to remain in power. The two major considerations for Washington were apparently the Chase loan and the success of the Congress.

Machado despatched Márquez Sterling, supposed to be a liberal-minded person, to the countries of South America to persuade them to attend the Pan-American Congress where Cuba would finally be freed from the Platt Amendment, our protectorate finally abolished.[2] Cuba pleaded that she needed their help.

And so, despite Nicaragua, despite previous boycott plans, for the first time in the annals of the Pan-American Union all the twenty-one republics of the New World sent delegates.

But the agenda had been carefully prepared to exclude all controversy. The delegates were banqueted in such lavishness as to recall the words of Seneca, "We have reached such refinement that we wish to walk treading precious stones." The people in the cafés murmured: "The crowning of General Machado as Emperor of the West Indies."

But not a word about the Platt Amendment was raised by the Cuban delegation—on express and severe orders of Machado. Márquez Sterling—discomfited and out of face with the other Latin-American delegates—made fruitless inquiries. Other Latin-American countries did give Mr. Hughes a bad day on the question of intervention—reports of which were carefully kept out of the American press and most of the Latin-American press. Even here, Orestes Ferrara, instead of living up to the program which had persuaded the Latin-American countries all to attend, backed

[2] Márquez Sterling, *Conferencias del Shoreham*, 56 ff.

up Hughes and burst into a poetic eulogy of intervention—
"Intervention is a word of honor, word of glory, word of
triumph and word of liberty." The sessions were hurriedly
lifted until five years later in Montevideo.

Washington without exactly fooling anybody, through
limiting the topics and discussions and connivance with the
Cuban delegates, carefully prepared press despatches from
dutiful American correspondents, had won a surface victory, hollow though it really was. And Machado had won
the right to overthrow the constitution; and the Chase
bank, the security of its past and forthcoming loans, the first
of the latter being promptly celebrated in June of that year.
Kellogg announced that he was pleased that the three parties (all under Machado's thumb by the means previously
described) gave unanimous consent to the alteration of the
constitution.

It was, as Márquez Sterling himself declares, "a coup
d'état, upheld from Washington through banking influ-
ences."

XVI MACHETE EDGE

I HAVE ALREADY RECOUNTED the killing of Vásquez Bello and the Freyre de Andrade brothers on September 26, 1932. That was a fatal day, for on it came tidings to Machado of the death of his most intimate American friend, Henry Catlin, who more than any one else, put him into power and did much to keep him there. This news had sent Machado to bed. At noon he was informed of the murder of his trusted friend, Vásquez Bello, who had continuously advised him regarding the political enemies to be eliminated and other matters, and in a state of hyperstatic frenzy, Machado paced the floor in his underclothes giving out orders. Within a few hours some of the most honorable and respected men in Cuban life who had had the temerity to oppose Machado, men who had no relation to the Vásquez Bello crime, were wiped out by Machado's secret Porra.

That afternoon, as before stated, I had an appointment with Leopoldo Freyre de Andrade, an authority upon the sugar question and an opponent of the catastrophic Chadbourne sugar plan.

I kept my appointment with a dead man. Before the sun set, not only Leopoldo, but his two brothers, Gonzalo and Guillermo, were lying in blood on the second floor of their house at No. 13 B Street. Machado gunmen had driven in an automobile to the police station adjacent to the Freyre house, then had swung around the corner to his residence.

They forced their way inside and mowed down the three brothers. The police, next door, close enough to hear all the firing, delayed fifteen minutes before appearing.

Guillermo was a sugar chemist, inactive in politics, but Gonzalo, a well-known lawyer, had dared oppose Machado in the Chamber of Deputies, had tried to defend political prisoners illegally held by the military authorities and just before his death had presented a petition to the diplomatic corps signed by leading Cuban women, calling upon them to act in behalf of yet unmurdered students. He and his brothers paid the usual penalty awaiting every lawyer who has attempted to defend political prisoners.

My friend Leopoldo was a victim of Machado and the banks which had foisted the sugar plan on Cuba. He had long strenuously opposed the Chadbourne plan and a few days before his death had published an article which treated of the Chase National Bank.

That same afternoon, Machado's henchmen murdered another opposition Congressman, also a professor and lawyer, Miguel Angel Aguiar, on his doorstep in the Vedado suburb. Dozens of other prominent Cubans, including the rector of the closed university, Ricardo Dolz, took refuge in foreign legations in order to escape a similar fate.

The bloodshed recounted did not complete the list of violences while I was on the island—occurrences common enough in Cuba for six years. Take merely a few of the bloody events of September, 1932. September 2 and 3 five persons were killed and sixteen wounded in so-called political riots in the Pinar del Río province. September 5 a school was dynamited. September 6, Lieutenant Echenique, military supervisor of a Havana suburb, was killed. Massip, Negro Chief of Police of Marianao, was killed and five more were wounded. In retaliation, the government riddled with bullets the three students Floro Perez, Antonio Perez and Juan Bautista Napoles. September 10, the Rural Guards, in a so-called battle near Havana, killed and wounded various people. An unexploded bomb was found near the home of bloodthirsty Major Arsenio Ortiz.

September 27 recorded the deaths of Vásquez Bello, the Freyre brothers, and others mentioned above, plus many wounded and many jailed. Three hundred pounds of dynamite were found in the Colón cemetery, a block from my home, near the Truffin family mausoleum where Dr. Vásquez Bello was expected to be buried.

September 30 a bomb smashed the façade of the brutal office-holder from Pinar del Río province.

For years no man's life or property has been safe at any time in Cuba. Human liberty has disappeared. Legal rights have disappeared. Since Machado has clamped the lid down upon all popular expression, since he has committed crimes terrorizing the Cuban nation, only individual rebellion of a violent nature has been left the Cubans as a weapon.

Despite these occurrences, Machado, as usual, fooled the American public by releasing to foreign correspondents the false news that the university would reopen, and that he would grant amnesty to eighty-four political prisoners. His frequent amnesties mean nothing; they are pure bluff. Those released are soon either assassinated or imprisoned again.

The assassination of the three students on September 6, recounted above, is typical. They were taken out of their cells September 6 and killed while in the custody of the Chief of Secret Service, Santiago Trujillo, and the Police Supervisor Arsenio Ortiz.

Long ago the murderous crimes of Ortiz became so scandalous and local fury against him so strong that he was indicted by the Supreme Court of Santiago for having committed forty-four political assassinations in ninety days. The total number of his victims is estimated at more than 150. All these charges have been minutely detailed in the court records by its president, Dr. Hechevarria, and in the magazine *Semana*. Many of these victims were tied up, and their heads were blown to pieces. At the time of the indictment, the populace tried to lynch two of Ortiz' aides.

Examine Ortiz' record.

Through Supreme Court Sentence No. 196, October, 1914, he was sentenced for "robbery with intimidation of persons, executed in an uninhabited place and in gang" to serve a term of seven years, ten months, and twenty-one days; on a homicide charge to a term of twelve years and one day, and on the charge of swindling, four months and one day.

An amnesty law released Ortiz and his accomplices. He enlisted in the army, rose in rank. November, 1930, he was appointed Military Supervisor of the Oriente police. December 26, Leopoldo Sánchez y Fernández, supposedly in jail, was found murdered on the Morro road. Four days later, December 30, José García, a Spanish friend of Sánchez, also supposedly in jail for political opposition, was found murdered at Once Street, Vista Alegre. In Olmos Park, January 3, was found the riddled body of the jailed Jamaican, José Ramón. January 14, Juan Cantero, another prisoner in Ortiz' custody, a friend of Ramón, was found strangled in Sueño suburb. February 8, the murdered body of prisoner Jorge Luis, another Jamaican, was located in Vista Alegre.

British Minister Morris protested, threatened to bring a battleship to Santiago de Cuba to protect British lives. (One was sent there and to Havana in March, 1933, news of which was suppressed in the American press.) The Machado government instructed the civil authorities to make a thorough investigation.

January 27, 1931, on Porfirio Valiente Street appeared the body of a man, head torn to pieces by a bomb. Autopsy revealed he had died by strangulation prior to the explosion. Señora Laura Gonzáles, resident of 85 Ninth Street, identified the man as her husband, Severino Pérez, employed at the Delicias sugar mill. Shortly before he had loaned a friend of Ortiz $5,000. Thus was the debt liquidated.

As a consequence of these and other crimes, an attempt against Ortiz' life was made. He ordered all nearby homes searched and the people therein arrested. Among them was a young shoemaker, "El Chinón," in business several years in the house in front of the place where the attempt occurred. Third degree cruelties drove him insane. Released three days later, he wandered about, a bag of skin and bones, and died in the public hospital.

Ortiz also had arrested Juan Flores, Alberto Echevarría, Fidel Rodríguez, Menéndez Castillo, and Angel Laguardia; also Señora Victoria Mustelier and her three small children, neighbors of Rodríguez. She was terrorized before being released. With no evidence against these prisoners, Ortiz ordered them murdered in pairs on consecutive nights. Menéndez and Rodríguez were thus murdered, before protests of local citizens, Americans and others, had any effect. The court investigated, calling upon Lieutenant Hernández, jail warden, to testify. He swore the two prisoners had entered the jail in Ortiz' custody, April 11. The following night, Ortiz, his son, an army sergeant and a municipal police sergeant, ordered jail-guard Bestard to bring the two prisoners out duly handcuffed, and they took them away in an automobile driven by Policeman Felizola. The Judge, Joaquín del Rio Balmaseda, boldly indicted Ortiz, his son and several others.

While the court was investigating these murders, Sergeant Aquilino Valle, jail supervisor, was murdered on the first floor of the Santiago jail so he could not testify. His body had three bullets, two in the chest, one in the right temple.

Though the judge ordered Ortiz' imprisonment to face trial, President Machado at once transferred him to Havana, flouting the court. In due time, Machado secured full amnesty from Congress, and promoted Ortiz military supervisor of Havana police—a flattering recognition.

This and similar promotions have proved to the police and army that the surest road to political favor is to murder Machado's opponents ruthlessly and without legal processes.

For this propaganda against Machado, the student Floro Pérez, resident of Santiago, was long persecuted by Ortiz and was obliged to hide in Havana under an assumed name. He was finally arrested on the upper floor of "La Filosofía" store, where he was talking to the employee Wycliffe B. Grafton. With him were apprehended his brother Antonio, Grafton, and Napoles. Grafton, supposed to be an English subject, was released and through the protection of the Uruguayan minister, escaped to the United States before it was discovered he was a Cuban. Prior to that, he, the two brothers, and Nápoles were held incommunicado in the secret police headquarters.

All efforts to obtain their release, even to ascertain their exact whereabouts, except in Grafton's case, proved fruitless.

It was later learned, through Grafton, that they were all given the third degree by Ortiz and Trujillo, that before dawn, September 6, 1932, the other three were led forth in different directions.

Floro was shot down on the Martín Mesa road near Mariel; his brother was similarly murdered on the Matanzas road near Mocha; Nápoles was assassinated near Jaimanitas. The bodies, when found, revealed terrible torture, including castration. The old father of the two boys tried to commit suicide; and a few days before I left Cuba—I had no time to verifv—it was rumored that their mother did kill herself.

Other killings of about that time were those of the three Alvarez brothers by Cuban army officials. The press reported them as "brigands" killed in a fusillade with soldiers.

As a matter of fact, they were sons of a brave soldier of the Independence Army, who still survives them, sick and despairing; and they perished because of the same love of liberty that led their father to fight Spanish rule. They had participated in the unsuccessful August, 1931, revolt, had been captured, granted amnesty. Though having settled down to pacific pursuits, one a dentist, the other two cultivators of the small Los Arabos ranch, a trumped-up horse-thievery charge was brought against them, but dismissed for lack of all evidence.

No sooner released than they were seized by the military authorities and spirited to San Severino Castle in Matanzas. Lieutenant Colonel Abelardo Herrera, Chief of the Matanzas district, and Captain Supervisor Sacramento del Castillo at once repaired to San Miguel Beach to confer with General Herrera, chief of the Cuban Army, taking a cure for intestinal troubles. Orders were given to put the three brothers to death.

In the castle records the three brothers were registered freed, then were taken at eleven-thirty at night by one Válido in Colonel Herrera's auto back toward Colón. Behind them followed Sacramento del Castillo with three machine-guns and ammunition. At Agijica (near Colón), in a narrow alley, they were delivered to soldiers under Lieutenant Vilches and Sergeant Vásquez, who trussed them up and killed them with machine-guns. Neighbors saw the prisoners struggling at their bonds, shouting to be allowed to fight even if only with bare hands.

The bodies were then trucked into Colón along with the three machine-guns and ammunition and exhibited to the populace—a glorious victory over the bandits and a capture of valuable booty.

On the death of the engineer, López Rubio, the press announced from official quarters that "in legitimate defense the authorities had killed an unknown person." Later it was reported he had been killed near the Almendares bridge near Havana because he had refused to answer an order to halt.

Neither version was true. López Rubio, former secretary of General Peraza, assassinated by Machado some years before, had long been suspected as a political opponent. One day the police arbitrarily seized him as a dangerous terrorist; he was taken to a lonely house near the bridge and assassinated. Autopsy revealed that the guns which killed him had been placed so close they had burned his clothing and had left powder traces on his mouth. The government thereupon refused to permit any further investigation.

2 MELLA

The strong arm of Machado reaches far beyond Cuba's borders, not only to suppress unfavorable news and unfavorable publications, but to murder opponents.

His tyranny has dispersed Cubans to all parts of the world. Many have fled to Mexico; there, too, have gone students unable to obtain an education at home because of the closing of the schools. The Cuban exiles published several magazines, the principal being *Cuba Libre*—FREE CUBA.

To Mexico went the student Julio Antonio Mella, jailed by Machado in 1925 on a false murder charge. After a hunger strike, he was released on condition he go into exile. In Mexico he at once became the leader of the exiled Cubans, just as previously he had been the leader of the students. I knew him well. Physically he was a young god; he had a razor-edge mind; and he was an excellent speaker with the power of moving multitudes.

For a long time the Mexican authorities disregarded the demands of the Cuban tyranny for persecution of the exiled Cubans. But one by one, Machado invited prominent Mexican officials to Cuba, fêted and banqueted them, showered them with attentions, and decorated them with medals.

Machado even rounded up a bunch of exiled Mexicans un-
friendly to Calles and shipped them home.

Presently *Cuba Libre* and other Cuban exile publications
were suppressed by the government of Calles and his successor Portes Gil. From then on the Cuban exiles frequently
found themselves in jail on one pretext or another. Others
were seized and shipped back to Cuba or to Europe. I knew
three such personally: Sandalio Junco, Alejandro Barreira,
and Manuel Cotoño (imprisoned during Coolidge's visit to
Havana). Barreira, penniless, very ill, was torn from his
wife and two children; and after considerable imprisonment
was shipped with the other two out of the country on the
Nord Friesland. Despondent over his family left penniless
behind, fearing to be taken off the boat in Havana and
thrust in prison or murdered, he attempted to commit
suicide.

Early the evening of January 10, 1929, in Mexico, I returned home to find a note scribbled on the back of an
envelope: "Julio has been shot. Come to the Red Cross
Emergency Hospital."

I jumped into a taxi, elbowed my way through the hushed
throng of Julio's friends in the vestibule, and after much
persuasion, was admitted to the operating room, where I
found present Diego Rivera, the painter, Francis Toor, editor of *Mexican Folkways,* and Tina Modotti, the Italian
photographer. Julio barely was alive.

Assassins had crept up behind him on Abraham González
Street in the dark. One bullet passed through his body, another smashed the whole bone of his right arm from elbow
down. After being shot, he ran across the street, then
pitched headlong unconscious. He regained his senses for
only a few seconds to murmur Machado had assassinated
him.

The Mexican Chief of Secret Police, Valente Quintana,
himself a bandit of the first order, had just visited Machado
in Havana, and in every way attempted to shield the real

assailants and throw suspicion on innocent persons. Friends of Mella accuse Quintana of having received money from Machado. He was temporarily removed from office, but no real attempt was made to catch the murderers.

Machado greatly feared the effects of this crime upon Mexican public opinion; serious demonstrations took place before the Cuban Embassy; and he also feared court disclosures. He called upon Márquez Sterling, well-known and beloved in Mexico because of his fine activities during the Madero-Huerta period twenty years earlier. Márquez Sterling's principal task in Mexico was to put a quietus on the Mella affair; and he permitted himself to be used for this purpose by Machado. The new Ambassador brought pressure to bear on the Mexican authorities that the tribunals should not "connect the government of Cuba with the murder of . . . Mella." [1] Why should the Cuban government, if not implicated, not have welcomed full investigation?

The Mexican government did not recognize the right of Cuba to dictate the conduct of its courts, but frankly admitted that probably because of Quintana's "mistaken or stupid handling . . . it had been necessary to liberate the one prisoner who might have thrown light on the affair, one Magriñat."

The matter lay in abeyance for several years. Last year, Mella's wife went to Mexico to seek justice and, after battling against great odds, had the case reopened. The Mexican government suppressed full accounts of the new trial, but the evidence which has piled up clearly implicates Quintana, Machado's secret police, and Machado and the Cuban Ambassador, Fernandez Mascaro. The assassins were receiving pay from the Cuban government, and took refuge in the Embassy after the crime.

It is impossible here to give the full testimony of or concerning Aurelio Alvarez de la Vega, Angel Otol, José

[1] Márquez Sterling, *Conferencias del Shoreham*, 65.

Magriñá, José Agustín López, Antonio Sarabia, Iturriaga, etc. Faint echoes of this trial drifted into the American press. On May 15, 1932, the *New York Times* outlined the testimony of Iturriaga that Machado had personally directed the assassination, which merely corroborated other testimony of the same import.

These revelations caused the National Students' Union of Mexico (July 26, 1932) to demand the breaking off of relations with Cuba. They laid Mella's assassination to the "direct order" of Machado with "the intervention of its [Cuba's] Ambassador accredited to Mexico"; and they further cited the Cuban government's assassination of two Mexican subjects, Raúl and José Sancho. More recently press reports have hinted that such a break would soon occur. Deaths have occurred in Cuba every January 10. Despite the terror, thousands of workers strike, and they and others demonstrate in memory of Mella. This year the parade was met with machine-guns, among those killed was the Jewish worker, Boris Waxman.

3 CALVIN

Calvin Coolidge, then still President, went to Havana in 1928 to address the Pan-American Congress, and in his speech on January 16, he said:

"The very place where we are meeting is a complete demonstration of the progress we are making. . . . Her [Cuba's] people are independent, free, prosperous, peaceful and enjoying the advantages of self-government. . . . They have reached a position in the stability of their government, in the genuine expression of their public opinion at the ballot-box, and in the recognized soundness of their public credit that has commanded universal respect and admiration."

Just before Coolidge's arrival, Cuba had suffered a most

brutal unfair election, was subjected to every sort of repression, and at the very moment Coolidge was pronouncing these words, Cuban student leaders were in jail, having been rounded up lest they lay their case before that august assemblage of bland words. On the eve of Coolidge's arrival in Havana to pat Machado's head, Claudio Brouzon, a Spaniard; Noske Yalob, probably a Pole, and two Cuban students, Puerta Reyes and Manuel Cotoño, were arrested for putting up anti-imperialist posters. Neither friends nor relatives were able to ascertain the whereabouts of the prisoners, presumably held by the military authorities in medieval Morro Castle. But shortly after Coolidge, Charles Evans Hughes, and the late Dwight Morrow had gone home, parts of a human body were found undigested in a shark's belly. The police unwittingly investigated. Mrs. Brouzon identified her husband from a coat, shirt, and initialed cuff-links found in the shark.

These details and a photograph of the shark may be found in the reliable paper, *El País,* of March 5, 1928; other accounts appeared in other papers. The details of Mrs. Brouzon's identification and the supporting testimony of friends, as related before the judge, are given in the oldest, most conservative paper of Cuba, *Diario de la Marina,* March 10. The widow and all the other witnesses were immediately deported to Spain.

Soon after this identification, the Port-Captain prohibited shark-fishing! This order is given in *El País* of March 15, along with news of the discovery of Yalob's body in a state of decomposition, half eaten by fishes, still weighted with prison chains, under one of the port *espigones,* apparently washed there by the tide.

Evidently the prisoners had been dropped, either dead or alive, through a medieval trap-door in Morro Castle, to serve as food for the sharks—an ancient Spanish custom.

No other fully authenticated cases of human shark-feeding exist, though the mysterious disappearance of other prisoners, combined with the prohibitory shark-fishing order, led Machado's opponents to believe that many held in Morro Castle probably met the same fate.

Scandal caused Machado for a time to abandon Morro Castle as a place of confinement, but recently the government has called for estimates to revamp its underground cells there to handle an excess of 1,000 prisoners from Oriente.

Too numerous to mention are those who have otherwise vanished—workers, political leaders, intellectuals such as the notable Venezuelan poet, Francisco Laguado Jayme. Laguado had never written or spoken against Machado, but an exiled opponent of Dictator Juan Vicente Gómez of Venezuela, he had circulated literature about his native country. He was seized March 18, 1929, and was last seen being taken to the prison-boat *Máximo Gómez*. The Cuban government, in reply to a query of the Unión Cívica Venezolana of New York, said that after arrest he was turned over to the Secret Police and March 23 embarked for Europe under the false name José García y García. When Márquez Sterling pressed for details to quiet anti-Machado propaganda in Mexico, the police refused to admit he had been taken aboard the *Máximo Gómez,* but in a series of contradictory statements, admitted that the entry of prisoners into Cabaña fortress and the *Máximo Gómez* was never recorded. The fact remains, Laguado has never been heard of since.

The deed was apparently executed as a favor to a fellow despot. Shortly after, Gómez decorated Machado and sent him gifts.

One of the first "disappearance" cases was that of Alfredo López, Secretary of the Workers Federation of Havana, an organizer of the Cuban National Federation of Workers and of the Textile Union. After being repeatedly threatened with death by the authorities, July 20, 1926, when on his way from his home to union headquarters on Gloria Street, he disappeared for all time.

March 29, 1927, Carlos Manuel de la Cruz, member of the Chamber of Deputies, declared before Congress that "since 1925 a policy of arresting and deporting workers has begun. Men have disappeared from their homes; many workers have entered military prisons."

In 1927, Dr. Armando Parajon and Octavio Seiglie were witnesses to the words of the Chief of Secret Police, Disidero Ferreira, who bragged he had initiated "the practice of disappearances, for this eliminates investigations, scandal, and even burial of the victims . . . and I arrest them when they are alone and no one sees it, and then they disappear and there are no disputes or bother."

More recently in the Marianao suburb, right near my apartment, quite often the bodies of respectable persons opposed to Machado were found mysteriously hanging from trees in the street-parking. This had been going on even earlier. At dawn of July 26, 1932, was found in Marianao the body of the youth Rafael Rodríguez Pool, horribly mutilated in the Arsenio Ortíz manner, with five bullet wounds in his mouth and on his body. He had taken part in a demonstration the previous day. The same morning in the same suburb the body of an unknown Jewish worker was found shot. The police have cynically declared themselves unable to account for these crimes.

The shark method threatens to be revived. But July 29, 1932, the Latin-American Trade Union Confederation issued a bulletin that during the previous two weeks four unknown corpses had been found floating in the sea near Havana. In Santa Clara four peasants were found hanging to a tree. Eight mutinous sailors had disappeared. October 11, Dr. Octavio Zubizarreta, Secretary of Interior, requested the Secretary of Public Works to submit an estimate of the cost of renovating the dingy underground cells of Morro Castle to house a surplus of 1,000 political prisoners which now crowd the jails of Oriente province. The old castle we wrenched from Spain is once more housing Cubans who have dared to cherish the liberty we helped to give them; and, remarks the heroic *Havana-American News* (October 11), "sharks will again gather among the rocks near the chutes, hoping that the old days have come again."

4 DEAD PATRIOTS

Some of the most distinguished patriots of Cuba's independence days have been murdered. Before daybreak of August 20, 1925, Commandant Armando André, editor of *El Pais,* and one of the bravest men of the independence wars, a Conservative Party leader, was foully shot down on his doorstep on Villuendas Street. Machado's aide, Llaneras, and Deputy Anselmo Alliegro and others were witnesses to Machado's statement in the Union Club, several days before André was killed, that he felt badly about "the necessity of having to kill him." The papers carried alongside the account of this murder an official statement that the government did not propose to suppress any newspapers. What need after such a warning?

May 28, 1928, Colonel Blas Masó, also of the army of independence, was shot down taking the air in the balcony of his own house. Estebán Delgado, also an independence veteran, was assassinated in his home at 78 Prenelles Street July 24, 1928, by Juan Ramón, Chief of Police Experts, accompanied by Lieutenant Pelaez and the two policemen, Nos. 202 and 1660. Simultaneously Delgado's chauffeur, evidently due to the belief of his assailants that he was accompanied by his employer, was killed in the very center of Havana on Cuba Street. Deputy Bartolomé Sagaró, independence veteran, and director of the periodical *Voice of the Teacher* was blackjacked to death, August 6, 1928.

Enemies of the bankers' Chadbourne sugar plan and of

precious governmental sugar policies have been killed. Besides Leopoldo Freyre de Andrade, might be mentioned, Manuel Luciano Hernández, a prominent sugar-land leaser, shot down in his home.

Many assassinations were really massacres. September 22, 1931, Congressman Carlos M. de la Cruz—who later had to take refuge in a foreign legation—accused the army of having murdered ten young men in the Artemisa district. April 4, 1926—two years before Coolidge praised Machado for his humanitarian régime—twenty-seven political enemies were tracked down and shot by the authorities in the province of Camagüey.

By decree, Machado created a censorship commission headed by Desiderio Ferreira. The Cuban constitution absolutely forbids censorship. Machado claims this step was requested of him "by the four largest papers of Havana." What they really wanted to avoid—even so, they were not spokesmen for all the papers—was arbitrary seizure and suppression by prior inspection of news. Machado was impelled to this step by recent publicity given the depredations committed in the military prisons against political prisoners, brutally tortured until death, or "bumped off" by shotguns in the Atares Fortress patio by prison chief, Captain Crespo.

In 1923 the Censorship Commission failed to prevent publication of the details and photographs of the murder perpetrated by the National Police on seventeen-year-old high-school student, Mariano Gonzáles Rubiera. Machado, in a rage, substituted army officers, putting in charge Colonel Guerrero, chief Army Auditor.

American newspapers and magazines containing any news of the government's terrorism are also confiscated; innocent venders even thrown into jail. Complete editions of the *New York Times, New York Herald Tribune, New Republic, Common Sense, Time, Plain Talk, Collier's, Reader's Digest,* and others have been seized. Foreign correspondents are also humiliated by having to go over to the Department of Interior frequently to explain their dispatches. This happens constantly with the able *New York Times* representative, J. D. Phillips. About the middle of April, 1933, the American correspondents in Havana were obliged to ask the American government for protection. On April 28, according to the *Herald Tribune,* the *Times* correspondent, threatened by the Porra, had to take refuge in the home of our Consul General, after being refused refuge in our Embassy, which later told him that he would be safe in the home of Minister of State Ferrara!

Among editors and newspapermen murdered by the régime might be mentioned: Mella, André, Captain Aguiar, Sagaro, Abelardo Pacheco, and Antonio López. Alfredo Santiago, editor of *El Heraldo Comercial,* was arrested February 2, 1929, and has never been heard of since.

Every newspaper in Cuba, except the officially subsidized *Heraldo de Cuba,* now edited by Orestes Ferrara, Secretary of State and of Finance, has been suppressed at one time or another. *Heraldo de Cuba,* for a time, was an opposition paper. Its properties were seized by Machado and his brother Carlos, called by *Time* "slow-witted," "bull-headed," and "a lover of cock-fighting," was installed as editor. Even the *Heraldo de Cuba* plant was occupied a few hours by soldiers, while I was in Havana, "for appearance' sake."

Among papers permanently suppressed might be mentioned *Karakato* (the editors, Julio Gaunard and Ramón Arroyo, were arrested, later exiled), *Cuba Libre* (editor assassinated), *El Día, Bohemia* (editor, Miguel Angel Quevedo jailed various times), *Política Cómica, La Estampa, Unión Nacionalista, La Semana* (editor, Sergio Carbó, arrested, exiled), *La Campaña* (director, Captain José Aguiar shot down at door of paper on San Ignacio Street), *La Voz del Maestro* (director assassinated), *La Voz del Pueblo* (editor,

Abelardo Pacheco, murdered getting off tram in Cerro suburb), *Siboney* (director—shameless police-official under Machado who subsequently turned against him—arrested; wife and daughter arrested eighteen times, merely for being related), *El Sol* of Marianao (director, Cesar San Pedro, jailed various times), *La Voz de la Razón* of Santiago de Cuba (director, José Llora Infante, murdered), *Havana-American* (owner and editor, John T. Wilford had to flee by plane to United States to batter on State Department doors; his son illegally held many months by military authorities; later Wilford republished as *Havana-American News*). A score of others were closed; many were sacked and burned. On suppressing *Karakato* fifty policemen led by the late Chief Captain Calvo, head of the Secret Service Experts (most of whom have committed any number of murders) attacked the building destroying the offices, furnishings, machinery and driving the staff out in a fusillade of bullets. One of the directors, Ramón Arroyo, was severely wounded in the face.

Calvo was called before a civil court (then not entirely stripped of authority) and sentenced to removal from his post. He appealed to the Supreme Court, and finally was amnestied by Machado so he might continue his crimes. Assassins' bullets finally took revenge on him.

Antonio López, editor of a paper in Sagua la Grande, Santa Clara province, was treacherously murdered by the authorities.

Toward the end of 1930 all papers were suppressed for one month by presidential decree, a wholly illegal procedure. The result was the temporary suspension of *Diario de la Marina* for the first time in its one hundred years of existence. It is one of the oldest, most reputable and brilliantly edited papers in the Western Hemisphere. Ex-Ambassador Guggenheim is reported to own bonds of this paper, and the editor always valiantly defended him.

Among Cuban exiles are men from nearly every publication in Cuba. Several of my letters of introduction were to newspaper men of high repute—for instance one of the editors of *Carteles*—but I discovered they all had to flee the country. Especially might be mentioned among the exiles, Ramón Zaydín, ex-director of *El País,* and Rogelio Rodríguez Blanco, director of *El Camagüeyano;* Manuel Marsal, literary editor, *El País;* Salvador Diaz Versín, writer for *El País.* The latter for having written up the Rubiera assassination was marked for death. One of the government agents detailed to murder him phoned a prior warning, and he fled on the *Cristobal Colón.*

All happenings of course are officially denied in the most categorical way, so that most Americans become utterly confused as to what is actually occuring in Cuba. Only occasionally is there a decided boomerang for the Cuban government, as occurred when Secretary of State, Orestes Ferrara, sent the following letter to the *New York Times,* which promptly published a conclusive reply that forbade further comment: [2]

"To the Editor of *The New York Times:*
"Your Mr. Porter in his article in *The Times* of Feb. 4, among other things, says:
" 'Evidence of the misuse of the ley de fuga was advanced recently by the publication of a picture of a murdered student in a Cuban newspaper. Although the police said that he had been shot when trying to escape, the picture showed him lying in the street with his hands and feet bound. The newspaper editor who published the picture took asylum immediately in a foreign legation under the Latin-American treaty providing this haven of refuge for political offenders.'
"Please ask Mr. Porter the name of the paper that published the picture, the name of the editor who took asylum

[2] *New York Times,* February 9, 1933.

and in what legation he took it. All is pure fiction. Porter could not prove anything of the kind.

"ORESTES FERRARA,

"Havana, Feb. 7, 1933.   *Secretary of State.*"

Mr. Porter's reply to Dr. Ferrara is as follows:

"The name of the paper which published the picture referred to by Dr. Ferrara is *El Pais* of Havana in its issue of Dec. 31, 1932.

"The picture, seven columns wide by four and one-half inches deep at the top of the first page, showed the body of the 17-year-old student, Juan M. Gonzáles Rubiera, lying in the street with his hands and feet bound.

"The name of the editor is Enrique Pizzi of de Porras, night managing editor of *El Pais*.

"Immediately following publication of the picture, he went into hiding, part of the time in the Uruguayan Legation and part of the time in private houses, and returned to work toward the end of January, telling his confreres that he had received assurances from Dr. Ferrara, through an intermediary, that he would not be molested by the police.

"According to reliable information in the writer's possession, he was arrested on Jan. 31 and is now held incommunicado in Principe Fortress in Havana."

It is impossible, for reasons of space, to give even a representative list of professors, lawyers, doctors, businessmen, students, labor leaders, political leaders, newspapermen, intellectuals and others held in jail for from two months to two years. Personally I know over one hundred labor leaders held for two years without trial. All are thus held, except those illegally sentenced by military tribunals, a procedure thrice declared unconstitutional by the Supreme Court. The number in jail is variously estimated at from 2,000 to 10,000 or more. If the government admits an excess of 1,000 political prisoners from Oriente province alone, and there are six provinces in Cuba not including the Isle of Pines, an approximate idea can be gathered of the total number affected. Yet Machado had the effrontery in March, 1926, to tell *New York Times* correspondent Russell Porter that only six political prisoners were behind bars. This number would not even include the student's directorate in jail since the closing of the university.

When the *New York Times* announces that eighty professors were arrested at one time, or that 52 arrests were made in a small town in Havana province, one can realize that arrests, like assassinations, are often wholesale. And when one reads in the *New York Times* (March 12, 1931) that of the 180 prisoners sent to the Isle of Pines penitentiary (a place inspected on its opening by the Pan-American Congress delegates in 1928) only 67 were reported to have arrived, some understanding of the possible fate of prisoners and their families, quite aside from torture, starvation and other trials, can be reached.

Among these prisoners are women from the best families of Cuba; one such, Mariana de la Torre, was condemned to death, a sentence reduced to fourteen years. Only the valiant efforts of Virginia Lee Boone of the Women's International League for Peace and Freedom and the American Spanish War Veterans threatening after a certain date to go to Havana and march in uniform on the prison, finally forced Ambassador Guggenheim to take action in her behalf and secure her release and deportation.

But there will not be so many prisoners in the future. Commandant Jomarrón of Oriente province has instructed soldiers and police to shoot without trial all persons found in possession of explosives or "materials from which explosives can be made. . . ." Machado has asked his hand-picked Congress to extend this as a law to the whole island.

Typical of Machado hypocrisy when such decisions are made are such press announcements as that in the *New*

York Times, December 1, that he had reëstablished constitutional guarantees, lifting martial law—except in the capital—for the first time in two years.

"Only the high responsibilities of maintenance of public order restrain me" from lifting it in Havana, he stated, and he pleaded that his opponents now organize an opposition political party under the terms of the law.

As a matter of fact no change was made in the administration of affairs by the army; military supervisors were appointed as usual; three new ones were named January 27 for Santiago, Iribara, and Caibarien; and official assassinations occurred in even greater number after this date.

Among prisoners released but forced into exile besides those already mentioned might be named ex-President Mario G. Menocal, any number of professors, some of whom have since hired out as common laborers; Dr. Eduardo Chibás, ex-President of the Rotary Club, and Dr. Pedro Herrera Sotolongo, long held incommunicado after successfully arguing the unconstitutionality of the military courts' jurisdiction over civilians, the arbitrary closing of the university, and executive decrees prohibiting political meetings.

The Cubans are now recalling the words of their negro patriot, General Antonio Maceo: "Liberty is not begged. It is won with the edge of the *machete*."

XVII BULLETS FOR BOOKS

1 FIAT LUX

BEFORE MACHADO COULD CON-
solidate his power, he had to destroy Cuba's educational
system almost in entirety.

The university was closed in 1927-28; again from
1930-33. During the latter years, the island has been deprived of nearly all educational facilities; professors and
teachers, if not in jail or in exile or murdered, are without
employment; the few still employed have not been paid.
The children of eight years of high-school and college have
been shut out into the street—not to mention those since
graduating from elementary schools—probably never to
complete their education. For three years no grammar-
school child has gone on to high-school, has had to abandon hope of further education. A generation of Cuba's
youth is growing up in darkness, schooled only in violence
and murder. The clique in power hates education, cares
only for military dictatorship but serious future problems
are being raised for stable responsible government in Cuba.

The University of Havana, on a high hill between the
center of the city and the aristocratic Vedado, has an imposing main stairway, impressive buildings amid beautiful
gardens. But to-day, for the first time since founded by the
Dominican Fathers in 1792, the buildings are closed and
deserted—something that did not even occur under Spain's
iron rule when daily the students were agitating for independence. To-day the students no longer sing their way up

and down the hill; the gardens are overrun with weeds. Armed soldiers guard the various entrances, lifting gun and bayonet against every one who approaches too close. Since September, 1930, the main patio has been converted into an encampment of tents.

This situation, according to the Guggenheim fellow, Herminio Portel-Vilá, is the result of "one of the most gallant and dignified struggles for freedom and decency ever fought on the soil of Cuba."

The Cuban students have a long tradition of fighting for good causes. They were the first, in their papers *Alma Mater* and *Youth,* to inveigh against the Machado excesses. As early as 1927 the entire Student Directorate, along with other students and leading intellectuals, were expelled and jailed, and the university closed. Again in 1928. During the Pan-American Congress, attended by Coolidge, Hughes and Morrow, to avoid any protests, students were temporarily jailed.

Shortly after, a gang of police entered the home of the aged philosopher and patriot, Enrique José Varona, to beat up a group of students visiting him. Soldiers seized the university. The rector resigned; Dr. Ramón Grau San Martín, professor of physiology, refused to continue teaching surrounded by soldiers; and he along with Dr. Guillermo Portela, law-professor, was thrown into the Isle of Pines penitentiary. Student proclamations were now issued from the "University Armory" to indicate that the institution had been converted into an army post. Many students were expelled. Machado had the student Mella assassinated in Mexico. Other student leaders had to go into hiding or exile.

Machado had been hopefully spending vast sums, "involving hundreds of thousands of dollars of useless graft" to erect new buildings and beautify the gardens—to build, as the students said, "a civilization of stones and cement." On the main tower a large tablet honored Machado for these enterprises; the students defaced it with mud and rocks. Machado could not find the culprits, but hurled all student leaders into jail.

During September, 1930, Cuban intellectuals planned to render national homage to Dr. Varona on the fiftieth anniversary of his philosophical teaching. Various professors and the students prepared to parade to his home. Unexpectedly the university grounds were surrounded by police; soldiers were hidden in the Crisántemo garden near Varona's home.

The students organized their parade outside, but after a few blocks were ridden down from ambush by mounted soldiers. Rafael Trejo, brilliant senior law-student, was shot in the back. Subsequently his father was arrested and sent to the Isle of Pines; and as Trejo became ever more a martyr figure, in February, 1933, his mother was sent to Principe Castle.

In the same mêlée in which Trejo lost his life, the student Pablo de la Torriente had his head split open, and after miraculous recovery, continued to be tortured in the Isle of Pines prison, where he remains to this day. Other students were wounded and maltreated. The professor, Dr. Juan Marinello, attempting to stop further beating of wounded Torriente, was arrested and put in a convict's uniform in Principe Castle. Marinello, subsequently released, was rearrested for defending as a lawyer twenty girl students who were sent to the Isle of Pines. He was condemned to one hundred days' imprisonment, but remained there until September, 1932, when I visited him. He then feared to stir from his home because of danger of assassination. In February, 1933, he was rearrested and after several weeks deported.

A few days after the Trejo incident, 300 professors met in the Engineering College to pledge their sympathy to the students and to back them in their fight for constitutional government. All these professors, including those of the preparatory schools—among them 70-year-old Dr. J. A. Rodríguez, for forty-two years professor of Spanish literature, and Dr. Méndez Pelayo, the outstanding authority on Spanish grammar in all Latin America—were immediately and illegally dismissed. Many were jailed or murdered. Dr. Costales Latau, eminent surgeon and teacher, Secretary of the Surgical Society of Cuba and member of the American Surgical Society, was thrust incommunicado in dark Principe Castle. Many of those jailed have been imprisoned ever since, despite the fact that this and the closing of the university which followed, were repeatedly declared unconstitutional acts by the Supreme Court. Many of these professors are to-day, if out of jail, in dire poverty; many are working at manual labor. Dr. Pedro Miguel, Cuba's leading mathematician, is doing bookkeeping; his children are being cared for in the homes of his former students. Dr. Victor Rodríguez, anthropologist, is now a baker; Dr. Rodríguez García depends on public charity. Among exiles are aged Carlos de la Torre, Ramón Grau San Martín, Dr. Carlos Findlay, son of the renowned Cuban doctor who discovered the cause of yellow fever, R. Márquez, Ramón Zaydín, Ramiro Capablanca, Fernández Conchesco, Pedro Cue, Guillermo Portela, Ricardo Dolz. Sixteen of Cuba's most brilliant professors are in exile in the United States, some of them literally starving.

The students of all high and normal schools, and of the commercial and industrial schools, although some of these institutions had already been put under military supervisors, continued to hold meetings and otherwise protest. Even girl students distributed manifestoes. Two girls had their ribs broken by the police. But despite the closing of all these institutions, despite police brutalities, opposition exasperated, Machado called out the army and swept the students off the streets, even broke up the religious services in memory of Trejo in Our Lady of Mount Carmel Church.

After Trejo's assassination, the government demanded

his body in order to obviate further student manifestations
at the funeral. The students armed themselves and swore
to die rather than comply. The government desisted, but
literally surrounded the cortege with machine-guns.

2 BORAH TO THE RESCUE

In behalf of three imprisoned
students, Rubén León, Ramiro Valdés Daussa and Rafael
Escalona, William Borah, April 11, 1932, humanely lifted
his voice in the American Senate. After describing the manner in which they were being held, he said: "On the 15th
of this month, they will be tried or court-martialed by a
military tribunal, and the lawyers retained by their families
for their defense have been given 24 hours for the examination of the proceedings and the constitution of their case.
The proceedings are spread over a stack formed by over
1,000 pages of foolscap paper. . . . I think it is a matter
which we cannot . . . owing to our connection with Cuba,
be indifferent. . . . I shall watch the procedure with interest, to see whether in this enlightened age the practices
of five centuries ago are revived." Machado personally
denied the facts, but despite Borah's protest, the students
were hurried through a drum-head trial, and to-day are on
the Isle of Pines; and as if in retaliation for Borah's protest, are subjected to especially vicious treatment.

Students of both sexes, under the legal age, are kept in
prison alongside of hardened criminals. All efforts to obtain
habeas corpus because of their minority have been barred.
Many students are held in grim Principe Castle. On the
night of December 30, 1931, the military authorities, wishing to do away with one of the students who had been a
witness to the government-seizure and assassination of the
student Félix Ernesto Apízar, armed the criminals in the
castle and launched them against the defenseless student
prisoners. César Andino had his intestines and kidneys cut

open and died; Manuel Varona Loredo was knifed in the back and his body stamped upon; Rafael Argüelles was knifed in the arm, had a wrist broken and suffered other injuries; four or five others were gravely wounded. At 11 o'clock the heavy bars of the castle were opened and a chain of ambulances packed with wounded men started, a sad caravan, toward the Columbia Military Hospital. There have been eye-witness and survivors. I quote Dr. José Fresnada, a young Havana lawyer who went through the horror of that night and lived to tell the tale:

"It is eight o'clock at night December 30, 1931. There is silence in the prison. In a long and narrow gallery, where the dampness is felt in all its intensity and where darkness prevails, there are sheltered about 70 political prisoners: young students whose only crime is that of being oppositionists to the Dictator's Government. The gallery is known as Gallery No. 2, but in the prison's argot it is called the 'lions' cage,' due to its tragic history and construction. There we are lying on small and uncomfortable canvas beds in a bitter cold that is making every one shiver. In the silence and tranquillity of the night something weird is felt. The phantom of frightfulness begins to worry us.

"It was exactly ten minutes past eight when Sergeant Ramón Cabrera entered the gallery in an aggressive manner. He went toward one of our companion's beds and, using harsh words and rough actions, tried to drive out the occupant. A group of the prisoners protested at this brutality and in less than a minute, upon an agreed signal, we received on our heads a shower of blackjack and hammer blows, the wounds of knives and other sharp instruments, inflicted by a gang of criminals.

"Three criminal prisoners, Antonio Cortizo, José Ramón and Ara, the first one secretary to the prison chief, Army Lieutenant Ambrosio Diaz Galup, with guns in hand, are commanding over 100 criminals in this assault. The order is clearly heard: 'Finish them quickly! Kill the whole bunch of them so that we will never hear them protest any longer of Machado!' And this gang of murderers, armed with knives, blackjacks, etc., were shouting like demons, hitting here and there and sweeping the gallery.

"No one remained on his feet. Shouts of horror filled the air; on the floor and in broken beds lay many of our companions, bleeding and broken. These tragic minutes will never be forgotten by us. The Government had mysteriously committed murders, had also hanged many defenseless citizens but the only thing missing from its records was a cowardly and premeditated assault on prisoners, within the prison walls."

Doctor Gonzalo Freyre de Andrade, who protested in Congress and out against this brutality, was subsequently assassinated. Other protesting professors were arrested.

High-school girls, even from the best families in Havana, were dumped into common criminal cells, as were also old ladies, such as Apolonia Gomila de Barcelo, mother of a student hiding from the police, and Señora Súarez Solís, guilty of the "terrible crime" of laying flowers on the tomb of Trejo. When the castle was filled up with students and professors, many were sent to the Isle of Pines penitentiary without trial. Most are held incommunicado.

Despite such jailings, the students continued their protests, especially the girls. One day a group of them appeared before the Palace with large placards: "RESIGN!" A few days later, the police released hardened women criminals and prostitutes and organized these harpies into the *Porra Femenina,* or Female Blackjack Gang, to attack such girl protesters. They descended on the girl students with tobacco knives, sliced up their flesh and stripped them in the streets.

One Machado official had the courage to speak out against such barbarism, M. M. Gómez, the Mayor of Havana, who still insisted that the police by law should take orders from him, not the army. He protested in his "double character of citizen and mayor" to the Secretary of Interior, bringing to his attention "the deplorable condition . . . that affronts our civilization. A group of women of low standing in society is stationed around the Presidential Palace, armed and perfidiously prepared by miserable men of their class to assault and attack the ladies of our best class, brutally wounding and tearing off their clothes, leaving them almost naked on our streets. The police show no desire to respond to their calls for help and stop the outrages. Such ignominious acts . . . [were] never registered in . . . our history, not even during the excess hate and drunkenness of the Colonial volunteers."

Cuban women have taken a brilliant part in opposition to the dictatorship. Among such is Señorita Clarita Porcet, a professional woman who had to hide out for her life in a foreign legation, and finally made her escape to the United States. "It is ambitious," she has stated, "this program of a country that realizes its past political shortcomings—and that suffers at this moment one of the cruelest tyrannies that America has ever known. It calls for sacrifices unlimited, but we are ready to do them . . . are doing them every day."

The most prominent women of Cuba have demonstrated and have signed various petitions to the diplomatic corps, and their manifesto, in which they protested against the conduct of Ambassador Guggenheim, was read by Senator Walsh in the Senate. For that manifesto many suffered tragic abuses.

To appease them, Machado hinted at offering woman's suffrage. But they have publicly denounced such a proposal at this time, holding that any motion passed by an illegal congress would be illegal and farcical at a moment when free elections are a myth.

THE CRIMES OF MACHADO

3 ATARES CASTLE

About 200 students have been killed. Among earlier ones in 1931 were Rafael Santiesteban, June; Eusebio Hidalgo, Leclere and Feleites, August; Apízar, December.

Apízar was "taken for a ride" after his arrest by the authorities. His official murder was witnessed. His mother visited every police-station in Havana, asking for his body on her knees; it never came to light.

In February, 1933, Mariano Gonzáles Rubiera, sixteen-year-old boy, Pío Alvarez Alvarez, and Mariano Gonzáles Gutierrez (engineering student) were taken to police headquarters. Later their bodies were found in different points of Havana, brutally mutilated. The police claimed they had tried to escape. But the body of the high-school student Gonzáles Rubiera was found with both legs bound. Gonzáles Gutierrez, a Spaniard, also a minor, was found shot at Carvajal and Leonor Streets in El Cerro suburb. Before having been killed, both wrists were broken, arms and belly sliced and his forearm veins severed. Alvarez' body was delivered at 12:20 in the morning at a hospital by persons unknown, powder showing on his temple wounds.

Machado assumed full responsibility for all these police-assassinations. He "insisted" to Russell Porter of the *New York Times* (February 4, 1933), "the killings were bona fide applications of the Ley de Fuga, necessitated by the fact that the student when apprehended, preferred death to arrest and chose to fight or try to escape rather than submit to arrest, justifying the police use of violence." Porter adds, but "the crude and brazen way in which many of the killings have been committed . . . has led the public to discount the official explanations."

On the outskirts of Havana, topping a hill overlooking the city, stands star-shaped Atares Castle, erected by the Spanish governor Antonio Maria Bucareli in 1776. There in 1851 Crittendon of Kentucky and his fifty volunteers, who came with López, were shot, and their bodies dragged at the heels of Spanish horses through the mire and over the cobbles. Many violent scenes have occurred under those ancient walls, but few surpass the horrors that are now enacted in its shadow by Cuban army officers.

Its broad naves have been selected as torture chambers by the Machado régime, and its narrow dark cells have harbored sixteen-year-old students, aged professors, men and women unsegregated, people of every category from prostitutes to society women, from murderers to philosophers. Many, after torture, come out bundles of rag and bones.

Many are the liberty-loving Cubans who have entered there; many have come out on a bier, their bodies lacerated and broken.

Let one of those sufferers tell his own tale, a letter of April 17, 1931, by Ramón Betancourt y Garcia, public proctor of Havana:

"I was taken to the Atares Castle. I was imprisoned in an underground cell. The door was of heavy bars. The cell was of triangular form, with heavy walls; horribly damp, full of cobwebs and insects and totally dark. Its floor was deep in mud.

"At night voracious rats came out of their holes and helped the mosquitoes and the cold, which goes into your bones, to make it impossible to get any sleep.

"In this Dante's hell I remained for several days.

"Then I was taken to a high officer who roughly questioned me:

" 'Who is Rogers and who is Cuco?'

"I answered: 'I do not know them.'

" 'To which one did you give the keys to the city hall, where the bomb exploded?'

" 'I never gave any keys to any one and I have not taken any part in this matter.'

" 'All right,' he said, 'you are trying to make a fool out of me but to-night we will be more explicit!'

"Night fell.

"A corporal and a sergeant took me into a dark chamber where my ankles were bound to my shoulders. Several of my bones were dislocated.

"I cried out in pain.

" 'Talk and I will set you loose,' said the officer. But, as I had nothing to say, they kept on pulling the ropes. A little later they put out all lights and left me there.

"I cannot say how long I remained there until I began to hear distant steps. Three men came in, and again the officer requested me to 'tell the truth.' I could hardly talk, but protested my innocence in a very low voice. Finally they untied the ropes!

"I remained prostrated.

"Twenty-one days have elapsed and I am still sick and showing in my body the black brands of the ropes and rifles."

Young Proenza, not a student, but close to a group of more radical students, had carried on considerable propaganda. Early in 1932, a neighborhood child was sent by a secret-police agent to Proenza's house with a package. It contained a bomb and when opened, the explosion blew the child to bits and horribly mutilated the face of one of the Proenza sisters.

Another sister hastened to take refuge in the Mexican Embassy, and after a near scandalous break in relations with Mexico, was given a passport to visit relatives in Guatemala. A third sister fled to relatives in Oriente province, but was arrested by two soldiers who drowned her in a nearby river and boasted about it unpunished.

In official communiqué, the rector of the university, Ricardo Dolz, brought various of these acts to the attention of the government. Machado, after originally closing the university and filling it with soldiers, subsequently to obey various Supreme Court decisions, declared it open, though no courses are given, the professors murdered or exiled, and no student allowed to pass by the armed guards. Dolz made an official statement showing why the professors could not function and ordered the university technically closed. According to law, his statement had to be published in the *Gaceta Oficial*. It was printed in *Edición Extraordinaria*, No. 15-A, July 13, 1932, but only one copy was circulated. Before the end of the year, Dolz had to take refuge in a foreign legation to escape the fate of Freyre de Andrade.

These students and professors are as much martyrs to the cause of Cuban liberty as those early patriots whose memory America has long honored. They are victims not of Bloody Weyler and Spanish rule, but of a high representative of American power, public utility and banking interests.

April 14, 1933, following the explosion of seventeen bombs in Havana, the government's blind and brutal reaction was immediate. Two of the Valdés Daussa boys, fourteen and fifteen years of age, brother of one of the students for whom Borah unsuccessfully raised his voice, and some fifteen others unreported by the press, were foully assassinated. The *New York Times* gives a vivid description by its correspondent, J. D. Phillips:

"The shooting took place at 2:45 P.M. on the Avenida de los Presidentes in the Vedado residential section. It was the first shooting of a student in the daytime as a reprisal by police.

"According to the usual custom of applying the dreaded ley de fuga the students were taken to the spot in an automobile by secret service men, pushed out of the car and told to run. Sharpshooters, mostly negroes, posted on a high cliff which overlooked both sides of the street at this point, where escape was absolutely impossible, opened a withering fire on the two youths.

"Your correspondent, standing on a balcony at his residence, was an eyewitness of the killing of one student. The first fusillade missed the boy and he started running and shouting, 'Don't shoot any more.'

"Despite his cries for mercy a second volley followed. The victim, hit in the head by bullets, staggered, ran some twenty feet and collapsed, as a third volley poured into his body.

"The ununiformed negroes who had done the fatal shooting came down the side of the cliff with rifles and revolvers in their hands, to inspect the body, after which they sauntered off, unmolested by the uniformed national police, who arrived on the scene immediately.

"At the same time other snipers, posted further down on the same cliff, had shot another student, who apparently ran in the opposite direction and was not in your correspondent's view. This youth, according to other eyewitnesses, is said to have been badly wounded, but, still alive, was immediately thrown into a car reported to have been from the Secret Service Department, which had brought them to the spot. He was taken to the emergency hospital, where, it is asserted, he died. However, police and hospital authorities refuse to give out any information concerning the victim.

"The Valdez brothers are said to be the sons of Leon Valdez, in the Paymaster Department of the treasury, who were suspected of being connected with the A.B.C. student revolutionary organization.

"Several other young students among those picked up by the police during last night's bombing campaign are reported to have been killed by government agents in the different parts of the city, but these reports so far are not confirmed. The police refuse to give out any information either concerning the names or the disposition of those detained, and all the departments of the government have combined in suppressing all possible news of terroristic activities.

"Local newspapers are rigidly censored by the military

authorities and are not permitted to print anything in regard to anti-administration activities throughout the republic. However, open warfare beween students and the police goes on, with many casualties on both sides, and the situation here is growing more alarming each day.

"Since the intensive bombing campaign began last night the reserve police have been equipped with rifles and stationed at strategic points. Those policemen patrolled the city to-day. . . .

"At least a score of other young students were taken into custody last night. Three of them were removed to-day to Atares Castle."

The list of such events grows wearisome. Only a small number are ever reported in the American press, principally those occurring in Havana.

XVIII DECLINE OF CUBA

1 DOWNHILL

SUMMARIZE THE MAJOR FORCES
at work in Cuba during the independence period:

Economic. Divorce of the Cuban people from the natural
resources on a scale far greater than during the Spanish
colonial period. 1900 to 1917 marks the gradual infiltra-
tion of American capital, the pace ever quickening toward
the end of the span. 1917 to 1922 marks a virtual tidal wave
of American capital investment. Those years also mark the
beginning of bankers' control over sugar and other resources. By the 1922 crisis J. P. Morgan and Company,
Chase National Bank, National City Bank, and allied Canadian institutions moved into dominance, ever expanding
their equities in the industrial and agricultural enterprises.
1922 to 1933 marks the definite consolidation of bankers'
control. Through the Electric Bond and Share Company
and the International Telephone and Telegraph Company,
close to the house of Morgan, public utilities were gathered into the fold. Most railroads, not in English hands,
are controlled by the Tarafa-Woodin-Rubens-Lakin-Rocke-
feller combination, closely harmonized with the American
Car and Foundry Company and the National City Bank.
Cubans own far less of the wealth of their country than in
1895.

Political. Cuba began with a government modeled on
American institutions. The United States, through the
Platt Amendment, has maintained an inefficient protec-

[295]

torate. Utilizing Menocal, American sugar-interests, close to the National City Bank, enjoyed almost personal rule. In 1917 we kept Menocal in office against the wishes of the Cubans better to help us make the world safe for democracy. Similarly, Zayas in 1921.

By 1925, Machado, though popular, directly represented the public utility interests. More and more alienated from the people, the government has become an armed institution to keep the people in subjection, increasingly tyrannical and corrupt.

Cuba has progressively declined since independence. Its best government was that of Estrada Palma; its worst, that of Gerardo Machado. Except as a mint for American exploitation, Cuba has gone down hill ever more rapidly; indeed greed of profits has so undermined its institutions and industries that it has deteriorated even as a place to be exploited. The rapidity and degree of decline, however, bears direct relation to the influx of and domination by American capital. Despite Insulls and Mitchells at home, most Americans retain the naïve notion that abroad they sprout wings and are only interested in great humanitarian efforts, setting backward peoples upon the road of civilization so perfected in these United States, never in mulcting other nations.

Cuba has been bled white. Every activity looking toward the benefit of the Cuban people, the building up of a sound and happy commonwealth, has withered at the roots. Cuba has become more worm-eaten ever since we released it after the strenuous Wood cleaning up. The canker has grown right through the Magoon administration to Machado in 1933. Cuba's brightest days were right after independence; her darkest days those of 1933.

One of our great American faiths is education. We started earnestly in Cuba, founded schools right and left, scrubbed and carbolic-acided and whitewashed and filled with benches old Spanish barracks. Since then the number of schools has decreased. Illiteracy has increased. The school system has become a source of graft, a political patronage machine.

We need but turn to the overwhelming data of Dr. Fernando Ortiz, Carlos Manuel Trelles and others. For before 1924, I use chiefly Ortiz' data. The Wood census revealed 66 percent of illiteracy. By 1908 this had been cut to nearly 30 percent. By Zayas it had risen to 53 percent; by 1924 to 50 percent for whites, 55 percent for blacks. It is now estimated at over 60 percent.

In 1900 16 percent of the population matriculated, a figure surpassing Norway, France, Australia and Japan; in 1924, only 9 percent; in 1932 5 percent. In 1900 under Wood, 75 children for every 1,000 inhabitants attended school; in 1920 only 50; in 1924, 32; in 1932, 12. By 1924 only one child in a hundred reached the fifth grade. To-day only one in 250. In 1919 out of 234,000 students, only 71 completed their studies, or 0.3 percent; in 1932, not one. By 1924 not a single school had been built in any town in Cuba, only eighty in the country. In that year, $750,000 annually had to be paid out to rent unsatisfactory locales. Machado built a few more schools, spent vast sums involving much graft on showy university buildings, now closed for three years.

Cuba does not have a single rural agricultural school and but one industrial school in Havana, now closed. The American negroes and Indians attend far better schools than the average Cuban child. To-day a whole generation is growing up in darkness, the masses no better fitted for self-government than when they came out from under Spain's heel. The number of teachers increased under Zayas, who spent far more than Wood, the number of schools and pupils declined. Everything educational has gone backward under Machado. Half the grade schools are closed or empty; teachers go unpaid. Only a few professors who accept the Machado tyranny still occasionally receive salaries.

Justice has steadily deteriorated. Given the arbitrary political practices, amnesties often are to be advocated. Yet these have increased in number and have included hardened criminals as well as political offenders. Indeed the former often are more favored than the latter. Such amnesties have occurred increasingly at election time in order to free criminals to intimidate the voter.

Through the period of Zayas, the republic passed sixteen amnesty laws, including every type of delinquency. Under Machado more amnesties have been granted than by any other predecessor. This has attested to both the severity and the hypocrisy of his régime, for while criminals were released definitively, political offenders were usually soon rearrested or otherwise disposed of. Estrada Palma granted six special pardons monthly; Magoon, 46; Gómez, 29; Menocal, 30; Zayas, 33. The Machado record will probably surpass that of Magoon. In 54 months Estrada Palma pardoned six assassins; Gómez in 52 months, 15; Menocal in 96 months, 50; and Zayas in his first 25 months, 55—more than Menocal in eight years. The Machado statistics are still incomplete; but he has released many more. In October, 1916, the month before election, Menocal pardoned 231 persons. In September, 1920, just before elections, 75, of which 19 were murderers. Zayas in October, 1922, just before elections, pardoned 63. Machado has used the same election tactics. Numerous hardened criminals have been released to attack opponents. His Porra is honeycombed with them, male and female. Criminals have been utilized to attack and kill student prisoners in their cells. In 1922 20 percent of all postulated candidates had penal records. In Cuba gangster elements have not merely supported candidates; increasingly they have become candidates and officeholders.

The Chamber of Deputies and Senate have become a refuge for criminal elements. Increasingly their members have been demanded by the courts for crimes, but increasingly, on the ground of Congressional immunity, this has been denied. Out of 700 court petitions up to the first part of Zayas' administration, only three members were turned over to be tried; Estrada Palma, 42 denials; Gómez, 32; Menocal, 279; the first part of Zayas' administration, 656. Judges under Machado have been too terrorized even to petition; besides for nearly two years they have been supplanted by drumhead army courts.

Justice in the courts has steadily disappeared, ever more difficult to convict any friend of the government, easier to convict any political enemy. Under Machado people are sentenced or murdered without trial.

Take the following quotation from the *Havana-American News* (December 31, 1932), telling about the police-murder of student Mariano Gonzales Rubiera:

"Judge Vianelo of Marianao, who started proceedings for 'murder against persons unknown' upon the finding of the corpse yesterday, and upon learning that young Rubiera was last seen in custody of the police, resigned jurisdiction over the case on the grounds that the police, being part of the military establishment under martial law, cannot be questioned for their acts by any but a military court."

For every 100 cases of murder or discharge of firearms up to 1924, but 27 convictions were obtained; and of all crimes, but 14. The record is far worse under Machado. The population of Cuba has increased at the rate of 3.3 percent per annum; murders at the rate of 20 percent up to 1924; 28 percent to date. Thieving has increased at the rate of 10 percent. Criminality has been steadily on the increase. The accentuating of despotic practices, leading to greater disrespect for abused authority, has merely increased crime. To-day the greatest illegal crime agent is the Machado government itself.

Although Wood attempted to modernize Cuban prisoners and introduce up-to-date treatment, Machado has reverted to the use of the worst prison-holes and medieval castles in the country, completely devoid of sanitation, dark, humid, and filthy. Male prisoners have been permitted to attack women political prisoners. The new prison constructed by Machado on the Isle of Pines, while sanitary, ignored most modern penology teachings.

Cuban morality has steadily been undermined, gambling ever on the increase. Wood started the ball rolling with his Jai Alai concession. Gómez introduced cock-fighting. Steinhart promoted the race-track and the Casino, outlet for the élite. The lottery has grown more corrupt, more linked with political spoils. This practice, begun by Gómez, became more vicious under Menocal and Zayas, and finally reached its worst phase as a means of corrupting deputies and senators under Machado.

In the recent Cuban national Sweepstakes lottery, sanctioned by the Cuban government and run off March 12, 1933, according to the *New York Times,* March 31, 6,500,-000 tickets were placed on sale with some 18,000 agents in the United States; more than 3,000,000 were estimated sold; but only 161,000 tickets were shuffled in the drawing, of which but 37,000 were of American ownership. All news of this gigantic fraud was suppressed in the Cuban papers.

Toward the end of Menocal's government, Asbert, Mayor of Havana, murdered a critic of his flagrant gambling dens in the very heart of the city. Under Machado these joints are run or profited from by high officials, and police, army and civilian.

Prostitution has been ever on the increase; Havana has more public prostitution in proportion to population than Paris, Berlin or Marseilles. Open cribs exist in the very heart of the city, interspersed with business houses and private dwellings. Open pornographic movies and naked rumba shows are maintained by public officials.

From 1913-14 crimes of corruption of minors increased fourfold. Rape doubled. From 1901 to 1923 suicides increased sevenfold. In 1899, 382 suicides were reported; in

1922-23, 985; in 1931-32 over a thousand; in New York the very high suicide rate is 132 to the million; in Cuba—and the suicide rate is very low in most Latin countries—328 in 1922-23.

This decline carries on through the economic scheme. In 1919, 27.4 percent of the sugar crop was from Cuban-owned Centrales, 13.9 from Spanish; 2.6 Cuban-American; 56.1 other foreign. By 1929, 69.9 percent was controlled by Americans, now about 80 percent. In 1923, Americans owned 35 percent of the values in sugar plantations; now through ownership or lease, about 80 percent. In 1923 Americans owned or controlled 16.72 percent of the territory of Cuba; to-day about 60 percent.

In 1926 Ramiro Guerra wrote: [1] "A people subjected politically but which owns the land and cultivates it, can go, as Cuba did, to independence and liberty; a free people which alienates its land and abandons its cultivation to others goes inevitably along the road of economic servitude and social and political decadence."

In 1923 the national debt crept up from nothing in 1902 to $140,000,000 under Zayas. Machado contracted $9,000,-000 from Morgan; $42,000,000 in sugar bonds; $80,000,000 from the Chase National viz., $20,000,000 serial work certificates; $40,000,000 bonds (out of an $80,000,000 issue); $20,000,000 credit; $20,000,000 gold certificates to public work contractors. The floating debt is estimated at $40,-000,000 excluding bank and work advances.

Budgets have steadily increased without proportionate public benefit. Though slightly less these later Machado years, he has spent far more than his predecessors by increasing the debt. Now, faced with the impossibility of floating a new loan, if he meets the foreign debt payments and pays the army, he will have scarcely any funds left the coming year for any other purposes. Cuba has spent about two billion dollars since the founding of the Republic, with no

[1] *Azucar y población*, 143.

proportionate collective benefit. Menocal, in eight years, spent $600,000,000, more than all his predecessors together, and this without counting in his $70,000,000 floating debt. Machado increased the public debt about four-fifths the amount ever contracted by all his predecessors combined. Cuba to-day owes more interest on the public debt than in the colonial epoch, when the fantastic charges abolished by the Treaty of Paris were chalked up against its exchequer.

Militarism has increased extravagantly. Estrada Palma began with a small police-force. Magoon started an army of 5,000. Gómez increased it to 10,000, Menocal to 18,000, Machado to 20,000 but in addition established various Rural Guard corps and militia and militarized the police, in all probably over 30,000. To-day it is the heaviest drain upon the public treasury next to foreign debt payments. It is not used to defend the country but as a personal body-guard to tyranny.

Cuban life and social organization are disintegrating. Cuba is descending rapidly toward barbarism, has been descending in that direction ever since independence. All our solicitude, our dollars, our meddling—since they but furthered economic subjugation—have but helped it down the chute. The more rapidly American capital has entered, the more rapidly Cuba has declined.

The words of Irene Wright, written in 1912, are even truer to-day than when penned: [2]

"At Roosevelt's command (not by the will of a non-existent Cuban people), the Cuban Republic rose in a night, on soil owned by others than its electors, swarming with a bureaucracy these foreigners and producing Cubans have had to support ever since. There it stands, tottering and pregnant with militant trouble as was the Trojan horse of old; when it finally collapses to its inevitable destruction, let Americans in hearing the crash recall distinctly that the Republic is not a creation of Cubans—it was neither fash-

[2] *Cuba,* 192-3.

ioned by them nor by them upheld—but on the contrary, it is of all-American manufacture. Americans built it, Americans set it up again when once it fell flat. *American influence is all that sustains it at this moment.* If they discover anything to criticize in it, or its failure, let Americans remember in so criticizing that they are dealing with the work of their own hands. . . ."

2 THE BOTTOM OF THE HILL

Judged by American standards, Cuban living conditions are atrocious. Judged by Cuban standards of 1900-27, they show a far worse drop than almost any country. Judged even by the standard of survival in a tropical country, they are deplorable. To-day the mass of Cuban people do not have enough to eat. Most are in ragged clothing. Many are without even a roof.

National income and money in circulation are falling lower. Wages have been cut to insignificant amounts; unemployment is widespread. One sugar company is feeding over 7,000 unemployed persons—not so much charity as to prevent sabotage and the burning of cane-fields.

Cuba passed the million-ton sugar mark even before becoming independent; its top record is nearly six million tons; to-day it is down to two millions; and if the Chadbourne plan continues without an agreement with American, Philippine, Hawaiian and Puerto Rican producers, must drop lower. The tobacco industry had decamped the country. Cuba's trade is as low as it was before the war for independence. Our sixth largest market has been practically wiped out.

Income, money, wages—all are declining, while the cost of living increases because of ever higher taxes and tariffs. A recent sales tax and food-consumption tax adds to the poor man's burden; the last shred above minimum current government expenses is absorbed by foreign debt payments and high military costs.[3]

The two largest items in the 1932-33 budget are $9,797,-844 for the army and navy payments; and $7,320,425 in national debt payments that come out of the regular (non-public work budget). The total debt payments, however, came to nearly $25,000,000. The deficit last year, though the expenditures were cut under budget figures, was over $10,000,000. In 1933 it is estimated that income—and the Guggenheim experts advised the government this was the highest possible figure—would not be over $40,000,000. If all public works are stopped—and some contracts cannot be abrogated—Cuba will have only $7,000,000 for general expenses after the army and the debt obligations are paid. A deficit of $15,000,000 is expected. Even so, the government must choose between cutting foreign debt payments or the army. The former is the least dangerous for its continued existence. In 1899 there were 5,700 Federal employees; in

[3] Salvador Massip pointed out in the *Diario de la Marina*, September 9, 1932, that Cuban national wealth in 1902 was $600,000,000; 1925, eight billion; 1931, two billion. Bank deposits, 1902, $200,000,000; 1919, $1,200,000,000; 1926, $414,-000,000; 1932, $48,000,000. Bank clearings 1929, $950,000,000; 1931, $400,000,000; 1932 (estimated), $250,000,000; 1933 (estimated) $150,000,000. Cuba's commerce in 1902 was $148,000,000; 1925, $651,000,000; 1931, $220,000,000. This year it will be back to the 1895 figure. Trade with the United States dropped from $460,-000,000 in 1925 to $140,000,000 in 1931.

In 1928 the per capita holding of money was $49.47; in 1930, $28; December, 1931, $19; June 30, 1932, $10. Money in circulation dropped from $180,000,000 in 1928 to $72,000,000 in 1932. The *Import and Industrial Record* of Cuba gave the money in circulation January 1, 1933, at $21,000,000, the per capita holding, $5.30. Banks have declined from 112 at the end of 1929 to less than 90 at present. In January, 1933, 300 business houses were being sold for taxes.

Production statistics give another angle of the story. Sugar production was, in 1902, 850,000 tons, $34,000,000; 1925, 5,171,000 tons, $260,000,000; 1931, 2,508,000 tons, $76,000,000; 1933, 2,000,000 tons, estimated price value $14,000,000. Tobacco exports were in 1902 $406,000,000; 1927, $170,000,000; 1933, probably not $60,-000,000.

The budget:

1902	$17,500,000
1925	84,800,000
1931	76,800,000
1932	66,000,000 (including public works)

1931, over 50,000. Except for the army, most of them have gone unpaid for six months.

The total funded public debt of Cuba January 1, 1933, excluding the floating debt, was $178,000,000.[4] Since June, 1931, the government has reduced it to this figure by payment of the enormous sum in comparison to the budgets, of $33,000,000 plus $12,000,000 for interest, the internal debt, etc.—a grand total of $45,000,000 in eighteen months.[5]

The floating debt is estimated at from $35,000,000 to $50,000,000; this will probably be settled at a discount; but the bankers hope that some day it will be funded. This would permit them to get the advantage of the discount rather than the government, as was accomplished in 1923 and 1927 with the Morgan $50,000,000 and $9,000,000 loans.

[4] Cf. Chapter XXII.

[5] $88,000,000 of the outstanding bonds represent a debt still to be paid on the public works program. At that the bankers prorogued the $20,000,000 5½ percent work credit of the Chase National, due March 5, 1931, until March of this year, when payment was again postponed. June 30, 1933, is due $1,250,000, final payment on serial work certificates; the last previous amortization called for $6,500,000. June 30 notes to contractors must be faced, the first payment required being $3,000,000, the final payment being due in 1935. Last year's unpaid balances on short-term loans to meet interest and amortization on the $1,650,000 borrowed from Chase, and $1,835,000 advanced by the Standard, Sinclair and Sell-Mex Oil companies against customs duties and taxes will fall due. The public works fund revenue has declined from $18,059,340 in 1928-29 to $10,756,-486 last year, and will be still lower this year, so that further inroads on the general treasury will become necessary. The $42,000,000 debt incurred to put into effect the Chadbourne plan, Chase and National City acting as fiscal agents, was reduced to $25,519,740 January 1, 1933. This is guaranteed by sugar in warehouses and compulsory payments to make up the difference from the sugar *colonos;* but general bankruptcy may oblige the government to contribute to this refunding.

The Morgan $50,000,000 issue has been reduced to $25,202,000 (January 1, 1933); amortization runs until 1953. The $9,000,000 issue now totals $4,500,000, amortization running until 1937. A previous 1914 $10,000,000 loan has been reduced to $5,085,000, amortization running to 1949. The first $35,000,000 Speyer loan at 5 percent in 1904 has been reduced to $10,023,500, amortization, 1944. The $16,500,000 Speyer 4½s issued in 1909 have been reduced to $10,772,000, amortization running to 1949. The internal 5 percent $11,250,000 issue of 1905 has been reduced to $7,816,400.

The drop in customs receipts tells the story. In 1902, $14,781,000; 1925, $46,961,000; 1931, under $20,000,000; 1933 (estimated), $15,000,000. In 1925 customs provided over half the national revenue. In 1933 they will provide little over a fourth.

Already customs duties dropped nearly $500,000 from November estimates; and the national lottery receipts, estimated at $100,000, were only $3,814. Every effort was made to lighten the tax burdens of foreign enterprises and throw the burden on the Cuban people. The present situation still further increases internal revenues, especially on consumable articles, to staggering amounts.

The 1931 emergency tax-law was expected to bring in $20,000,000 extra; it gave $5,000,000; and it brought about business stagnation. Business taxes are now so cumbersome and heavy that operation costs are almost prohibitive. They require an army of collectors; and large amounts vanish en route to the treasury.

These burdens and the loans sanctioned by the United States government have contributed, along with the collapse of sugar and tobacco, high taxes, and political tyranny, to increase the burden of the people and precipitate them into greater misery.

Even Havana, far better off than the interior, shows much wear and tear. Centers of trade and amusement are almost empty, dull instead of joyous. The hotels are running three-fourths empty; the Sevilla-Biltmore, Inglaterra and lesser hotels have closed their doors. This year at the height of the tourist season one of the swank hotels had fewer guests than employees. Beggars and peddlers swarm, annoying people in cafés and on the streets. In previous years the government, during the tourist season, put the beggars in stockades. The past two years no funds have been available for this. The lottery venders for the national government represent the world's prize ragamuffin army. The streets are dilapidated, dirty; traffic is reduced.

Universal discontent is ever in evidence. Even three years ago when I made one of my many visits to Cuba, my taxi-driver, who did not know me from Adam, exploded hotly that the only solution for Cuba was to kill Machado. That was before the terrorist movement had even begun. Though Cubans fear to be seen in a foreigner's company for any extended time, lest police suspicions be aroused, to a foreigner even on chance acquaintance they are apt to whisper their hatred of the despotism. If this is true of the employed, it is doubly true of the unemployed.

The 1932-33 budget provides $7,239,894 for education and but $2,834,535 for sanitation; but even these meager amounts have not been spent for these purposes; most of these sums have gone to the army and to pay the foreign debt.

All public services have been curtailed, even abandoned. The sanitation budget is now too low to curb epidemics of malaria and other fevers, though news of these is strictly censored. All public hospitals have been closed. Even the leper hospital was shut down three years ago, casting the lepers back into the community.

The newspapers published a report early last year by a medical inspector of the department, that since the closing of public clinics and the lack of sanitary precautions, in some parts of the provinces 95 percent of the population was afflicted with malaria; and that an epidemic attacking 25,000 persons was raging in Pinar del Río. The government immediately ordered all further news of sanitary conditions to be censored; and shortly after the archives of the Department of Health were burned, an occurrence the government immediately laid at the door of the terrorists. This report stated that bad sanitary conditions, stagnant water, bad drains were responsible. A large percentage of the population was said to be suffering from intestinal parasites.

XIX YOUNG CUBA

1 TERRORISM

In a large business office in Cuba, in a firm composed partly of Americans, partly Cubans, sits a prominent young professional man. Though his firm has important relations with the Machado government and with large American corporations, this man's secret life is dedicated tirelessly to the overthrow of the Machado tyranny.

On a certain October day, 1932, in a certain sea-cooled restaurant, we sat quietly while I expounded my firm belief that the throwing of bombs and the assassination of government officials could only lead to more brutalities, would provide no satisfactory solution to the Cuban problem; for this man, in perfect standing in the community, a man for whom Ambassador Guggenheim even intervened when he subsequently got into trouble, is one of the major heads of the present terrorist movement which has sprung up as a result of Machado's illegal violences.

"We want to prove to the United States, which is the real master in Cuba," he declared, "that a tyrannical régime such as that of Machado does not pay even for the powerful interests; that it is dangerous and unprofitable to do business in Cuba while open violence is constantly going on. Not until the United States withdraws its support of Machado can we hope to find any solution for Cuban problems."

"The State Department declares that it is completely neutral with regard to Machado."

"Pure camouflage!" was his retort.

Some time ago Machado published an article in the *New York American* in which he accused all of his opponents, particularly the terrorists, of being Communists. But Mr. X, with whom I was so discreetly dining, declared that the Communists could not succeed in Cuba because of their lack of organization and the complete antagonism of the United States. "Your government would stamp out Communism in this country with force within a week." My companion at that time, as well as the rest of the terrorists in Cuba, as a matter of fact are not Reds, but are younger members of the oldest, most aristocratic families of Cuba. Mr. X belongs to the most exclusive clubs; he is accepted in high society; his connections are with the upper classes. Yet even those classes are bitterly against Machado.

My informant continued: "We have a list of twenty-odd government officials to be 'suppressed.' Five have already been disposed of. Those names range from police-killers to high government officials, such as Vásquez Bello, President of the Senate, intimate adviser of Machado, who was killed two days ago, and General Herrera, head of the army."

My answer was: "In retaliation for the killing of Police-Commissioner Calvo, the government jails innocent people right and left and killed over forty people. No sooner was Vásquez Bello killed than government agents again murdered and jailed."

"We Cubans, unfortunately, have to learn to kill and be killed before the tyranny of Machado can be ended. You have not had your sons, your father, your brothers cold-bloodedly assassinated by the government, otherwise you would understand why we are obliged to resort to violence. We have no press, we have no vote, we cannot assemble, we cannot raise revolt, because only Machado is allowed to buy arms in the United States. We did not start these tactics until we had been abused, trampled upon, the constitution overthrown—with the connivance of your State Department. The first bombs were placed by police provocateurs to serve as an excuse to arrest and kill us. We might as well have the game as well as the name—"

Only seven men in Cuba know Mr. X's name in connection with his present activities; and even these seven may not all know of the terroristic end. Yet his orders, at that time, were carried out by thousands. A clandestine newspaper, *La Denuncia,* is published; and he communicated to his followers by a secret code known to the members of the shock brigades of his organization. The system of organization is as follows: Mr. X is the king-pin of a group of eight persons—Cell A. Each of these seven are in turn king-pins of subordinate cells of eight members, Cells B, C, etc. Hence the name of the organization, A.B.C. None of the members of the seven subordinate groups know more than one man of the original group, none know the big king-pin. Each of the forty-nine men, other than the king-pins, of the subordinate groups, in turn organizes other cells of eight. In this second lower tier no new man knows any one in authority except his own king-pin, and no one at all in the top tier. Thus are established a series of hermetically sealed cells. Even the king-pin of each cell does not know more than seven men on the tier of cells above him. The main king-pin can transmit his orders through a whole series of minor king-pins who do not even know who he is. If the organization were to develop seven tiers, it would contain over five million people, more than Cuba's entire population—like a chain-letter from an unknown writer. It is almost impossible for the police to break through the mesh and discover the responsible persons. A state within a state. The government will never end terrorism so long as Machado remains in power. Cuba is destined, sadly enough, to go on from violence to violence.

Unfortunately the government, instead of using legal

methods to combat such activities, has resorted to open assassination of its enemies regardless of their sobriety in the community, whether or not they are terrorists.

The Cuban opposition consists of other elements than terrorists; indeed Machado hasn't a friend left to-day in Cuba except those on the government pay-roll and the large foreign financial interests. The opposition includes all social classes, all shades of opinion.

To the newcomer in Cuba, who does not get the present conflict in perspective, it might seem that the government should be fully justified in opposing the terrorists by any means within its power. For the terrorists, any measure is legitimate against a despotism, which knows no legality. But the government began assassinating its citizens, the government left the rails of legality before the A.B.C. And obviously terrorism is always a symptom of brutal tyranny. Free states and legal states who attempt to operate with justice according to law are not afflicted with terrorism. Terrorism is to be criticized, but ere criticizing it, the honest person must first criticize its source and cause—the illegal terrorism of the government.

As all legal means of expression and all rights have been abolished, as they are ruled by iron-handed militarism, as they cannot get arms for an uprising, as they are held in the leash of the Platt Amendment, the Cubans have resorted to the only form of armed revolt left to them—organized terror—and this revolt has been going on ever more actively for three long bloody years, until to-day the whole country is unsafe, and miles of cane-fields have gone up in smoke. Cuba is back in the days of '95.

According to a secret police report in my possession, given to me by Machado's private secretary, between November 12, 1930, and November 8, 1931—when the terrorist movement had scarcely begun—the police discovered 2,940 bombs, an average of eight a day; at least 78 persons were wounded or killed. During the same period, according to a reliable Cuban, who has kept close tab, over eight times that number were cold-bloodedly murdered by the police, in jail and out. Since then the toll has been much heavier; the violence far more frequent; the loss of life ever greater. April 14, 1933, in Havana alone, seventeen bombs exploded. Only a fraction of these occurrences seep into the American press.

The first of these bombs, set off by police provocateurs a few years back, often in the homes of oppositionists, gave an excuse to lay hands on and accuse every critic of the administration. The police are apparently still simulating many such terroristic activities.

Some months before I arrived in Havana this last time, a man had his arms blown off by a bomb he was placing in public toilets. Before it was discovered that he was a secret police employee, suspects were seized wholesale, probably none of whom had any connection with violent acts. Originally the police planted guns, dynamite or other sinister weapons in the home or the auto of the person they wished to get. But now, reliable newspaper reporters of Havana tell me, the police do not bother, but merely announce that dynamite or bombs were discovered in his possession, and if necessary present such material as evidence in court-martials. Rarely now does the government even bother about a court-martial—jail or death without trial is the rule.

2 AFTER MACHADO?

Most of those who have looked into the Cuban situation have asked, But who are the leaders of the Cuban opposition? What is their program?

Those not accustomed to examining the phenomenon of a dictator feel nonplused. Who can take Machado's place?

The very creation of dictatorship always makes dictatorship apparently irreplaceable, for dictatorship destroys all possibility of opposition leadership. For an opposition leader to become the least bit prominent would immediately spell his doom.

Another characteristic of dictatorship is that it befuddles all social problems, leads to a concentration by oppositionists on the one slogan—Get rid of the dictator. "All paths seem closed," wrote the well-known Spanish writer, Ariquistain, as early as 1928, "but the New Cuba will have to open some way, legally or against the law, with words or with the machete, to reconstruct the State and the nation . . . Only this Cuba, without foreign limitations for its sovereignty, without large landlords, without predatory capitalism, without peasant generals, and without sinecure professionals, will be truly free and merit the moral respect and love of all free men of the world." [1]

Examine the opposition elements. First there is the typical political "out," who conceives of the problem as merely one of how personally to get back into power, with little comprehension of political or social problems.

Foremost among these is ex-President Menocal, who of all the oppositionists was Ambassador Guggenheim's pet. He gave Cuba one of its most corrupt governments, closely allied with foreign sugar interests. His tactics closely resembled those of Machado. He was kept in office by Washington against the wishes of the Cuban people. In addition he delivered over his government to the most reactionary white aristocrats. He is in exile in Miami. Types like Menocal can do nothing more than befog present Cuban problems. Why get rid of Machado to put into power a little Machado?

Another wing of the "outs" is the Miguel Mariano Gómez group, led by the former Mayor of Havana, son of ex-President José Miguel Gómez. His administration in Havana was unexpectedly upright; he had the courage to oppose

[1] *Agonía Antillana,* 293-4.

Machado's ruthless and illegal projects. He is now in exile in New York. A good rotarian type.

Long prominent in forward-looking politics have been Carlos Mendieta and Mendez Capote, exiled nationalist leaders, both of very high reputation. Both served long unjust terms in prison under Machado "for reasons unknown," but are now in exile.

We have already analyzed the labor movement which though driven underground is a bitter enemy of Machado and with each day of suppression grows more radical.

Gradually the younger generation is building up a program and a tactic, which have much in common despite differences in groupings and outlook.

The real shock-troops of the opposition have been the students. The original student directorate broke into two wings, Communist and non-Communist, practically all of whom have been in jail for two years. New directorates have conserved the same division.

3 A.B.C.

In addition, students and professors formed the nucleus of the new A.B.C. group in 1931 after the premature August revolution. Its November platform, a pamphlet of 41 pages, states, "No civic movement was ever inaugurated under worse circumstances." The government was strengthened by suppression of the revolution, public spirit depressed, revolutionary resources wiped out, the opposition discredited."

The A.B.C. carries on propaganda, terrorism and other activities. Its tactics are multiple. It even has a Gandhi wing, "the Militia of Decency," [2] which boycotts luxuries and carries on passive resistance.

The A.B.C. "aspires to effect an integral renovation of Cuban public life." Its aim is not merely to end this régime

[2] Cf. *Denuncia*, Supplement 5, February 10, 1933.

(of Machado) but also to "remove its causes and maintain sane public opinion as a permanent force."

It is primarily a youth movement which has discovered that the generation of '95 has sequestered for itself control of public affairs, systematically excluding the Cubans who control their civil majority during the Republic. This past generation, which served "as a bridge between the colony and the Republic," has demonstrated "utter lack of aptitude for the civil labor of organizing and defending the new state." To-day only those willing to bow to its terms and accept its vices, "an inverse selection of the worst elements," have been able to enter public life. "General renovation of men" in the government and even in the ranks of the opposition is demanded.

Present conditions arise primarily from economic causes —the displacement of the Cuban from the wealth of his country. The first colonial phase of Cuba systematically excluded Cubans from public posts but not from the sources of wealth, such as sugar, tobacco, cattle-raising, mining. But they sacrificed their properties during the independence wars.

The Americans, who denied the Cubans even a seat at the Paris peace discussions, were recompensed for the war by their "booty" of Puerto Rico and the Philippines; the Cubans received no economic recompense. The veterans, peasants, workers and middle-class were left helpless. "The Yankee administrator" did not bother about these great problems. Estrada Palma tried to face the veteran question by pensions and a foreign loan, but failed, went down in revolution.

A second American occupation further retarded natural evolution. Gómez opportunistically stalled off the problems by giving away government jobs, cutting the people off still more from a solid economic basis. "An entire people cannot live as parasites." Graft became rampant.

The Conservative Menocal government continued this

vicious system, and Machado "from the first moment carried this policy of looting and lack of foresight to its extreme."

Thus Estrada Palma began the subjection of the government to foreign capital and closed all doors to native development of fields, mines, industries, the wealth of the country; so Cuba has had "a nation of bureaucrats and proletarians instead of property owners." The foreign bank "extends its tentacles everywhere. Master of credit, it is also master of production and commerce." The government has docilely executed the imperative demands of foreign capitalists, and aided by the state has disinherited the Cuban. Less than 200 mills control more than 5½ million acres. One company alone owns nearly an eighth of all Cuban sugar lands. The large plantations are more extensive than the counties (*municipios*) and their governments. Whole towns, as Banes in Oriente, are inside the foreign estates, and obey only the law of the American administrator. Officials and citizens are vassals, often are denied admission to the town after certain hours. A state within a state. Private company railways make every one completely dependent for miles around. Private ports are centers of contraband and put the companies in a privileged competing position. "If this process is carried to completion, all Cuba will be converted into a vast sugar plantation with a population of West Indian negroes, a cowardly native bureaucracy; a government receiving orders from Wall Street, and a flag—symbol of its independence."

The political causes of Cuba's present plight are equally discernible. Both the Captain General and the Yankee Governor (the latter more benign) established the system of absolutism, engendered mass submission to the governing. Each president transformed himself into an omnipotent Captain General. In imitating the constitution of the United States, the Republican government gave the executive branch complete power, for the checks existing in the

American commonwealth were for Cuba fictitious. The Cuban executive remains immune from all popular control.

Public will is further vitiated by dependence on foreign capital. Foreign companies oppose any participation of their employees in public affairs.

As Cubans have no economic resources, public posts become extraordinary prizes, to be fought for at the point of the gun and "ferociously" held when won. Positions won by force can only with difficulty be taken away. To hold on to a position, all methods are considered justifiable from bribery to violence and appealing to the Yankee government.

Since power is a prize, the government organizes a professional army to retain it. The privileged army is another means of living off the State, for it is paid and fed well, though the rest of the population may starve. Cuba, not having to defend itself against any foreign enemy, the army's mission is purely political—to uphold presidential imposition. Automatically an instrument for oppressions, hence it has impunity to commit the most repellent crimes.

Thus protected, the President may dispose of public funds and legislate as he wishes. Congress is subjected by shameful lottery graft. He names and controls the judges. With force he subjects the people, with corruption his subordinates.

The pauperization of cultural life has proceeded in direct relation to the alienation of the country's resources. The university has become not a center of learning, but of political sinecures and unworthy diplomas granted by pseudo-professors.

Even the students could no longer endure this. Protests in academic matters led directly to protest against all public wrongs. As early as 1927 the student directorate had the temerity to resist Machado. The spirit of the 1930 directorate raised public spirit by "its courage, its enthusiasm,

[317]

its abnegation," and has gained "the eternal gratitude of Cuba." Bad governors know the great power of thought and culture.

The platform goes on to recite the crimes committed against students, professors, newspapers, and other forces of enlightenment.

Machado is merely the typical culmination of all these evils in Cuban life, one of the most characteristic examples of the Hispano-American despot. The document gives a bitter pen-portrait, physical and psychological, of Machado, and recites the financial and political history of his tyranny, and then adds that thanks to short-term loans with juicy commissions he has won the support of the foreign banks. One example of favoritism toward the banks at the expense of Cuba is the Chadbourne plan. Machado continues skinning the Cuban people to pay the interest promptly to continue in power "even if this means exercising it over a prostrate and famishing people."

An extensive program of thirty-five measures is presented by which the people of Cuba can regain control of the national wealth and their government, and retain it after it is regained. Some of these steps are unnecessarily nationalistic. The A.B.C. proposal of universal military service seems a wrong-headed approach to the extirpation of militarism, and its political program too theoretical and too bureaucratic, with too much elaborate machinery.

The general trend of the A.B.C., both with respect to personnel and program, is "National Socialist" and semi-Fascist.

An offshoot organization of the A.B.C. is the *Organización Radical Revolucionaria Cubana,* with a program of more direct land-distribution and more extensive socialization of resources. While the A.B.C. is more of an urban phenomenon, the O.R.R.C. is more rural, includes labor and peasant leaders, and has endeavored to arm the people of the countryside on the theory that terrorism is not in itself a sufficiently potent weapon, but is merely a preliminary for the uprising of the Cuban people.

Meanwhile a new development has taken place on the exile-front in the United States, the formation of a unified revolutionary Junta with the venerable and noble Dr. Carlos de la Torre, former president of the university, at its head.

More than 1,000 exiles are now living in Miami in quarters ranging from the garden cottages of Grove Park to the four *Campos,* or barracks, that the less fortunate have taken over in different parts of the city. *Campo* No. 1, in downtown Miami, bears a huge sign: CUBAN EXILES, and at the entrance to its living quarters an unarmed but husky sentry is always on guard. Among the exiles are representatives of a half dozen different parties joined for the most part by nothing stronger than a common hatred of President Machado. To work more effectively they met early in April and formed a new revolutionary Junta in which each party will have one vote. It numbers:

Nationalists: Col. Carlos Mendieta, Col. Roberto Méndez Peñate, Col. Aurelio Hevia.

Menocalists: General Mario G. Menocal, Dr. Santiago Verdeja, Dr. Pedro Martínez Fraga.

Professors: Dr. Carlos de la Torre, Dr. Raimundo Grau San Martin.

Students: Guillermo Barrientos, Luis Barreras.

Political Adviser: Dr. Miguel Mariano Gómez.

A.B.C.: Carlos Saladrigas, Alfredo Botet.

Toward the end of April the new Junta held continuous secret sessions in New York to lay a joint program of action before the semi-official American commission which would attempt to arrange a satisfactory solution. The only basis for the beginning of such negotiations is the elimination of Machado. How far Roosevelt will assume any responsibility for such a step remains to be seen.

In the meantime, besides the customary city violence,

[319]

conditions in the interior ever since the O.R.R.C. got under way, have grown more unsettled. For months armed bands have been roving at large; cane-fields have gone up in smoke; towns and barracks have been seized, railway bridges blown up, trains fired upon, even wrecked, the highways blocked, telegraphic communications repeatedly cut.

It now seems a race between the efforts of the New York Junta to settle the problem diplomatically and the possibility of a spontaneous popular uprising, into which the army would inevitably be swept. In these two divergent solutions are involved far-reaching racial, economic, class and political differences.

PART V
AMERICAN PENETRATION

"Peoples are not merely chess-boards."

"We are men and are not going to want any paper-doll governments."

JOSÉ MARTÍ

XX "HANDS-OFF" GUGGENHEIM

OUR CUBAN POLICY HAS FLUC-
tuated from the "preventative"—i.e., intimate control over
every act, with the inevitable purpose of placing a new
loan—as during the Crowder-Zayas days—to the apparent
hands-off policy of the present moment. But the Platt
Amendment, ever a conditioning instrument, is raised like
a policeman's club. All the time the subtle forces of American financial and sugar interests are in play, American
troops are encamped eternally on Cuban soil in territory
ceded to us under compulsion. Cuba lives under a permanent threat, her independence ever more nominal than real.

Whatever policy has been pursued, every government
has owed much of its origin to American business interests
or to the direct intervention of the United States, or both;
and these governments have been maintained in power,
legally or illegally, by these same factors constantly operating. The main objective of American capital in Cuba has
been to reap the largest profits possible without regard for
the welfare of the Cuban people; the main objective of the
State Department has been to maintain the status quo, to
insure stability often regardless of the wishes of the Cuban
people. The Platt Amendment, subject to innumerable and
conflicting interpretations, has always served the two ob-
jectives just cited. There have resulted a score of diplomatic
interventions and three in armed interventions, not to mention numerous landings of marines—for order, loans, Amer-

ican property, not for liberty, justice, or Cuban independence. American troops have been in Cuba—aside from the naval stations granted us—fifteen years out of Cuba's independence period since 1902. Four American governors ruled the island. Crowder had almost as much power as President Zayas; so that direct American control over Cuban affairs covers a period even longer than fifteen years. The present situation or any other situation cannot be disentangled from our responsibility. The Cuban people know perfectly that since the State Department sets stability above considerations of humanity or justice, that they are never really free to run their own affairs. Free Cuba is a textbook myth.

Every decisive interpretation of that amendment has resisted every effort of the Cuban people to change usurping and tyrannical régimes. Every ruler, safe from effective domestic attack because of our dislike of revolution, has proceeded to mulct the country as quickly as possible. Thus, the great Cuban scholar Dr. Fernando Ortiz can say, "Notwithstanding the statements of Root and Platt, the Platt Amendment has served only to support *improper* governments in Cuba and never to correct them." [1] We have our cake and eat it too.

Cosme de la Torriente states that the right of intervention accorded by the Platt Amendment has ever been "useless to prevent violations of the most sacred individual rights when persons disposed to violate them have occupied power; and in contrast the intervention or possibility of intervention has been taken advantage of by unscrupulous persons to promote their own interests. . . . If this continues and the Cubans become accustomed to this tutelage, they will end by never deciding anything for themselves. The third article of the treaty which refers to the maintenance of a government adequate to protect life, property and liberty, does not serve, either in spirit or in applica-

[1] *American Responsibilities for Cuba's Troubles*, 8.

tion, in any way except to help destroy any good Cuban government and keep in power rulers who in one form or another violate the constitution and laws to perpetuate themselves in power." [2]

Márquez Sterling declares that intervention springs "fatally" from the political clause of the amendment, which "provokes tyranny as a cause and terrorism as a result." "Credit" is but the "conventional device of this system: interventionist concessions to prevent intervention." What "the Dictator is trying to salvage (by paying his debts) is the tolerance of the American chancellory." [3]

Thanks to the amendment, "the hands-off policy tends to strengthen Machado," declared the *New York Herald Tribune,* February 1, 1933, "regardless of the State Department's wishes in the matter."

In ways unnoticed by the average American, but perfectly intelligible to all Cubans, we have—despite our recent "hands-off" pose—definitely and repeatedly intimated to the Cuban people that Machado has our full support. When President Coolidge visited Cuba in 1928—on the heels of brutal unfair elections, when Machado's tyrannies were already in full bloom—and declared to the whole world that the Cubans had reached "genuine expression of their public opinion at the ballot-box": when he announced at a time when the Cubans were being jailed or murdered, and their constitution overthrown, that they were "independent, free, prosperous, peace-loving and enjoying the advantages of self-government," the people knew that such Uriah Heep dishonesty, however much it may fool Americans, cloaked unflinching support of Machado's bloody tactics. When President Hoover received the new Cuban Ambassador, Oscar Cintas, Vice-President of Woodin's American Car and Foundry Company, and stepped beyond diplomatic good usages to express his "good wishes" for Machado's "personal safety," the Cuban people believed that

---

[2] *La enmienda Platt,* 58 ff.   [3] *Conferencias de Shoreham,* 253.

Hoover was definitely committed to the régime which beats them into the dust. Hoover ever showed singular eagerness to demonstrate his friendliness for "out-damned-spot" Machado and went out of his way to send Machado birthday greetings.

In May, 1930, the American government made special arrangements to participate in Cuba's independence celebrations. By that date the Chase National Bank, among others, was heavily involved financially in Cuba; Ambassador Guggenheim had appeared on the scene to save the day for dollars and beauty; plans were being laid for a new debt arrangement. At the same time serious criticism of Machado, despite press-suppression in this country and Cuba, was leaking out. Opposition to him was growing rapidly. Official murders were increasing.

The financial and economic situation was entering upon a more unstable and disastrous phase. And so, to celebrate independence—no more significant than other years—marines paraded down the Havana streets, American planes circled overhead, and Lieutenant Colonel F. M. Andrews made a non-stop flight to the Havana air-port—the best Guggenheim could do to match Morrow's Lindbergh flight.

All this, say the Cubans, was merely definite warning to them not to bother Machado. July 12 of the following year, Captain J. Bream and Lieutenant Hodgeson were granted the order of military merit for organizing Cuba's air forces, not to fight any foreign invader, but to keep the Cuban people under heel.

For the Cubans, the slightest word of an American diplomatic representative has significance, his faintest suggestion carries worlds of meaning. It is therefore vitally necessary to clarify our policy and analyze the actions of our Embassy and the State Department during the development of the worst phases of the Machado tyranny.

Recent Ambassador Harry F. Guggenheim is a member of the family so prominently connected with Anaconda

Copper and the American Smelting and Refining Company and the scandalous Chile nitrate deals. The family is represented among the seventy-odd individuals said by ex-Ambassador Gerard to "manage" the United States.

Guggenheim was appointed September 15, 1929, after an interview with Hoover concerted, it is said, by a prominent New York bank official; but his appointment was held up by Foreign Relation Committee inquiries until October 10. He arrived in Havana November 18.

Declared the *Washington Daily News:* "Two reasons for sending Guggenheim to Havana are obvious. He is a business man with Latin-American interests. . . . He is a pioneer in commercial aircraft development. . . . Havana is the natural focal point—strategic place, certainly, for a Guggenheim. . . . He will report and interpret the dictatorship for Washington. If he sees clearly and reports fearlessly, there should be a reversal of the administration's policy toward Machado very soon."

What were Guggenheim's interests? Percy Rockefeller, a fellow director with Guggenheim of the Chile Company, also a director of Anaconda, is closely connected with the National City Bank controlling a large share of Cuba's sugar. Rockefeller is not only a director of most of those sugar companies but is particularly interested in American railway interests in Cuba; Bethlehem Steel, which owns most of Cuba's vast iron deposits; Remington Arms, which has sold Machado army supplies; and Air Reduction, which controls Cuban Air Products; various sugar companies and other Cuban interests.

Another Chile and Anaconda Copper director was the good Charlie Mitchell, of the National City, who was also connected with American and Foreign Power, the Electric Bond and Share subsidiary controlling the Cuban company of which Machado was Vice-President; the International Telephone and Telegraph Company, enjoying luscious Cuban concessions; and Cuban sugar companies. The responsibility of the Electric Bond and Share and American and Foreign Power for Machado's election, their subsequent concessions, fantastic rates and ferocious military protection give triple significance to the fact that besides Mitchell and Rockefeller, this company has as officers and directors numerous high Guggenheim officials and directors such as: W. C. Potter, Lewis Eugene Pierson, John D. Ryan (recently died), George H. Howard. Of the foregoing, Pierson is also a director of the Freeport Texas Company completely controlling the Cuban-American Manganese Corporation, owning 10,000 acres of mineral lands in Cuba.

Another close Guggenheim tie-up was with Horace Havemeyer of Chase National Bank and the big Lowry sugar interests.

Nor should we neglect to mention Guggenheim's mutual mining and aviation interests with Charles Hayden (director of seventy companies) of the Chase executive committee, interested in Coca-Cola (two plants in Cuba), International Cement (owning the Cuban Portland Cement), the big Cuba Cane Company, and Cuban sugar companies.

Through aviation and other interests, Guggenheim was close to Thomas L. Chadbourne, closely connected with Chase bank officials.[4]

The list is far from complete, but even these few names link up, not only with nearly every important American investment in Cuba, but with the financial forces which have directly sponsored the Machado régime.

Did Guggenheim, as the *News* suggested he might, report clearly and fearlessly?

2 "GENTLEMAN'S WORD"

Personal rivalry had existed between Guggenheim and Dwight W. Morrow in connection with patronage of Lindbergh and other matters, and

4 Cf. Chapter XXIII.

Guggenheim moved on Cuba to achieve fame by bettering Morrow's tactics in Mexico. Just as Morrow hired numerous private experts, so did Guggenheim. This partook of a knight-errant effort to straighten out all Cuba's economic and political ills, hence meant propping up the hated Machado to prevent impending collapse from bankruptcy and the gale of popular wrath. We have not heard that Guggenheim began his Cuban career of friendliness to Machado with ham and egg breakfast, but Cubans claim "Ambassador Guggenheim has often been photographed with Machado and some of his photographs show him in bathing attire with the President of the Cuban senate, Dr. Clemente Vázquez Bello. He is the first to admit he lunches and dines with President Machado occasionally and has attended many official functions with him, always prominently seated at his side." Guggenheim and especially Secretary Reed revolved in a little clique of Machado supporters.

Our Acting Secretary of State Castle hastened to declare May 14, 1931, that Guggenheim was merely maintaining those "cordial relations" which should be maintained with the head of the Cuban government. The Cubans retorted that Guggenheim went far beyond customary official cordiality.

One hundred leading Cuban women signed a joint accusation that Guggenheim's intervention had been "indubitable, continuous and hypocritical." This document, read in the Senate by David I. Walsh of Massachusetts and combated by Walsh of Montana, declared that Guggenheim was "one of the principal supporters of an illegitimate situation . . ." that he had tried to make "his government and the American people believe that all is well in Cuba and that the people here support the government," that it is opposed by "only a small group of malcontents."

He was "functioning as the axis of a plot hatched by private banking interests of the United States" to deliver

[329]

"an illegitimate government to those interests," and "moved the machinery so successfully as to crush the Cuban people. . . ."

Cubans firmly believe that Machado's success in remaining in power has been largely due to Guggenheim and the State Department, "contrary to the knowledge of the American people."

Machado frequently utilized and boasted about the Ambassador's presence at his side to frighten the Cuban people with the specter of possible armed intervention.

May 19, 1930, on orders personally transmitted by Machado (admitted by him publicly), troops broke up the Artemisa political meeting of the Nationalist Union, killing and wounding innocent men, women and children quietly assembled. On the following day, May 20, Machado, reviewing troops, stated that "before resigning the Presidency of the Republic, I will drown the island in blood." According to reports, Guggenheim, probably unwittingly, joined in the applause. At a banquet in Santa Clara, Guggenheim sat complacently while Machado declared, "My government is an honest and just one, and here is the American Ambassador by my side to prove it." Machado never missed an opportunity to cite the name of Guggenheim in defense of his policies.

Though the Communists are too weak in Cuba even to own a typewriter, Machado—stressing the dangers to Cuba of "the snake of Russian Communism . . . spitting its venom"—stated in the *New York Sun*, "On my word as an officer and a gentleman, on my word as President of this Republic, this is the truth and your own American Ambassador, Señor Harry F. Guggenheim, knows that it is the truth." Guggenheim never disavowed such improper uses of his name, even when the facts were wrong and it threw slander on the opposition.

Machado, in his own blundering way, attempted to put the Ambassador in a better light: "It is publicly known that the Ambassador, each time he wants to come to the Palace, asks for an audience, and if it is not, for numerous reasons, granted, he reiterates his request and waits until he is able to obtain it and then interviews the President. . . . He has no advantages of any kind over his colleagues."

In other words, Machado cleverly utilized Guggenheim's name as a pillar of support and conversely attempted to show the Cuban people that though Guggenheim supported him, the President really had the upper hand—a gratifying arrangement to which Guggenheim never once objected, though in secret channels he attacked the opposition for elucidating these matters.

3 FIND THE DOLLARS

Guggenheim, from time to time, circulated various secret statements giving his position and bitterly attacking the opposition. In one of these prepared at the request of Dr. Hubert C. Herring, Executive Secretary of the Committee on Cultural Relations with Latin America, Inc., and sent out by the latter as a "document" to a few key persons, the Ambassador stated that "in an effort to induce the United States to take action against the Machado government in Cuba, the Cuban oppositionists and their American sympathizers have been . . . seeking to discredit the American Ambassador . . . and the policy which he has been instructed to follow," viz., that of no intervention, no meddling.

Practically all the Cuban oppositionists, time and again, have merely demanded the United States remain neutral, have inveighed against intervention. Guggenheim thus tried to stigmatize the Cubans as interventionists, at the same time putting himself forward as the paladin of Cuban independence, more patriotic than the patriots—"fiery Cubans," he calls them.

Guggenheim thereupon quotes the intervention article

of the Platt Amendment and misquotes the Root interpretation of "no intermeddling" to emphasize that we have "no
obligations" in Cuba, merely "rights." Secretary Stimson,
he added, reaffirmed this Root interpretation in October
and December (the Chadbourne sugar-bond proposals were
being approved) but neglects to state that Stimson left the
loophole, "The United States . . . reserves the right to
judge every case in the future on its own merits"—tacit
approval of the Machado régime.

Guggenheim himself in the very next breath egre-
giously lets the whole cat out of the bag: In the "fulfillment" of the Root interpretation "it was believed at the
same time a continuous and thorough study of Cuban economic and political conditions should be made, so that the
mission could be in a position at all times to give, when
desired and without obligation, unofficial [blessed word]
advice and assistance to the Cuban government, in order
to help Cuba's progress." To "give . . . unofficial advice
and assistance to the Cuban government" can only mean
support of that government. Guggenheim has given such
advice. Has it helped Cuba's progress?

On this basis, American authorities, paid by Guggenheim or the United States government, "unofficially" nosed
into the Cuban archives in a way the Cuban government
would scarcely have tolerated except for *official* pressure.
As we see in this statement, this work was done by express
authorization of the State Department.

A *New York Times* article (February 8, 1933) by Russell Porter, obviously prepared after proper interview with
Guggenheim, stated that due to the Root interpretation
of the Platt Amendment, "Whereas Ambassador Guggenheim had been unable to bring official pressure to bear
upon the Cuban government in internal political matters,
he has exercised the rights of the United States over the
Cuban government's financial affairs under Article 2 of the
Platt Amendment, which reads as follows:

" 'That said government [of Cuba] shall not assume or contract any public debt, to pay the interest upon which, and to make reasonable sinking fund provision for the ultimate discharge of which, the ordinary revenues of the island, after defraying the current expenses of government, shall be inadequate.'

"With government revenues falling, despite heavy tax increases, Ambassador Guggenheim, beginning in 1930, has consistently used his influence against the government's embarking upon any increased public spending that would mean new foreign loans." Yet in 1930 two new loans were arranged and approved!

All this is equivalent to saying we shall—so that you pay all your international bills—see that all your finances are sound, hence see that your government is quite solid; but we don't prevent that after thus strengthening your position, you violate the constitution at your heart's desire, that you jail or murder your opponents. A very handy division of labor.

Why we should enforce the financial provisos of the Platt Amendment and ignore the political provisos is not a great mystery. Why one should be considered not "meddling" and the other "meddling" is a bit more mysterious—for this hairsplitting offends the intelligence of even a schoolchild. Let us clarify the sequence of events:

1925-27

Labor movement destroyed.
Students arrested; university closed.

1927

Feb. 19. Chase Bank work loan.
March. Chester Wright reports 147 official murders.
April. Thomas Lamont declares Machado should remain in power by any means. Woodin eulogizes Machado.
July 1. Morgan $9,000,000 loan.
Nov. Machine gun elections.

1928

Jan.-Feb. Pan American Congress. Coolidge eulogizes free Cuba. Students jailed.

March. Brouzon and Yalob thrown to sharks.

May 28. Colonel Blas Masó officially murdered.

June 22. Chase Bank $60,000,000 revolving credit loan.

July 24. Esteban Delgado officially murdered.

August 6. Bartolomé Sagaró officially murdered.

Nov. Machado seizes power for six years. Kellogg voices approval.

1929

Jan. 10. Mella murdered in Mexico City.

Increased official terrorism.

Nov. 18. Guggenheim arrives.

Dec. 12. Luis Blanco Neuman murdered by police for presenting petition to American Embassy.

1930

Jan. Official murders.

Feb. 26. Chase $80,000,000.

May 20. Guggenheim arranges friendship celebration. Marines march through Havana.

Sept. 30. Trejo murdered.

Oct. Stimson enunciates hands-off policy.

Nov. Guggenheim sets "unofficial" approval on illegal elections.

Dec. Stimson revoices "hands-off."

Dec. 16. Chadbourne $42,000,000 sugar bonds authorized.

1931

Jan. Students and professors jailed and murdered.

A storm of protest in 1930 prevented the refunding of the Cuban debt at $300,000,000, a scheme Guggenheim, after unfavorable publicity, hotly disavowed. Guggenheim's experts had been delving into Cuba's finances to set them in order. The prior iniquitous Chadbourne sugar bond issue and the Chase $80,000,000 loan had been put across.

At the time of the proposed $300,000,000 loan, Representative Louis T. McFadden declared: "Cuba is on the verge of bankruptcy. The government of Cuba is in a precarious position. . . . The international bankers are preparing to unload the bad obligations they have in Cuba on the innocent American public. . . .

"We have a minister in Cuba, Ambassador Guggenheim, who is representing these international houses and has been engaged in negotiating the present $300,000,000 refunding loan. Ever since Guggenheim went to Cuba, he has had two expert accountants down there. Now he has returned, and we have the announcement of the flotation by J. P. Morgan and Company of $300,000,000 Cuban bonds."

This sprang out of the investigations being carried on by Guggenheim's investigator, Grosvenor M. Jones of the Department of Commerce. In *El Pais*, September 22, 1930, the Treasury Department reported that the plan of an economic commission headed by Mr. Jones would eliminate all difficulty "in carrying out a financial operation with the North American banks." The *New York Times* (September 23) reported: "It is believed Wall Street will not hesitate to place at the disposal of Mr. Jones any sum he may deem advisable to bring about Cuba's economic reconstruction." September 27, the *Diario de la Marina* was informed by Treasury officials Aizcorbe and Altunga that Guggenheim's adviser had secured information looking toward the funding of the debt. Juan Maspons, head of the National Economic Commission, stated that when Machado went into office, Cuba's debt was $97,000,000; it had risen to $270,000,000, and it was planned to fund the same at $300,-000,000, leaving Machado a small remnant for current expenses.

In any case, Jones and his assistants and Guggenheim were compiling information to set Machado's financial house in order. The real project was the Chadbourne sugar plan and sugar bonds.

Among others who labored along similar lines were Professors R. A. Seligman and Carl Schoup, who drew up the ideal tax-system plan for Cuba, a heavy 470-page tome with exhaustive statistics and charts. The volume does not clarify who footed the bills, but the Seligman study was correlated with Guggenheim's constant efforts to control Cuban finances.

Despite good modernization features, detailed examination soon reveals Seligman's fundamental concern was to increase taxes mostly at the expense of the general public and reduction of public works and salaries. It dodges increases on large foreign capital. Seligman proposes as a satisfactory substitute for an income-tax, a levy based on house-rent (which ignores special factors in the Cuban situation) and which reminds us of medieval assessments on doors and windows. "Urban property," protested a Cuban pamphlet, "is the one wealth still . . . in the hands of Cubans or residents in Cuba." To bring real-estate taxation under Federal control would also further curtail local liberties, further concentrate power in tyrannical government. Was this to put the government on a footing to continue paying up on its onerous debt?

Early in 1931 a new scheme was afoot to create an American-controlled commission with "final jurisdiction in all financial matters" which would "obviate the necessity of political intervention," i.e., keep Machado in power with American control over customs collections and governmental disbursements "as the only means of protecting the great foreign investments involved." The details of this appeared in the first edition of the *Washington Evening Star*, June 5, 1931, under William H. Fort's signature; and was amply commented upon by Roig de Leuchsring in *Carteles*, whereupon a new and ferocious censorship was clamped upon the Cuban press.

Cuba was to be kept paying through the nose, but none of these schemes were concerned with the welfare of the Cuban people, and were to aid Machado with no check upon his brutalities.

[336]

Guggenheim's right hand was labeled "official;" his left hand, "unofficial."

4 CLAIMS

Americans, unless they belong to the clique of bankers and public utility interests with whom Guggenheim played, received no proper protection against illegal persecutions.

Aristides Betencourt, a youthful cigar-maker of Key West, Florida, was imprisoned six months in the Isle of Pines penitentiary and Principe Fortress without trial.

I have already cited the Arthur Tagle case, the murderer of whom, protected by the government, is now back on the police force unpunished.

Even more important Americans not within the charmed circle of specified financial and public utility interests were in a bad way. Lacking proper backing against illegal violations, they are afraid to take their cases to the Embassy or to the State Department for fear of brutal retaliations. The vice-president of one of the biggest American productive companies of Cuba told me his concern dared not protest to the State Department regarding flagrant abuses against which they had no recourse.

"Why?" I asked.

"Because Machado would smash our mills and burn our cane-fields."

Mr. John T. Wilford, American twenty-year resident of Cuba, children born in the country, had his printing plant raided and damaged by the police, his newspaper suppressed. He had to flee the country. According to his final estimate, business and good-will losses totaled $23,500.

Guggenheim savagely berated this claim as "unscrupulous," even declared the police committed these depredations "with due legal formality," that the paper only had a circulation of "a few hundred copies," and estimated the damage at $100, "substantially in accord with the Cuban government's estimates." No allowance, no sympathy, for the closing of Wilford's business, the expense and strain of his forced flight to the United States, his time and money trying to get redress, or the difficulties of reëstablishing his paper under a new name. But Wilford had been "bitterly hostile to the American Embassy in Cuba and the Machado government." (Curious bracketing!)

Wilford wrote in the *Havana-American News* (April 3, 1933): "In some matters which I considered of importance to the good relations between Cuba and the United States . . . the Ambassador had by omission at least, placed the matter before the State Department in Washington in the wrong light. . . . Mr. Guggenheim has done many things detrimental to me and my property interests, even . . . directly misrepresenting the facts. I have never . . . criticized Guggenheim except in his official capacity. I . . . have refrained from giving currency to any of the many deplorable and uncomplimentary 'rumors' of his personal activities while residing in Havana."

Machado finally promised to make amends to Wilford, but failed to keep his word. October, 1930, long after the event, Wilford filed a claim for diplomatic interposition. He was asked to submit documentary evidence; but by that time, even if he could still collect evidence, no one would run the personal risk attached to testifying; and besides Wilford, rightly or wrongly, was convinced of Guggenheim's utter bad faith.

Subsequently Wilford complained to the Embassy against a censorship glaringly discriminatory. He was told to "exhaust his legal resources" under a régime in which the Ambassador himself confessed inadvertently he could not obtain fair trials.

Nor did Guggenheim, up to the time I left Cuba, lift a finger in behalf of Wilford's young son, long illegally held by the military authorities.

Among others whom Guggenheim included in what he called "the claims racket," was the Joseph E. Barlow $9,-000,000 claim, particularly annoying to Machado because his son-in-law, Rafael Jorge Sánchez, was exploiting the property from which Barlow had been illegally ejected.

Whatever the justice of the claim, May 22, 1929, Stimson dispatched a note to the Cuban government requesting it to restore Barlow's property—a note prepared after seven months' exhaustive research by Mr. Reuben Clark, one of the most honorable men ever in the American State Department service.

Eight days later Mr. Herbert C. Lakin, a relative of Stimson by marriage and president of the powerful Cuba Company (in which present Secretary of Treasury Woodin was also deeply interested), hurried to Washington to combat the Barlow claim. Lakin had such close relations with Machado, according to Barlow, "he was able to have Machado sign a decree closing ports for the shipment of sugar served by the railroads competing with the railroad of which Lakin was president, thus permitting Lakin to ship 18 million bags of sugar at 50 cents per bag, for a total of $9,000,000."

The State Department, after Lakin's arrival, immediately cooled off concerning Barlow's claim. Barlow pointedly asked Stimson, "Do you realize the position you are placed in by the action of your relative, the friend of President Machado, whose son-in-law has part of my property?"

But Barlow was no longer backed up. For Lakin, besides being active himself, engaged Colonel John Carroll, star-witness in the 1929 lobby investigations, paying him a $10,-000 retainer and a monthly salary of $4,500 to buck the Barlow claim.

Later Carroll was put on the mat by a Senate investigating committee. Senator Walsh asked, "What difference does it make to them [Lakin and the Cuba Company] whether or not Barlow sustains his claim?"

Colonel Carroll replied, "They tell me they are not interested *per se* in the Barlow claim but are interested in the
Machado administration. . . . Lakin said his company was
interested in defending the Machado administration and
that was why he got me. . . . These charges . . . detail
facts that if true would compel another intervention which
these American property owners don't want."

Instead of pressing restoration of Barlow's property pending suit (the State Department's original position), Guggenheim on his arrival "was able to put an end to the
agitation by preparing a scrupulously fair plan of arbitration . . . calling for an American and Cuban arbitrator
and, if necessary, a third neutral appointed by the Permanent Court of International Justice at The Hague. Barlow's opponent accepted the plan, while Barlow himself re-
jected it," said Guggenheim. "This indicated the weakness
of his case and removed it from the status of an international claim."

Guggenheim does not state the way in which the arbiters
were to be chosen, nor other jokers, nor the likelihood that
Machado's representative at The Hague would be chosen.
Barlow, whatever the justice of his claim, was a beaten man,
told to "exhaust his legal resources in Cuba," where no
legal resources existed.

Against him, in possession of his property, was Machado's
son-in-law; against him was Mr. Stimson, supporting his
wife's relative who was reaping benefits from the Machado
régime; against him were the Woodin-Lakin-Rubens-
Rockefeller railway interests, the powerful Cuba Company;
against him was the mighty National City Bank. Senator
Caraway accused Vice-President Rentschler, after the latter's eulogy of Machado's "sound, stable government," that
his institution had paid its part toward financing the efforts
against the so-called Barlow claim. In short, Barlow was
outside the charmed circle of special interests; and he had
dared attack Machado. The Barlow case clearly demon-

strated the great concern all these and other interests had in upholding the Machado régime to the last ditch.

The last time Barlow went to Cuba, he was thrown into prison, put into a convict's uniform; and because he refused to perform hard labor, was housed with maniacs. He literally died of starvation.

The Harrah claim was settled for $350,000, then cut down to $14,000. Some day the story may be revealed as to who pocketed the difference between these two amounts.

5 ILLEGAL ELECTIONS

We have seen how the loan-racket prospered before and after Guggenheim's arrival. Despite the so-called "hands-off" policy, Guggenheim also meddled politically.

For the November 1, 1930, elections, Machado nominated family members, several cabinet ministers and many intimate friends. This, crowed officials, was to be a "unanimous" election, no opposition permitted; only the official "Coöperationists" would be allowed to go to the polls.

July 17, just before his vacation to the States, Guggenheim announced "signal progress in the affairs of the nation," making possible new electoral legislation. The President, "because of unofficial persuasion by Guggenheim" (*New York Times*), promptly issued a statement beneath that of the Ambassador declaring the legislation would be embodied in a message to Congress. "Even the Nationalist would be allowed to vote."

But in August Congress, which does not brush its hair without Machado's consent, defeated the bill, 86 to 1. When some one suggested Congress was turning against him, Machado retorted (*El País*, August 13, 1930): "Ah! You also believe Congress repealed the Presidential message against my will? Well, you are mistaken! The House repealed it in agreement with me. Congress and I are in perfect accord. No, I promised the legally organized parties [all controlled by him] to pay no more attention to the Nationalists, and, as a man of my word, I had to keep my promise."

Was his promise to Guggenheim less binding? Was Guggenheim merely helping Machado preserve his mask? Or was he beaten? Was Guggenheim a Machiavellian? Was he dumb? Or was he weak?

He returned October 5, after two and a half months' absence, but made utterly no comment on the collapse of his proposed legislation. *El Heraldo de Cuba* merely published across eight columns his statement: "It is time to work for the betterment of Cuba, not to talk." In other words, "Take your medicine and shut up!" No political campaigning, no opposition, no free voting—"Let Machado alone to rule as he wishes."

Was not this a species of collaboration with Machado on the basis of existing illegal and unfair electoral machinery in the forthcoming machine-gun election? Did not this condone the Artemisa slaughter, the jailing of students and Nationalists? Was it to save millions for the banks that Machado and his illegal terroristic elections had to be backed up? Was it to put across the Chadbourne sugar loan?

November 5, 1930, in *El País,* the Ambassador openly commented that the elections had been peacefully held [sic] throughout the Republic, that the efforts of the Nationalists and Conservative Menocalistas to keep the people away from the polls had found "very limited following."

This statement was equivocal, misleading. In Havana, by recounting the same votes many times, electoral participation was brought up to 30 percent, in the rest of the island scarcely 15 percent. The Electoral Board of Havana, under a mayor since kicked out, moved for indictment of more than four hundred persons, mostly government employees, for voting two, three, even four times.

Guggenheim publicly ratified these illegal elections.

6 NEW OUTRAGE

On various occasions, Guggenheim unofficially (blessed word!) tried to draw the teeth of the opposition, asked it to postpone activities "until the economic situation" of the country grew "normal" again, promised conditions would improve, that Machado would enact reforms. But he warned them also (cf. *Herald Tribune,* August 18, 1931) that they "would have small chance of success against President Machado's army."

Finally flatly told by the opposition sector with which he was dealing that the *sine qua non* was a thorough remedy of existing conditions, he replied "that would be intervening." To Dr. Domingo Méndez Capote, then President of the Cuban revolutionary Junta in New York and former Vice-President of the Republic, Guggenheim "refused to consider any proposal which looked to Machado's resignation"—as that would mean "the defeat of my policy." (*Herald Tribune,* August 15, 1931.) The *New Republic* said, August 26, 1931: "Unofficially . . . he seems to have done his best to convince the opposition leaders that they should not revolt, but should rather consent to a compromise program of reform which would keep Machado in office longer. It is sometimes difficult for patriots to distinguish between the official and unofficial character of the Ambassador."

Invariably following Guggenheim's unsuccessful attempts to reconcile the opposition with Machado came new terror by the government.

Publicly he prognosticated that the Cuban government was about to balance its budget without new taxes by the reduction of employees' salaries, gave full faith to the dictator's promises of financial reform. The Cuban people are still waiting for economic improvement.

Incidentally Guggenheim's negotiations were for the most part carried on with the most reactionary intriguing "outs," principally with Menocal, the best previous American tool, most similar to Machado in misuse of power. But sincere patriotic and disinterested oppositionists such as the scholarly and statesmanlike Dr. Fernando Ortiz, he damned bitterly on every possible occasion, even stooped to cast slurs on his unquestioned scholarship.

To fortify his "liberal" position in the United States, Guggenheim would declare there was "general approval of a government plan which had done much to alleviate political tyranny;" of late "no criticism of the lack of freedom of the press"—opinions on the face of them not borne out by the facts.

Guggenheim moved heaven and earth to block the 1931 revolt.

Plans were afoot for a new "financial plan." When it broke, Guggenheim advised Washington it was "a secret conspiracy." Some Cubans and resident Americans charged him with having betrayed Menocal's confidence, thus leading to prompt suppression and execution of hundreds. Guggenheim stated, according to Washington releases, that "the cause of Cuba's latest uprising was the fear of the opposition that their chief argument against Machado would be removed with the passage of Cuba's new constitutional reforms . . . to-morrow," which would have "removed the principal causes of political discontent."

But these joker reforms, framed and sponsored with his assistance, distinctly tended to strengthen Machado. They were being enacted under martial law and press censorship, no public discussion permitted. They could not even be debated in Congress, for most opposition deputies had been eliminated, jailed or murdered. They were to be put through, not in the legal manner of amending the constitution; and they would be made law by the illegal Congress in control due to the previous illegal reforms of 1928 (sponsored by Washington) and the illegal elections Guggenheim had approved. A manifesto against them, which no Cuban paper was allowed to print, signed by distinguished Cubans, called them a "new outrage."

It was even proposed—as was later effected—to extend the term of Senators to twelve years, and to make Machado, should he ever abandon the Presidency, a Senator without election for the same period. None of these proposed changes satisfied the Cuban people, not in any way consulted. They were a contributing cause of the unsuccessful 1931 revolt.

If reforms were calculated to improve the situation, why were they, after revolt, dropped into the waste paper basket by Guggenheim and Machado? Apparently Guggenheim accepted Machado's thesis that having dominated by brute force, he could do as he pleased. Governmental terrorism increased. In November the United States authorities, at the behest of the Cuban government, which provided evidence and witnesses, dug up old charges against Cubans in this country, a folly not ended until March, 1932.

Guggenheim asserted his "complete impartiality" during the August, 1931, revolution. He is mistaken or else the department misquoted him. He branded the revolt "a secret conspiracy."

August 18, the *New York Times* stated, "The point of view and the actions of the United States Department of State have been the center of only a little less controversy here [in Cuba] than the actions of President Machado himself. This has been marked by open accusations by members of the opposition that the United States government and specifically Ambassador Guggenheim have been supporting Machado régime and that it would fall but for this support. To-day with the chief leader of the opposition in jail, there is no lessening of these accusations both here and in the United States; and the Havana papers are carrying declarations that Mr. Guggenheim is the 'man of the hour' and strongly intimating that future developments depend on him. . . ."

Guggenheim in the *Havana-American News* (April 3, 1933) quoted a United Press dispatch obviously inspired by him personally to prove he was absolutely neutral, a pat-on-the-head for not having precipitated intervention at that time.

State Department releases do not confirm this impartiality, but were preparing the American public for probable intervention. And via the *New York Times* (August 18) the War Department announced: "When the trouble first assumed serious importance, the General Staff brought its Cuban plans up to date," though without determining who should head the opposition. Acting Secretary of State Castle could not conceal his final elation from Márquez Sterling "that the revolution had been completely beaten."

Guggenheim declared that despatches from Havana in the New York papers stated that both *El Mundo* and *Diario de la Marina* and "the Cuban press in general, approved the Ambassador's neutrality and good handling" of the situation, his prevention of intervention. The following citation, from the *New York Times,* indicates how much the opinions of the Havana press at that time were worth:

"The censorship on Cuban papers is even closer and more complicated. It begins in the local telegraph offices in the interior, where reports are subjected to a strict censorship before they start on their way to Havana. An army officer and soldiers are stationed in each newspaper office and more army men stand guard in the press-room. After the newspaper is made up, page-proofs are taken to the Palace for examination in the office of the Chief of Staff. The newspapers must make such changes as ordered. When the presses finally are started, the first three copies must be taken to the Palace for still another examination, and the presses are not permitted to run off more papers until the first three receive the government's stamped O.K."

Not only did Guggenheim try to sidetrack the opposition which he believed most powerful, but bitterly and secretly attacked other sectors of it. The Cuban Patriotic League, he said, was headed by claims racketeers; one of its leaders, Octavio Seigle, had been "repudiated" by the opposition.

Seigle was merely "repudiated" by a few politicians with whom Guggenheim was playing ball. The President of the League, Alfred Betencourt, stated that he abandoned a claim years before; Guggenheim "never" had had to exert any action for him.

Guggenheim also attacked the Cuban-American Friendship Council composed of a few professional Cubans of unimpeachable character. Guggenheim did not know its correct location, falsely accused it of circulating a letter with which it had no connection, ascribed to it a member who was not a member. "Other inexactitudes," said the President of the Council . . . "demonstrate the little-to-be-recommended judgment of Mr. Guggenheim."

7 MACHADO'S COPS

When I stepped into the gray American Embassy on the plaza near the Malecón in September, 1932, I was greeted not by a proper employee, but by a Cuban policeman in blue uniform and black braid. Another Cuban policeman sat at the Embassy switchboard listening in on all conversation. A policeman communicated visitors' names to the Ambassador or, in his absence, to the dapperly dressed, handsome Chargé Reed. The effect on a visiting Cuban, harassed by brutal persecutions, of such an encounter with a policeman of the ruling tyranny—at a time when all policemen have been militarized and are part of the army, who will thus instantly know his name and can communicate it to higher authorities—can well be imagined. It is not especially agreeable even to an American.

Legally an American Embassy is sacred American soil. Guggenheim in various secret communiqués has argued that these policemen within the Embassy were even paid

$25 monthly by the Embassy, because substitute messengers, and switch-board operator, cannot be afforded, that they had been there twenty years. In 1920 when I was in Havana, they were not *within* the Embassy, nor have the same policemen been there for twenty years. Other Embassies and Legations have Cuban police guards, but they are not admitted into the interior as part of the staff to carry on intimate functions. Of course, such countries as Haiti, Brazil, Uruguay, etc., are not so deucedly poor as the United States.

Did the Embassy ever frown upon the murder of Machado's opponents? When Vásquez Bello was assassinated, and the government retaliated within a few hours with the assassination of national Congressmen Aguiar and Gonzalo Freyre de Andrade, our embassy immediately sent its condolences for the death of Machado's intimate, Vásquez Bello, but sent none for opposition Deputies Aguiar and Freyre. Did these merit no recognition from the American Embassy? Was it because they were opposed to Machado? All Cuba seethed with horror at our cynical partisanship.

Incidentally Deputy Freyre when murdered had just presented a document in behalf of Cuban women and the students to the diplomatic corps. Morally our Ambassador should have inquired whether this document had any relation to this murder.

November 26, 1929, Luis Blanco Neuman was caught with a copy of an appeal to the American Embassy in his possession. Was the government informed through the Cuban policemen Guggenheim installed in the Embassy? Blanco was thrown from a second story window by the police. He recovered from his injuries in prison, and there "committed suicide" December 12, 1929. (At that time the Chase Bank was negotiating their $80,000,000 loan.)

Herrera Sotolongo, outstanding Cuban attorney, comparable in Cuban life to Mr. Hughes in America, brilliantly and successfully argued the unconstitutionality of the closing of the university, of usurpation of civil functions by military courts, and other abusive decrees. He was seized and held incommunicado for months.

He appealed for protection under the Platt Appendix in a letter smuggled out to his wife to be presented to the American Embassy. Chargé d'Affaires Reed declined to see her, but by a ruse the letter was personally placed in his hands. He did not even telegraph her plea to Washington.

Señora Herrera then determined to appeal directly to the State Department. When I queried Reed about this, he replied coldly, "That is the customary procedure with such complaints." But warned that if she took this step, her husband would be tortured in prison, perhaps murdered, that she herself would be arrested, she was obliged to desist.

While I believe the Platt Amendment a very undesirable instrument, legally it exists. Machado has violated it openly by titling such appellants as "traitors," and he boasted publicly, "Máximo Gómez shot traitors in war-time; I shoot them in peace times." Deputy José Ramón Cruells, at Machado's behest, even introduced a House motion assigning severe penalties to those appealing to the United States.

Toward the end, stung by criticism of indifference, Guggenheim did attempt to prevent student Alvarez being murdered—with ill success: for despite prior promises to him from Secretary of State Ferrara (into whose care Reed recommended *Times* correspondent Phillips), the student was foully murdered by the police.

January 13 the *Havana-American News* records that "Ambassador Guggenheim has received as token of the high regard in which he always has been held by President Machado, a fine black thoroughbred horse, said to be of Arabian stock."

Guggenheim had hastened to this futile effort probably because of the exposé published in the *Havana-American News,* December 31, 1932, and elsewhere that the mother of the high-school student Mariano Gonzáles Rubiera, murdered by the police, had in her desperation previously but unsuccessfully requested the Embassy to exercise its good offices. She asked that its influence be exerted to obtain for her son a fair trial and to protect him against irregular and illegal retaliatory aggression.

"Sra. Rubiera was told that the Embassy could not intervene in any way, due to the fact that the youth was not of American nationality. From the Embassy she went to the Uruguayan legation where she was promised that such friendly intercession as diplomatic procedure permitted would be made for the safety of the boy.

"At two o'clock a bullet-riddled and otherwise disfigured body was found on the corner of 6 and 15 streets, Miramar. Later this was identified by Sra. Rubiera as the remains of her son who had last been seen in the custody of the police in Havana."

Rubiera had been held fourteen months in the Isle of Pines penitentiary; but two weeks after his release—one of Machado's fake festures of generosity—he was seized again by the police.

According to the *Havana-American News,* Señora Julia Rubiera "reaffirmed to-day that she had called on the American Embassy in a vain attempt to obtain mercy for her son. . . ." Her statement "was denied to-day at the Embassy, but Mrs. Rubiera tells her story with a wealth of detail that substantiates the truth." Other sources of information also confirm Señora Rubiera's story.

Guggenheim states that "he interceded time and again to request a fair trial"—queer commentary on Cuban justice —"for the arrested oppositionists." "No statement can be issued as to the number of Cubans whose lives have been spared by this humane and unofficial intercession; and the rescued Cubans, while privately grateful, are reluctant to admit they appealed to the American Embassy." We have already seen how people are murdered and maltreated when it is discovered they have appealed to the Embassy.

After prolonged careful inquiries high and low, I have

been able to find no one, except Mariana de la Torre de Mendoza (for whom he acted only after scandalous publicity), Alvarez and Martínez Saenz (employed by a National City Bank law-firm) and several revolutionists after the August, 1931, fracas. Alvarez was murdered; Martínez and two other lawyers were sent to the Isle of Pines; Mariana de la Torre is in exile. Even to ask drumhead court-martials to give fair trial is a travesty in itself. The Guggenheim release goes on to state that "of course a number . . . were killed before he [I] could take any action." Why does he thus attempt to minimize the many hundreds of worthy Cubans officially murdered? Further to show his good faith, he seizes upon a technicality to refute Menocal, who stated in the *New York Times,* "Every Embassy except that of the United States is sheltering political refugees. Although the American Embassy is the one to which Cubans should turn most readily for protection in such times as these, I do not know of one Cuban who has gone there. Surely there is a reason for that." Guggenheim cried, "Another deliberate distortion of fact," and pedantically split hairs—"there are only three Embassies in Havana." Menocal neglected to say "Embassies and Legations." In addition Guggenheim denies that Cubans took refuge in the Spanish Embassy. The contrary is true. The British, Mexican, Uruguayan, Brazilian, and Panama representatives have repeatedly and indefatigably done far more to help persecuted Cubans in the name of humanity than Guggenheim; nor have they ever been accused of meddling. The Spanish Ambassador in addition has had to protest against the wanton police-murder of his nationals, much as we protested to Spain in the colonial days.

Another evidence of Guggenheim's good faith may be deduced from his action in the case of the aged Professor Carlos de la Torre put under arrest in his home. News of Torre's arrest aroused universal criticism in the United States. On the State Department's inquiry, the armed guards were at once removed. Guggenheim then made the simple public announcement that De la Torre was not under arrest. The true facts would have discredited Machado.

The President of the Cuban Patriotic League, in a pamphlet, "Ambassador Guggenheim and the Machado Program," states, "When Mr. Guggenheim mentions a series of murders on both sides," he is openly upholding and sheltering Machado. He knows that the latter commenced his wholesale murder on August 20, 1925, when he had Editor Armando André killed. . . . Then followed the harrowing assassinations of labor leaders, Antonio López, Varona, Villafuerte, Cuxart, Editor Aguiar, and many others. All through 1926 he continued . . . (a long list of names). Camagüey Islanders were "bumped off" by the hundreds. "El Día of April 14, 1926, listed twenty-seven murders of 'Islanders' up to that day . . . 1927 compiled a frightful list . . . [many names]." And he adds that Chester Wright returned to the United States with "147 substantiated cases of assassination. . . . In 1928 he [Machado] broke out with renewed fury. . . . El Heraldo de Cuba [official paper] reported nineteen [prisoners murdered] in one bunch. Machado started 1929 with Julio Antonio Mella, and kept up at full blast during that year and 1930. [Long lists follow for 1930, 31, 32.] Seven years of uninterrupted pogrom. . . ." The ratio in favor of the government, concludes Betencourt, is 500 to 1. The fact that the Ambassador has or has not saved two or three persons out of the hundreds upon hundreds officially murdered, is basically irrelevant. The effort expended in curbing the sanguinary instincts of the Havana police in this or that case could better be expended in rectifying our whole policy so that Cuba might, through the expressed will of its people, return to normal conditions with general guarantees. As it is the Cuban oppositionist marked for death had a very slim chance in the personal ticket he held in the lottery of the American Ambassador's good-will.

[352]

8 ARMS TO MACHADO

Our neutrality laws prevent the opposition from acquiring arms and ammunition to recover their government; but Machado, to hold Cuba helpless under his criminal tyranny, though he cannot pay his teachers, is permitted to buy any amount of arms and ammunition in the United States. A large shipment of machine-guns entered while I was there, and the decks of the steamer *Tela* on which I sailed from New Orleans had been converted into stables for horses to put more men in the saddle to maintain the present iniquity. Heavy purchases of bombing planes have also been made.

Those opposed to Machado can buy no arms. They have been shadowed and arrested in this country. Nothing, for instance, was crueler than the recent deportations of striking Cuban tobacco workers from Tampa to Cuba which inevitably meant for them persecution, imprisonment and danger of death. They were held by Machado in a stockade, a fact inadvertently revealed by the flight from the place of José González Cosuegra.

Interviewing Secretary of State Ferrara, I inquired if there was anything in the rumor that the oppositionists in the United States planned to launch a new armed expedition. He pulled out a letter from the chief of the Cuban secret service in the United States which stated that with the coöperation of the American authorities, all the Cubans were being closely watched and would be arrested at the sign of the first move.

In his 1902 report, Secretary of War Root said, on the occasion of Cuba finally being given independence: "I . . . hope that this strong and well-deserved friendship of Cuba may be permanent," that it might "never be alienated by our treatment of the smaller and weaker power," that the United States might "never lose their deep interest in the welfare of the new republic which they have called into being with so much labor and sacrifice."

Of all Latin-American countries, the people of Cuba have ever been most friendly to the United States; but this feeling is rapidly changing.

In 1931 a circular asked the Cuban people to show their displeasure "of the Ambassador's dealings" by consuming "no product of the United States if substitutable by other Cuban or foreign products. Do not travel in steamships under the American flag. Do not enter moving picture shows exhibiting American films, or any other establishment, hotel or American business place in Cuba. Do not consume electric current which is American. Do not deposit a single cent in any American bank, substituting the same with the Cuban or Canadian banks doing local business."

A boycott exists in some 64 Cuban cities against the American Utilities Company. The Havana Electric railways came to a standstill for several weeks, paralyzed by a strike of its employees and refusal of the public to ride on the tramways. The main offices of the Electric Company have been bombed in Havana and in cities in the interior and considerable damage done. The American Five-and-Ten-Cent store was partly wrecked by a bomb. The largest American Hotel, the Sevilla-Biltmore, has had to close its doors.

Other American business in Cuba is feeling the pinch. Anti-Americanism is showing considerable growth.

This is the tragic finale of Root's hope in 1902 that the good feeling between the two countries might never be disturbed; that we, the powerful, should never do anything to destroy Cuban faith and friendliness.

XXI GOOD DEMOCRATS

1 WOODEN MONEY

CUBA PROVIDES AN EXCELLENT
springboard to dive into the troubled waters of the new
administration. Four important names, high in Democratic
councils, are closely linked with Cuban affairs: Owen D.
Young, Norman H. Davis, Daniel C. Roper, and William
Hartman Woodin.

Does the intimate Cuba tie-up of new high officials, Secretary of Treasury Woodin and Secretary of Commerce
Roper, not to mention the great influence of Young and
Davis, augur any hope of change? Or will Roosevelt carve
out his own independent policy?

Woodin, until accepting office, President of the American Car and Foundry Company, had most intimate relations with the Machado régime. Because of this connection,
the Vice-President of the American Car and Foundry Company, Oscar B. Cintas, was appointed Cuban Ambassador
at Washington.

Why should Woodin, on accepting the office of Secretary
of Treasury, have dined at the Cuban Embassy?

On the north side of Cuba in Camagüey province, set
among horizon-stretching silver-green cane-fields and humid
banana groves, is the once-thriving town of Woodin. Years
ago, the place was renamed after our sweetly-smiling, cultured Secretary of Treasury. The event was properly celebrated with fireworks, bands and banquets. Mr. Woodin,
then as since interested in business, music, numismatics—

"Coins are the metallic footprints of nations"—and the uplift of poor but beautiful theater artists, could find no time to visit the scene of the source of much of his fortune and greet the people thus honoring him for his enterprise in railway and sugar development in our Cuban colony. But Mrs. Woodin journeyed thither.

Present was handsome young Oscar B. Cintas. To be handsome for some people spells ruin, for others success. For Cintas, not endowed with striking intellect, his good looks and winning ways have meant unusual success. He was born into a poor, middle-class family of a small interior town of Cuba; and in that mongrel oppressed world of the backward Spanish colony, people of fine physique were rare enough to excite attention.

A prominent English railroad man sent him to England to be educated. He came back modishly dressed, speaking English. His patron found him a position in the Banco Nacional of Cuba. But not having great interest in bank-balances not his own, Cintas presently found himself on the street.

But as salesman of sundry imported products, his handsome build and eager personality found proper outlet. Presently he was selling American Car and Foundry products. In those days the booming sugar industry was laying four thousand miles of track from the Centrales out through the cane-fields—limitless business for Woodin's company.

From managing the Cuban end, Cintas was brought to the United States. His sensitive interest in painting and beauties of the spirit attracted the refined composing sensibilities of Woodin; his handsome bearing brightened the Woodin home; enduring friendship resulted.

When a boy Woodin's father made him clean castings at ninety cents a day—so grievous a task for such a young esthete, he fled to Europe to study music and became a composer not jealous of Wagner. But ultimately he stepped into full charge of the American Car and Foundry Company. Soon his interests expanded into allied lines. Despite his obvious gentility, during the War he converted his plant to make murderous munitions. He also manufactures one-third of all the carburetors for General Motors, sundry other rail supplies, and builds ACF cruisers. When Federal agents began pot-shotting innocent yachtsmen as rum-runners, Woodin turned violently Wet. Until taking government office, he was chairman of the American Locomotive Company, run by his cousin, and director of its subsidiary, the Montreal Locomotive Works. The American Locomotive Company controls half a dozen mighty subsidiaries and over ten years ago made a contract on a fifty-fifty basis with the General Electric Company to turn out electrical engines. Woodin is also a director of the Remington Arms Company, which produces one-third the small arms and ammunition manufactured in this country, and in Cuba found excellent market; anyway people there had to be kept in their places so as not to throw stones at Woodin's railroad or blow up bridges.

Woodin's interest in Cuban railways is far-reaching. Till accepting office, he was director of the Cuba Company, a large holding concern, estimated by its president, Mr. Herbert C. Lakin, before the Senate Judiciary Sub-committee in 1929, to own properties in rail and sugar valued at $175,-000,000. Of its 640,000 shares, only 2,000 were then owned by Cubans. It controlled through its subsidiaries, the Cuba Railroad, the Cuba Northern, and other companies (1,000 miles of public service railroad, inventoried a few years earlier at $165,000,000); it owned directly 300,000 acres of land; and subsidiaries, 250,000 more. Thirty-three thousand acres of this was under cultivation, largely through leases running for ten years and worked by laborers whose maximum wage was then $1.50 a day, and is now almost nil. Woodin is not only on the board of directors of the Cuba Company, but is a director of the Cuba Railroad

Company, the Consolidated Railroad Company and the Compañia Cubana.

More important fellow directors are Herbert C. Lakin, a relative by marriage of former Secretary of State Stimson; and Horatio Seymour Rubens, who after helping free Cuba, became president and director of the Cuba Consolidated, the Cuba Railroad and Cuba Northern. Under Machado he has received two Congressional decorations, one especially created, "Great Friend of Cuba." Equally important as directors are Percy Rockefeller, George E. Devendorf (vice-president American Founders Corporation, president and director of the American and Overseas Corporation, director of the Public Utilities Holding Corporation); and R. C. Tripp (Curtis Aeroplane and Motor).

Lakin, "for old times' sake," has lobbied ardently for Machado in Washington on the Barlow case and sugar questions. For that purpose he collected $100,000 and expected to raise $50,000 more. At first he contended to the Senate investigation that he represented merely the American Chamber of Commerce in Cuba and the United States Sugar Association,[1] founded in 1922 or 1923, the president of which was George A. Zabriskie, close Hoover friend. But cross-examination forced Lakin to disclose he also represented the Cuban mill-owners and Machado. He was asked "specifically and directly" by Cuban Secretary of Agriculture (whose son was a son-in-law of Machado) to go to Washington to lobby; and he remained constantly in touch with Machado by letter, cable and personal emissaries.

The leading attorney hired by Lakin was Edwin P. Shattuck of the Shattuck, Bangs and Davis firm—promised

[1] Among others the following companies were members: Antilla Sugar Company, Atlantic Fruit and Sugar, Caracas Sugar, Cuba Cane, Cuban American, Cuban Dominican, Czarniskow-Rionda, Elia, Fidelity, Francisco, Fulton Iron Works (St. Louis), General Sugar, Hershey Corporation, Hormiguero Central Corporation, Ingenio Porvenir Company, W. J. McCahan Sugar Refining and Molasses Company, Manati Sugar, National Sugar Refining Company (New Jersey), New Niquero Sugar, Soledad, Sugar Estates of Oriente, Sugar Planters Operating Company, Tiunicu Sugar.

$100,000 for his efforts. Lakin constantly stressed to all his backers that Shattuck had daily entrée to Hoover.

Shattuck had long been associated with Cuban sugar activities. In 1923, he received a fee of over $20,000 from H. B. Hawley, president of the Cuban American Sugar Company, and from 1922-23, $60,000 or more from the Czarniskow-Rionda Company. He had been employed by our government Sugar Equalization Board from 1917-1919 and collected fees from it as late as 1927.

At Machado's direct request, and paid by Cuban mill-owners, as well as receiving nearly $2,000 in expenses from Lakin, Enoch Crowder also lobbied.

Another Lakin employee (paid by the Cuba Company) was Colonel Carroll (presented to Lakin years before by Crowder), who was given $10,000 for lobbying, "talking with everybody," and $4,500 monthly up to a total of nearly $30,000 for investigating and opposing the Barlow claim. In addition Carroll had for ten years been attorney for the Cuban Embassy ($4,800 monthly). It was he who went in his private car to Cuba, got Machado right after he was elected President, and brought him to this country to see Coolidge—"took him over to the White House." For, as Carroll put it, "I intend to try in whatever way I can to maintain and sustain . . . the Machado government as I would if an assault were made upon my own country." (After all a stipend of over $100,000 with a liberal expense account should command some loyalty.) In addition Carroll was attorney for the United Fruit Company ($15,000 annually) with heavy Cuban investments, not to mention his phenomenal salaries as attorney for the Northern Pacific, Great Northern, etc. (good customers of Woodin), and for the Royal Dutch Shell.

Carroll was outspoken. The Barlow claim was fought because it cast aspersions on the "justice in Cuban courts . . . dominated by President Machado." The Woodin-Lakin Cuba Company had, said Carroll, "an investment of

. . . $170,000,000 in Cuba. They were greatly interested in the administration of Machado. They . . . think he is making a fine President . . . they like the administration of Machado, think it the best they have ever had down there, and they want to sustain it," for "the orderly proceeding of Cuban government" was "very important to the prosperity of those interested in Cuban affairs."

Lakin, speaking reverently of the "broad and capable shoulders of President Machado," admitted he would always do whatever he "might be called upon to do by the [Cuban] government in behalf of the Cuban interests," and he proposed "to take some people to Cuba to prove to them that Cuba is not in the desperate state that some people have believed."

He got Cuban and American Masons in Havana to come to Washington and interview influential fellow-Masons in the government and elsewhere, and to write letters in behalf of honorary 33d degree Mason Machado. Though Machado has imprisoned and murdered fellow Masons, Masonry has been one of the most ardent secret defenders of Machado in this country.

Similar undercover action was obtained through the Rotary Clubs.

Percy Rockefeller, also associated with the Woodin rail interests, is likewise a director with Woodin in the Remington Arms Company. We have already noted his connection with Guggenheim and ramified Cuban enterprises.

His banking connection in New York is the National City Bank (he is a director). Charles E. Mitchell, until recently Chairman of the Executive Board of that institution, was a director, along with Woodin, of the Federal Reserve Bank of New York, and has been director of numerous Cuban sugar companies.

Associated with Woodin in the powerful Remington Arms Company, besides Rockefeller, should be mentioned F. P. Adams (also of Air Reduction), V. E. S. Griswold (treasurer, W. & J. Sloane Company and director of Chase); Frederick Winthrop Allen (of Woodin's subsidiary Transamerica Company, of Lee Higginson, and director of Chase, International Telephone and Telegraph, Otis Elevator, Vanadium Corporation, etc.); Seward Prosner (Chase corporation, General Motors and Kennicott Copper, a Guggenheim interest).

Mr. Charles Hayden, connected with seventy companies, a member of the Chase executive committee, is associated with Woodin in the American Locomotive Company and the Montreal Locomotive Works, as was also Wiggin, former head of Chase. Hayden also has relations with Woodin through numerous American railways. The Ward Bakery Company also claims Hayden as a director, and is related to milk and other Cuban monopolies sustained by military authority. Hayden is also interested in Coca-Cola Company which has two Cuban plants; the Cuban Portland Cement Company, owned by the International Cement Corporation; and the Matanzas (along with Chadbourne) and Punta Alegre sugar companies.

Some of these names tie up with the Electric Bond and Share Company and its subsidiary, American and Foreign Power, of Owen D. Young fame, so instrumental, via Catlin, in helping Machado into office, which have received enormous favors from Machado, both in legislation and tax-favoritism and the shooting of people in consumers' strikes.

Three of Woodin's directors of the American Car and Foundry Company are also directors of Electric Bond and Share Company: W. C. Potter, Lewis Eugene Pierson, John D. Ryan (just died). We have already mentioned their connection with the Guggenheim interests. Pierson is also connected with the Freeport Texas Company which runs the Cuban American Manganese Corporation.

Woodin is thus, through interlocking directorates, loans, concessions and privileges, closely linked with all the financial, public utility, sugar and mining interests, directly or indirectly responsible for upholding Machado. We have seen that the president and lawyers of the company in which Woodin is most deeply interested in in Cuba have testified that they would do anything to keep Machado in power and stop the slightest criticism of him.

Woodin's most direct approach is through the Cuba Company and affiliated railways and sugar companies.

In defiance of the Foraker Amendment prohibiting our first occupation to grant concessions, Sir William Van Horne incorporated the Cuba railway under a New Jersey charter, with only 160 shares of $50,000 each—one of the most aristocratic companies on record. Later the shares were split up. By December 1, 1902, the road, running eastward from Santa Clara to Santiago and to Antilla on Nipe Bay was opened for operation. President Gómez, as he said, "relying on the support of Congress and, above all, the aid of Divine Providence," subsequently gave the Cuba railway a $6,000 kilometer subsidy to build the Martí-Manzanillo branch and east to San Luis north of Santiago.

Various manipulations later took place to extend this company's control. The leading Cuban instrument of the Woodin-Lakin rail manipulations was Colonel José Miguel Tarafa (now dead), father of Cintas' wife.

The ambition of the Cuba railway precipitated one of the most tangled complications in Cuba's history, what Professor Chapman calls a "major grafting deal." The so-called Tarafa law—to benefit the Cuba railroad—was enacted in 1924, signed in final form by Machado and netted the concern at least $9,000,000 extra profit. Apparently to create a great Cuban railway consolidation to liberate the island from the clutches of foreign capital, the project played hugely upon the nationalistic sentiment Zayas had fomented during and after Crowder's departure. The "patriotic" enterprise was to merge the Cuba railway with two Cuban lines, the Cuba Northern and the Camagüey and Nuevitas; the "patriotism," according to La Discusión, consisted in "ditching" the Cuban minority stockholders of the smaller companies and turning over the Cuban lines to the Woodin-Lakin-Rockefeller corporation.

That the new patriotic company might have greater success, all sugar enterprises were obliged to abandon their ports—some 47 in all—from which they had previously shipped, so the railway might have the revenue of transporting sugar to officially designated ports, thus increasing shipping and wharfage costs at the expense of independent Cuban growers and the general interests of Cuba. A system of rebates permitted enterprises controlled by or friendly to Woodin and associates to out-compete other interests.

Admittedly the passage of the law was bought. The Veterans and Patriots Association charged that a minimum of $6,000 was paid to the Congressmen; $20,000 to Senators, and $500,000 to President Zayas. Certainly the bill was shoved through with practically no discussion.

Immediately the sugar people raised a hue and cry, denouncing the law as confiscatory, censuring the graft and secrecy with which it had been enacted. The issue was carried to the State Department. The Cuban government hastened to validate the Santa María port belonging to the General Sugar Company, i.e., the National City Bank, so that this powerful concern withdrew as an opponent. Washington lost interest, urged the contenders to compromise. But the Cuban Minister in London, through Washington pressure, was removed for making declarations against the merger. Further compromises were finally effected, but the railroad was given a strangle-hold on all new port development and sugar expansion. Machado put the final seal on this great Cuban welfare work. Perhaps Mr. Woodin then composed his famous ditty on bluebirds:

> Oh, hear the happy bluebirds singing in the rain.
> They're singing to the rainbow shining there again.
> So let us be like bluebirds, happy all day long,
> Forgetting all our troubles in a sunny song.

Daniel C. Roper of the new administration is also close to the elements which help keep Machado in power. Before taking office, he had been a representative of the following sugar companies, for the most part closely connected with the National City Bank, Mitchell and Rockefeller, a few with the Chase National: Cuba Cane, Punta Alegre, Guantánamo, Cuban American, Matanzas, Francisco, General Sugar, Caribbean Sugar, Fidelity, Cuban Dominican, etc.

2 NORMAN DAVIS

Another man high in Democratic councils, Norman H. Davis, also used Cuba as a crutch to rise to wealth and power. He arrived there broke, but in time became connected with various contracting companies and president of his own bank, the Cuba Trust Company.

The most exorbitant deal in the annals of Cuba is closely associated with his name—the notorious Ports Company of Cuba concession, granted by President Gómez, January 25, 1911. Designated ports were to be dredged and kept in condition for thirty years in return, during the entire period, for a levy of 68 cents a ton (70 cents for American) merchandise and 25 cents a ton on coal. The company, purely a paper concern, issued $10,000,000 stock which went to the backers and prominent members of the Liberal Party in power, including Miguel Céspedes and Orestes Ferrara. Eight hundred and twenty-five thousand dollar first mortgage bonds were also parceled out. The Ports Company also gave good sinecures to politicians. A law-partner of Orestes Ferrara, speaker of the Cuban Chamber, was made a director; Ferrara headed the legal department, which also included Céspedes. Ferrara and Céspedes are the two big guns to-day in the Machado cabinet.

In September, 1913, the *Times of Cuba,* pointing out why the Ports Company should not suffer loss by having any privileges curtailed, declared that it probably had "paid out a large amount of money to get the concessions, scores of Cuban officials and lawmakers—from President down to common policemen—receiving their share of the spoils. . . ."

Revenue returns for the first year were estimated at one million dollars and were expected to increase during the next twenty-nine years. Though work of a value of only $10,000,000 was to be performed, Davis' bank, the Trust Company, which loaned a million dollars, appraised the concession at $25,000,000. Davis journeyed to London, bag stuffed with $6,000,000 in bonds. Sperling and Company offered them to the public in May, 1911, the prospectus stating that the works plus bond interests would be entirely paid off within fifteen years, leaving the income of the remaining fifteen years, less maintenance costs, entirely to the stockholders.

The contract for the entire job was sublet to T. L. Huston Contracting Company. This company had been incorporated in Havana, September 27, 1904, by Tillinghast L'Hommedieu Huston (ex-U. S. Engineers) and Norman H. Davis, who together turned in $19,900 in materials and contracts to pay up the bulk of the $20,000 capital. The venture prospered. Affiliated subsidiaries, such as the Huston Concrete Company and the Huston-Trumbo Dredging Company were formed; it acquired the inexhaustible Camoa quarry near Havana. At Concha, by 1913, it had the largest concrete pipe-plant in the world.

The New York bankers were concerned over this raid on customs lest loan-payments suffer. The State Department advised the Cuban minister, June 23, 1911, that this was a "highly improvident and dangerous fiscal policy." The following year it took the matter up with the Ports Company direct, also brought pressure to bear on Cuba at the moment when marines had landed to suppress the negro rebellion.

Eight days before leaving office, Gómez published a decree, approved by the Ports Company and the American legation, allowing the Cuban government to purchase outstanding stock at a valuation set by three appraisers, one of whom would be appointed by the United States. Stock issue was limited to $10,000,000. The Ports Company received new favors, was relieved of performing part of the assigned work, was granted title to reclaimed lands; its mortgages and contracts were recognized. In such wise did the United States reform the iniquitous concession—by increasing apparent legality, without imperiling expected profits.

The scandal refused to subside. Menocal voided the last Gómez decree and seized the properties. The company had already done about $5,000,000 worth of work, but port dues had largely covered this amount. The bond-holders and State Department at once brought pressure; and though the courts had upheld the confiscation, Menocal ordered indemification, but delayed until 1916. By that time Menocal's election was in doubt; he also needed funds. Fifteen million dollars was promised him as a reward for Cuba's declaration of war against Germany.

Norman Davis had become a dollar-a-year man in the Treasury Department, in charge of recommending Allied loans; and the United States and Davis' bank became doubly insistent upon a settlement of the ports concession. It was soon clear without such settlement to his company, Davis would hold up the "patriotic" loan.

A Menocal decree authorized the exchange of $7,000,000 5 percent Cuban bonds for the same amount of company bonds. The properties of the company, valued at $18,000,-000, including 831,044 square meters of Havana waterfront, were returned to it. The Cuban government, in short, returned the company its assets and assumed its debts. Thus, the United States, aided and advised by patriotic Mr. Davis, helped save Cuba from improvident squandering of her resources. Shortly after Congress authorized this arrangement, Cuba received her anticipated "Liberty" loan.

This holy concern of the United States government over the improper ports concession was stripped of its good front by our championship of two of the most high-binder concessions in all of Cuba's history: the McGiveny-Rokeby concession for the sewering and paving of Havana and the Reilly concession for the Cienfüegos aqueduct, pushed through by the Magoon administration. The sewerage system was inadequate before it was laid; the poor paving "made American contractors the jibe of Cubans for a decade."

While these connections of Woodin, Roper, Davis and Young do not augur favorably for any solution of Cuba's fundamental problems by the new Democratic administration, present indications are that since the sugar industry is now largely owned by the Chase National Bank and the National City, reduction in our tariff toward Cuba is almost inevitable, together with steps to pool Cuban, Hawaiian, Filipino and Puerto Rican sugar. Chadbourne's preëlection attacks on Roosevelt are not likely to add to President Roosevelt's faith in the preposterous sugar plan now in force. And of course the Woodin-Lakin-Rockefeller rail interests have suffered tremendously by the economic policies of Machado, his favoritism to a narrow clique of American interests, the central highway, the decline of sugar, and the disorder which has stopped almost all passenger traffic. It is doubtful if to-day Lakin would sing such high praises for the Machado tyranny.

Such steps would improve economic conditions and restore some of our own lost trade, but without a political clean-up, will be merely dangerous "soothing-syrup." Political bitterness has become so deep rooted that no lasting stability can be achieved until Machado is driven from the island, and even then months and years may be required to straighten things out. To buttress up Machado with economic reforms, however capable, will lead the new administration into the same pitfalls as Guggenheim; and will in the end merely aggravate the difficulties he helped promote.

Unfortunately Sumner Welles, the new ambassador, has already indicated this will be precisely the policy which will be followed. The only new device being proposed is the hoary trick of dictator Porfirio Díaz of Mexico to fool the public into believing he intended to resign; viz., the creation of the office of a Vice-Presidency.

XXII DOLLARS

1 SCHMIDLAPP AND SOLDIERS

THE STATE DEPARTMENT'S RE-
sponsibility for Cuban loans is clearly defined. Mr. Lamont
testified before the Senate Finance Committee, December
18, 1931, that the Platt Amendment required the Cuban
government to secure special approval of the American government before it could float any foreign loans. American
bankers have always secured such approval. The department has given its consent to all loans allocated there—is
directed involved.

The long history of American loans to Cuba is full of
complicated and dubious twistings which would require
volumes.[1]

[1] Prior to the Machado régime the following bank loans were floated:
1904 Estrada Palma—Speyer & Co., $35,000,000, 5% tax-free.
    Security: Excise taxes, 15% customs.
    Purpose: Veteran payments, $28,281,181.
1909 Gómez—Speyer, $16,500,000, 4½% tax-free.
    Security: Prior customs lien.
    Purpose: Retire $2,196,585 internals.
        Havana sewerage.
        Cienfüegos aqueduct.
1914 Menocal—J. P. Morgan, $10,000,000, 5% tax-free.
    Security: 10% customs, if insufficient other revenues.
1921 Zayas—Morgan, $5,000,000.
1923 Zayas—Morgan, $50,000,000, 5½% tax-free.
    Security: 10% revenues exceeding $50,000,000.
    Purpose: Retire $5,000,000 loan.
        Past services, $7,000,000.
        Fund of Special Accounts, $9,000,000.
        Pensions, $2,000,000.
        Back public work obligations, $18,000,000.
        Internal bonds, $3,000,000.
        Repair, carry on public works, $6,000,000.

In addition to the Chadbourne sugar bonds, to be considered in the last chapter, July 1, 1927, J. P. Morgan and Company made a 5½ percent $9,000,000 loan due serially, 1928-1937. Prior to this loan, Lamont at a banquet to Machado in New York, April, 1927, is reported by the press to have stated: "We do not care by what means, but we should like to see such a good administrator remain in power." This money was used to take up at par previous credits of the Zayas government which Machado, Catlin and other associates had bought up at a few cents on the dollar. It is estimated that $6,000,000 were cleaned up on this deal.

February 19, 1927, the Chase Bank signed a contract to loan Cuba $10,000,000 at 6 percent for four years in return for deferred payment public works certificates and a $400,000 commission. It also made later loans on the same basis, to build the famous east-to-west road and the capitol building (mentioned in the first chapter), though some later funds were utilized to construct private roads to Machado's private haciendas, for constructing new towns owned body and soul by Machado, including one named after himself, an enterprise in which Guggenheim was especially interested.

June 22, 1928, the Chase people arranged for a revolving credit of $60,000,000 by the exchange of each successive $10,000,000 bloc of work certificates (up to a total of $50,000,000) in 5½ percent tax-free serial certificates.[2]

This issue was then converted, February 26, 1930 (after Guggenheim's arrival), into an $80,000,000 loan at 5½ percent due June 30, 1945.[3]

[2] These were retirable in nine $6,250,000 installments between December 31, 1931, and June 30, 1935—these to be offered to the public. The bank was granted 1.80 percent on all retired work certificates and 1 percent on the $50,000,000 principal. Cost of transmission of funds to New York was to be paid for by the government. Of these new certificates two $10,000,000 installments were floated on the New York market, thirty-odd million dollars being retained by the bank.

[3] The Chase Company turned in $37,723,348.83 serial certificates in portfolio and took $40,000,000 bonds at 95 and interest, which were then floated at 98,

The gross profit of these multiple transactions, according to Mr. Schmidlapp, vice-president of the Chase National Bank, was $3,317,666, or about 5½ percent, a spread —if his figures are correct—which cannot be considered exaggerated. But the $80,000,000 issue was taken at 95 and is retirable at 105. Also, to avoid defaulting, the Cuban government has had to obtain from Chase advance money for payments, at exorbitant interest and discount rates. The Chase was asked by the Senate Finance Committee early in 1932 to produce some of these short-term advance contracts, but they were never included in the subsequently printed evidence.

Obviously none of the public works, certainly not the capitol, has returned anywhere near this cost and interest, even in indirect benefit to the nation, and of course, nothing directly. Schmidlapp estimated that the road cost $100,-000,000 alone; at that it is unfinished, has been narrowed beyond specifications, and is breaking down. This is about $135,000 a mile instead of a normal cost of a few thousand dollars. An American company previously offered to build the entire road for $35,000,000. Considering this last as somewhere near a normal price, the road represented a loss in graft of $65,000,000, or 65 percent in the utilization of the money.

Schmidlapp testified to the Senate Finance Committee that he had paid no attention to the manner in which this money was spent. Senator King retorted, "Were you not interested . . . [in] making any investigation as to the purpose of the loan and the application of the funds?" Schmidlapp admitted he did know the purpose.

Part of this road contract was granted to Warren Brothers Company fighting suit, as Machado was previously advised,

or, plus the 1.80 charge and excluding the 1 percent commission ($500,000), a gross 4.35 spread. In addition, the government paid the bank for serving as fiscal agent, and some $207,470 for various services, plus cost of transferring funds and mailing notices.

in three American cities. But Machado, Céspedes and others were investing in stock of the favored company, at the time very depreciated; it jumped immediately afterward.

All of this perhaps explains why Machado was willing to violate his solemn preëlection promise not to increase the public debt.

To secure the Chase loan, over $500,000 was paid to José Emilio Obregón y Blanco, Machado's son-in-law, as manager of the Chase's Havana subsidiary, in which capacity he received a $19,000 salary, while simultaneously serving as head of the Havana clearing house and major-domo at the Palace (salary $2,400). The $500,000 was paid out by presidential decree.

Schmidlapp admitted that Obregón had been hired as "a man who had contacts in Havana; that had contacts throughout the island, that could perhaps be helpful in bringing business to the bank." How helpful, we have seen.

Senator King: Your organization knew that he was the son-in-law of Mr. Machado?

Mr. Schmidlapp: They did.

King: . . . Was not your company advised repeatedly that Mr. Machado was not a *de jure* President, or even *de facto,* but was holding position by reason of usurpation and violation of the constitution of Cuba?

Schmidlapp: No. . . .

King: Well, did you not know that Mr. Machado had prorogued his office; that is, prolonged it by unconstitutional or allegedly unconstitutional methods?

Schmidlapp: No.

King: . . . that Mr. Machado . . . had suppressed all political parties and was governing by military rule? . . .

Schmidlapp: No.

King: You knew that he had a rather large standing army?

Schmidlapp: I did not give it a thought. . . . I did not know what the Army of Cuba was.

What great concern over the security of the millions paid out by American bond-buyers! March 31, 1933, these bonds were quoted at 33 1/8.

Senator Johnson: Do you know where Mr. Obregón resided during the time that he was in your employ . . . whether he resided at the Presidential Palace?

Schmidlapp: I do not know.

Mr. Williams (vice-president of the Chase-Harris Forbes Corporation): I know, as a matter of fact, he did.

Among others who received commissions for the Chase loan contract would be mentioned Mr. Catlin of the Cuban Electric Company with whom, as we have seen, Machado was intimately connected, personally, politically and in business deals.

2 CUBAN PROTESTS

In 1930 prior to the $80,000,000 loan, the Cuban Patriotic League (attacked so heartily by Guggenheim) sent out a circular to all members of Congress, the President of the United States, and his cabinet as well as to all banks, banking firms, and brokers. It therefore was received by Schmidlapp's company, the Chase National Bank. It declared:

1. That the Machado government was illegal and despotic; that these loans were to be paid by the people of Cuba, who had had no say in the issuance thereof.

2. That there was a large deficit in the Cuban budgets, which started back in 1926. Machado was and is sustaining an immense army and bureaucracy to hold power and his budget outlay was and is more than Cuba can bear. Taxes are unbearable. The loans allowed him to remain in office by covering his budget deficits and the Chase Bank was thus merely handing out money which the Cuban people would

have to pay and which was being utilized for their detriment and the suppression of their liberties.

3. A large part of the money advanced by the Chase Bank was pilfered by the Machado administration. It was chiefly used to build a 680-mile road at a cost of over $100,-000,000 which could have been built for 40, or, at the utmost, 50 millions. The capital, originally bid out for $3,500,000, cost over $20,000,000. Although it is considerably larger than the original project, in any event, it is a monument to the extravagance of the Machado dictatorship, financed by the Chase Bank.

4. The money which is now being paid to the Chase Bank is sorely needed by the Cuban population. Widespread misery reigns in Cuba to an incredible degree; it is directly imputable to the Machado régime and in nowise to the price of sugar. Salaries of government employees are three months in arrears, that the Chase Bank may be paid. The market price of 38, which represents an immense loss to American investors, is proof that Cuba is at the end of the rope and cannot pay. But for the Machado iron rule, a moratorium, highly beneficial to the Cuban people, would have been already declared.

5. The Chase Bank has actually given the Machado dictatorship a two years' lease on life. It has permitted the wholesale murder and exploitation which has characterized the Machado despotism.

It now becomes clear why Guggenheim hurried to Cuba to salvage the Machado régime, why such efforts have been made to gag the press and magazines not merely of Cuba but of this country, why every effort to return the Cuban government to the Cuban people will be resisted to the last ditch by American official and financial power.

Orestes Ferrara, Guggenheim's close friend (he even provided servants for his home), has declared: "In the name of the government I ratify the proposal to fulfill its international obligations even if the people have to cut down on their food [they have done that to the starvation point], even if their economy leaves them naked."

Cuba might well remember the words of González Roa, representative of Mexico in the special 1923 Arbitration Commission: "To consider that the foreigner, for the sole circumstance of owning bonds of a loan for which is responsible a determined nation that has suffered severe internal calamity, should be placed in a privileged position with reference to its nationals, not only is contrary to the elemental spirit of justice but also to scorn the fundamental principles of the law of nations."[4]

The United States, for its part, might well recall how it forced Spain to cancel all of Cuba's debts. The full responsibility of the banks for Cuba's present tragic situation should be clarified preliminary to scaling down the island's debt.

3 CAPITAL PENETRATION

One-third of Cuba's territory, nearly 90 percent of the cultivable lands of the island, is owned or controlled by long-time leases by Americans or American corporations. The remainder is largely mortgaged to American banks and creditors. Eighty percent of the sugar industry belongs to citizens of the United States; the rest is controlled chiefly by American creditors. Cuba's second industry—tobacco—is also mostly American. Nearly all the banks, railroads, street-car lines, electric plants, telephone systems and other public utilities are owned by capital from the United States. The dominant position in all this American enterprise has, during recent years, been assumed by the banks, principally the National City, the Chase National and the House of Morgan.

Nowhere else, certainly not in the United States, has rugged capitalism had a freer hand than in Cuba. Yet in few places in the world to-day are conditions quite as bad.

4 *La responsibilidad internacional del estado,* 22.

Denied economic justice, the people can only be kept down by brutal despotism, iron-heeled militarism. Thus all political doors are closed to the honest and capable.

Our share of responsibility for this situation is clearly demonstrable.

American commerce with Cuba dates back to Spanish colonial days of smuggling and piracy. Clandestine commerce flourished before our own independence, but not until the early 'nineties of the eighteenth century were Cuban ports opened to neutral ships carrying food and clothing.

The first railway (Havana to Güines, 1837) was the work of Americans with English money. Quite early American planters, near Matanzas and Cárdenas introduced improvements and machinery into the sugar industry. By the 'fifties one-third the island's trade was with the United States; we bought $12,000,000, sold back $8,000,000—greater than Cuba's commerce with Spain. Over half the vessels entering Havana from 1851 to 1855 carried the American flag. By the 'eighties, one-fourth our foreign-trade tonnage was engaged in Cuban interchange.

Thus various periods are discernible in American penetration of Cuba. Up until the end of the nineteenth century, our stake was largely trade, more or less clandestine. Toward the close of Spanish rule, some American investments —largely due to small private initiative—appeared in Cuba.

Early independence was predominately the concession and settler period. Through the administrations of Estrada Palma, the second intervention under Magoon, the epoch of Gómez and Menocal, American concessionaires buzzed around the government buildings for fat contracts and other privileges. To-day these Wallingfords are overshadowed by large-scale capital developments.

The American sugar industry in Cuba began to gain control during the Gómez period, consolidated its position under Menocal. The second term and the subsequent administration of Zayas and Machado represented the financial consolidation of American interests, a shift of control from the sugar barons to the banks and public utilities. The opening of the Panama Canal made Havana far more important as an international trade-depot. Under Menocal the Spanish banks were looted and smashed, control came into the hands of Morgan and Company, the National City, the allied Royal Bank of Canada, and the Chase National. Rapidly these banks sucked in the sugar industry, a process hastened to completion under Machado.

These shifts, as we have seen, were paralleled by political changes and the development of a paternalistic Caribbean policy by the United States. The earlier concession-sugar period was represented by the Taft-Magoon intervention. Financial concentration was featured by the meddling or "preventive" policy of Crowder. Full financial consolidation coincides with the hypocritical hands-off policy begun with Harding, carried on by Coolidge, Hoover and Ambassador Guggenheim. In other words financial rule, become more direct and powerful, needs to call upon the State Department only in subterranean ways or in times of crisis.

4 LIGHT ON DARK PLACES

We have already considered the pleiad of names revolving around Guggenheim, Woodin, Roper, Young, Davis and others.

The Electric Bond and Share Company, so responsible for Machado, is a great holding company which in October, 1932, owned 49 percent of American and Foreign Power common; 31 percent of American Power and Light; 59.6 percent Electric Power and Light; 46.6 percent of National Power and Light; 18.9 percent American Gas and Electric Company. It also controls the Phœnix Utility Company and the United Gas Corporation. Its subsidiary, the American and Foreign Power, controls the Cuban subsidiaries;

and in 1930 they supplied light, power, gas, water and ice to 1,520,000 Cubans. Later in 1930 (besides the rate and tax-privileges previously indicated, the brutal suppression of consumers' strikes) the government used its good offices in helping them garner in thirteen more communities in Santa Clara, Matanzas, Camagüey and Oriente.[5]

A significant connection of these power interests is with the International Telephone and Telegraph Company (I. T. and T.), through Sosthenes Behn, Charles Mitchell, and Clarence Dillon.

The I. T. and T. controls the Cuban Telephone Company, the Radio Corporation of Cuba, Cuban-American Telephone and Telegraph Company, the Cuban All-American Cables, and at the end of 1926 had Cuban assets valued at $28,300,000.

With Sosthenes Behn in the I. T. and T. are Hernand Behn, and these, through Orestes Ferrara, were helped to acquire not only the Cuban monopoly but also the much-discussed Spanish monopoly (Compañia Telefónica Nacional de España, etc.), of which former Minister of Public Works Indalecio Prieto has declared, "a high personage received a 500,000 peseta bribe for arranging a contract with the Primo de Rivera government." The Behns also control the Havana Docks Corporation.

The relation of Orestes Ferrara with the I. T. and T. and

[5] This company and the American and Foreign Power have among their officers and directors besides Owen D. Young and others, the following men: On October 13, 1932, F. H. Brownell, chairman of the Guggenheim interests, the American Smelting and Refining Company (A. S. R. Co.) was added to the board of directors of Electric Bond and Share; other directors prior to that were Clarence E. Groesbeck (also an A. S. R. Co. man and director of the American Gas and Electric and United Gas); John D. Ryan (recently died), head of the Guggenheim Anaconda Copper interests; Lewis E. Pierson (A. S. R. Co.); W. C. Potter (A. S. R. Co. and Guggenheim Exploration Company).

The National City Bank is tied up to the Electric Bond and Share through director Charles Mitchell, S. S. Colt (former vice-president National City); George S. Roberts (vice-president, 1919-21, since a director).

The Chase National Bank is tied up to them through Clarence Dillon, George H. Howard, Brownell, I. T. Parkinson.

the Behns is important. Ferrara was an exiled Italian anarchist who fought, mostly with his wits, in Cuba's independence struggle, became a Cuban citizen by act of Congress, and gradually insinuated himself into high Cuban politics by fighting duels for important officials. Former Cuban Ambassador at Washington, to-day he has two portfolios in the Machado government, Secretary of State and of Finance. He is a great admirer of Machiavelli, of whom he had shadow-written a massive biography and critical study; and he bases all his own procedure on the wily Italian's doctrines.

Ferrara was also utilized to try to secure a similar concession in Japan. The whole machinery of the Cuban government was put into motion to bring this about. Various Japanese commissions appeared in Cuba. Soon adroit Japanese diplomats whispered in susceptible ears that the United States government was the natural enemy of Cuba; some day she would need Japan's aid. Strangely enough the Cuban officials seemed impressed. Diplomatic relations were set up between the two countries, and for the first time in Cuba's history, a Japanese representative, Mr. K. Uchuyama, arrived on the island. June 25 Cuba signed what ordinarily might have been considered an affront to the United States—since there was no especial need for such an arrangement—a favored nation treaty.

At the same time, Uchuyama spent all of his free time visiting the landlocked bays adjacent to Havana harbor, and for some time past, the Cuban authorities had winked their eyes at the activities of a Japanese fishing fleet, enjoying a very curious and favored concession, which under this guise had been taking careful soundings and plans of all out-of-the-way harbors which abound on both sides of the island. Memoranda of these activities, especially of the fishing fleet, is on file with the American State Department, and therefore I presume also with the Navy Department and the Intelligence Department. Whether the fact that these activities between Cuba and Japan were tied up with the expansion plans of a large American corporation, and whether these same plans deterred the State Department from taking any action with Machado regarding Japanese activities on the island, I am unable to state. Señor Ferrara was given the absurd appointment of Ambassador to the United States and Extraordinary Envoy and Minister Plenipotentiary to Japan.[6]

5 BANKS AND SUGAR

The Chase National Bank reveals the following connections:

José Obregón (manager Chase branch, Havana, son-in-law of Machado).

G. M. Dahl (vice-president, 1917-23, now a director; associated with Hayden Stone; interested in New York traction).

Albert W. Wiggin (close to Woodin interests).

I. T. Parkinson (Electric Bond and Share, interested in New York traction).

Carl Jacob Schmidlapp (vice-president, connected with companies dealing with Woodin interests; and director of various sugar companies close to the bank).

Charles Hayden.

George H. Howard (public utilities, Electric Bond and Share).

E. V. R. Thayer (former Chase president, many sugar companies, director of railroads doing business with Woodin interests).

The leading sugar companies closely connected with

[6] Other important links of the I. T. and T. are with Morgan (R. C. Leffingwell and Arthur M. Anderson); with National City (Allan Gray Hoyt, Charles Mitchell, Gordon S. Rentschler); with Chase (F. W. Allen, of Lee Higginson); with United Fruit (V. M. Cutter, since eliminated); and Bradley W. Palmer.

Walter G. Olgivie, another I. T. and T. director, is president of the Havana Terminal Railroad and an officer of the Havana Central Railroad, Cuban Pan-American Express Company, American Cuban Estates Company, etc.

Chase through actual control of stocks, interlocking directorates, special financing, etc., are Lowry and Company which absorbed the Punta Alegre interests; the Cuban Trading Company, Cuba Cane, Eastern Cuba Company, Francisco Sugar Company and Matanzas Sugar Company.

Among the directors of Cuba Cane should be mentioned Mr. E. W. Stetson, who is connected up with the tobacco industry and with Coca-Cola. Also Irene Dupont of the E. I. du Pont de Nemours Company; and Mathew Chauncey Brush of the Boomer-Du Pont Property Corporation, and of New York traction.

The National City Bank has already been thrown into relief.

Without making this a Biblical list, besides Mitchell, Roberts, Rockefeller, Sosthenes Behn, Gordon S. Rentschler (sugar companies), should be mentioned J. A. Stillman, director of the board of the National Hotel of Cuba; and James Howell Post.

Post, one of the biggest sugar men in Cuba, is director on most of the bank's sugar concerns. He is also interested in New York traction. He has been decorated by Machado.

Among the leading sugar companies close to the National City, in most of which Post is found as an official or a director, are General Sugar (Colonel Edward Deeds, president); George Houston, president (close to Woodin); Cuban Dominican (F. P. Adams, president); Atlantic Fruit and Sugar; Cuban American; National Sugar Refining; Guantánamo, New Niquero, Vertientes, San Chistóbal, Camagüey, Sugar Estates of Oriente.[7]

6 JUSTICE

The net result of all our good-will, our capital, our advice, our marines, our outlay of talent, enterprise, human life and money has been—

[7] See Appendix.

abysmal failure. Despite American dollars poured into Cuba to buy out the island, despite all the technical knowledge we have bestowed, despite the good advisers and experts paid for by the American and Cuban treasuries, all this sanctimonious effort has merely helped precipitate our protectorate into its present tragic economic and political condition. Why?

Our major purpose in Cuba has been profits, not justice.

XXIII CUBA'S WHITE GHOST

1 BITTER SWEET

Ex-ambassador marquez Sterling wrote: [1] "Sugar-cane does not make colonies happy, or a people cultured, or republics opulent; and the independence we won in the war against Spain, we must consummate in a war against sugar-cane, which perpetuated in the golden island, as an inexhaustible tradition, the despotism of the major-domo and the hatred of the slave." [2]

Sugar and geography made Cuba declare war on Germany. Geography and sugar made Cuba more than ever an American vassal. Both have cost Cuba dearly, most subsequent disasters being due to her willingness to coöperate with us during the War, to bend every effort to expand her sugar production at the expense of all other crops—to let us reap the cream of the profits and subsequently protect ourselves at her expense. Of all our foreign allies, we treated Cuba, the best of them all, the worst.

After the brief post-War "Dance of the Millions" in 1920 Cuba plunged to economic disaster, a prostrate rôle of economic invalidism; she has remained bed-ridden until this day—thirteen long years.

The banks tumbled down the ditch with sugar. They could not unfreeze their sugar assets. Those assets had, for the most part, depreciated beyond recovery.

In October, 1920, the banks folded up. A run on the *Banco Mercantil Americano de Cuba* soon spread to other

1 *Las Conferencias de Shoreham,* 26.
2 Cf. appendix.

institutions. October 11, Menocal declared a moratorium. A system permitting certified checks allowed the large depositors—as is usual in such cases—to loot the banks at the expense of small depositors.

Before any plan could be worked out, Albert Rathbone, our former Under-Secretary of Treasury, arrived unannounced even to Secretary of Treasury Cancio, who at once resigned. Rathbone installed himself in his office. After two weeks, he submitted a 14-point memorandum, sailed for New York, and billed Cuba for $50,000. His unique proposal was a gigantic foreign loan.

The moratorium continued while the *colonos* and their *guajiros* harvested a bumper crop at falling prices.

Enoch C. Crowder hurried down to pave the way for Rathbone's suggested loan. Cuba vainly protested.

Crowder supported the Cosme de la Torriente bill for the gradual lifting of the moratorium through successive percentage payments to depositors; other Crowder bills were jammed through. "He [Crowder] cannot compel me, not even with the guns of the *Minnesota,* to vote in the Cuban Congress for any law which appears to harm us," shouted Majority Leader Senator Aurelio Alvarez, withdrawing from that body. Crowder ended the moratorium, but did nothing to strengthen credit or improve the economic situation. The major banks headed directly into quicker ruin.

And early in April, Cuba—who had sacrificed her whole national economy to sugar production to aid us in the War —now at its most disastrous moment since independence, received a body blow under the belt from her erstwhile Big Brother—the Emergency Tariff bill raised the duty on Cuban sugar from 1.0048 to 1.60 cents.

Crowder's optimistic bank reports now proved doubly wrong. A new board of directors replaced Merchant, head of the Banco Nacional with Porfirio Franca, former manager of the Havana National City. Merchant fled from the country. José López ("Pote," the wealthiest man in Cuba, personally owing the bank $7,000,000 without security) hung himself by the neck from his balcony. April 9 the institution closed its doors. J. I. Lezema, calling a meeting of sugar creditors to investigate, was immediately ordered arrested for forgery and skipped the country. His failure revealed $24,000,000 liabilities, much of it in the bank.

During May eight banks with 123 branches, headed by the Banco Internacional, crumpled up. Three more in June. June 6, Banco Español handed itself over to the Liquidation Commission, and Marimón joined Merchant and Lezema in terrified flight overseas. Eighteen banks failed in rapid succession. The National City, the Royal Bank of Canada, and the Chase National remained in command of the carnage field. At last American finance had won the victory over Spanish financial influence in the island. Wise statesmanship would have averted the Banco Nacional crash. Its failure and the victory of National City and Morgan influence in Cuba through Crowder is one of the great monuments of our political idealism, part of our sacrifices for shouldering the white man's burden.

This victory, as time went on, meant the absorption of the entire sugar industry by American banks, who were to precipitate it into new disasters for their own ends.

The National City Bank opened its Havana branch in 1915 or 1916. Up until 1921 the bank's interest in the sugar industry was solely as a lender to the sugar planters. In that year it lost its first loan. By then $30,000,000 to $35,000,000 had been chalked up by it as slow or doubtful. From the 1920 deflation on, the enforced sugar expansion of the institution was rapid.

Vice-President Rentschler, who handled the National City sugar business from July, 1921, went to Cuba to organize the General Sugar Company ($25,000,000 stock) to take over all the bank's frozen loans and sugar properties acquired during the crash. George Houston became president, Rentschler vice-president. By foreclosure it took over the Centrales Astraya, Pilar San Cristóbal and the stock of the Santa Clara Sugar Company, then purchased the Camagüey and Vertientes properties to round them out. In all it had nearly 330,000 acres and in 1928 produced 683,500 pounds of sugar.

2 LAST GASP

Cuban sugar was down to 1¾ cents a pound. A commission was sent to Washington to lobby for favorable tariff rates. There they encountered the beet-sugar interests strongly intrenched with Boss Reed Smoot, Beet Sugar Chairman of the Senate Finance Committee, and Beet Sugar Boy Fordney, Chairman of the Ways and Means Committee. Secretary of Commerce Hoover told the Cubans to come to some agreement with the beet-growers.

Horatio Seymour Rubens of independence fame, who had rewarded his services in the cause of liberty by acquiring Cuban interests, now head of the wealthy Cuba Railroad and other corporations, rushed hither and yon in behalf of Cuban sugar. Havemeyer, stakes at both ends, strove to bring the two groups together. But all their pleas were thrown back from the stone-wall of a narrow vested interest in an artificial American industry. Beet-sugar politicians, buttressed by farm-bloc allies, refused to listen to the heads of the great American sugar companies in Cuba. The beet-sugar people demanded Cuba limit her crop to 2,500,000 tons for 1922, about 60 percent of the previous three-year average—a colossal blow, but would promise nothing regarding the tariff. Crowder, close to Smoot, was very ardent for restriction. Neither world efficiency, the price of sugar to the consumers, nor any other sound economic motives were at stake—merely the profit-greed of the beet-growers.

Cuban restriction merely meant that sugar would be grown less economically elsewhere. Crop limitation could have only one result—disaster for Cuba. The people first to be hit would be the Cuban workers, then the small native producers, the *colonos*. The last to be affected would be the large American Centrales. Cuba decided against restriction, despite Crowder.

The Fordney tariff at once jumped the duty to 2.30 cents on world sugar, 1.84 cents on Cuban sugar, the highest schedule since the 1890 trade war with Spain. More of our eternal gratitude!

But by April, 1923, despite the Fordney tariff, the price rose to six cents. Cuban sugar made a brief effort to revive. For the moment the Fordney tariff merely passed the cost on to the American consumer.

But this was merely the last gasp of the corpse. Soon the price tumbled again. Cuba could not hurdle the tariff.

3 CUBA, THE PAWN

To-day, the white ghost of Cuba is sugar. This dread specter of Cuba's once flourishing industry stalks the sun-drenched land, striking fear through every heart. Her consort is black-robed tyranny; behind her is a trail of murder and desolation. The rhetorical eloquence of these sentences is fully justified. Step into the armed camp that is Cuba, where men and women are jailed, tortured, murdered for attempting to exercise their legal rights. Go out into the provinces and see the hordes of half-naked emaciated wretches roaming the countryside with unkempt hair and falling like beasts on the slightest morsel of food.

Largely on the advice of American bankers, alarmed for their loans to the Cuban growers, President Machado in 1925 began a policy of paternalism, which if not wholly to blame for wrecking the industry, has aggravated every evil beyond immediate remedy.

But he preferred to play in with the financial powers for whom he might expect loans to carry on his government. Sound industry be damned. Money in the cash-box was the thing.

The scheme was to bring the sugar industry under state control, restrict output and attempt to bolster up the price. At first glance this might seem a statesman-like move to further prosperity. But every step was to redound, not to benefit Cuba and her industry, but to every one else on the checkerboard. Cuba has been the dupe and Machado the instrument of interests not Cuban.

When in 1926 Dwight W. Morrow—who incidentally during the bank crisis period attempted to arrange the most liberal loan in Cuba's history—visited Machado in 1926 in the company of the local Morgan lawyer, the President asked him, "What do you think about sugar restriction?" Morrow replied with a twinkle, "I would limit to eight million tons"—three million in excess of Cuba's maximum production. He clearly foresaw that Cuba should not tie her own hands and leave her world competitors with teeth and claws free for action.

But the restrictionists had the upper hand. Among supporters close to Machado were also Cuban interests who hoped their backward *ingenios* would be protected against the competition pushing them to the wall. Nor were they disappointed. When in 1926 a ten percent cut in the prospective mill output was ordered, Machado, exercising dictatorial powers in granting the quotas, did not neglect his friends. In 1926-27 the crop was arbitrarily limited to 4,500,000 tons; again great favoritism was shown. In September, 1927, Colonel José Tarafa, father of Cintas' wife, the man previously interested in the Woodin-Lakin rail deal and other political schemes of high finance—persuaded the government to limit the 1927-28 crop to 4,000,000 tons and to create the National Sugar Defense Commission to market that part of the crop not to be sold in the United States or used domestically.

Tarafa journeyed to Europe to form a cartel of beet-sugar producers of France, Germany, Poland, Holland (Java), Belgium and Czechoslovakia. Three of these countries made agreements. As a result Cuba reduced her crop nearly half a million tons, while curiously the other countries were allowed to increase their output to an extent their producers could not even fill their assigned quotas. The new control was to last six years. The up-to-date sugar mills of Oriente and Camagüey were now reduced fifty percent, while favored mills, many of them antequated, in the hands of politicians in western Cuba, were allowed to grind even beyond their maximum.

The price of sugar was not bettered, nor world production reduced. The Cuban financial situation was growing ever worse. Restriction was lifted, and a monopoly selling organization—El Vendedor Unico—set up. The 1928-29 crop was 5,156,315 tons. Neither the creation of this body nor its prompt abolition prevented any drop in the sugar price. Cuba, the following year, produced 4,671,260 tons. With lowering prices, the backward producers were again threatened with extinction; the banks ever more alarmed at the possibility of losing loaned money. Already they were stacked high with purchased or foreclosed sugar. Restriction was desirable but without iron-clad world agreements was as foolish as before.

4 BANKERS' PLAN

At this juncture there appeared in Cuba a man with a glittering project to rehabilitate the industry. Thomas Lincoln Chadbourne arrived toward the end of 1930, shortly after Stimson had reiterated the "hands-off" policy and Guggenheim had put his seal of approval on recent brutal elections. Cuba was to be saved—for the bankers.

Who is Chadbourne?

He had a common basis of understanding with Guggenheim because of common interest in aviation and mining; and he had been previously in touch with Lakin and Shattuck during the sugar lobbying. Along with Charles Hayden (Chase Bank Executive Committee), Wiggin (former Chase head), and Frederick W. Allen (Chase director), he was a fellow director of the Otis Elevator Company. Hayden was interested in the Cuban Portland Cement Company, Coca-Cola and various Chase sugar subsidiaries. Hayden, Wiggin, and Chadbourne's law firm had had close connections with New York subway affairs. Both Hayden and Chadbourne are directors of the Matanzas Sugar Company in Cuba.

Allen, a member of Lee Higginson, with loans in Cuba, was a director of the I. T. and T., the powerful Air-Reduction Company, the Woodin Transamerica Company and the Remington Arms.

Chadbourne's connection with New York traction also brought him in close touch with T. I. Parkinson (Chase), Matthew Chauncey Brush (Dupont connections), G. M. Dahl (Chase, partner of Hayden, former vice-president of Electric Bond and Share); James H. Post (big shot in Chase Bank sugar properties).

Can there be any doubt in the Chase Bank's interest in the subsequent scheme?

Cuba was told there was a gentlemen's agreement with American producers to restrict production. It was a gentlemen's agreement apparently with respect to Chadbourne and no one else. Later, November 5, he wrote Machado that he would not hold the Cuban government responsible for his personal compensation, he would collect this from "the American side of the industry." As a matter of fact, according to the official *Gaceta*, he received heavy expense money from Cuba and presented them with a heavy bill. Chadbourne proceeded to take Cuba for a ride on a scheme differing little from its predecessors and which has since proven ruinous. As he was first housed in the American Embassy, official color was given to his mission. According to the protest of Cuban women, Guggenheim was "one of the initiators and prime movers of the Chadbourne plan so fatal to our economy."

Shortly before he came Leopoldo Freyre de Andrade wrote, "The only partisans of restriction left in Cuba are those individuals who have sugar because they did not sell it in time at speculative prices, and a few banks which shortsightedly prefer to collect their debts quickly even though they lose their non-sugar investments which they undoubtedly will [as time has proven] if the country is definitely ruined by restriction."

The famous plan created a corporation to be responsible for the expenses of the sugar producers—in reality for the bankers' loans—through the emission of $42,000,000 in bonds to be used to buy 1,500,000 tons of sugar from existing supplies, largely impounded by the banks, and retire it from the market. The final agreement between the Republic of Cuba, the New National Sugar Exporting Corporation, the Chase National Bank and the National City Bank, was signed December 16, 1930.

It has been charged that $4,000,000 went out in mysterious payments. Recipients of money were Chadbourne and various law firms, and for beating the big drums of publicity, among others, Mr. Ivy Lee and Karl Byoier (editor of *Havana Post,* a paper stoned by the irate Cubans). The whole scheme was devised apparently (1) to permit the banks to get back their bad loans; (2) to permit the large foreign Centrales to break their contracts with the growers. In addition, it benefited American beet-sugar growers and cane-growers in Hawaii, the Philippines and Puerto Rico, Secretary Stimson reportedly being personally interested.

Subsequently Cuba, Java, Germany, Czechoslovakia, Poland, Hungary, and Belgium, through Chadbourne and sugar representatives, entered into a new agreement that for the 1930-31 crop Cuba would cut production 33 percent, Poland and Hungary, 14 and 5 percent respectively. All the other countries were permitted to increase their output from 3 to 27 percent! The exportation from all these countries was restricted, save from Germany (allowed to export 150 percent more than the previous year). The 1931-32 quota saw, however, a general European and Java cut averaging 22.6 percent over the 1929-30 crop; but Cuba was cut 51 percent.

Cuba was further weakened by an executive decree which forced the companies—otherwise liable under American laws of a combine in restraint of trade—to form a sugar pool to hold in reserve 700,000 tons in addition to that to be bought by the corporation. This, also, was another bankers' maneuver to jockey up temporarily the price and get out from under regardless of subsequent effects on the industry as a whole.

5 ECONOMIC SUICIDE

The Chadbourne plan, still in force, has meant economic suicide. It would be too optimistic to suppose Cuba would not have been hard hit by the economic crisis which has submerged the world, but ordinarily a man does not cut his throat because he has corns on his toes. Cuba, the major sugar country of the world, with costs of production as low or lower than nearly every other country, should have been the last to have restricted her crop. By doing so she has opened the door to less worthy competitors, who could more economically engage in other activities, except for the artificial advantage created—the old story of growing lemons in Scotland. The production of world sugar has increased instead of diminished. For every pound of sugar Cuba holds off the market, other countries rush in to provide. Thus while Cuba furnished 21.6 percent of the world's supply in 1925, in 1931 she provided but 11 percent, this year probably less. The logical outcome of her present policy will be to keep on reducing her output until the Cuban sugar industry is all but wiped out, with higher prices for the consumer. The world's most efficient sugar mechanism has been effectively broken across the back.

It is true that Cuba should have more diversified crops and should not be so dependent upon the price fluctuations of one commodity, but this is no argument for having helped ruin an existing flourishing industry.

Mr. Chadbourne, to put over his plan, used other persuasion besides the gentlemen's agreement. In the *New York Times,* June 7, 1931, he declared that the law of supply and demand and the survival of the fittest belonged to the "laws of the jungle." But this does not mean that you defeat jungle laws by tying yourself to a stake and letting all the wild beasts run loose. Mr. Ivy Lee glibly asserted that the Chadbourne plan was to bring order out of chaos and adjust production to consumption; in reality it was to let loose bigger wolves on little wolves and innocent babes. But the press and magazines of the United States, thanks to high-pressure salesmanship of special articles, blazoned with glowing reports of the enlightened rationalization of one of the world's major industries. This is exactly what the Chadbourne plan did not do; only 40 percent of the world's production was brought into that agreement; and this 40 percent was crippled in order to further special interests in the United States; and of that 40 percent, Cuba was the worst hit.

The important thing for Cuba was not to salvage her sugar already made, but to salvage her future sugar; not to salvage banks speculating in produced sugar, but to keep going to the extent possible the industry which provides sustenance to the greater part of Cuba's workers. The plan benefited everybody but Cuba and the Cubans.

For Cuba it would have been more advantageous to have burned the sugar outright than to hold it a wet blanket over the market. Producers and consumers certainly would have suffered far less. As it is, the cost of storage, handling, interest and overhead of the government sugar corporation —which has provided many fat political jobs—will practically wipe out the value of the sugar held. This cost is paid by the producer in addition to his original producing costs; the banks get paid, but no one else. The banks had already taken a heavy slice out of the producer by foreclosing on his sugar; they now forced the producer to foot the additional loss of depreciated sugar.

From the standpoint of the Cuban *colono* the transaction is still more disastrous. It means, for him, the practical destruction of 40,000 *caballerias* of sugar which will require $60,000,000 to replace. The hacendado, or owner of the Central, in most cases a large American company, merely loses the profits he would otherwise have gained, plus continued overhead, plus serious deterioration because his machinery is not being utilized; and probably he would have been as well off, his losses no greater, had he continued to have produced even at prevailing low prices. Thus, while he would have lost temporarily in either case, the Cubans, whose only return from the industry, since 80 percent of it is in American hands and the profits are shipped abroad, resides in the share split with the *colonos* and the wages paid the workers and revenues received by the government, all of which would have benefited by unhampered production. The government by its own policy has lost millions of revenue and set up costly instruments of control, and the *colono,* whose contracts have been arbitrarily destroyed by government edict, not only fails to make his customary cutting, but his cane is deteriorating rapidly. While his contract with the Centrales is arbitrarily thrown overboard, cutting off his whole means of livelihood, at the same time he must pay full taxes based on previous prosperity values, must pay the lease on his lands (up until the very recent moratorium), and the full interest on his loans from the bank. None of his expenses have been restricted along with his producing restriction. Hundreds have thrown up their hands and abandoned their properties to the jungle, the insects or the banks.

The worker is still worse off. Crop restriction brought immediately wholesale unemployment and increased competition for jobs with frightful lowering of wages. Cane-cutting, instead of beginning in November or December, is postponed until February and lasts but one month. Not only the number of workers, but also the number of working days, has been reduced. The Chadbourne plan meant the largest deliberate labor lock-out in history, and has reduced the greater part of the 500,000 workers dependent upon the industry to semi-starvation. As Freyre wrote, "While all countries are trying to solve the unemployment problem, in Cuba we are restricting the work we naturally have in a vain effort to control our sugar price."

The Cuban countryside is to-day in a pitiful state of misery, which we in the United States, with all our unemployment, would have difficulty in visualizing. Ordinarily the cane worker received $1.50, even up to $2.50, a day; now, wages for the one month of cutting do not exceed 25 cents a day; in Camagüey the worker can earn but nine cents, in some places only three cents. This means that he is starved even during the month he does work—if he is lucky enough to have a job—and the rest of the year he must beg, steal, live on roots, or sleep in the city streets. At the normal proportion of the estimated $2.15 wage cost for each 325-pound sack of sugar, the wage outlay for an average Cuban crop would have resulted in about $535,000,000 wage cost for the period of the plan. Just the restriction means a loss of $180,000,000 at normal rates. But with the concurrent drop in wages, the loss in five years will come close to $400,000,000 to save a paltry $38,000,000 for the banks.

Most of this, as well as part of the company's expenses and profits, was formerly spent for American products, which means corresponding loss to American industries. Our sixth largest market, which meant at one time a total trade of nearly a billion, is almost destroyed by these stupidities. Every Cuban worker out of a job means an American worker out of a job.

A sad side-product has been the favoritism in the apportioning of the quotas. These are announced at the last moment so those in the industry can make no proper preparations for the future crop and do not know what labor force to keep employed. Even after President Machado personally publishes the list of quotas, these are secretly altered to favor political friends. Thus while the growers in Camagüey province, which boasts the most up-to-date equipment in the world, are cut about fifty percent, such favorites as the recently murdered Vásquez Bello, President of the Senate, Tirso Mesa, the dissolute mayor of Havana, Colonel Alberto Herrera, chief of Machado's staff, and Secretary of Communications Aballi are permitted to grind up to 100 percent of capacity, or even more, with inferior equipment. This is equivalent to closing down the Ritz-Carlton Hotel because the chop-suey Chinaman on the corner happens to be a friend. The government argues it is protecting Cubans against the rapacious foreigners, but far more Cubans derive their living from the rapacious foreigners than from the few backward Cuban mills; favoritism to inefficiency is never a patriotic gesture.

The sugar industry, in other words, is not like petroleum or silver or gold, which often can be left in the ground until ready to be taken out. Sugar is a perishable industry. A cane-field uncut one year seriously deteriorates; in a few years is lost. Expensive machinery deteriorates; knowledge deteriorates. A few years ago the Cuban entrepreneur was alert for new methods, new fertilizers, new ways of promoting his output with decreasing costs. All that initiative has been destroyed by the Chadbourne plan and still more by the capriciousness and graft in its administration.

In addition it has hit the railroads badly, causing wage-cuts and discharge of workers. It has thrown port-workers out of employment, and has stopped most imports, until despite soaring duties the customs revenues have become insignificant.

The bankers have been so shortsighted they have lost far more than they gained by the destruction of an industry and of profits on other normal business transactions.

On the other hand probably over 80 percent of the sugar properties are in their hands through default. But the banks, in raiding the industry, failed to look toward their future profits in a prosperous Cuba. They were interested only in the Shylock pound of flesh.

Even Machado's son-in-law, in his paper, the *Mercurio* (December 9, 1932), declared that Chadbourne should be immediately fired from the presidency of the National Sugar Export Corporation as a "traitor." Even the Cuban head of this corporation, once one of its most ardent supporters, Señor Viriato Gutiérrez, November last, admitted the whole procedure a dire failure.

6 PRICE OF SUGAR

This conversion of Cuba from a great sugar emporium to a great sugar warehouse with nobody but the warehouse keeper to foot the bills has significance for Mr. Average Man in the United States. All this is sad, not merely for Cuba, but for us. Sugar, which in the middle ages was considered merely a rare spice and a medicine, is to-day one of the most important products of man, and each of us in the United States in normal times consumes over 100 pounds a year.

For those hundred pounds each and every one of us, despite world over-production, pays far more than he should. Our tariff, in the past responsible for unjustly increasing the price of sugar for the consumer to benefit the artificial beet-sugar industry, has by the Smoot-Hawley schedule been increased, and now stands shoulder to shoulder with the Chadbourne plan to further prejudice the real interests of our own country. These factors have added $247,000,000 of annual cost to the American consumer.

We should be the first to desire that Cuba, rather than Hawaii, the Philippines or Porto Rico become great sugar producers. We cannot supply our own demand; and sugar is also an indispensable commodity in war time, not merely as food but for essential war industries and chemical products. Cuba is the only sugar country with which we can guarantee our communications in case of international war. The destruction of the Cuban industry now occurring cannot be replaced in many years. Thus, besides destroying a valuable market, we have helped destroy part of our national security—one more instance, of so many in recent years, of private interests placing their own profits above the needs of the country at large. They are even willing to jeopardize our security in a troubled world.

Our own beet-sugar industry can never satisfactorily fill the bill. It is an artificial industry the existence of which depends upon the caprice of Congress and cheap labor. Only 2.3 percent of our agriculturists cultivate beet-sugar, but all consume sugar.

All this is quite apart from the sentimental fact that we brought the Cuban republic into being, that we have obligations as well as rights in Cuba, that Cuba came loyally to our aid during the World War. The only gratitude we have shown is to pursue a policy which has helped drive her to despair and ruin, and which if not checked will drive her ere long to the folly of a bloody revolution, costly in marines, property and international good-will.

Beneath the tropical opulence of Cuba, hidden in the tangled jungle of her present cruel political tyranny, are the fangs of bitter discontent. Cuba, unless a remedy is soon found, will be reaped to the holocaust of civil war. Thousands of acres of American sugar-cane will go up in smoke, and the hammers of revolution will smash the mills which have become merely symbols of misery. Under Cuba's calm blue sky stalks the white ghost of sugar, sad memory of better days.

APPENDIX

Other interests worthy of mention are:

On May 15, 1920, was organized the Cuban Air Products Company, a subsidiary of Air Reduction. The latter also controls the Liquid Carbonic Corporation of Cuba. Here we find familiar names: Percy Rockefeller, John McHugh (Chase), F. W. Allen (close to Woodin, I. T. and T. Lee Higginson and Chase); M. C. Brush (Duponts, New York traction).

One of the powerful companies in Cuba is the United Fruit, new directors of which November 22, 1932, were Odlum, Davison, E. K. Hall. William Clark Bradley connects it up with Coca-Cola; George Cabot Lee, with United States Smelting and Refining; Victor M. Cutter (ousted president) with I. T. and T. Orestes Ferrara has been active in various activities of this company.

The Hershey interests control large sugar acreage, the Rosario Sugar Company, a modern refinery, and the Hershey Cuban Railway Company.

The second largest agricultural activity on the island is tobacco.

Prior to independence, our tobacco relations with Cuba had been largely mercantile. Cuba, Key West, and Tampa enterprises, largely owned by Cuban, Spanish and German proprietors, were thriving. The largest, however, was Henry Clay and Bock, Ltd., an English concern managed by a resident German. We merely traded.

The industry, smashed during independence struggles, soon revived. H. B. Hollins of New York promoted the Havana Commercial Company—the Cuban-American Rafael R. Govin being a member—and purchased thirteen cigar factories and one cigarette factory, uniting them in one organization, with the leaf-mercantile business of F. G. Garcia Brothers. Plantations were bought, and by the end of 1901 advances to planters totaled $1,300,000.

In 1901, the American Tobacco Company, "the Trust," under James B. Duke, Thomas F. Ryan, P. A. B. Widener, Anthony N. Brady and Grant Schley combined some twenty American factories into the American Cigar Company, and in 1902 forced the British tobacco interests into a world-combine marketing arrangement. The Trust then turned to Cuba; but openly bucking the Trust the Havana Commercial Company bid in the Henry Clay and Bock Company, only to be themselves absorbed through purchase by the Trust of $3,500,000 in bonds and two-thirds of their stock. Thus 90 percent of Cuba's cigar exports, or nearly half the Cuban production, was concentrated under the control of the American Cigar Company, which watered the value of its Cuban holdings up to $41,860,000. The independents banded together to defend themselves, by 1905 handled 52 percent of the export business.

[401]

APPENDIX

The Trust was also greatly handicapped by strikes; the most notable, that of 1907, Magoon, if anything, protected. This and depression caused the Trust to expand its Tampa and Key West business—tobacco exports dropped in one year from $31,286,000 to $20,931,000. In 1914 they reached $32,000,000 again, but with the World War dropped once more to $22,000,000.

Now, after a quarter century of American capital penetration, the Cuban tobacco industry has declined. In 1893 Cuba exported 147 million cigars; the prewar independence average was 147 million (196 million in the banner 1919-20 year). But from 1920-33 the average is far below 100 million. By 1930 it had dropped to 72 million, and is still declining. Cigarette exports rose from 38 million packages in 1893, but declined to an average of less than 3 million from 1925-7; it was under 5 million in 1930, and now has reached its lowest level this century.

During the past few years new labor troubles, Machado's prima donna taxes, and the American 100 percent tariff on manufactured tobacco products have practically forced complete withdrawal of the Trust's factories from Cuba, save that of Henry Clay and Bock, which produces Coronas only for the Cuban trade. Plantations are still owned or controlled; but to-day Corona cigars are manufactured in New Jersey.

Before the World War Cuba produced 2½ percent of the world's leaf tobacco. Since the War this has fallen to ½ percent in 1927, is now even less. In 1906 our tobacco investment—unwatered—was estimated at $30,000,000. Twenty years later it had dropped to $20,000,000 and in 1933 to $17,261,559. By 1930 gross earnings of the Cuban Tobacco Company had dropped to $406,469.

Wood ruled that the Foraker Amendment, prohibiting concessions during the American occupation, did not apply to mining grants; and a feverish filing of claims began. Most proved worthless; and it was not till about a decade later that big American companies began to interest themselves greatly in Cuban mineral resources.

The Spaniards had worked gold and silver, later copper. El Cobre mine (British) was started in 1835 and long was the largest source of copper in the world. Iron production began in 1883. But not until 1909 was it discovered that Cuba was one of the largest iron-bearing regions in the world, with reserves comparable to Mesaba Ridge in Minnesota. A 1913 estimate by Charles F. Rand, president of the Spanish American Iron Company, puts reserves at 3,331,000,000 tons.

But there has been little actual development—perhaps due to lack of contiguous coal deposits.

To-day Bethlehem Steel is the largest holder. In 1913 the Spanish American Iron Company and Bethlehem Iron Mines Company controlled 1,775,000,000 tons, with surface ownership on 134,569 acres and control over 150,986 acres more. A 1916-17 consolidation—which took in the Spanish Iron Company for $32,000,000—brought into the net 20,000 additional acres with estimated reserves of 300,000,000 tons. In 1929 6,000 more acres were controlled with one-third interest owned by Witherbee, Sherman and Company of New York.

Their property in Santiago is equipped to produce 280,000 tons per annum; that on Nipe Bay (north coast), 500,000 tons nodules annually. Important figures in Bethlehem Steel, with reference to Cuba, are Percy Rockefeller (Cuba Company, National City, Air Reduction, Remington Arms, Guggenheim interests), and W. C. Potter (Electric Bond and Share Company).

The United States Steel Company has 200 million tons reserve through the

[402]

APPENDIX

Piloto Mining Company, acreage, 15,000. Eastern Steel Company of Pottersville, 12,000 acres Moa District, reserve 50 million tons; Guantánamo Exploration Company (Knickerbocker Trust), 18,000 acres, 210 million tons in 1913.

The Matahambre copper mines were opened in 1912 by Gómez' Minister of Public Works. In 1921 the majority stock was acquired by the United States Metal Refining Company of Carteret, New Jersey.

APPENDIX TO CHAPTER XXIII, SECTION 1

The whole sugar question and its solution is tied up with land-tenure, which has varied with the needs of the industry.

First Governor Valásquez ceded few lands because of the small number of Conquistadores. His successors made no new grants, but the total authorities gave away vast pasturage acreage.

In 1729 a Royal Cédula had stressed the necessity of providing for "an abundance of food-stuffs and bread-working" that small properties for agriculture be granted, even within the private cattle grants. Thus was built up a class of small firmly rooted proprietors alongside of a few large cattlemen.

The sugar industry—introduced about 1560, fifty years earlier than in Barbados—accelerated land division. The first capital for the industry came from Mexico, a loan authorized by Philip II to the cultivators at the petition of the Havana Cabildo. But the industry grew slowly. Spain, Cuba's only outlet, provided little market; cane had been cultivated there since the Arabs. By 1763 Cuban exportation had reached only half a million pounds.

Shift in Cuba's development came with the English seizure of Havana for several months in 1762—a gust of outside ideas, temporary removal of trade restrictions, new sugar machinery, ten thousand new black slaves. Independence of the United States in 1776 provided a new adjacent, if contraband, market. Revolution, disorder, flight of the French hacendados to Cuba, ruined the Haitian sugar industry. Before 1800 Cuba had caught up the fallen scepter. Vast acres of woods were hacked down or burned to be substituted by cane, coffee, and other products. Practically all bars were lifted against the blacks; negro population rose temporarily to 66 percent.

But all this development prevented large land-holding. The 1827 Vives census showed Cuba had 1,000 sugar *ingenios*, 2,067 coffee plantations, 76 cotton plantations, 60 cacao properties, 3,090 pasturage estates, 5,534 tobacco *vegas*, 13,957 small farms. The island's population was 286,942 slaves, 311,051 whites; i.e., a piece of rural property, barring duplication in holding, for every twelve white persons.

Towards 1800 the sugar expansion was halted by one of its customary collapses, rapidly giving the industry the name of the "lottery of the Indies." The United States' 1807 embargo continued and aggravated the situation.

Even after 1820 when steam-machinery was brought in to turn the mills and *trapiche* presses, sugar was not greatly stimulated. Cane is bulky, wood required for fuel is bulky, both hard to transport. Primitive ox-carts restricted the available supply of both with reference to each mill. Just to have enough ox-carts meant the maintenance of pasture lands more extensive than those devoted to cane. The costly upkeep of a large slave personnel during many idle months added to the cost. In 1827 there were 1,000 sugar *ingenios;* in 1860 about 2,000. Smaller units were more profitable.

APPENDIX

From 1840, the railroad having been introduced, sugar production jumped up; the size of the *ingenios* increased. The 1856-59 annual average was 375,000 tons. Coffee declined. Evolution in the sugar industry no longer consisted in increasing the number of mills, but their size. Between 1860-1877, in part due to the devastating Ten Years' War, the number of *ingenios* dropped from 2,000 to 1,197.

The larger *ingenio*, the introduction of the railroad and an expanding world market developed the *colono* system, that of promoting independent growers and leasers, who received their payment in a portion of the raw sugar. Such mills, utilizing many growers, came to be called Centrales.

The industry was also stimulated by new methods and by new developments in the United States. In 1888 Henry O. Havemeyer combined nineteen sugar refineries, the nucleus for the creation in 1890 of the American Sugar Refining Company, the famed "Sugar Trust," which absorbed most of Cuba's sugar for years to come.

By 1885, 200 Bostonians were working on Cuban sugar estates. The Ten Years' War smashed up the industry and Americans picked up properties at low prices. Sugar merchants E. Atkins and Company of Boston made the first important investment through foreclosure on the Soledad estate of the bankrupt Sarria family. The property was at once enlarged and provided with new equipment. The Sugar Trust (which absorbed this property) and the 1891 free-entry treaty with the United States boosted new enterprises. By 1893 Soledad itself comprised 12,000 acres, nearly half of which were planted to cane; 23 miles of private railway; 1,200 employees harvested the *zafra*. About this time Havemeyer and Atkins jointly invested in a Central near Trinidad. Hugh Kelly and Franklin Farrel started the Santa Teresa Central near Manzanillo. In 1893 the Rionda family organized the Tuinucuá Cane Sugar Company and commenced milling near Sancti Spiritus and Tanamo. By 1899 efficiency and concentration had reduced the number of mills from 1,197 in 1877 to 207.

Raw sugar production passed the million ton mark. But the Wilson tariff restored raw sugar to a stiff schedule. Cuba production dropped back to 225,000 tons, about a third of what it had been in 1885.

The independence war completed prior tariff destruction, ruined practically all plantations, prostrated Cuba. The beet-growers in the United States (encouraged by our Dingley tariff) worked overtime. Sugar in Central America expanded. European countries were piling on bounties to beet-growers. Previous to 1899 Cuba had supplied from 12 to 14 percent of the world's total sugar supply; 30 percent of all its cane sugar; in 1900, only 3½ percent of all sugar and 10 percent of the cane supply. Her production, less than 300,000 tons, had a market value of less than $20,000,000.

The sugar people feared worse calamities if our occupation ceased. Before the industrial commission, July 18, 1899, Atkins announced, "If Cuba is made an independent nation, Cuba is ruined by our tariff." J. H. Post (B. H. Howell and Son) told the commission of the rosy prospects if Cuba remained American, the industry would provide an outlet for southern negroes to work on the plantation, who would also Americanize the island—though strangely enough the negroes have not yet Americanized our own South. It was not seriously believed Cuba would be made independent.

All went ahead blithely purchasing new properties. Post and his friends were making vast improvements in the sugar mills. New projects required larger capital, creating larger producing units than Cuba had ever known. In 1901, the

[404]

APPENDIX

United Fruit Company, through a syndicate headed by its president, Andrew W. Preston, bought close to 200,000 acres more on Nipe Bay for approximately $400,000. The Rionda family resuscitated its Tuinucuá estate; and in 1901 joined with the Philadelphian McCahan refining interests in developing the 80,000 acre Francisco estate on a wild spot on the southern coast. Stuyvesant Fish of the Illinois Central backed a company which bought the Constancia Central near Cienfüegos and combined it with the Louisianan Gramercy Refinery. H. B. Hawley, first Republican Congressman from Texas, already interested in Louisiana sugar, hied himself to Cuba, met young Mario G. Menocal, Cornell-trained, of high connections, and on his advice bought 66,000 acres near Puerto Padre, a north-coast harbor, where he constructed Chaparra, the largest mill yet, initial capacity 200,000 bags, i.e., 10 percent of the entire 1900 crop. Menocal remained in charge from its opening in 1902 until elected President of Cuba in 1912. In 1914 it produced 195 million pounds; by 1926 controlled over 250,000 acres. In 1901 the Hawley interests added a refinery at Cárdenas; in 1902, with $7,500,000 new capital, they restored Tingüaro, a 7,000 acre Matanzas estate, three smaller plantations, and the Mercedita mill on Cabañas Bay, sixty miles west of Havana. In 1906 Chaparra and the other properties were consolidated into the powerful Cuban-American Sugar Company.

Yet as late as 1905 there were only 29 mills owned by American citizens, producing but 21 percent of the island's sugar.

When obviously Cuba would not be annexed, delegations of planters and merchants beseeched Washington day and night to protect them, above all in the arrangement of commercial reciprocity. This was advocated by Roosevelt and Root, but the Republican majority was not willing to cede one jot on the principle of high protection. President Oxnard of the United States Beet-Sugar Association strutted through the corridors of Congress like an arrogant king.

Representative Weeks of Michigan, his feet firmly planted in the beet fields of his own state, gazed aloft and demanded, "Where, under the broad canopy of the sky, rises our moral and legal obligation to Cuba?" Ten million dollars, said his Michigan colleague, H. C. Smith, had been invested in the sugar business of that state, "in the faith of the pledges and principles of the Republican Party."

"Cuba," retorted Roosevelt in special message, June 13, 1902 ". . . has assumed certain special obligations as regards her international position in compliance with our request. I ask for special economic concessions in return."

Congress scorned his message. Said a Louisiana Congressman rooting in the precious cane-fields of his own state, "After the war, it was 'Root, hog, or die.' And we rooted. Let Cuba root awhile."

But Roosevelt, unauthorized, sent Colonel Trasker H. Bliss to Havana to negotiate a treaty, giving twenty percent preference to Cuban sugar. Bliss' assistant, Captain Fletcher Smith, toured states hostile to reciprocity to tell the manufacturers their interests were in jeopardy.

Senator Sereno E. Payne sponsored the treaty: "Let Cuba become prosperous. . . . Let American capital go down there to develop the island and employ the islanders. . . . Multiply the buying capacity of the people as we have multiplied it in the last five years under the Dingley Tariff law, so that people want more, buy more, and are ready to give bigger prices because they get larger wages." Three hundred million dollars a year would be bought from the United States— "Why there are millions in this bill to the farmers and manufacturers of the United States. . . ."

APPENDIX

But not the lard and ten-penny nail sellers turned the scales for reciprocity, nor concern for America's welfare, but a truce between the Sugar Trust and the beet-growers. During 1902, Havemeyer and the American Sugar Refining Company invested heavily in beet-sugar company stocks, bought the largest Michigan company outright. Sugar solidarity!

The Michigan representatives jumped through the new tissue-paper loop, and much to the confusion of our enlightened electorate, the treaty was ratified December 17, 1903.

Down to 1910 reciprocity meant better prices to Cuban producers, perhaps a twenty-million-dollar total. The United States could buy sugar cheaper there than in any other foreign country. Cuba's production expanded till she supplied all our imported needs. By 1905 her sugar harvest exceeded any year of the colonial period. By 1912, Cuba for the first time since the crisis of the 'eighties, produced 14 percent of the world's supply. By 1914, 35 percent of the Cuban *zafra* was milled in the forty or so Centrales under American ownership or control, 100,000 bags average per mill as compared to the Cuba-owned mills averaging 50,000 bags (325 pounds). But as world production also increased, Cuba—despite preferential treatment—was forced to accept the current world price. Cuba was closer, dominated the market; freightage cost less, but if the reciprocity treaty enabled Cuba to seize the American market as an exclusive prize, the 20 percent reciprocity tariff margin between Cuban and other foreign sugar was corralled by monopolistic seaboard refineries at the expense of Cuba and the American consumer.

In 1913, Cuba slid into the world-depression mud puddle, the sugar price dropped lower than any time since 1902.

But soon German armies were smashing through the Belgian and French beet-sugar regions; England was deprived of German and Austrian sugar; everywhere else in the world, the sugar industry boomed.

July, 1914, raw sugar had sold in Havana under two cents a pound; in August the average price jumped to 3.66 cents. The first year of the War Cuba sold 2,600,000 tons at an average of 3.31 cents a pound. New plantations boosted the 1915-16 crop to over three million tons—average, 4.37 cents a pound. A similar crop 1916-17 sold at 4.62 cents. The sugar income of Cuba had tripled. By the end of 1917 39 new mills had been built or were soon to open.

Atkins fused two new mills with his Trinidad property and founded the Punta Alegre Sugar Company (1916). The Warner Sugar Refining Company erected the Central Miranda in Oriente. The West India Sugar Finance Corporation (connected with the National Sugar Refining Company interest) financed and managed Alto Cedro, Cupey and Palma properties in far eastern Cuba. In 1916 there were 72 American mills. By 1920 consolidation and superior methods reduced this to 55 super mills. The largest investment was made by Manuel Rionda and Miguel Arango, who in 1912 interested a New York syndicate in a 70,000 acre estate at Manati. An enormous new mill was ready to reap boom profits; at the close of 1915 Rionda and his friends swung their properties—14 mills at nearly 100 percent of pre-war cost—into the $50,000,000 Cuban Cane syndicate (J. and W. Seligman, bankers); an additional $50,000,000 common stock was given away with the preferred shares. A race to open new sugar lands in the east began; whole forests of valuable woods were ruthlessly hacked or burned down; cane was planted between the smoking stumps without plowing. New contracts, at very favorable rates for the Centrales, were made. Despite exclusion laws a great flood of ignorant black labor from Haiti and Jamaica and

APPENDIX

Chinese coolies poured in and were driven to their tasks without the least regard for sanitation or health.

In 1917 Herbert Hoover returned from feeding Belgian babies to become food-administrator for the United States. May 9 he told the Senate Committee on Agriculture and Forestry that by October the country would have exhausted its sugar supply, that new supplies were not large, that the Cuban crop might be down "a million and a quarter tons below the 4 million normal," a statement "so false, so ignorant, so injurious" that it has astonished later-day historians.

Everybody dashed to buy sugar. The price of Cuban sugar in New York zigzagged up violently from 3.81 cents a pound (February, 1917) to 6.75 cents. The Lever Act promptly provided control over food-stuff marketing. The International Sugar Committee, thereby established, forced Cuba, as a price of receiving ships and food, to accept a price maximum of 4.60 plus freight to New York. Cuban producers held off. The Senate investigated. The United States put the screws on by withholding flour to Cuba. Cuba suffered breadless days. Finally a contract was signed with Hawley (Cuban-American) and Rionda (Cuban Cane), and the necessary Cuban decree was passed. Flour and other urgent supplies steamed for Havana.

In 1918 closer control was created by the Sugar Equalization Board, Inc.—Woodrow Wilson, President of the United States, principal shareholder; Herbert Hoover, chairman; Edwin Shattuck, attorney. It bought the entire Cuban crop outright. At the behest of the beet-growers, the board pegged up the sugar price to 9 cents a pound on refined sugar, a price which they declared would not permit all of them to make a profit.

But we demanded Cuban sugar for only half a cent advance over the price of the previous year. The Cubans were finally forced to sell for 5.50 cents. The profit on Cuban sugar was to pay the expenses of the equalization board and compensate American producers unable to make a profit of one cent a pound, for of course only patriots were making the great sacrifice of raising sugar which should not and could not be raised otherwise. On the 1918-19 Cuban sugar crop, the board cleared $42,000,000 profit, nearly 10 percent. No list of American producers compensated has ever been published, but had the market remained uncontrolled, Cuba would have enjoyed the profits we yanked out of her by superior military and political leverage without a cent more cost to the consumer. Hoover nevertheless informed the world his policy had saved the American consumer four cents a pound less than the world price.

Armistice came about two weeks after the equalization board had purchased Cuba's 1918-19 crop. By January 26, 1919, all special regulations governing manufacturers and refiners in the United States were annulled. Only Cubans were not yet freed from the shackles; a very slight concession was made them—they could independently ship some small quantities of sugar directly to Spain, France, Canada, and other countries.

The board was worried over Cuba's coming crop, 4,000,000 tons. Should it buy it at the contract rate, 6½ cents a pound plus duty, freight and refiner's margin? Wilson hesitated. Meanwhile the Cuban producers nettled that the board had sold 150,000 tons of the 1918-19 sugar to foreign countries at higher than the obligatory price for Cubans, began to hold out some already contracted sugar. August, 1919, an association of *hacendados* and *colonos*, representing some 22 Centrales in addition to Cuba Cane and the Rionda interests, compelled withdrawal of the 6½ cent proposal in September.

APPENDIX

The equalization board threw the gates down, which alarmed the beet-growers and the Louisiana cane people. Attorney General Palmer, property custodian, and, like Hoover, a member of the Society of Friends, jumped into the breach, announced November 8, 1919, he would not prosecute any one for selling *Louisiana* sugar as high as 17 cents!

Prices skyrocketed. Cuban sugar on the New York market jumped from 9⅛ cents (February 18, 1920) to 22½ cents (May 19), then sank slowly to 3¾ cents (December 13).

A dance of the millions! Already war production had passed prosperity to many groups in Cuba, higher wages, higher standards of living, larger turnover profits on all merchandise. The dance of the millions now—in common with the post-war plunder spirit of the world—introduced piratical and dazzling pyramiding of credit. The mania was communicated from sugar to financial geniuses, from banks to sugar geniuses; between them they rode the chute to disaster.

Sales of Centrales occurred at fabulous prices. At the peak of the boom about 50 mills, nearly 25 percent of the total, changed hands. Many shifts of capital control were taking place. The Coca-Cola and similar bottling companies, utilizing the Norit process for raw Cuban sugar, put up two factories. The Charles E. Hires Company purchased the Dos Rosas mill in Santa Clara province at three times its 1914 cost. Percy Rockefeller, Charles Hayden and others promoted the Air Reduction Company's interests in Cuba. Amos Hershey was expanding operations in Matanzas.

Cuba also went into refining. Closed refineries were put back into commission. Several were brought by Atkins and the Czarniskow-Rionda Company. Ex-President Gómez and Orestes Ferrara founded a new concern.

Extravagant bids for cane set exorbitant rates for a decade to come: in some cases the *colonos* received as high as two-thirds of the extracted sugar. A few even became millionaires. Some branched out into mills for themselves or became partners in mills. They flaunted their new wealth in baronial Vedado homes; in baroque palaces in the Marianao suburbs, bought expensive furniture, European cars, jewels, art, kept mistresses, took junkets to Europe, developed social snobbery.

In 1908-09 Cuba had produced 10 percent of the world's sugar supply; in 1918-19, 25 percent. In 1908 the export of cane products was 54.1 percent of all the island's exports; in 1919, 88.6 percent. Cuba was headed for disaster.

The collapse caught everybody on a limb. Speculators who had bought at 10 to 20 cents were ruined. *Colonos* and Centrales could not pay off their bank loans. The banks scampered around trying to liquidate their assets, were drawn head over heels into the sugar business, sat hopelessly on the wreckage. From this time on the story of sugar in Cuba becomes a bankers' story.

SELECTED BIBLIOGRAPHY

Alger, Russell A. The Spanish American War. New York, 1901.

Antiga, Juan. Escritos políticos y sociales. 3v. Madrid, 1927.

Arango y Pareño, Francisco de. Discurso sobre la agricultura y medios de fomentarlo. Havana, 1792.

Ariquistain, Luis. La agonía antillana. El imperialismo yanqui en el mar Caribe. Madrid, 1930.

Arnao, Juan. Páginas para la historia de Cuba. Havana, 1900.

Atkins, Edwin Farnsworth. Sixty Years in Cuba. Cambridge, 1926.

Ballou, M. M. History of Cuba. Boston, 1854.

Bangs, John Kendrick. Uncle Sam Trustee. New York, 1902.

Barbarrosa, Enrique. Patria y libertad. Havana, 1899.

—— El proceso de la república. Havana, 1911.

Betencourt Agramonte, Ignacio. Agramonte y la revolución cubana. Havana, 1928.

Betencourt, Gaspar. Cultura y civildad. Havana, 1932.

Buell, Raymond. Cuba and the Platt Amendment. New York, 1929.

Cabrera y Bosch. Los partidos coloniales. Havana, 1914.

Calcagno, Francisco. Diccionario biográfico cubano. 4v. New York, 1878; Havana, 1885, 1886.

Calderón, Carlisle. Reports to E. Dupuy de Lome. Washington, 1896-97.

Callahan, J. M. Cuba and International Relations. Baltimore, 1899.

Canini, I. E. Four Centuries of Spanish Rule in Cuba. Philadelphia, 1898.

Carbonell y Rivero, José Manuel (Ed.). Evolución de la cultura cubana (608-1920). 18v. Havana, 1928.

Carricate, Arturo R. Martí en Isla de Pinos. Havana, 1923.

Castellanos, Gerardo. Francisco Gómez. Havana, 1933.

Centro de la propriedad urbana de la Havana, Informe sobre el Plan Seligman. Havana, 1932.

Certero, Julio M. Los estados unidos y las antillas. Madrid, 1931.

Céspedes, Benjamín. La prostitución en la ciudad de Habana. Havana, 1888.

SELECTED BIBLIOGRAPHY

Chapman, Charles E. A History of the Cuban Republic. New York, 1927.
Collazo y Tejada, Enrique. Cuba independiente. Havana, 1900.
—— Cuba intervenida. Havana, 1910.
—— Desde Yara hasta el Zanjón. Havana, 1933.
Concepción, Pablo de la. Prisioneros y deportados cubanos en la guerra de independencia, 1895-98. Havana, 1932.
Consuegra, Wilfredo I. Hechos y comentarios. Havana, 1920.
Corporación exportadora nacional de azucar. Reglas. Havana, 1932.
—— Leyes creando el instituto cubano de estabilización del azucar. Havana, 1931.
Cuba. Ley y reglamento para la estabilización del azucar. Havana, 1930 (Republished from Gaceta extraordinaria, Nov. 15, 1930, and Gaceta Oficial, Nov. 17, 27, 1930).
—— Convenio internacional sobre la estabilización de la industria azucarera firmado en Bruselas el 9 de marzo de 1931. Havana, 1931. (Republished from Gaceta Oficial, June 13, 1931, and Edición extraordinaria, No. 14.)
Cruz, Manuel de la. Obras. 7v. Madrid, 1927.
—— La revolución cubana y la raza de color. Key West, 1895.
Davis, Richard Harding. Cuba in War. New York, 1897.
—— The Cuban and Porto Rican Campaigns. New York, 1898.
Delafosse, Mauricio. Las civilizaciones negro-africano. Madrid, 1927.
Domingo, Marcelino. Viajando por America. Madrid, 1923.
Dumont, Henri. Antropología y patología comparadas de los negros cubanos. Havana, 1887.
Estévez y Romero, Luis. Desde el Zanjón hasta Baire. Havana, 1899
Estrada Palma, Tomás. La invasión de Occidente. Partes oficiales. New York, 1896.
Falco, Francisco Federico. Veinte años después del grito de Baire. Genoa, 1915.
Fernández de Castro, José Antonio. Medio siglo de historia colonial de Cuba. Havana, 1923.
Fernandez de Castro, Rafael. Para la historia de Cuba. Havana, 1899.
Fernández Prieto, Florindo L. Terrorismo, 1930-31. Havana, 1931.
Ferrara, Orestes. Las enseñanzas de una revolución. Preface by Clemente Vásquez Bello. Havana, 1932.
—— Tentativas de intervención europea en America. 1896-98. Havana, 1933.
Ferrer y Martínez, Miguel. El general Tacón. Marqués de la unión de Cuba y el conde de Villanueva . . . Madrid, 1838.
[410]

SELECTED BIBLIOGRAPHY

Freyre de Andrade, Leopoldo. La intervención gubernamental en la industria azucarera. Havana, 1931.
— La restricción de la zafra. Havana, 1931.
Flint, Grover. Marching with Gómez. Boston, 1898.
Forbes-Lindsay, Charles Harcourt Ainslie. Cuba and Her People of Today. Boston, 1911.
Funston, Frederick. Memories of Two Wars. New York, 1914.
Garrigo Salido, Roque E. Historia documentada de la conspiración de los soles y rayos de Bolívar. 2v. Havana, 1929.
Giberga, Eliseo. Obras. 3v. Havana, 1931.
Gómez, Fernando. La insurrección por dentro. Madrid, 1900.
Gómez, Máximo. Convenio del Zanjón. Jamaica, 1878.
— Mi escolta. [?]
Guerra y Sánchez, Ramiro. Azucar y población en las antillas. Havana, 1927.
— Historia de Cuba. 2v. Havana, 1921, 1925.
Guillén, Nicolás. Motivos de son. Archivos del folrklore cubano. V. 3, Havana, 1928.
Guiteras, Pedro J. Historia de la isla de Cuba. 2v. New York, 1865-66.
Halstead. The Story of Cuba. New York, 1898.
Haggedorn, Herman. Leonard Wood. 2v. New York, 1931.
Humboldt, Alexander von. The Island of Cuba. London, 1856.
— Versuch über den politischen zustand der Insel Cuba. Stuttgart, 1807.
Iglesias Vásquez, Eduardo. Cuba independiente. Havana, 1906.
Irisarri, José Miguel. La meneada cubana y los problemas económicos. Havana, 1930.
Iznaga, R. Tres años de la república . . . 1902 á 1905. Havana, 1905.
Jenks, Leland. Our Cuban Colony. New York, 1929.
Johnson, Willis Fletcher. History of Cuba. 5v. New York, 1920.
Jones, Chester Lloyd. Caribbean Interest of the United States. New York, 1916.
Lee, Fitzhugh. Cuba's Struggle Against Spain. New York, 1899.
Lizaso, Félix. Cf. Martí.
López Leiva, Francisco. El bandolerismo en Cuba. Havana, 1930.
Loynaz del Castillo, E. La Mujer Cubana. Havana, 1922.
Maceo, Antonio. . . . De la campaña. Havana, 1916.
Mañach, Jorge. Estampas de San Cristóbal. Havana, 1926.
— Indagación del choteo. Havana, 1928.
Marinello, Juan. Sobre la inquietud cubana. Havana, [1930?].

SELECTED BIBLIOGRAPHY

Márquez Sterling, M. Las conferencias del Shoreham. El cesarismo en Cuba, Mexico, 1933.

Márquez Sterling, M. y Loret de Mola, Manuel. Alrededor de nuestra psicología. Havana, 1906.

Martínez Ortiz, Rafael. Cuba: los primeros años de independencia. 2v. Paris, 1921.

Martí, José. Articulos desconocidos. Introd., Félix Lizaso. Havana, 1930.

—— Espistolario. Introd., Lizaso. 3v. Havana.

—— Obras. 12v. Havana.

—— El presidio político en Cuba. Madrid, 1871.

Mayo, Lawrence S. America of Yesterday as Reflected in the Journal of John Davis Long. Boston, 1923.

Memoria del I. Congreso Industrial Cubano. Havana, 1930. II. Congreso. Havana, 1931.

Millis, Walter. The Martial Spirit. Boston and New York, 1931.

Miro, José. Cuba—crónicas de la guerra. 2v. Havana, 1909.

Miso Márquez, Barolomé. A los habitantes de terriotrios cubanos no ocupados aun por las fuerzas del ejercito libertador. Havana, 1898.

Montero, Rafael. Obras. 3v. Havana, 1933.

Morales y Morales, Vidal. Iniciadores y primeros martires de la revolución cubana . . . 3v. Havana, 1931. (Intro. by Fernando Ortiz.)

Musgrove, G. C. Under Three Flags in Cuba. Boston, 1899.

Navas, José. La convulsión de febrero . . . revuelta de 1917. Matanzas, 1917.

Ortiz, Fernando. Las actuales responsibilidades políticas y la "nota" americana. Havana, 1919.

—— Los cabildos africanos. Havana, 1923.

—— La crisis política cubana. Havana, 1919.

—— La decadencia cubana. Havana, 1924.

—— Las relaciones económicas entre Cuba y los Estados Unidos. Havana, 1927.

—— Alejandro de Humboldt y Cuba. Havana, 1930.

—— Glosario de afronegrismos. Havana, 1924.

—— Historia de la arqueologia indo-cubano. Havana, 1923.

—— Hampa afro-cubana. Los negros brujos. Madrid, 1906, 1917.

—— Historia de Santiago de Cuba. Havana, 1912.

Palma y Romay, Ramón de. Cuentos cubanos. Havana, 1928.

Peraza y Sarausa, Fermín. Bibliografía de Enrique José Varona. Havana, 1933.

SELECTED BIBLIOGRAPHY

Pérez Cubillas, José Martí. Economista ú sociólogo. Havana, 1932.

Pezuela, Jacobo de. Diccionario geográfico, histórico . . . de la Isla de Cuba. 4v. Madrid, 1866.

Polavieja, Marqués de. Relación documentada de mi política en Cuba. Madrid, 1898.

Ponte Domínguez, Francisco J. La personalidad política de José Antonio Saco. Havana, 1932.

Portell-Vilá, Herminio. Narciso López y su época. Havana, 1930.

Quesada y Miranda, Gonzalo de. Martí periodísta. Havana, 1929.

Report of the Provisional Administration. 2v. Havana, 1908-09.

Ribo, José Joaquín. Historia de los voluntarios cubanos. 2v. Madrid, 1872-74.

Rhodes, J. F. McKinley and Roosevelt Administration. New York, 1922.

Robinson, Albert Gardner. Cuba, Old and New. New York, 1895.

Roig de Leuchsenring, Emilio. La ley del dragado. Havana, 1915.

Roosevelt, Theodore. The Rough Riders. New York, 1899.

Root, Elihu. Military and Colonial Policy of the United States. Cambridge, 1916.

Rousset, Rivardo V. Historial de Cuba, 3v. Havana, 1898.

Saco, José Antonio. Biografía de cubanos distinguidos. London, 1860.

Sanguilly, Manuel. Discursos y conferencias. 2v. Havana, 1918-19.

—— Victoria de las tunas. New York [?].

Sanjenís, Avelino. Tiburón. Havana, 1915.

Sellén, Francisco. Hatüey. New York, 1891.

Seigle, Octavio (Anon.). Cuban Information Bureau. Ambassador Guggenheim and the Cuban Revolt. Washington, 1931.

Seligman, Edwin R. A., and Shoup, Carl S. Informe sobre el sistema tributario de Cuba. Havana, 1932.

Serra y Orts, Antonio. . . . Recuerdos de las guerras de Cuba. Santa Cruz de Teneriff. 1906.

Sixto de Sola. Pensando en Cuba. Havana, 1917.

Torre, José M. de la. Lo que fuimos y lo que somos.

Trelles, Carlos Manuel. Biblioteca histórica cubana. 2v. Matanzas, 1922, 1924.

—— El progreso (1902 á 1905) y el retroceso (1906 á 1922) de la república de Cuba. Havana, 1923.

Torriente, Cosme de la. En defensa de los derechos del hombre y del ciudadano. Havana, 1930.

—— Cuba y los Estados Unidos. Havana, 1929.

—— La enmienda Platt. Havana, 1930.

Ubieta, Enrique. Efemerides de la revolución cubana. 4v. Havana, 1911-20.
—— La mujer en la revolución cubana. Havana, [1911?].
United States, Senate. Hearings before the Committee on finance. 72nd Cong. S. Res. 19. Sale of Foreign Bonds and Securities in the United States. 4v. Washington, 1932.
—— State Department. Consular correspondence respecting the conditions of the reconcentrados in Cuba, the state of the war in that island, and the prospects of the projected autonomy. Washington, 1898.
Valverde, Antonio L. Jurisconsultos cubanos. Primera serie. Havana, 1932.
Varona, Enrique José. De la colonia a la república. Havana, 1919.
Vasconcelos, Ramón. El Gral. Gómez y la sedición de mayo. Havana, 1916.
Villaverde Cirilio. Cecilia Valdés . . . Late edition. Havana, 1923.
Vogt, Paul. The Sugar Reform. Philadelphia, 1908.
Wright, Irene A. Cuba. New York, 1912.
Weyler y Nicolau, Valeriano. Mi mando en Cuba. 5v. Madrid, 1910-11.

ARTICLES.

Aguayo, Alfredo. Factores cualitativos de nuestra decadencia escolar. *Revista Bimestre Cubana*, XIX, March-Apr., 1924.
Brooks, Sydney. Cuba. *Fortnightly Review*, XLIV, November, 1910.
Castro y Bachiller, Raimundo de. La obra educacional de la sociedad patriotica en Cuba republicano. *Revista Bimestre Cubana*, XXXI, Mar.-Apr., 1933.
Crowder, Enoch H. El memorandum No. 13. *Heraldo de Cuba*, Aug. 5, 1922.
Entralgo, Elías. El caráctar cubano. *Revista Bimestre Cubana*, XXVII, 2 and succeeding issues. March-April, 1931.
Fernández de Castro, José Antonio. Tres entrevistas con José Antonio Saco. *Revista Bimestre Cubana*, XXXI, 2. Mar.-Apr., 1933.
García Hernández. Reformas políticas y económicas que necesita Cuba. *Revista Bimestre Cubana*, XXXI, 1. Jan.-Feb., 1933.
Maetzu, Ramiro de. El espiritu de la economía ibero-americana. *Revista Bimestre Cubana*, XXVII, 2. Mar.-Apr., 1931.
Marvin, George. Keeping Cuba Libre. *World's Work*, XXXIV, Sept., 1917.

Menocal, Mario G. Cuba's part in the world war. *Current History,* IX, 315-18. Nov., 1918.

Ortiz, Fernando. Humboldt y Cuba, *Revista de la Havana,* I, 5 and 6. May and June, 1930.

—— La reforma electoral de Crowder en Cuba. *Reforma Social,* XX, 214-225. July, 1921.

Ponte Domínguez, Francisco J. La mujer en la revolución de Cuba. *Revista Bimestre Cubana,* XXXII, 2. March-April, 1933.

Varona, Enrique José. Los circulares del General Gómez. *Patria,* IV, 205. New York, December 8, 1895.

—— Los cubanos en Cuba. *Revista Cubana,* X, 97-114. Aug., 1889.

—— Un nuevo partido político en Cuba. *Repertorio americano.* San José, Costa Rica, Dec. 15, 1919.

—— El imperialism yanqui en Cuba. *El Repertorio americano.* San José, Costa Rica, Jan. 30, 1920.

—— Martí y su obra. *El Mundo,* XXIX. Havana, May 19, 1929.

INDEX

A.B.C., 194, 293, 310-318
A.B.C. countries, 218
Abacuá, 49
Aballi, 396
Abraham González Street (Mexico
    City), 267
Abreu, Madame, 224
Absenteeism, 22, 209
Absolutism, 98, 208
Academy of History, 245
Academy of Science, 245
Accident insurance, 214
Acción Socialista, 249
Acevedo, Guillermo, 216
ACF cruisers, 357
Adams, Charles Francis, 115
Adams, F. P., 360, 382
Adams, John Quincy, 123
Adjutant General, 166
Africa, 20, 55, 57, 58, 65, 159, 172, 190
Agramonte, Dr., 168
Agramonte, General, 104
Agijica, 265
Agonía Antillana, 56, 206, 313
Agrarian problem, 193
Agricultural loans, 160
Agriculture, 66, 162, 198, 403
Agüero, Joaquín de, 101
Aguiar, Captain José, 275, 352
Aguiar, Miguel Angel, 39, 260, 348
Aguiar Street, 23
Aguilera, Francisco, 102
Aguinaldo, 161, 174
Air-craft development, 327
Air Reduction, 327, 360, 390, 401, 402,
    408
Aizcorbe, 335
Alabama, 176
Alameda Michaelson (Santiago), 32-33
Alcoran, 73
Aldrich, Senator, 135
Alfonso XII, 101
Alfonso XIII, 106, 116
Alger, Russell A., 135, 143, 153, 156
Alhambra Theater, 36
Allen, Frederick Winthrop, 361, 380,
    390, 401

Allen, Senator, 139
Alliegro, Anselmo, 273
Allison, Senator, 135
Alma mater, 282
Almendares Bridge (Havana), 265
alpargatas, 64
Alto Cedro Estate, 406
Altunga, 335
Alvarez, Aureleo, 384
Alvarez Alverez, Pío, 289, 349, 351
Alvarez brothers, 264-66
Alvarez de la Vega, Aurelio, 268
Amadeo, 101
America, cf. United States
American and Foreign Power Com-
    pany, 327-28, 364, 377-78
American and Overseas Corporation,
    358
American bankers, 157, 255, 295, 333-
    35, 337, 365, 369, 375, 380, 387-88
American banking interests, 84, 258,
    292, 323, 329-30, 361, 376-77, 380-
    81, 385-6, 401-3
American business, 67, 164, 170, 174,
    235
American capital, 70, 74, 116, 126, 164,
    174-75, 192-93, 199, 206, 295-96,
    302, 316, 317, 323, 327-28, 357-82,
    401-3, 404-8
American Car and Foundry Company,
    295, 325, 355-57
American Chamber of Commerce
    (Havana), 358
American Cigar Company, 401
American claims, 121, 337-41
American colony, 210
American Club (Havana), 251
American colonies, 91
American Consul General (Havana),
    275
American Cuban Estates Company,
    380
American domination, 74, 194
American Embassy (Havana), 217, 224,
    252, 275, 326-54, 347-48, 349, 350,
    351, 391
American Experts (cf. Crowder, Hord,

[417]

INDEX

Rathbone, Guggenheim, experts, etc.), 382
American Federation of Labor, 247-48
American fleet, 138, 145-49
American forces, 142-45, 149-53
American Founders Corporation, 358
American Gas and Electric Co., 377-78
American interests, 36, 115, 173, 240, 323, 377
American intervention, 125, 170, 172, 192, 196-97, 202, 203-11, 220-23, 226, 234, 256-58, 323, 377
American investments, cf. American capital
American land-owners, 209
American Locomotive Company, 357, 361
American occupation, 103, 160-72, 173, 180, 181, 189-90, 196, 198, 200, 315, 324, 362, 377, 404
American officials, 222, 315, 316
American Power and Light Company, 377
American property, 22, 33, 62, 121, 126, 170, 206, 219, 221-22, 223, 307, 324, 375-81, 404-8
  destruction of, 122, 276, 337-38
American revolution, 107
American Smelting and Refining Company, 327, 378
American Sugar Refining Company, 404, 406
American Surgical Society, 284
American Telegraph, 202
American Tobacco Company, 401-2
American women, 35, 36
Americans, 24, 35-36, 77, 83, 126, 131, 133, 174, 203, 221, 232, 263, 301, 303, 337-41, 375, 376
  killing of, 116, 124-25, 251-52
Amnesty, 103, 217, 222, 261, 262, 263, 265, 267, 298
Anaconda Copper, 327, 378
Anarchists, 247-48
Andalusia, 24
Anderson, Arthur M., 380
Andalusian language, 86
Andino, Cesar, 285
André, Armando, 236, 273, 275, 352
Andrews, Colonel F. M., 326
Anglophiles, 120, 139
Anglo Saxons, 163, 228
Annexation, 100, 121, 123-25, 137, 159, 173, 206
Anti-Americanism, 256
Antilla, 362
Antilla Sugar Company, 358

Antilles, cf. West Indies
Apia, 117
Apizar, Felix Ernesto, 285, 289
Aponte, José, 30, 60
Aponte Rebellion, 30, 59, 99
Ara, 286
Arabos (Los) Ranch, 265
Arabs, 58, 403
Aragón, 110
Arango, Miguel, 406
Arango y Parreño, 188
Araunuz, Miguel de (pseud.), 32
Arawaks, 21
Arbitration Commission (Mexico-U. S., 1923), 375
Arévalo, Juan, 249
Argentina, 106
Argüelles, Rafael, 286
Ario, 73
Ariquistain, Luis, 56, 206, 313
Aristocracy, 23, 74, 77, 79, 120, 218, 309, 313
Arizona, 149
Arkansans, 144
Arkansas, 176
Armantó, Ricardo, 170
Armistice, 133-34
Army (Cuban), 72, 225, 247, 250-52, 255, 262, 264, 265, 279, 280-82, 284, 301-2, 304-5, 309, 317, 346-47
  (Spanish), 111 (cf. Spanish forces)
  (United States), 119, 142-45, 147-54, 161, 190, 197 (cf. American forces)
Army officers, 250, 274, 290
army supplies, 182, 215, 221, 234, 309, 353
Arroyo, Ramón, 275-76
Artemisa District, 274
Artemisa Massacre, 330, 342
Artillery, 150-51
Asbert, Ernesto, 217, 219, 300
Assassinations, 201, 213, 216, 244-94, 299, 308-12, 325, 326, 333-34, 348, 351, 352
Association of Commercial Employees of Havana, 252
Astor, John Jacob, 144
Asturian Club, 79
Asturias, 73
Atares Fortress, 274, 289-91, 294
Atkins, Edwin F., 103, 115, 121, 128, 130, 135, 404, 406, 408
Atkins and Company, 221, 404
Atlanta Federal Reserve Board, 230
Atlantic Fruit and Sugar Company, 358, 381
Atlantic Monthly, 120, 141
Australia, 120, 297

[418]

INDEX

Autonomist Law, 128
Autonomist Legislature, 134
Autonomists, 197
Autonomy, cf. Home-rule
Avenida de los Presidentes, 292
Avenida Presidente Machado, 240
Aviation, 327-28

Bacon, Assistant Secretary of State, 203-4
Baire, 31, 95-96, 179
Baire, Revolt of. Cf. Revolt of '95
Balmaseda, Joaquín del Río, 263
Banco Español, 385
Banco Internacional, 385
Banco Mercantil Americano de Cuba, 384
Banco Nacional, 228, 356, 384, 385
Banes, 316
Bank clearings, 304
Bank deposits, 304
Bank liquidating acts, 228
Bank Liquidation Commission, 385
Bank of Spain, 157
Bankers, 34, 68, 116, 229, 231, 234, 273, 305, 335, 392, 397, 406, 408
Bankers' loans (private), 385-6, 390-91. Cf. Loans
Banking laws, 230
Banks, 69, 75, 209, 224-5, 229, 243, 260, 304, 316, 342, 373, 375, 376, 380, 383-6, 389, 391, 394, 408
Spanish, 377, 383-85
Bar Association, 245
Baracoa, 95-6
Barbados, 193, 403
Barbarossa, Enrique, 207
Barbour, Major George, 164-65
Barcelo, Apalonia Gomela, 287
Barlow, Joseph E., 339, 358-60
Barreira, Alejandro, 267
Barreras, Luis, 319
Barrientos, Guillermo, 319
barrios, 68
Barroque, 78
Barton, Clara, 164
Basques, 81
Batabanó, 29
Batambo, 178
Batëyes, 28
Battle Hymn of the Republic, 138
Bayamesa (La), 197
Bayamo, 102, 107
Behn brothers, 242, 378-79
Behn, Hernand, 378
Behn, Sosthenes, 378, 381
bejuco ubi, 49
Belgium, 389, 392

Belknap, Reginald R., 221
Belmont, 119
Berlin, 300
Bestard, 263
Betencourt, Alfred, 347, 352
Betencourt, Aristides, 337
Bethlehem Iron Mines Company, 402
Bethlehem Steel Company, 221, 327, 402
Bible, 73, 139
Biltmore Hotel, 244
Bishop of Barcelona, 111
Bismarck, 117
Black Eagle Legion, 99
Black Vomit, 72
Blanco, Eusebio, 110
Blanco Neuman, Luis, 334, 348
Blanco y Erenas, Ramón, 106, 128, 129, 132, 154, 161
Blasco Ibañez, 110
Bliss, Colonel Trasker H., 405
blockade, 142
"bluff," 119, 153
Bohemia, 275
bohios, 28, 63, 90
Bolivar, 99, 124, 226
Bolivia, 125
bombs, 260-61, 291, 294, 398, 310, 311-12, 354
Bonsal, Stephen, 31
Boomer-Dupont Property Corporation, 381
Boone, Virginia Lee, 279
Borah, William, 285, 292
Boston, 404
Bostonians, 115, 404
Boston Journal, 133
botellas, 208. Cf. Graft
Botet, Alfredo, 319
Boycotts, 244, 314, 354
Boza, General, 109, 198
Bozal, 81
Bradley, William Clark, 401
Brady, Anthony N., 401
Brazil, 193, 348
Brazilian Minister (Havana), 351
Bream, Captain J., 326
Bribery, 363, 378
British Minister, 262, 351
Britishers, 362
Brokers, 373
Brontë, Emily, 32
Brooke, John R., 161-63, 166-68, 171, 195, 207
brothels, 78
Brouzon, Claudio, 270, 334
Brownell, F. H., 378

[419]

INDEX

Brush, Mathew Chauncey, 381, 390, 401
Brujo, 57
Bryan, 225
Bryce, A. C., 129
Bucareli, 289
buccaneers, cf. pirates
Buchanan, 124
budget, cf. finances
Bureaucracy, 302, 304, 316, 318
Byoier, Karl, 391

Caballero, Colonel Rogerio, 251
Cabaña Fortress, 21-22, 31, 104, 271
Cabañas Bay, 405
Cabinet, The (American Occupation), 67
Cabinet, The (Cuban), 200, 208, 231-32
Cabinet, The (U. S.), 135, 142, 373
Cabra, 89
Cabrera, Ramón, 286
Cacao, 403
caciques, 26
cafés, 23, 33, 36, 76, 78, 306
Café Venus, 164
Caibarien, 280
Caimito, 191
Calabar Coast, 58
Calabar River, 57
Calatrava, 99
Calles, Plutarco Elías, 74, 267
Calvo y Herrera, Miguel, 240, 276, 309
Camagüey (city), 101, 231
Camagüey (province), 24, 102-3, 108, 199, 223, 231, 274, 352, 355, 378, 389, 395
Camagüey and Nuevitas Railway, 362-63
Camagüey Sugar Company, 381, 386
Camagüeyano, El, 277
Camargo, José (pseud.), 69
Camoa quarry, 365
Canada, 407
Canary Islanders, 24, 59, 63, 79, 352
Cancio, Secretary of Treasury, 384
cane fields, cf. sugar cane fields
Cannon, Joe, 134
Canovas del Castillo, 107
Cantero, Juan, 262
Capablanca, Ramiro, 284
capital, cf. American capital
capital and labor, 188
capitol (Havana), 27, 37, 38, 370, 371, 374
Captain General (cf. Viceroy, Governor General), 98, 132, 316
Carabalí, 57
Carabalí lodges (cf. *ñañigo* lodges), 57

Caracas Sugar Company, 358
Caraway, Senator, 340
Carbó, Sergio, 275
Cárdenas, 101, 376, 405
Caribbean, 24, 27
Caribbean Sugar Company, 364
Caribbean Sea, 17
Caribs, 27
Carlist Wars, 100, 157
Carnegie, Andrew, 146
Carrol, Doctor, 168
Carroll, Colonel John, 339-40, 359
Carteles, 277, 336
Carteret, 403
Carvajal Street, 289
Casanova, Emilia, 78
Casas, Bartolomé de las, 26
Casas, Luis de las, 59
Cascorro, 111
cassava, 28
Castle, Assistant Secretary of State, 329, 346
Castile, 28
Castillo, Commissioner, 158
Castillo, Sacramento del, 265
Castro, Dictator, 106
Catholic Church, cf. The Church
Catholicism, 75
Catlin, Henry, 242-44, 259, 361, 370, 373
cattle-raising, 315, 403
caudillaje (cf. militarism), 71
Cecilia Valdés, 61
Celts, 81
Censorship, 165, 170, 179, 216, 234-45, 253, 273, 274-78, 307, 309, 318, 346, 374
Censorship Commission, 274
Census, 55-56, 72, 99, 129, 190, 219, 297, 403
Central America, 182, 189, 404
  Treaties of 1907, 182
  Treaties of 1923, 182
Central Astraya, 386
Central Pilar San Cristóbal, 386
Centrales, 75, 301, 356, 381, 391, 394, 404, 406-8
Cerro suburb, 276, 289
Cervantes, Agustín, 170
Cervera, Admiral, 32-33, 145-47, 154, 198
Céspedes, Carlos Manuel de, 26, 31, 102, 104
Céspedes, Miguel, 364, 372
Cetrino, 81
Chadbourne sugar bonds, 301, 305, 332, 334-35, 370

INDEX

Chadbourne sugar plan, 38, 146, 259, 367, 389-99
Chadbourne, Thomas Lincoln, 361, 367, 389-99
Chamber of Deputies, cf. Congress (Cuban)
Chango, 189-91
Chaparra sugar plantation, 200, 218, 405
Chapman, Charles E., 207, 209, 227, 233, 362
Chapultepec, 101
Charcoal burning, 66
Charles I, 55
Charles III, 98
Charles IV, 73
Chase-Harris Forbes Corporation, 373
Chase National Bank, 37, 242, 246, 256-58, 260, 295, 301, 305, 326, 328, 333-34, 348, 361, 364, 367, 370-75, 377, 378, 380-81, 385, 390-91, 401
Chat, Mrs. Ormiston, 127
Chibas, Dr. Eduardo, 280
Chicago World's Fair, 119
Chickamagua camp, 156
Chile, 117, 125, 193
Chile Company, 327
Chile nitrates, 327
China, 135
Chinese, 68, 81, 407
Chinese slums, 78
Chinese trade, 121
"Chinón" El, 263
chot, 86
chota, 86
choteo, 85-92
Christ, Jesus, 51, 133, 139, 156
Christianity, 26, 130-31, 141, 174
Church, The, 75, 116-17, 134-5, 189, 232
Church and State, 116, 189
Church annuities, 116, 189
Church claims, 189
Church property, 189
Cienfüegos, 147, 179, 203, 213, 247, 367, 369, 405
Cienfüegos Aqueduct, 367, 369
Cigar workers, 246
Cintas, Oscar B., 325, 355-57, 362, 388
Cipangu, 30
Circuit Court of Santiago, 254
Cisneros Betencourt, Salvador (Marquis de Santa Lucía), 102, 178
Civil War, 143
Claiborne, Governor, 123
Clark, Ruben, 339
Clay and Bock, Ltd., Henry, 401

Cleveland, Grover, 115-16, 119, 121, 125, 141
Message of (1896), 126
Clothing, 376
coaling stations, 181
Coca-Cola Co., 361, 381, 390, 401, 408
Cock-fighting, 214, 275, 300
Coffee, 193, 403, 404
plantations, 403
Collier's Magazine, 274
Colombia, 124, 125
Colón, 129, 226, 265
Colón, cf. Cristobal Colón
Colón cemetery, 126
Colonial régime, cf. Spanish rule
Colonos, 69, 90-91, 305, 384, 387, 394, 404, 407
Colono System, 404
Colt, S. S., 378
Columbia Military Hospital, 286
Columbus, Christopher, 27-28, 30, 155, 157, 226
commerce, cf. trade
Commercial and Financial Chronicle, 138
Committee on Cultural Relations with Latin America, Inc., 331
Common Sense Magazine, 274
Communism, 246, 309, 330
Communists, 247-48, 309, 314
Compañía Cubana, 358
Compañía Telefónica Nacional de España, 378
Concessions, 170-72, 209-10, 215, 231-32, 243, 361, 364-67, 376, 377, 402
Concha, 365
Confederación Nacional Obrera Cubana, 248
Conferencias de Shoreham, Las, cf. Márquez Sterling
Conga dances, 225
Congo, 24, 30, 35
Congos, 46, 58
Congress (Cuban), 63, 197-98, 200-02, 205, 208, 227, 229, 235, 239, 243, 245, 251, 255, 260, 272, 279, 288, 298, 341-42, 344, 349, 362, 364, 367, 379
Congress (United States), 115, 118, 121, 125, 135-38, 140, 171, 175-76, 256, 389, 405
farm bloc in, 386
Congress of Vienna, 117, 192
Congressmen, 245, 252, 260, 363
Conquest, The, 26
Conquistadores, 28, 403
Connecticut, 175
Connecticut (U.S.S.), 222

INDEX

INDEX

INDEX

INDEX

Food (*Cont.*)
rice, 53-4
snakes, 28, 150
yuca, 28
cassava, 28
Food Administrator, 407
Foraker Amendment, 171-72, 362
Fordney, Senator, 386
Fordney Tariff, 387
Ford, Henry, 22
Fort, William H., 336
Fortune Island, 96
Franca, Porfirio, 384
France, 102, 156, 160, 182, 297
Francisco, 60
Francisco Estate, 405
Francisco Sugar Company, 358, 364, 381
Franklin, Benjamin, 60
Freeport Texas Company, 328, 361
Free Trade, 404
French, 26, 32, 81
French patois, 27
French revolution, 59
Fresnada, Dr. José, 286
Freyre de Andrade, Fernando, 161, 201
Freyre de Andrade, Leopoldo, 38, 259-60, 261, 274, 391, 395
Freyre de Andrade, Gonzalo, 38, 253, 259-61, 287, 292, 348
Freyre de Andrade, Guillermo, 38, 259-60, 261
Frontier, 118, 193
Frontón, 79
Fruit Industry, 208
Fruits (cf. Trees)
Frye, Alexis Everett, 168-69
Fulas, 58
Fulton Iron Works, 358
Funerals, 89-90
Furniture, 77, 90, 408

Gaceta Oficial, 172, 244, 292, 390
gacha, 28
Gallego Club, 79
gambling, 224, 300 (cf. Lottery)
Gangá legends, 51
Gangás, 51-54, 58
Gangsters, 239, 298
García Brothers, F. C., 401
García, Calixto, 103-9, 148, 150, 153, 155, 165, 218
García, José, 262
García Vélez, General, 234-35
Garibaldi, 97
Gaunard, Julio, 275
Gelabert, Sebastián, 229
General Electric Company, 357

General Motors, 357
General Sugar Company, 358, 363, 364, 381, 385-6
Gerard, Ex-Ambassador, 327
German Fleet, 117
Germany, 120, 135, 220, 223, 266, 383, 389, 329, 406
Gandhi, 314
Ghost Fleet, 148
Gloria Street, 272
Godkin, E. K., 117
God, 130, 139, 156, 158, 163, 179, 362
Gods, Chango, 191
pebble, 20, 50
stick, 20, 48
Gold, 71, 396, 402
Gold Coast, 24
Gómez, Francisco, 112
Gómez, José Miguel, 55, 62-63, 199, 200, 202, 210, 219, 222-27, 231, 235, 247, 298-302, 313, 315, 362, 364-66, 369
Government of, 210, 212-18, 242
Gómez, Juan Gualberto, 60, 104, 161, 178
Gómez, Juan Vicente, 271
Gómez, Máximo, 70, 78, 95-97, 103-13, 125, 142-43, 161, 194, 196, 198, 199, 218, 349
Gómez, Miguel Mariano, 287-88, 313-14, 319
Gonzáles, Laura, 262
Gonzáles, Minister William Elliot, 209, 220-23, 236
González Cosuegra, José, 353
González, Roa, 375
González Rubiera, Juan Mariano, 274, 277-78, 289-99, 349
González, Señora, 349-50
Gonzalo de Quesado, 196, 204
Gordo, El, 216
Gorgas Mayor Street, 168
Gould, Helen, 144
Govín, Rafael R., 401
Government employees, 246, 250, 304-5, 311, 343
Graft, 116, 125, 130, 195, 198, 208, 213-15, 224, 227, 230-32, 234, 245, 256, 282, 297, 315, 317, 362-367, 370, 371, 374
Grafton, Wycliff B., 264
Grammercy Refinery (Louisiana), 405
Grant, President U. S., 125
Grau San Martín, Ramón, 282, 284, 319
Great Northern Railroad, 359
Green, William C., 248
Grimes, Captain, 150

INDEX

Griswold, V. E. S., 360-61
Groesbeck, Clarence E., 378
Grosvenor, General, 139
Guáimaro Assembly, 61, 102
guajiros, 24, 63, 209
Guanabacoa, 27, 202
Guanabacoa Hills, 18
Guanabacoa Springs, 27
Guanamaquillo, 101
Guanguancoa, 50
Guantánamo, 37, 90, 221-22
Guantánamo Exploration Company, 403
Guantánamo Naval Base, 223
Guantánamo Sugar Company, 381
Guaribos, cf. Caribs
Guas, Rafael, 245
Guatemala, 106, 291
Guerra, Faustino ("Pino"), 202, 216
Guerra, Ramiro, 301
Guerrero, Colonel, 274
Guggenheim, Harry F., 38, 183, 246, 276, 279, 288, 304, 308, 313, 316-54, 360, 367, 370, 373-74, 377, 389-91
Guggenheim experts, 304, 329, 332, 335
Guggenheim Exploration Company, 378
Guggenheim family, 326-27
Guggenheim Fellow, 282
Guggenheim interests, 361, 378, 402
Guggenheim officials, 328
Guianas, 27
Guillén, Nicolás, 65-66
Güines, 376
Güines District, 109
Guipúzcoa, 105
Gun-running, 126
Gussie, 145-46
Gutierrez, Mariano Gonzáles, 289
Gutiérrez, Viriato, 397
Gutiérrez Quiroz, Dr. Juan, 253-54

hacendados, 30, 108, 234
haciendas, 30, 59, 62
habeas corpus, 169, 253-4, 285
Hague, The, 340
Haiti, 27, 30, 32, 59, 81, 99, 190, 222-23, 348, 406
Haitian immigration, 56, 406
Haitians, 55-6, 58
Hale, Senator, 135
Hall, E. K., 401
Hang General Weyler to a Sour Apple Tree, 138
Hanna, Mark, 114-15, 122, 135, 168, 171
Hanna, Matthew, 165, 168

Hapsburgs, 116
Harding, President, 231, 377
Harding, W. P. G., 230
Harrah claim, 341
Harrison, President, 118
Harvard University, 168
Hatüey, 26, 30-31
Havana (city), 18-23, 26-27, 33, 36, 40, 51, 67-68, 72, 76, 78, 82, 99, 100, 105, 109, 125, 127, 131, 132, 134, 143, 162, 167-69, 173, 178, 179, 190, 199, 203, 207, 213, 216, 224, 227, 230, 240, 243, 247, 252, 256, 262, 263, 265, 267, 269, 270, 272-75, 278-80, 286, 287, 289, 294, 306, 312, 313, 326-28, 342, 345, 346, 348, 350, 360, 365, 367, 370, 376, 385, 396, 403, 405-6
  Embassies and Legations in, 348, 351
Havana (province), 110, 201, 216, 227
Havana American, 276, 297, 300
Havana American News, 273, 276, 299, 338, 346, 349, 350
Havana Bridge, 215
Havana Casino, 300
Havana Central Railroad, 380
Havana Clearing House, 372
Havana Commercial Company, 401
Havana Country Club, 23
Havana Docks Corporation, 242, 378
Havana Electric Light and Power Company, 242
Havana Electric Railway Company, 242, 354
Havana Harbor, 31, 203, 215, 366, 379
Havana Police-station, 202
Havana Post, 211, 391
Havana Terminal Railroad, 380
Havana Yacht Club, 20, 23, 38, 69, 246
Havemeyer, Henry O., 404
Havemeyer, Horace, 328, 386, 406
Hawaii, 117 (cf. sugar)
Hawkins, General, 152
Hawley, H. B., 359, 405, 407
Hawley interests, 405
Hay, 139
Hayden, Charles, 328, 361, 380, 390, 408
Hayden, Stone firm, 380
Hayes, Rutherford B., 220
Hearst, William Randolph, 119-20, 127, 132, 144, 154
Hechevarría, Dr., 261
Henequén, 193
Henry, Guy, 145
Heraldo Comercial, 275

[426]

INDEX

INDEX

INDEX

INDEX

quez Sterling, University of Havana, United States policy, Herbert C. Lakin, Horatio S. Rubens, H. W. Catlin, Vasquez Bello, Julio Antonio Mella, William C. Green, Russell Porter, etc., etc.)
machetes, 120, 143, 280
Machiavelli, 245, 379
McHugh, John, 401
McKinley, William, 93, 114, 116, 118, 122, 128, 131-37, 142, 156, 160, 167, 173-75, 179
McKinley, Mrs. William, 127
Madero, Francisco, 268
Madison Square Garden, 127
Madrid, 22, 116, 129
Maeztu, Ramiro de, 196
magic, 57, 58, cf. Maja cult
Magoon, Governor Charles E., 55, 61, 63, 160, 190, 207-13, 228, 231, 233, 296, 298, 302, 367, 376, 377
Magriná(t), 268-69
maguey, 28
mahogany, 72
Maine (U.S.S.), 37, 128, 131-36, 140 (new ship), 211
  Monument to, 241
Maize, 28
Maja cult, 58
Malaria, 95, 109, 307
Malecón, 20, 22, 23, 74, 79, 112, 240, 241, 347
Malongo, 64
Mal-Tiempo, 109
Mañach, Jorge, 20, 76, 80, 85, 88-89, 92
Managua, 34
"Manana," 78
Manati, 406
Manati Sugar Corporation, 221, 358
Mandingás, 58
Manganese, 328
Manhattan bar, 34
Manila Bay, 145
Manresa, Mariina, 78
Manufactures, 116
Manzanillo, 90, 96, 214, 222, 362, 404
Marcy, Secretary of State, 124
Marianao, 23, 109, 272, 276, 299, 408
Marimón, 385
Marinello, Juan, 80, 283
Marines, 31, 203, 221-22, 223, 256, 324, 365, 381, 399
Márquez Sterling, M., 64, 208-9, 257-58, 268, 271, 325, 346, 383
Marsal, Manuel, 277

Marshal, Edward, 149
Martí (town), 214, 362
Martí y Pérez, José Julián, 15, 80, 93, 95, 97, 104-107, 184, 187-89, 196, 197, 237, 253, 321
Martial Law, 62, 280
Martín Mesa Road, 264
Martínez Campos, Governor General, 103, 107, 109, 110
Martínez Fraga, Pedro, 319
Martínez, Ortiz, 162
Martínez, Saenz, 245, 351
Marvin, George, 218
Masó, Andre, 244
Masó, Blas, 273, 334
Masó, Bartolomé, 31, 96, 104, 160, 196, 197
Mason and Dixon area, 191
Masons, 105, 360
Maspons, Juan, 335
Massip, Chief of Police, 260
Massip, Salvador, 304
Matahambre Copper mines, 403
Matanzas (City), 60, 101, 131, 265, 376
Matanzas (Province), 109, 110, 128-29, 226, 265, 377, 405, 408
Matanzas Road, 264
Matanzas Sugar Company, 361, 364, 381, 390
Mauretanians, 81
Mauru, 52-54
Mauser rifles, 149-50
Máximo Gómez, 271
Maya (La), 26
Mayas, 27, 81
Mayor Gorgas Street, 34
Maza y Artola, José de la, 219
Mazariego, Diego de, 27
Mazzini, 97, 188
Meat, 116
Mella, Julio Antonio, 266-69, 275, 282, 334, 352
Méndez Capote, Domingo, 179, 196, 200
Méndez Pelayo, 284
Méndez Peñate, Colonel Roberto, 314, 319
Mendieta, Carlos, 212, 219, 235, 314, 319
Mendoza Domenech, Teresa, 78
Menéndez Castillo, 263
Menocal, Mario G., 55, 62, 182-83, 202-3, 217-27, 231, 233, 235-36, 243, 247, 280, 296, 298, 299, 300, 302, 313, 315, 319, 343-44, 351, 366, 369, 376-77, 384
Menocalistas, 314, 343
Merced, 51

INDEX

Pongué dialect, 86
Pope Leo, 116
Pope, the, 134, 206
Popular Party, 134, 206
Porcet, Clarita, 288
Porfirio Valiente Street (Santiago), 262
Porra, 38, 245-6, 251-52, 259-61, 298
Porra Femenina, 287
Port Arthur, 135
Port Workers (Cuba), 396
Port Workers (New York), 247
Ports Company of Cuba, 364-66
Portel-Vilá, Herminio, 282
Portela, Guillermo, 282, 284
Porter, Robert, 173
Porter, Russell, 277-78, 279, 289
Portes Gil, Emilio, 267
Post, James Howell, 381, 390
Potter, W. C., 328, 361, 378, 402
Pottersville, 403
Powell, Cadet Joseph, 33
Power Trust, 235, 244 (cf. Electrical Interests, Electric Bond and Share Company, American and Foreign Power, etc.)
Pozos Dulces, Count of, 81, 188
Prado, 36, 37, 76, 79, 99, 103, 214, 215, 251
Prenelles Street, 273
Prensa, La, 216
Press (cf. Yellow Journalism)
  American, 144, 211, 257, 262, 269, 274, 370
  Cuban, 165-66, 170, 234, 264, 345-46
  of Santiago, 165-66
Preston (town), 222
Preston, Andrew H., 405
Prieto, Indalecio, 378
Prim, General, 157
Primo de Rivera, 378
Principe Fortress, 278, 283, 284, 285, 337
Prisoners, 252-54, 260, 270-71, 274, 278-79, 285-87, 300
Prisons, 254, 285-89, 299-300
  torture in, 285-87, 289-91
Prœnza, 291
Professors, 239, 278, 281, 283, 290, 292, 297, 317-18, 319, 334
Profintern, 248
Proletariat, cf. Labor
Pro-Patria, 198
Prosner, Seward, 361
Prostitutes, 112, 287
Prostitution, 300
Public assemblage, 245, 247, 252, 280, 309

Public clinics, 307
Public utilities, 235, 354, 375
Public Utilities Holding Corporation, 358
Public Utility Interests, 75, 243, 354, 361, 376-78, 380, 392, 396
  of Ohio, 114
Public works, 165, 198-99, 209, 213-15, 229, 233, 236, 246, 256, 304, 305, 336, 369, 371
Public Works certificates, 256, 305, 370
Puche, 28
Puerta Reyes, 270
Puerto Padre, 405
Puerto Principe, 101
Puerto Rico, 145, 146, 174, 197, 204, 315 (cf. Sugar Production)
Pulitzer, 119, 141
Punta, La, 22, 31, 79, 241
Punta Alegre Sugar Company, 361, 364, 381, 406
Puritanism, 181

Queen Regent, 116
Quesada, General, 125
Quevedo, Miguel Angel, 275
quinine, 109
Quinta de los Molinos, 198
Quintana, Valiente, 267-68
Quitman, Governor, 101

R. F. C., 209
Race prejudices, 192
Race question, 17, 20, 24, 25-29, 30, 40, 55-66, 67-69, 73-74, 79-80, 81, 99 (cf. Negroes)
Race War of 1912, 62, 217
Radio Corporation of Cuba, 378
Railways, 172, 214, 235, 295, 316, 339, 356, 357, 360, 362-64, 375, 376, 380, 388, 397, 404
  interests, 327, 340, 367
  rebates, 363
  subsidies, 214, 362
Railway Workers Brotherhood, 248-49
Ramón, José, 262
Ramón, José (2), 286
Ramón, Juan, 273
Rand, Charles F., 402
Rape, 300
Rasco, Colonel Federico, 251
Rathbone, Albert, 384
Rathbone, Estes G., 168
Rattenbury, J. Freeman, 123
Reader's Digest, 274
Real estate, 336
Reciprocity, 125, 199, 405, 406
Reconcentrado, El, 170

INDEX

[435]

INDEX

INDEX

Smoot-Hawley Tariff, 398
Smugglers, 72
Smuggling, 376
Socialists, 117
Socialization, 318
Society of Engineers, 245
Sol, El (Marianao), 276
Sol y Ortega, Deputy, 110
Soledad Estate, 404
Soledad Sugar Company, 358
Son, 24
Sóngoro Cosongo, 64-6
Sores, Jacques, 72
Soule, 124
South America, 106, 124, 189, 257, cf. Hispanic America, Latin America
Soviet Union, 158
Spain, 20-21, 24, 32, 40, 60, 70-72, 78, 98, 100, 105, 114, 116, 118, 120, 121, 124, 125-32, 134-36, 139, 141, 156-58, 174, 181, 188-89, 194, 198, 209, 239, 241, 297, 375, 376, 383, 403, 407
ambassador in Cuba, 351
authorities, 32, 115, 116, 190
constitution of 1812, 100
diplomatic corps in Americas, 157
exchequer, 72
fleet of, 32, 115, 145, 146-48, 154-55
forces of, 102-13, 149-53, 161
literature of, 79
Minister of Marine, 146
officials of, 155
rule of, 32, 34, 68, 70-74, 114, 116, 157, 191, 195, 281, 292, 302, 356, 376
spies of, 114
Spaniards, 26, 74, 79, 81, 84, 95, 128, 131, 142, 171, 197, 402
Spanish American Iron Company, 402
Spanish American War, 93, 119, 133, 134, 138-56
causes, 114, 117, 121-38
peace-terms, 156-59
Spanish casino, 80
Spanish Crown, 72
Spanish-Cuban bonds, 116
Spanish Immigrants, 68, 74
Spanish language, 20, 24
Spanish merchants, 173
Sperling and Company, 365
Speyer and Company loans, 198, 213, 214, 305, 369
Spinden, Herbert G., 225, 226
Sports, 75
Springer, Joseph A., 129
Springfield rifles, 150

Standard Oil Company, 305
Standards of Living, 303
Star-Spangled Banner, 167
State Department (U. S.), 84, 95, 122, 128, 131, 222, 227-28, 240, 256, 276, 309, 310, 323, 325, 326, 330, 332, 337-40, 345, 351, 363, 365, 369, 377, 379-80
Stegomyia mosquito, 168
Steinhart, Maximiliano, 162, 203, 204, 208, 209
Stetson, E. W., 381
Stillman, J. A., 381
Stimson, Secretary of State, 183, 332, 334, 339-40, 358, 389, 391
Storey, Moorfield, 174
Strikes, 249
consumers', 243-44, 378
Pullman, 119
railway, 247
tobacco, 402
Students, 239, 260, 266, 270, 278-94, 314-20, 333-34, 349
Students Directorate, 279, 282, 314, 317
Suárez Solís, Señora, 287
Suarez y Romero, Anselmo, 60
Sueño suburb (Santiago), 262
Suez Canal, 144
Sugar, 25, 71, 116, 229, 248, 374, 380, 383, 386-408
bounties on, 404
cane, 19, 356, 383, 403; cutting of, 395; destruction of, 115, 162, 223, 311, 397, 399
Cartel, 389
companies, 68, 327-28, 358-60, 362, 363, 406-8
consumption of, 397-98
crops, 208, 220, 301, 392, 406, 407, cf. *zafra*
industry, 55, 64, 193, 198, 273, 295, 306, 315, 316, 327, 367, 375, 377, 385-86, 391-99, 403-8; beet, 198, 391, 398, 404, 405; destruction of, 392-99; of Haiti, 403; workers in, 392-99
interests, 115, 231, 313, 316, 357, 361, 380-81, 390; beet, 198, 391, 398, 404, 405-8
machinery, 403
mills, 62, 95, 163, 202, 389, 396-7, 404-8, cf. *ingenios*
owners, 108, cf. sugar interests, sugar mills, etc.
planters, 69, 385, cf. *colonos*; American, 376
Pool, 392

[437]

INDEX

INDEX

INDEX

Vertientes Sugar Company, 381, 386
Vest, Senator George, 130
Veterans (Spanish-American War), 279; (Cuban), 193-4, 196-99, 217, 234, 273, 315
Veterans and Patriots Association, 202, 234, 363
Veterans' bonus, 161, 369, cf. pensions
Vianelo, Judge, 299
Viceroys, 71, 72, cf. Captain General, Governor General
Vice-presidency, 368
Victorianism, 68, 78
Vidaurreta, Dr. José Luis, 253
Vilches, Lieutenant, 265
Villafuerte, 352
Villanueva lands, 215
Villaverde, Cirilio, 61, 78
Villuendas, Enrique, 201
Villuendas Street, 273
Virginius, 32, 125
Viriato, 44-46
Virtudes Street, 251
Visigoths, 81
Vista Alegre, 262
Vivanco, Doctor, 254
Vives, Francisco Dionisio, 99, 239, 403
Vizcaya, 146
Voice of the Teacher, 273, 275
Volantes, 72
Voltaire, 73
Voluntarios, 107, 288
Voodoo, 20, cf. ñañigo
Voodooism, 75
Voz de la Razón, 276

Wages, 34, 246-47, 303, 357, 314, 395-96
Wagner, 356
Wall Street, 114, 117, 138, 143, 316, 335
Walsh, Senator David I. (Massachusetts), 288, 329, 340
Walsh, Senator (Montana), 329
War Department, 142, 143, 144, 146, 153, 170, 175, 346
Ward Bakery Company, 361
Ward Line, 127
Warner Sugar Refining Company, 406
Warren Brothers, 371-72
Washington (City), 95, 136, 137, 147, 179, 205, 248, 358, 360
Washington (U. S. Government), 114, 122, 124, 126, 135, 144, 170, 171, 172, 174, 175, 203, 210, 213, 215, 221, 222, 223, 225, 229, 255, 256, 257, 258, 313, 327, 363, 405
Washington, George, 160
Washington Daily News, 327-28
Washington Evening Star, 337

Watterson, Henry, 210
Waxman, Boris, 269
Wealth, 219, 295, 304
Weeks, Congressman, 405
Welles, Sumner, 368
West India Sugar Finance Corporation, 406
West Indies, 27, 316, cf. Antilles
West Point, 143, 144
Weyler y Nicolau, Valeriano ("The Butcher"), 21, 33, 95, 102, 111, 113, 121, 126, 128, 130, 138, 156, 162, 193, 226, 239, 292
expedition of, 116
Wheeler, General, 149, 152
Whigs, 175
White House, 114, 224, 359
Whites, 67-80, 188, 297, 403, cf. Creoles, Spaniards
Widener, P. A. B., 401
Wiggin, Albert W., 361, 380, 390
Wikof brigade, 151
Wilford, John T., 276, 337-38
Williams, 373
Williams, John Sharp, 158
Wilmington, 117
Wilson, Woodrow, 167, 189, 236, 407
Wilson Tariff, 404
Windward Passage, 27
Witherbee Sherman Company, 402
Woman's suffrage, 228
Women, 74-77, 260, 283, 284, 287-88, 291, 329
Women's International League for Peace and Freedom, 279
Wood, Governor General Leonard, 55, 61, 120, 143-45, 148-49, 152-3, 163-64, 166-72, 173, 177-80, 189, 191, 193, 195-99, 207, 212, 224, 240, 296-97, 299
Woodford, Stewart, 116, 129, 131, 135, 136
Woodin (town), 355-56
Woodin, William Hartman, 235, 295, 325, 333, 339-40, 355-57, 359-63, 367, 377, 380, 381, 388, 390, 401
Workers, cf. Labor
Workers Federation of Havana, 271
Workers' homes, 214
Workers Insurance, 243
World War, 74, 84, 167, 218, 223, 357, 383, 398, 402, 406
armistice, 407
Wright, Chester, 247-48, 333, 352
Wright, Irene, 211, 302

Yalob, Noske, 270, 334
Yara, 26, 31, 178

INDEX

CUBA
A PORTFOLIO OF PHOTOGRAPHS
BY WALKER EVANS

1. HAVANA STREET

18. BREADLINE

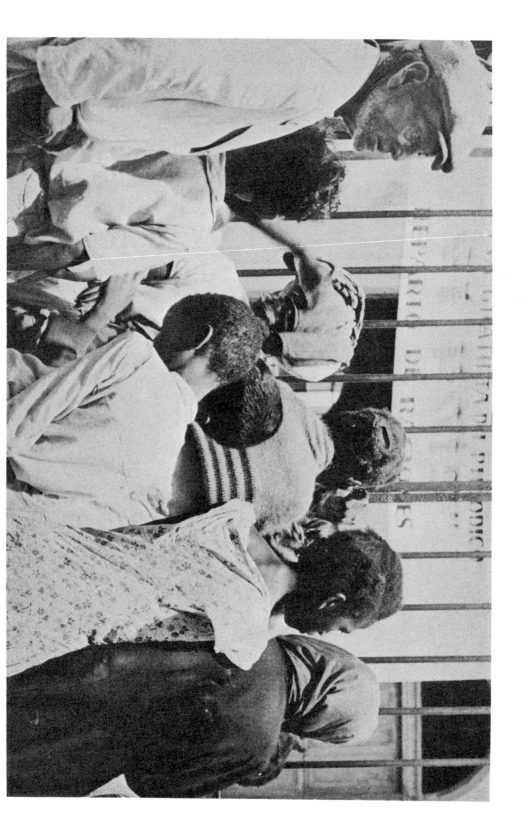

19. PATIO

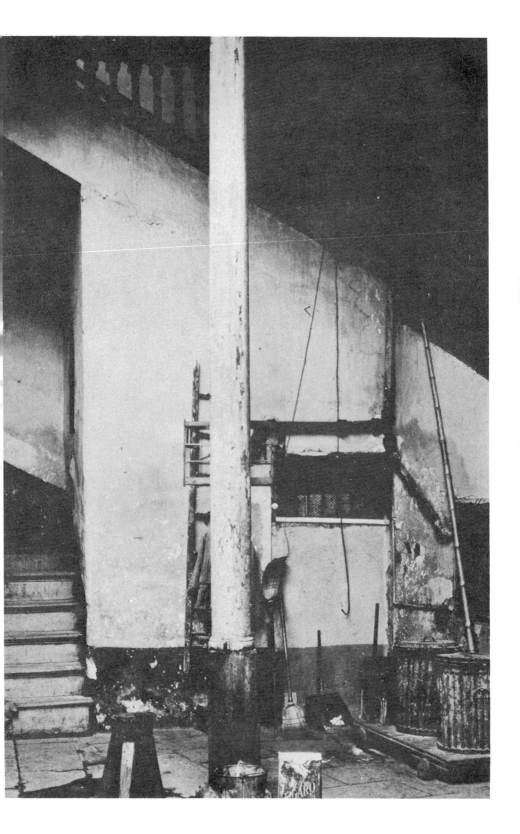

20. SMALL TOWN

21. COUNTRY TOWN

22. UNOFFICIAL VILLAGE OF HAVANA POOR

23. BOHIO

24. SUGAR PLANTATION. OFF-SEASON

26.   A DOCUMENT OF THE TERROR
Anonymous Photograph

27. PATROL

28. GONZALEZ RUBIERA
Anonymous Photograph

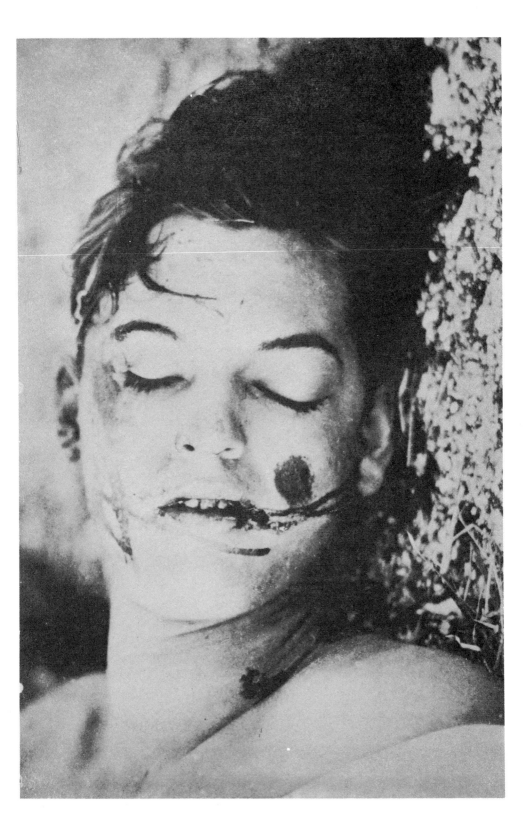

29. NEWSBOYS

30. TERRORIST STUDENTS IN JAIL
Anonymous Photograph

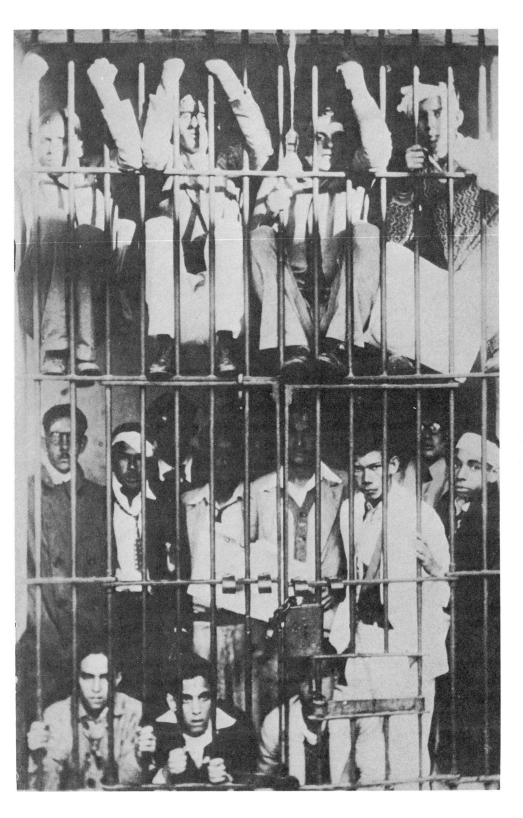

31. WALLWRITING

| We support the strike of the cigar workers | Down with the Imperialist War |

APOYEMOS
LA HUELGA DE
LOS CIGARREROS
DOI.
ABAJO
LA GUERRA
IMPERIALISTA
PC

2. WOMAN

3. PATRON SAINT

4. PUBLIC SQUARE

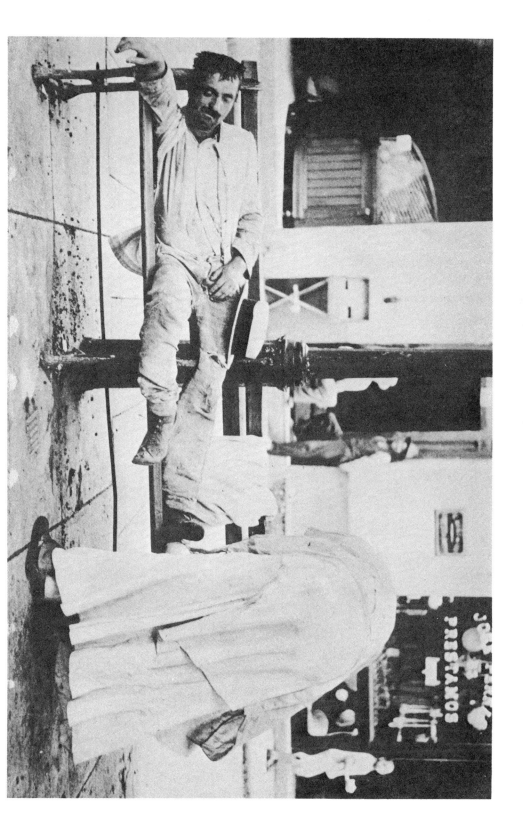

5. LOTTERY-TICKET VENDORS

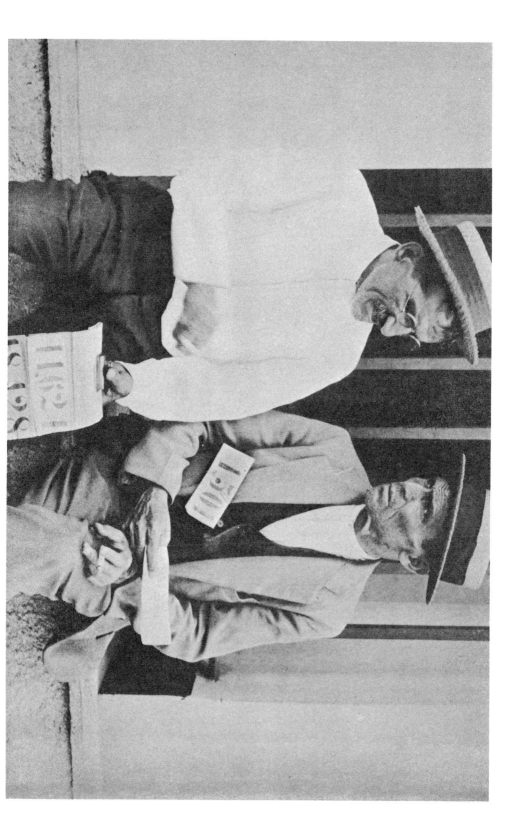

6. PARQUE CENTRAL I

7. PARQUE CENTRAL II

8. CINEMA

9. BEGGAR

10. STREET CORNER

11. FAMILY

12. PUSHCART

13. CITY PEOPLE

14. BUTCHER SHOP